Practicing Health Standards

As you read this introduction, you will learn about the seven health standards. A **health standard** is something you must know and be able to do to be healthy. These are the health standards.

1 Comprehend Health Facts

2 Access Valid Health Information, Products, and Services

3 Make Health Behavior Contracts

4 Analyze Influences on Health

5 Communicate in Healthful Ways

6 Make Responsible Decisions

7 Be a Health Advocate

HEALTH STANDARD 1 | Comprehend Health Facts

Students will comprehend concepts related to health promotion and disease prevention.

1. Study and learn health facts. A **health fact** is a true statement about health. Health facts help you know what you need to do to be healthy. This textbook is organized into ten units to help you find health facts easily. For example, one unit is called Nutrition. It has health facts about nutrition and diet. These health facts help you know how to plan a healthful diet. Suppose you want to reduce your risk of heart disease. You will learn health facts about the relationship between diet and heart disease. You will learn that broiled chicken is more healthful than fried chicken.

2. Ask questions if you do not comprehend health facts. As you study health facts, you might have questions. For example, you might ask, "Why is broiled chicken more healthful than fried chicken?" The answer is that fats from frying chicken can build up on artery walls. This reduces blood flow. This answer gives you a better understanding of health facts.

3. **Answer questions to show you comprehend health facts.** Your teacher or someone else might ask a question to learn what you understand. For example, you might be asked, "Is broiled fish or fried fish more healthful for the heart?" Your answer should be broiled fish. You comprehend health facts. You understand that eating fried foods increases the fats you eat. These fats can build up on your artery walls.

4. **Use health facts to practice life skills.** A life skill is a healthful action that is learned and practiced for a lifetime. This textbook contains a list of life skills. Each lesson in the book begins with one or more life skills. This is one of the life skills: *I will plan a healthful diet that reduces the risk of disease.* Suppose you want to practice this life skill. You rely on health facts. You know that eating fried foods increases the risk of heart disease. You also know that broiled foods do not have as much fat. You order a broiled chicken sandwich rather than a fried chicken sandwich at a fast food restaurant.

Students will demonstrate the ability to access valid health information and health-promoting products and services.

1. **Identify health information, products, and services you need.** Suppose you are going to be in the sun and want to protect against skin cancer. You need health information. You need to know about harmful rays from the sun. You need health products. A **health product** is something that is produced and used for health. If you are going to be in the sun, you need sunscreen lotion. You need health services. A **health service** is the help provided by a health care provider or health care facility. A **health care provider** is a trained professional who provides people with health care. Some health care providers are dentists, doctors, pharmacists, and police officers. A **health care facility** is a place where people receive health care. A hospital and a mental health clinic are health care facilities.

2. **Locate health information, products, and services.** Suppose you need health information. Use **Some Sources of Health-Related Information.** Suppose you need health products. You can get health products from a health care provider. You might purchase health products at a store. Most likely, your parents or guardian get you health products. Suppose you need health services. You might find health services in the telephone directory. Most likely, your parents or guardian help you get health services.

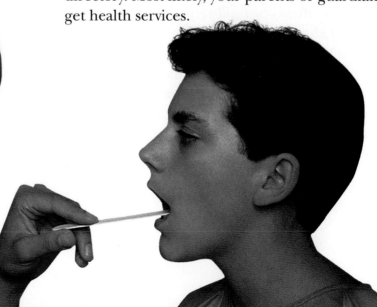

Some Sources of Health-Related Information

- Health care professionals, such as your physician or dentist
- Centers for Disease Control and Prevention (CDC)
- National Health Information Center
- Professional organizations, such as the American Red Cross, American Heart Association, American Cancer Society, American Medical Association, American Association for Health Education
- Books, such as this textbook
- Medical journals
- Computer products and services such as CD-ROMs and the World Wide Web
- Your health teacher
- Videos and television programs

You might have to get help for an emergency. An emergency is a serious situation that occurs without warning and calls for quick action. Learn the emergency telephone numbers in your area. There might be a 9-1-1 emergency number to get help from the fire department, police, and emergency medical services. If not, dial the operator (the number 0).

How to Make an Emergency Telephone Call

- Remain calm and give your name.
- Tell the exact place of the emergency.
- Tell what happened, the number of people involved, and what has already been done.
- Give the number of the telephone you are using.
- Listen to what you are told to do. Write down directions if necessary.
- Do not hang up until you are told to do so.
- Stay with the person or persons needing help until emergency care arrives.

3. Evaluate health information, products, and services. Sometimes you need help deciding if the health information you got is reliable. Use **A Guide to Evaluating Health-Related Information.** Sometimes you need help evaluating health products and health services. Use **Questions to Help Evaluate Health Products and Services.**

A Guide to Evaluating Health-Related Information

- What is the source of the information?
- What are the qualifications of the researcher, author, speaker, organization, or group providing the information?
- Is the information based on current research and scientific knowledge or is it the opinion of certain individuals or groups?
- Have reputable health care professionals evaluated the information and accepted it?
- Is the purpose of sharing the information to inform you or to convince you that you need to buy a specific product or service?
- Is the information provided in a way that educates you without trying to appeal to your emotions?
- Are you able to get additional information if you request it?
- Does the information make realistic claims?

Questions to Help Evaluate Health Products and Services

- Do I really need the product or service?
- Do I understand what the product or service does and how to use it?
- Is the product or service safe?
- Is the product or service worth the price?
- Is the product or service of high quality?
- What can I do about the product or service if I am not satisfied?
- What do consumer agencies have to say about the product or service?

4. **Take action when health information is misleading. Take action when you are not satisfied with health products and services.** You might hear, read, or see inaccurate health information. Suppose you are not satisfied with health products or health services. You might write a letter of complaint or contact a federal agency.

Federal Agencies to Help You with a Complaint

- The Food and Drug Administration (FDA) checks and enforces the safety of food, drugs, medical devices, and cosmetics. The FDA has the authority to recall products. A product recall is an order to take a product off the market because of safety concerns. The FDA Consumer Affairs Information Line is 1-800-532-4440.
- The Federal Trade Commission (FTC) checks advertising practices. The FTC can stop certain advertisements or force an advertiser to change the wording in advertisements.
- The Consumer Product Safety Commission (CPSC) establishes and enforces product safety standards. The CPSC has the authority to recall products.
- The United States Postal Service (USPS) protects the public when products and services are sold through the mail. Contact your local post office or call the Postal Crime Hotline at 1-800-654-8896.

Make Health Behavior Contracts

Students will demonstrate the ability to practice health-enhancing behaviors and reduce health risks.

Use a health behavior contract to practice healthful behavior and reduce health risks. A **healthful behavior** is an action that

- promotes health;
- prevents illness, injury, and premature death;
- and improves the quality of the environment.

A **health behavior contract** is a written plan to develop the habit of practicing a life skill. When you practice life skills, you reduce health risks.

1. **Tell the life skill you want to practice.** Decide on a life skill. For example, you might want to manage stress. **Stress** is the body's reaction to the demands of daily living. Too much stress is a health risk. You practice healthful behavior when you make a health behavior contract for this life skill: *I will follow a plan to manage stress.*

2. **Write a few statements describing how the life skill will affect your health.** Explain how practicing this life skill helps you to reduce health risks. Write a few statements about these health risks.

3. **Design a specific plan to practice the life skill and a way to record your progress in making the life skill a habit.** Tell what you will do to practice the life skill. Choose actions and write them on your plan. Then make a calendar or other way to record what you do. Set a time frame.

4. **Describe the results you got when you tried the plan.** After the end of the time frame, review how well you did. Did you follow the plan you made? Did anything get in the way? What did you enjoy about the plan? How might you improve the plan?

Health Behavior Contract

Name: _____ **Date:** _____

Life Skill: I will follow a plan to manage stress.

Effect on My Health: If I manage stress, I will be less likely to have a headache and stomachache. I will keep my body strong. Then I will be better able to resist colds and flu. I will be less likely to have an accident.

My Plan: I will deal with stressors. I will talk to my parents or guardian about the cause of stress. I will protect my health. I will take a brisk walk each day. I will keep a journal for a week. I will staple my journal to this health behavior contract. I will record the stressors I experience and tell if I spoke to my parents or guardian about them. I will keep a record of the days on which I took a brisk walk.

How My Plan Worked: (Complete after one week). I talked with my parents about stressors on two days. I took a brisk walk on three days. I feel better when I talk with my parents and take a brisk walk. I will take these actions more often.

Analyze Influences on Health

Students will analyze the influence of culture, media, technology, and other factors on health.

Students will analyze the influence of culture, media, technology, and other factors on health.

1. **Identify people and things that might influence you.** Be aware of people and things that influence you. For example, what people influence you? Your parents or guardian? Other family members? Friends? Heroes from television or sports? What things influence you? Do the media influence you? **Media** are the various forms of mass communication. Are you influenced by ads on TV? On radio? In magazines or newspapers? Does technology influence you? **Technology** is the use of high-tech equipment to communicate information. Are you influenced by computer games? Ads or articles on the World Wide Web? CD-ROMs? Videos? Does culture influence you? **Culture** is the arts, beliefs, and customs that make up a way of life for a group of people at a certain time. Do family customs influence you?

2. **Evaluate the effects the influence might have on health.** Use the **Guidelines for Analyzing Influences on Health®.** Answer Yes or No to each question. Note: All six questions might not apply.

Guidelines for Analyzing Influences on Health®

1. Does this influence promote healthful behavior?

2. Does this influence promote safe behavior?

3. Does this influence promote legal behavior?

4. Does this influence promote behavior that shows respect for myself and others?

5. Does this influence promote behavior that follows the guidelines of responsible adults, such as my parents or guardian?

6. Does this influence promote behavior that shows good character?

3. **Choose positive influences on health.** Review your answers to the six questions. Did you answer YES to the questions that applied? If so, the influence has a positive effect on health. For example, you might see a TV ad that encourages teens to be drug-free. You use the six questions to evaluate the effects of this TV ad on you. You answer YES to all six questions. It is a wise use of your time to view this ad.

4. **Protect yourself from negative influences on health.** Did you answer NO to one or more of the six questions? If so, the influence might have a negative effect on health. For example, you might listen to a song on the radio. The lyrics might encourage violence and include bad words. Your NO answers to the questions indicate this is a negative influence. It does not mean that you will be violent or use bad words. But you still must protect yourself from the potential that it might. Avoid listening to this song. Change the radio channel. Do not buy the CD that has this song on it.

Communicate in Healthful Ways

Students will demonstrate the ability to use interpersonal communication skills to enhance health.

Communication is the sharing of feelings, thoughts, and information with another person. How well do you communicate with others? Are you able to say NO to an action? Are you able to leave a situation? Are you able to settle disagreements without fighting? These are skills you can use.

Use Resistance Skills

What would you do if someone asked you to do something that was harmful? Unsafe? Illegal? Disrespectful? That did not follow the guidelines of responsible adults? That did not show good character? You can use resistance skills. **Resistance skills, or refusal skills,** are skills that are used to say NO to an action or to leave a situation.

1. Say NO in a firm voice.

2. Give reasons for saying NO.

3. Be certain your behavior matches your words.

4. Avoid situations in which there will be pressure to make wrong decisions.

5. Avoid being with people who make wrong decisions.

6. Resist pressure to do something illegal.

7. Influence others to make responsible decisions rather than wrong decisions.

Use Conflict Resolution Skills

Have you ever had a conflict or disagreement with someone? Did communication break down? Did you settle the disagreement without fighting? Did you settle the disagreement in a responsible way? **Conflict resolution skills** are steps that can be taken to settle a disagreement in a responsible way.

1. **Remain calm.**

2. **Discuss the ground rules with the other person.**
   - Do not blame.
   - Do not use put-downs.
   - Do not interrupt
   - Do not use threats.

3. **Describe the conflict.**
   - Tell what you think happened.
   - Be honest about what you have said or done to cause the conflict.
   - Use I-messages to express your feelings about the conflict.
   - Allow the other person to describe what (s)he thinks happened.
   - Listen without interrupting.
   - Respond to the other person's feelings.

4. **Brainstorm a list of possible solutions.**

5. **Use the six questions from** *The Responsible Decision-Making Model*™ **to evaluate each possible solution.**
   - Will the solution lead to actions that are healthful?
   - Will the solution lead to actions that are safe?
   - Will the solution lead to actions that are legal?
   - Will the solution lead to actions that show respect for you and others?
   - Will the solution lead to actions that follow the guidelines of responsible adults, such as your parents or guardian?
   - Will the solution lead to actions that show good character?

6. **Agree on a solution.**
   - Keep your word and follow the solution on which you agreed.

7. **Ask a trusted adult for help if you cannot agree on a solution.**

HEALTH STANDARD 6
Make Responsible Decisions

Students will demonstrate the ability to use goal-setting and decision-making skills that enhance health.

The Responsible Decision-Making Model™ is a series of steps to follow to ensure that decisions lead to actions that promote health; protect safety; follow laws; show respect for self and others; follow guidelines set by responsible adults, such as a person's parents or guardian; and demonstrate good character.

1. Describe the situation that requires a decision.

2. List possible decisions you might make.

3. Share the list of possible decisions with a trusted adult.

4. Evaluate the consequences of each decision.
Ask yourself the following questions:

Will this decision result in actions that
- are healthful?
- are safe?
- are legal?
- show respect for myself and others?
- follow the guidelines of responsible adults, such as my parents or guardian?
- demonstrate good character?

Note: All six questions might not apply to each situation. Write or say "Does not apply" if a question does not apply to this situation. If you answer NO to any of the six questions, the decision is a wrong one.

5. Decide which decision is responsible and most appropriate.

6. Act on your decision and evaluate the results.

Be a Health Advocate

Students will demonstrate the ability to advocate for personal, family, and community health.

1. Choose an action for which you will advocate. A health advocate is a person who promotes health for self and others. Consider actions that protect and promote health. For example, cigarette smoke contains a drug called nicotine. Nicotine raises blood pressure and increases heart rate. People who smoke might become addicted to nicotine. It is very difficult for them to quit smoking. It is best never to try smoking. You have chosen to advocate for NO smoking.

2. Tell others about your commitment to advocate. A health advocate is willing to make a commitment. This involves being able to tell others where you stand. You are willing to say, "I am against cigarette smoking." "I will be a health advocate and encourage others not to smoke." "I will encourage others to avoid breathing cigarette smoke."

3. Match your words with your actions. Show others that you believe what you say. For example, suppose you are with friends at a restaurant. You must wait 15 minutes to be seated in the nonsmoking section. There are seats available in the smoking section. You wait rather than sitting in the smoking section.

4. Encourage others to choose healthful actions. Think of ways you encourage others and promote your cause. You might make a poster encouraging others not to smoke. You might collect money for the American Cancer Society. You might write a letter or email a child you know. You might tell the child why you do not smoke. You might encourage the child to pledge not to smoke.

Practice
Health Standards
for Success

Each health standard is important. To be successful, you will need to practice each of the health standards. This textbook includes several activities that will help you practice the health standards. With practice, you can master all seven health standards. When you master all seven health standards, you will reach your goal– Totally Awesome® Health.

Macmillan/McGraw-Hill

Totally Awesome® Health

Linda Meeks
The Ohio State University

Philip Heit
The Ohio State University

Macmillan McGraw-Hill

New York   Farmington

Credits

Cover Design and Illustration: Devost Design

Cover Photo: PhotoDisc

Photos: *All photographs are by Macmillan/McGraw-Hill (MMH); Roman Sapecki; Lew Lause; Ken Karp for MMH; and Dave Mager for MMH, except as noted below.*
Front Matter: S1: Bob Daemmrich/The Image Works; S2: Richard Hutchings/Photo Edit; S3: mr. Tony Freeman/Photo Edit; tc. Michael Newman/Photo Edit; S4: Blair Seitz/Photo Researchers; S7: David Young-Wolff/Photo Edit; S8: Bob Daemmrich/Stock Boston; S11: Dennis O'Clair/Stone; S12: Jonathan Nourok/Photo Edit; S15: David Young-Wolff/PhotoEdit; S16: Jeff Greenberg/Visuals Unlimited.

Illustrations: Jennifer King, Dave Odell

Unit 10 outlines emergency care procedures that reflect the standard of knowledge and accepted practices in the United States at the time this book was published. It is the teacher's responsibility to stay informed of changes in emergency care procedures in order to teach current accepted practices. The teacher can also recommend that students gain complete, comprehensive training from courses offered by the American Red Cross.

learning through listening

Students with print disabilities may be eligible to obtain an accessible, audio version of the pupil edition of this textbook. Please call Recording for the Blind & Dyslexic at 1-800-221-4792 for complete information.

Macmillan/McGraw-Hill

*A Division of The **McGraw·Hill** Companies*

Published by Macmillan/McGraw-Hill, of McGraw-Hill Education, a division of The McGraw-Hill Companies, Inc., Two Penn Plaza, New York, New York, 10121.

Printed in the United States of America

ISBN 0-02-280439-0 / 7

4 5 6 7 8 9 055/027 07 06 05 04

About the Authors

Professor Linda Meeks   Dr. Philip Heit

Linda Meeks and Philip Heit are emeritus professors of Health Education in the College of Education at The Ohio State University. Linda and Philip are America's most widely published health education co-authors. They have collaborated for more than 20 years, co-authoring more than 200 health books that are used by millions of students preschool through college. Together, they have helped state departments of education as well as thousands of school districts develop comprehensive school health education curricula. Their books and curricula are used throughout the United States as well as in Canada, Japan, Mexico, England, Puerto Rico, Spain, Egypt, Jordan, Saudi Arabia, Bermuda, and the Virgin Islands. Linda and Philip train professors as well as educators in state departments of education and school districts. Their book, *Comprehensive School Health Education: Totally Awesome® Strategies for Teaching Health,* is the most widely used book for teacher training in colleges, universities, and school districts. Thousands of teachers throughout the world have participated in their Totally Awesome® Teacher Training Workshops. Linda and Philip have been the keynote speakers for many teacher institutes and wellness conferences. They are personally and professionally committed to the health and well-being of youth.

Advisory Board

Medical Reviewers

Albert J. Hart, Jr., M.D.
Mid-Ohio OB-GYN, Inc.
Westerville, Ohio

Donna Bacchi, M.D., M.P.H.
Associate Professor of Pediatrics
Director, Division of
  Community Pediatrics
Texas Tech University
  Health Sciences Center
Lubbock, Texas

Reviewers

Kymm Ballard, M.A.
Physical Education, Athletics,
  and Sports Medicine
  Consultant
North Carolina Department of
  Public Instruction
Raleigh, North Carolina

Kay Bridges
Health Educator
Gaston County Public Schools
Gastonia, North Carolina

Lillie Burns
HIV/AIDS Prevention
  Education
Education Program
  Coordinator
Louisiana Department of
  Education
Baton Rouge, Louisiana

Deborah Carter-Hinton
Physical Education Health
  Resource Specialist
Joliet Public Schools
Joliet, IL

Anthony S. Catalano, Ph.D.
K–12 Health Coordinator
Melrose Public Schools
Melrose, Massachusetts

Galen Cole, M.P.H., Ph.D.
Division of Health
  Communication
Office of the Director
Centers for Disease Control
  and Prevention
Atlanta, Georgia

Brian Colwell, Ph.D.
Professor
Department of HLKN
Texas A&M University
College Station, Texas

Tommy Fleming, Ph.D.
Director of Health and
  Physical Education
Texas Education Agency
Austin, Texas

Denyce Ford, M.Ed., Ph.D.
Coordinator, Comprehensive
  School Health Education
District of Columbia Public
  Schools
Washington, D.C.

Elizabeth Gallun, M.A.
Specialist, Comprehensive
  Health Education
Maryland State Department of
  Education
Baltimore, Maryland

Mary Gooding
Health Instructor
Tom Joy Elementary School
Nashville, Tennessee

Linda Harrill-Rudisill, M.A.
Chairperson of Health
  Education
Gaston County Schools
Gastonia, North Carolina

Janet Henke
Middle School Team Leader
Baltimore County Public
  Schools
Baltimore, Maryland

Russell Henke
Coordinator of Health
Montgomery County Public
  Schools
Rockville, Maryland

Susan Jackson, B.S., M.A.
Health Promotion Specialist
Healthworks, Wake Medical
  Center
Raleigh, North Carolina

Robin Kimball
Belle Isle Enterprise Middle
  School
Oklahoma City, Oklahoma

Joe Leake, CHES
Curriculum Specialist
Baltimore City Public Schools
Baltimore, Maryland

Mary Marks, Ph.D.
Coordinator, Health and
  Physical Education
Fairfax County Public Schools
Falls Church, Virginia

Darlene Y. Nall
Health and Physical Education
  Instructor
Metro Nashville/Davidson
  County Public Schools
Nashville, Tennessee

Debra Ogden, M.A.
Coordinator of Health,
  Physical Education, Driver
  Education, and Safe and
  Drug-Free Programs
Collier County Public Schools
Naples, Florida

Michael Schaffer, M.A.
Supervisor of Health
  Education and Wellness
Prince George's County
  Public Schools
Upper Marlboro, Maryland

Merita Thompson, Ed.D.
Professor of Health Education
Eastern Kentucky University
Richmond, Kentucky

Linda Wright, M.A.
Project Director
HIV/AIDS Education
  Program
Washington, D.C.

Mental and Emotional Health

Unit 3

Growth and Development

Unit 4
Nutrition

Unit 5

Personal Health and Physical Activity

SAY NO!

Unit 6
Alcohol, Tobacco, and Other Drugs

Communicable and Chronic Diseases

Unit 8

Consumer and Community Health

Unit 9

Environmental Health

Unit 10

Injury Prevention and Safety

UNIT 1
Mental and Emotional Health

Lesson 1
How to Take Charge of Your Health

Lesson 2
How to Make Responsible Decisions

Lesson 3
How to Develop Good Character

Lesson 4
How to Develop Mental Fitness

Lesson 5
How to Manage Stress and Be Resilient

PRACTICE
HEALTH STANDARD 2

Access Valid Health Information, Products, and Services

Practice this standard at the end of this unit.

1. **Identify health information, products, and services you need.** Suppose you have a friend who is under a great deal of stress that is affecting her study habits.

2. **Locate health information, products, and services.** Name sources of help in your school and community your friend might use.

3. **Evaluate health information, products, and services.** Review who the sources of help are, the location in the community or school where the sources can

be found, and the time that the sources are available.

4. **Take action when the health information is misleading.** Suppose the school counselor is not available at the times your friend has a free period. Write a note to the school counselor explaining the situation and asking if (s)he can make adjustments to his or her schedule to meet with your friend.

How to Take Charge of Your Health

Life Skills

- ◆ **I will take responsibility for my health.**
- ◆ **I will practice life skills for health.**
- ◆ **I will gain health knowledge.**

Imagine that you are in a room filled with gifts. Each gift is something you have wanted. Imagine that you are giving yourself a gift. Choose which gift you would give yourself. Did you think about good health as a gift to give yourself? Or do you take good health for granted? Good health is a gift you should give yourself. Your parents or guardian, physician, dentist, and teacher can help you appreciate the gift of good health. However, you must learn to take charge of your own health.

The Lesson Objectives

- Tell the difference between a healthful behavior and a risk behavior.
- List and discuss ten factors that influence health status.
- Explain how and why you would use a *Health Behavior Inventory*.
- Design a health behavior contract.
- List and describe four skills you need to be a health literate person.

Vocabulary

health
physical health
mental health
social health
holistic effect
quality of life
healthful behavior
risk behavior
health status
The Wellness Scale
premature death
optimal health
heredity
random event
unnecessary risk
life skill
Health Behavior Inventory
health behavior contract
health knowledge
health literate person

What Is Health?

Health is the condition of a person's body, mind, emotions, and relationships. **Physical health** is the condition of a person's body. **Mental health** is the condition of a person's mind and emotions. **Social health** is the condition of a person's relationships.

A behavior that affects one kind of health—physical, mental, or social—can affect the others. The **holistic** (hoh·LIS·tik) **effect** is a term used to describe the effects one health behavior can have on total health. An example may be helpful. Suppose you work out to improve your physical health. As you work out, your blood circulates more easily to your brain. As a result, you think clearly and thus improve your mental health. When you think clearly, you can make better decisions about your relationships. As a result, you improve your social health.

This example shows how one healthful behavior can improve the quality of your life in several ways. **Quality of life** is the degree to which a person lives life to the fullest capacity.

A **healthful behavior** is an action that:

● promotes health;

● prevents illness, injury, and premature death;

● and improves the quality of the environment.

A **risk behavior** is an action that:

● threatens health;

● increases the likelihood of illness and premature death;

● and harms the quality of the environment.

Unfortunately, choosing even one risk behavior can harm the quality of your life in several ways. Suppose a teen is rude and, as a result, has no friends. Having no friends means poor social health. This teen might feel stressed and be unable to sleep. Physical health declines due to tiredness. When (s)he is tired, the teen cannot work quickly to solve problems. His or her mental health is affected.

How Can I Achieve Optimal Health Status?

Health status is the condition of a person's health. To consider a person's health status, use *The Wellness Scale*. *The Wellness Scale* is a scale that shows the range of possible health conditions from premature death to optimal health. **Premature death** is death that occurs before a person reaches his or her life expectancy. **Optimal health** is the highest level of health a person can achieve. The health conditions between premature death and optimal health are: major illness or injury, minor illness or injury, average health, and above average health.

Let's look at how *The Wellness Scale* works. Suppose you were going to rate the condition of a male teen. This teen smokes cigarettes and does not work out. He huffs and puffs when he climbs stairs. He coughs in the morning. How might you rate his health using *The Wellness Scale*? Because his health status is not what you might expect for someone his age, his rating is low. He chooses behaviors that are likely to lead to illness and premature death.

Now, suppose you have an 80-year-old grandmother who lives with you. She has good relationships with your family. She spends time with friends. She eats a balanced diet and walks daily. She takes prescription medicine only according to the directions. She has a hearing aid to correct her hearing loss. Could your grandmother have optimal health? Yes. Her health status is what you might expect for someone her age. She does everything possible to take charge of her health.

You can have optimal health. You can do everything possible to take charge of your health. Read through the list *Take Charge: Ten Factors That Influence Your Health Status*. There are some factors over which you have little control. For example, you have no control over your heredity. **Heredity** is the passing of characteristics from biological parents to their children. You might not control parts of the environment in which you live. A natural disaster or an accident might occur and affect your health. These are random events. A **random event** is an event over which a person does not have control. But, the good news is that you have a great deal of control over six out of the ten factors that affect your health status.

100

Optimal Health

Above Average Health

Average Health

Minor Illness or Injury

Major Illness or Injury

Premature Death

0

The Wellness Scale

Take Charge: Ten Factors That Influence Your Health Status

1. Your heredity

Take charge: Gain health knowledge about your biological parents and make the most of who you are.

2. The quality of the environment in which you live

Take charge: Strive to improve your environment.

3. The random events that occur in your life

Take charge: Do the best you can with what you have.

4. The health care available to you

Take charge: Get health care when you need it. Have regular checkups.

5. The behaviors you choose

Take charge: Choose healthful behaviors and avoid risk behaviors.

6. The quality of the relationships you have

Take charge: Choose friends who encourage you to choose healthful behaviors and make responsible decisions.

7. The decisions you make

Take charge: Make responsible decisions about your health.

8. Your ability to say NO to wrong actions

Take charge: Say NO when someone pressures you to act in ways that are harmful, are unsafe, are illegal, are disrespectful of yourself or your parents or guardian, or that lack character.

9. The kinds of risks you take

Take charge: Do not take unnecessary risks. An **unnecessary risk** is a chance that is not worth taking after careful consideration of the possible outcomes.

10. Your ability to bounce back from difficult times

Take charge: Make adjustments when difficult times discourage you.

What Are 100 Life Skills I Should Practice?

A **life skill** is a healthful action that is learned and practiced for a lifetime. To take charge of your health, you need to practice life skills. There are 10 units in this book. Ten life skills are recommended for each unit. A *Health Behavior Inventory* is a personal assessment tool that shows which life skills a person practices. The *Health Behavior Inventory* on the following pages includes the 100 life skills that are in the 10 units in this book. Use this *Health Behavior Inventory* to learn about your health behavior.

Health Behavior Inventory

Directions: Number from 1 to 100 on a separate sheet of paper. Read each life skill carefully. Write YES or NO next to the same number on your paper. Each YES response indicates a life skill you are working on right now. Each NO response indicates a life skill you are not working on right now. Leave a blank if you do not understand what the life skill involves. Some life skills may not relate to your life right now. Some may not apply to you. You will learn more about each life skill as you read this book. The listed life skills are not of equal value. You will learn that some life skills affect your health more than others.

Mental and Emotional Health

1. I will take responsibility for my health.
2. I will practice life skills for health.
3. I will gain health knowledge.
4. I will make responsible decisions.
5. I will develop good character.
6. I will use resistance skills when appropriate.
7. I will communicate with others in healthful ways.
8. I will choose behaviors that promote a healthy mind.
9. I will follow a plan to manage stress.
10. I will be resilient during difficult times.

Growth and Development

21. I will keep my body systems healthy.
22. I will achieve the developmental tasks of adolescence.
23. I will recognize habits that protect female reproductive health.
24. I will recognize habits that protect male reproductive health.
25. I will learn about pregnancy and childbirth.
26. I will provide responsible care for infants and children.
27. I will practice abstinence to avoid teen pregnancy and parenthood.
28. I will develop habits that promote healthful aging.
29. I will develop my learning style.
30. I will share with my family my feelings about dying and death.

Family and Social Health

11. I will develop healthful family relationships.
12. I will work to improve difficult family relationships.
13. I will make healthful adjustments to family changes.
14. I will use conflict resolution skills.
15. I will develop healthful relationships.
16. I will develop skills to prepare for dating.
17. I will recognize harmful relationships.
18. I will practice abstinence.
19. I will develop skills to prepare for marriage.
20. I will develop skills to prepare for parenthood.

Nutrition

31. I will follow the Dietary Guidelines.
32. I will eat the recommended number of servings from the Food Guide Pyramid.
33. I will plan a healthful diet that reduces the risk of disease.
34. I will evaluate food labels.
35. I will select foods that contain nutrients.
36. I will develop healthful eating habits.
37. I will follow the Dietary Guidelines when I go out to eat.
38. I will protect myself from foodborne illnesses.
39. I will maintain a desirable weight and body composition.
40. I will develop skills to prevent eating disorders.

Personal Health and Physical Activity

41. I will have regular examinations.

42. I will follow a dental health plan.

43. I will be well-groomed.

44. I will get adequate rest and sleep.

45. I will participate in regular physical activity.

46. I will develop and maintain health-related fitness.

47. I will develop and maintain skill-related fitness.

48. I will follow a physical fitness plan.

49. I will prevent physical activity-related injuries and illnesses.

50. I will be a responsible spectator and participant in sports.

Alcohol, Tobacco, and Other Drugs

51. I will follow guidelines for the safe use of prescription and OTC drugs.

52. I will not misuse or abuse drugs.

53. I will be aware of resources for the treatment of drug misuse and abuse.

54. I will choose a drug-free lifestyle to reduce my risk of violence and accidents.

55. I will choose a drug-free lifestyle to reduce my risk of HIV, STDs, and unwanted pregnancy.

56. I will practice protective factors that help me stay away from drugs.

57. I will use resistance skills if I am pressured to misuse or abuse drugs.

58. I will avoid tobacco use and secondhand smoke.

59. I will not drink alcohol.

60. I will not be involved in illegal drug use.

Communicable and Chronic Diseases

61. I will choose behaviors to prevent the spread of pathogens.
62. I will choose behaviors to reduce my risk of infection with communicable diseases.
63. I will keep a personal health record.
64. I will choose behaviors to reduce my risk of infection with sexually transmitted diseases.
65. I will choose behaviors to reduce my risk of HIV infection.
66. I will choose behaviors to reduce my risk of cardiovascular diseases.
67. I will choose behaviors to reduce my risk of cancer.
68. I will recognize ways to manage chronic health conditions.
69. I will recognize ways to manage asthma and allergies.
70. I will choose behaviors to reduce my risk of diabetes.

Environmental Health

81. I will help keep the air clean.
82. I will help keep the water safe.
83. I will help keep noise at a safe level.
84. I will precycle, recycle, and dispose of waste properly.
85. I will help conserve energy and natural resources.
86. I will be a health advocate for the environment.
87. I will stay informed about environmental issues.
88. I will protect the natural environment.
89. I will take actions to improve my visual environment.
90. I will take actions to improve my social-emotional environment.

Consumer and Community Health

71. I will evaluate sources of health information.
72. I will develop media literacy.
73. I will make a plan to manage time and money.
74. I will choose healthful entertainment.
75. I will recognize my rights as a consumer.
76. I will take action if my consumer rights are violated.
77. I will make responsible choices about health care providers and facilities.
78. I will evaluate ways to pay for health care.
79. I will be a health advocate by being a volunteer.
80. I will investigate health careers.

Injury Prevention and Safety

91. I will practice protective factors to reduce the risk of violence.
92. I will practice self-protection strategies.
93. I will respect authority and obey laws.
94. I will participate in victim recovery if I am harmed by violence.
95. I will stay away from gangs.
96. I will not carry a weapon.
97. I will follow safety guidelines to reduce the risk of unintentional injuries.
98. I will follow guidelines for motor vehicle safety.
99. I will follow safety guidelines for severe weather and natural disasters.
100. I will be skilled in first aid procedures.

How Do I Design a Health Behavior Contract?

Suppose you have just completed the *Health Behavior Inventory* on pages 8 through 11. You might have responded NO to some of the life skills.

Your NO response indicates that you are not working on these life skills. Suppose a life skill to which you responded NO was: *I will get adequate rest and sleep.* To have optimal health status, you must practice this life skill. A **health behavior contract** is a written plan to develop the habit of practicing a specific life skill. Look to the right to learn how to design a health behavior contract.

There is something else you need to make a health behavior contract work for you. You need health knowledge. **Health knowledge** is facts about health. You need health knowledge so you can complete the second part of the plan by writing a few statements to describe how the life skill will affect your health. You also need health knowledge for the fourth part so you can evaluate how your plan worked.

- **This book helps you gain health knowledge.**
- **You will learn how life skills affect your health.**
- **You will learn how to make a plan to practice a specific life skill.**

How to Design a Health Behavior Contract

There are four parts of a health behavior contract.

1. Tell the life skill you want to practice.

2. Write a few statements to describe how the life skill will affect your health.

3. Design a specific plan to practice the life skill and way to record your progress in making the life skill a habit.

4. Describe the results you got when you tried the plan.

Activity

Health Behavior Contract

Copy the health behavior contract on a separate sheet of paper.

DO NOT WRITE IN THIS BOOK.

Name: _____Your name_____ **Date:** _Today's date_

Life Skill: I will get adequate rest and sleep.

Effect on My Health: Someone my age needs eight to ten hours of sleep. When I sleep, my heart rate slows by about 10 to 15 beats per minute. My blood pressure decreases. I take fewer breaths per minute. When I wake up, I have energy for the day. I perform well in school. My immune system is strong, so I get sick less often.

My Plan: I will establish a sleep schedule. I will go to bed at 10:00 p.m. and get up at 7:00 a.m. I will record how much sleep I get. I also will be careful about what I eat and drink before going to bed. I will not eat or drink anything that contains caffeine. Caffeine is a stimulant and will make me restless. I will complete a chart for a week. I will write down the time I went to bed and the time I got up. I will write down the foods and drinks I had in the evening.

My Calendar	M	T	W	Th	F	S	S
	Bed 10 p.m.	Up at 7 a.m.; bed late, 11 p.m.	Slept in; drank cola after 8 p.m.; couldn't sleep.	Bed 9 p.m.	Up at 6 a.m.; to bed late.	Tired all day; to bed on time.	Up early; drank milk before bed.

How My Plan Worked: I got enough sleep five out of the seven nights. I was tired both days after I did not get enough sleep. One evening I drank a cola beverage that kept me awake.

What Skills Do I Need to Be Health Literate?

The goal of your health class is to motivate you to practice life skills and to become health literate. A **health literate person** is a person who has skills in:

1. effective communication;
2. self-directed learning;
3. critical thinking (also called problem solving);
4. and responsible citizenship.

The symbols below show the skills you need to be health literate. The descriptions tell what you can do to develop and practice the skills.

You can write, speak in front of a group, make a graph, or use technology to express yourself.

You can investigate situations in order to solve your problems. You can use *The Responsible Decision-Making Model*™ in Lesson 2 of this book.

You can gather and use health facts on your own. You can visit a Web site to learn facts. You can check the card catalog in the library and check out books to read. You can attend a speech or contact an organization. Of course, you must be careful to choose reliable sources.

You can investigate ways to promote health in your community, nation, and world.

Review

Vocabulary Words

Write a separate sentence using each vocabulary word listed on page 4.

Health Content

1. What is the difference between a healthful behavior and a risk behavior? **page 5**

2. What are ten factors that influence your health status? **page 7**

3. Why might you complete a *Health Behavior Inventory?* **page 8**

4. What are the four parts to include when you design a health behavior contract? **page 12**

5. What are four kinds of skills you need to be a health literate person? **page 14**

The Responsible Decision-Making Model™

Your classmate explains that he might as well smoke cigarettes. "What's the big deal?" he says. "After all, I could get struck by a car and die young. What's in the cards is in the cards." Write a response for your classmate to read. Explain the difference between a random event and a risk behavior. Then, answer the following questions on a separate sheet of paper. Write "Does not apply" if a question does not apply to this situation.

1. Is it healthful to smoke? Why or why not?

2. Is it safe to smoke? Why or why not?

3. Is it legal to smoke? Why or why not?

4. Will he show respect for himself and others if he smokes? Why or why not?

5. Will his parents or guardian approve of his smoking? Why or why not?

6. Will smoking demonstrate good character? Why or why not?

What is the responsible decision for your classmate to make in this situation?

Health Literacy

Effective Communication

Look at the symbol for effective communication. Create another symbol for that skill. Use a computer, markers, colored pencils, paints, or other media. Share your symbol with classmates.

Critical Thinking

Suppose you eat a healthful breakfast every morning. How might this healthful behavior have a holistic effect on your health? Suppose you skip breakfast every morning. How might this risk behavior have a holistic effect on your health?

How to Make Responsible Decisions

Life Skill

◆ **I will make responsible decisions.**

Consider how many decisions you make during a typical day. How do you make those decisions? Do you consider possible decisions you might make and then evaluate each? Do you check out decisions with your parents or guardian? Do your friends influence the decisions you make? Do you put off making decisions as long as possible? You need to know how you can make responsible decisions. You need to know when it is responsible to take risks and dares.

The Lesson Objectives

- Tell the difference between a responsible decision and a wrong decision.
- List and discuss ways to prove to yourself and others that you are responsible.
- Use *The Responsible Decision-Making Model™* to determine what action to take in a given situation.
- Tell the difference between an unnecessary risk and a calculated risk.
- Identify six questions to ask to evaluate the possible outcomes of a risk or dare before you take it.

Vocabulary

responsible

responsible decision

wrong decision

restitution

The Responsible Decision-Making Model™

risk

calculated risk

unnecessary risk

dare

What Are Ways I Can Show I Am Responsible?

To be **responsible** is to be accountable and dependable. There are five ways to prove to yourself and others that you are responsible.

1. **Make responsible decisions rather than wrong decisions.**
   A **responsible decision** is a choice that leads to actions that:
   - are healthful;
   - are safe;
   - are legal;
   - show respect for self and others;
   - follow the guidelines of parents and other responsible adults;
   - and demonstrate good character.

   A **wrong decision** is a choice that leads to actions that:
   - harm health;
   - are unsafe;
   - are illegal;
   - show disrespect for self and others;
   - disregard the guidelines of parents and other responsible adults;
   - and do not demonstrate good character.

2. **Take responsibility for wrong decisions.** Remember, you have control over what you say and do. If you make a wrong decision, do not blame others. Do not make excuses. Admit you were wrong.

3. **Make restitution for wrong decisions, if possible. Restitution** is making good for any loss or damage.

4. **Recognize that some wrong decisions cannot be "fixed."** Show and tell others you are truly sorry for a wrong decision you made. Reassure others that you do not intend to repeat the same wrong decision.

5. **Listen to the advice of responsible adults.** Adults have experienced the outcomes of the decisions they made as teens. They want you to experience positive outcomes. They want to help you avoid wrong decisions that result in negative outcomes.

How Do I Use The Responsible Decision-Making Model™?

The Responsible Decision-Making Model™ is a series of steps to follow to assure that decisions lead to actions that:

- promote health;
- protect safety;
- follow laws;
- show respect for self and others;
- follow guidelines set by responsible adults, such as a person's parents or guardian;
- and demonstrate good character.

The Responsible Decision-Making Model™

1. Describe the situation that requires a decision.
2. List possible decisions you might make.
3. Share the list of possible decisions with a trusted adult.
4. Evaluate the consequences of each decision. Ask yourself the following questions.

Will this decision result in actions that:

- are healthful?
- are safe?
- are legal?
- show respect for myself and others?
- follow the guidelines of responsible adults, such as my parents or guardian?
- demonstrate good character?

Note: All six questions may not apply to each situation. Write "Does not apply" if a question does not apply to this situation. If you answer NO to any of the six questions, the decision is a wrong one.

5. Decide which decision is responsible and most appropriate.
6. Act on your decision and evaluate the results.

Activity

Use The Responsible Decision-Making Model™

Life Skill: I will make responsible decisions.

Materials: paper, pen or pencil

Directions: A situation in which you need to make a decision is described below. Use the six questions from *The Responsible Decision-Making Model™* to help you make a responsible decision. Answer YES or NO to each question. Explain each answer. Write "Does not apply" if a question does not apply to this situation. Write your answers on a separate sheet of paper.

Situation: You stay home from school because you have the flu. Your physician said you could easily spread flu germs to others. After school, your friend calls. You are bored and want some company. You do not tell your friend that you could spread flu germs. Should you ask your friend to come over and watch a videotape with you?

1. Is it healthful for your friend to come over and watch the videotape with you? Why or why not?

2. Is it safe for your friend to come over and watch the videotape with you? Why or why not?

3. Is it legal for your friend to come over and watch the video-tape with you? Why or why not?

4. Will you show respect for your friend if you do not tell him or her you could spread flu germs? Why or why not?

5. Will your parents or guardian approve if you ask your friend to come over and watch the video-tape with you? Why or why not?

6. Will you demonstrate good character if you ask your friend to come over and watch the video-tape with you? Why or why not?

What is the responsible decision to make in this situation?

When Should I Take Risks and Dares?

Calculated Risks Have Benefits

A **risk** is a chance that a person takes that has an unknown outcome. A **calculated risk** is a chance that is worth taking after careful consideration of the possible outcomes. Calculated risks can yield benefits. For example, you might call a new classmate to begin a friendship. You might try out for the soccer team or take a higher-level math course. Even if you do not succeed at these tasks, you benefit from trying. The risk is worth taking.

Unnecessary Risks Can Be a Disaster!

An **unnecessary risk** is a chance that is not worth taking after careful consideration of the possible outcomes. Unnecessary risks can be disasters. The Centers for Disease Control and Prevention (CDC) has identified behaviors that are unnecessary risks for teens.

Six Categories of Risk Behaviors for Teens

1. Behaviors that result in unintentional and intentional injuries
2. Tobacco use
3. Alcohol and other drug use
4. Sexual behaviors that result in infection with HIV or other sexually transmitted diseases
5. Diet choices that contribute to disease
6. Lack of physical activity

"I dare you. I double-dare you!"

A **dare** is a request to do something as a test of courage. If someone dares you to run for class president, go for it! The person has dared you to take a calculated risk. Even if you lose, the outcome will be positive because you tried. However, if someone dares you to cheat, lie, or engage in risk behaviors—say NO. These are unnecessary risks. The outcomes will be negative.

Check Out Risks and Dares

Use the six questions from *The Responsible Decision-Making Model™* to make decisions about any risks and dares you are tempted to take. The six questions will help you evaluate the possible outcomes of a decision before you make it.

Vocabulary Words

Write a separate sentence using each vocabulary word listed on page 16.

Health Content

1. What is the difference between a responsible decision and a wrong decision? **page 17**

2. What are five ways to prove to yourself and others that you are a responsible person? **page 17**

3. What are six questions to ask yourself to evaluate the possible consequences of a decision *before* you make it? **page 18**

4. What is the difference between a calculated risk and an unnecessary risk? **page 20**

5. How can you check out risks and dares before you decide to take them? **page 20**

The Responsible Decision-Making Model™

A classmate dares you to place a firecracker in a friend's mailbox. When you say NO, he says he will accept any dare you give him if you take his dare. Answer the following questions on a separate sheet of paper. Write "Does not apply" if a question does not apply to this situation.

1. Is it healthful to place a firecracker in a friend's mailbox? Why or why not?

2. Is it safe to place a firecracker in a friend's mailbox? Why or why not?

3. Is it legal to place a firecracker in a friend's mailbox? Why or why not?

4. Will you show respect for your friend and his or her family if you place a firecracker in their mailbox? Why or why not?

5. Will your parents or guardian approve if you place a firecracker in a friend's mailbox? Why or why not?

6. Will you demonstrate good character if you place a firecracker in a friend's mailbox? Why or why not?

What is the responsible decision to make in this situation?

Health Literacy

Effective Communication

On a small card or piece of paper, write the six questions to use to evaluate the possible consequences of a decision. Keep it in your purse or wallet.

Critical Thinking

Suppose you are having difficulty making a decision. Why would it be important for you to listen to the advice of responsible adults?

How to Develop Good Character

 Life Skills

- ◆ I will develop good character.
- ◆ I will use resistance skills when appropriate.

Vocabulary

responsible value
character
self-control
reputation
self-respect
peers
peer pressure
resistance skills

Imagine that you are an architect designing a skyscraper. Your design includes unique windows, stairways, and other unusual features. However, the builder asks questions about the foundation you are planning. The builder knows the foundation of a building is more important than the appearance. Do you realize that you already are a kind of architect? You are designing a premier product—the kind of adult you will be. Your appearance, your clothing, and your abilities all influence the kind of adult you will be. But, these are like the windows and stairways of a building— necessary, but not the foundation. Your character is the foundation that will determine the kind of adult you will be.

The Lesson Objectives

- Explain how you can develop good character.
- Explain why it is important to have a good reputation.
- List and discuss three ways to do a character checkup.
- Use resistance skills if you are pressured to do something wrong.
- Explain what you should do if you give in to negative peer pressure.

How Can I Develop Good Character?

Your character is related to your values. A value is a standard or belief that is important to you. A **responsible value** is a standard or belief that guides a person to behave in responsible ways. For example, honesty is a responsible value. If honesty is one of your values, you tell the truth.

Character is a person's use of self-control to act on responsible values. **Self-control** is the degree to which a person regulates his or her own behavior. Let's use the example of honesty again. Suppose honesty is one of your values. When you have good character, you use self-control if you are tempted to lie. You do not lie, even if lying might be easier than telling the truth.

Your character influences your reputation. A person's **reputation** is what most people think of the person. Again, let's use the example of honesty. When you are honest, other people notice your actions. You will develop a reputation for being honest. Because you have a reputation for being honest, people will trust you. Responsible people will respect you.

Now let's examine what happens if a teen does not have good character. She does not behave in responsible ways. Taking care of her health is not one of her values. As a result, she does not use self-control and does not choose healthful behaviors. Instead, she goes to parties where teens use alcohol and other drugs. She uses alcohol and other drugs, too. Other teens notice her actions. She develops a reputation for misusing and abusing drugs. Responsible teens avoid her. Their parents or guardians do not believe she is a good choice for a friend.

To develop good character, choose responsible values and use self-control to regulate your behavior.

Character Values

loyalty

honesty

responsibility

commitment

self-discipline

trust

respect

integrity

What Are Ways I Can Do a Character Checkup?

Developing good character helps you develop self-respect. **Self-respect** is a high regard for oneself because one behaves in responsible ways. It is wise to do a character checkup every now and then. Here are three ways to check on your character.

1. **Consider how you would feel to have your name discussed for actions on the six o'clock news or mentioned in the headlines of a story in your local newspaper.** For example, would you be proud to have your name in any of the headlines below? For some headlines, the answer would be "yes." For others, "no."

2. **Make a list of ten of your values and evaluate each.** Do you have responsible values? Do you use self-control to act on these values?

3. **Ask responsible adults, such as your parents or guardian, to help you do a character checkup.** Listen carefully to their feedback and suggestions.

Dylan volunteers to help at cancer society

LaShawn refuses to get in an automobile with a driver who was drinking

Kayley steals a bookbag from locker

Tori talks behind the back of best friend

Jeremy cheats on math test

Activity

Newspaper Headlines

Life Skill: I will develop good character.

Materials: piece of butcher paper, pen or pencil, computer (optional), photograph of yourself (optional)

Directions: Write a story about something you have done of which you are proud. Imagine that the story will appear in your local newspaper. Follow each of the steps described below.

1. **Think of something you have done that shows you have good character.** Write a story describing your actions.

2. **Imagine that your story will appear on the first page of your local newspaper.** Create an eye-catching headline for your story.

3. **Create a newspaper page using the butcher paper or a computer.** Include your newspaper headline and your story (see the sample). Be creative.

4. **Share your newspaper story and headline with your classmates.**

5. **Discuss the following questions with your classmates.** How does having good character affect a person's reputation? Why is it important to have a good reputation?

The Character Gazette | Cloudy 62°

Teen returns wallet to senior citizen

xxxxxxxxxxxxxxxxxxxxxxxxxxxxxxxxx
xxxxxxxxxxxxxxxxxxxxxxxxxxxxxxxxx
xxxxxxxxxxxxxxxxxxxxxxxxxxxxxxxx

How Can I Resist Pressure to Do Something Wrong?

Peers are people of similar age or status. The friends with whom you hang out are peers. Students at your school whom you do not know well also are peers. **Peer pressure** is influence that peers place on others to convince them to behave in certain ways. Some peers may pressure you to do something wrong, such as cheating on a test or stealing something from a store. This kind of peer pressure is negative peer pressure.

When you have good character, you know the difference between right and wrong. However, you still must resist negative peer pressure. What can you do if someone calls you a chicken? What can you do if someone dares you to do something unsafe? What can you do if someone you really like pressures you to do something that will harm your health? You can use resistance skills. **Resistance skills** are skills that are used to say NO to an action or to leave a situation.

Resistance Skills

1. Say NO in a firm voice.
2. Give reasons for saying NO.
3. Be certain your behavior matches your words.
4. Avoid situations in which there will be pressure to make wrong decisions.
5. Avoid being with people who make wrong decisions.
6. Resist pressure to do something illegal.
7. Influence others to make responsible decisions rather than wrong decisions.

No one will know if you do it just this once!

Don't be a chicken! Try it! You'll really like it!

What's the big deal?

I dare you.

Everyone else does it.

Activity
Lines, Lines, and More Lines

Life Skill: I will use resistance skills when appropriate.

Materials: paper, pen or pencil

Directions: Resistance skills are skills you can use to say NO to an action or to leave a situation. Follow the steps below to practice resistance skills with your classmates. Your teacher will divide your class into groups of five students.

1. **Select one student in your group to write the group's responses.**

2. **Make a "Top Ten List of Pressure Statements."** Your group will brainstorm statements peers might use to pressure others to do something wrong. An example might be, "Everyone our age does it." Review your group's list of pressure statements. As a group, select the ten most persuasive statements. List these in order from the most persuasive to the least persuasive statement.

3. **Assign one of the following risk behaviors to each student in your group.**
   - Smoking cigarettes
   - Joining a gang
   - Getting into a car driven by a drunk driver
   - Cheating on an exam
   - Hitchhiking home from school

4. **Review the reasons to resist pressure to participate in risk behaviors.** One or more of the following reasons can be used to say NO to a specific risk behavior.
   - The risk behavior harms health.
   - The risk behavior is unsafe.
   - The risk behavior is illegal.
   - The risk behavior does not show respect for myself and others.
   - The risk behavior does not follow the guidelines of responsible adults, such as my parents or guardian.
   - The risk behavior does not demonstrate good character.

5. **Use pressure statements to persuade a student in your group to participate in the risk behavior to which (s)he was assigned.** For example, one student in your group was assigned "smoking cigarettes." The other students in your group should use pressure statements from your group's "Top Ten List of Pressure Statements" to try to convince this student to smoke.

6. **Allow the student who is being pressured to practice using resistance skills.** The student should say NO and then give a reason. The student should use one or more of the reasons given in step 4. For example, the student might say, "NO. Smoking cigarettes harms health."

7. **Repeat this process, allowing each student in your group a chance to practice using resistance skills.**

What Should I Do If I Give In to Negative Peer Pressure?

Make a U-turn and get back to responsible behavior!

If you are doing something wrong, stop and change directions. The sooner you change directions and return to responsible behavior, the better. Be honest and do not blame others for your mistake. Forget the excuses. Never think your wrong behavior will be OK as long as your parents or guardian or other responsible adults do not find out what you have done. Admit your wrong behavior. Try to correct any wrongdoing you might have caused. Make restitution if possible. Restitution is making good for any loss or damage.

Try to figure out why you gave in to negative peer pressure. What "pushed your button?" Was it important to you to feel accepted? Did you want to appear grown up? Were you seeking a thrill? One way to develop good character is to continue to evaluate what motivates you to do something. Remember, you want to be motivated by responsible values, not by negative peer pressure.

Think ahead to the next time you are likely to be pressured in the same way. Make a plan to handle the pressure. Rehearse what you will say and do. Ask a parent, guardian, or other responsible adult to help you.

Vocabulary Words

Write a separate sentence using each vocabulary word listed on page 22.

Health Content

1. How can you develop good character? **page 23**

2. Why is it important to have a good reputation? **page 23**

3. What are three ways you can do a character checkup? **page 24**

4. What are seven resistance skills you can use if you are pressured to do something wrong? **page 26**

5. What should you do if you give in to negative peer pressure? **page 28**

The Responsible Decision-Making Model™

A classmate invites you to a party where teens will be drinking alcohol. Your classmate says you should go to the party and lie to your parents or guardian about where you are going. Answer the following questions on a separate sheet of paper. Write "Does not apply" if a question does not apply to this situation.

1. Is it healthful for you to attend the party and lie about it? Why or why not?

2. Is it safe for you to attend the party and lie about it? Why or why not?

3. Is it legal for you to attend the party and lie about it? Why or why not?

4. Will you show respect for your parents or guardian if you attend the party and lie about it? Why or why not?

5. Will your parents or guardian approve if they find out that you attended the party and lied to them? Why or why not?

6. Will you demonstrate good character if you attend the party and lie about it? Why or why not?

What is the responsible decision to make in this situation?

Health Literacy

Effective Communication

Write a six-line poem about good character. Use at least three vocabulary words from this lesson.

Self-Directed Learning

Go to the library. Find two books that address the topic of good character. Copy the correct bibliographical information about each book on a separate index card.

How to Develop Mental Fitness

Life Skills

- ◆ **I will communicate with others in healthful ways.**
- ◆ **I will choose behaviors that promote a healthy mind.**

Many people talk about the importance of fitness. Usually, they mean physical fitness. Physical fitness is the condition of the body that results from regular physical activity. Regular physical activity helps the parts of the body function at their best. You do not hear many people talk about mental fitness. Mental fitness is the condition of the mind. When you achieve mental fitness, you communicate well with others. You know what to do when you feel angry and insecure. You know that you need to avoid addictions.

The Lesson Objectives

- List and discuss positive personality traits you might develop.
- Explain four things you can do to communicate effectively.
- List and discuss steps you can take to stay in control of yourself when you are really angry.
- Explain how you can carry on when you are feeling insecure.
- Explain how you can feel good about yourself without turning to an "instant fix" or addiction.

Vocabulary

personality

sense of humor

optimistic

gratitude

communication

nonverbal communication

feeling

I-message

you-message

anger

anger cue

insecure

self-esteem

instant gratification

addiction

denial

codependence

phobia

How Can I Develop a Terrific Personality?

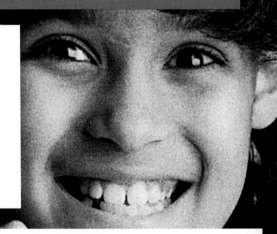

No two people are alike. They differ in the traits they inherited from their parents, as well as in the traits they have developed. A trait is a distinguishing quality or characteristic. **Personality** is a person's unique blend of traits. To develop a terrific personality, you need to work on two areas. You need to make the most of your inherited traits, and you need to develop the positive personality traits that are listed and discussed below.

Positive Personality Traits

- Having a sense of humor
- Having knowledge on different topics
- Avoiding put-downs
- Being optimistic
- Showing gratitude
- Having good manners

A **sense of humor** is an ability to see the funny side of a situation. If you have a sense of humor, you do not take yourself too seriously. You are able to laugh and make others laugh. A sense of humor helps keep you and others from becoming stressed.

Having knowledge on different topics helps you grow mentally. You can contribute meaningfully to conversations. You are able to comment on a wide range of topics. Other people will find you interesting and well-informed. They will like to be with you.

Avoiding put-downs allows other people to feel comfortable in your presence. Other people can enjoy being with you without feeling you will insult or attack them. Being **optimistic** is tending to expect positive outcomes. If you are optimistic, you are upbeat. You see the good in things and people around you. Other people will not feel like you are a "downer" when you are around them.

Showing **gratitude** is feeling thankful for a favor or for something that is pleasing. If you show gratitude, other people know that you have noticed something they have done for you. They feel appreciated rather than taken for granted. Having good manners helps you feel confident. You know when to say please, thank you, and excuse me. Other people notice that you are considerate of them.

How Can I Communicate Effectively?

Communication is the sharing of feelings, thoughts, and information with another person. Verbal communication is the use of words to express oneself. The words you use and how you say them are both important. For example, you might express yourself during conversation or in a letter. The words you say and the tone you use will both be considered by the other person. **Nonverbal communication** is the use of actions to express oneself. For example, you might frown, smile, or shake your head to convey a message to another person.

To communicate effectively:
- have knowledge on different topics;
- express feelings in healthful ways;
- listen carefully when other people are speaking;
- develop a balanced conversation style.

Have knowledge on different topics.

Being knowledgeable is very important. You have so much more to offer other people when you have an active mind. So, gain knowledge by reading books and magazines. Stay up-to-date on current events. Know what is going on around you. Develop hobbies of interest to you that you can discuss with others. Make a point of learning something new every day.

I-message

Express feelings in healthful ways.

A **feeling** is an emotion. Love, happiness, sadness, disappointment, and anger are feelings everyone experiences. It is important to recognize what you are feeling and why you feel the way you do. You also need to express your feelings in healthful ways by using I-messages. An **I-message** is a statement or message that contains:

1. a reference to a specific behavior or event;
2. the effect of the behavior or event;
3. and the feelings that result.

Suppose you have worked all weekend on a history project. On your way to school, you drop your papers, and they land in a puddle. At the dinner table, your parent or guardian asks about your day. You share your disappointment with the following I-message.

1. On the way to school, I dropped my history project in a puddle. (the event)

2. The ink ran and muddled the page. (the effect)

3. I was so disappointed I could have cried. (your feeling)

This I-message does not threaten anyone. Now, consider how an I-message also might be used to express your feelings in a tense situation. A friend of yours tells you that another friend talks behind your back. You are furious. You see the friend who gossips about you after school. You share your anger with the following I-message.

1. I learned that you have talked behind my back. (the event)

2. I am having difficulty trusting you. (the effect)

3. I am both angry and hurt. (your feeling)

The friend can respond to your I-message. (S)he does not feel threatened, and feels free to respond. The friend might explain that (s)he did not talk behind your back. The friend might affirm that (s)he did and is sorry. The I-message opens up the lines of communication. It helps both of you focus on what happened. A you-message does not open up the lines of communication. A **you-message** is a statement or message that blames or shames another person. For example, suppose you said, "You are a lousy friend for talking behind my back." Your friend would feel attacked, and his or her response would not be a positive one.

Listen carefully when other people are speaking.

Look directly at someone who is speaking to you. This allows you to see the person's facial expressions and actions. You are better able to hear what the person is saying. In addition, you show the other person that you care and are paying attention. Make certain you know what has been said. Ask the person questions if you do not understand something. Repeat what you think the person said.

Develop a balanced conversation style.

Think about your conversations with other people. Who does most of the talking? Who does most of the listening?

You have a balanced conversation style when you participate by both talking and listening. Don't hog the conversation. But, at the same time, don't sit back and remain silent most of the time.

You-message

How Can I Keep from Losing Control When I Am Angry?

Anger is a feeling of being irritated or annoyed. Everyone gets angry at times. You may get angry if you are frustrated or if someone hurts your feelings. It's OK to get angry, but it's not OK to lose control and do something you later regret. How can you stay in control of yourself when you get really angry?

1. **Recognize anger cues.** An **anger cue** is a body change that occurs when a person is angry. When you are angry, your heart rate and blood pressure might increase. You might breathe more rapidly and begin to sweat. Your mouth might become dry. You might feel depressed.

2. **Take a deep breath through your nose and blow it out through your mouth.** This action will relax you and counteract the anger cues or body changes you are experiencing.

3. **Express your anger in a healthful way. Use I-messages to express your anger.** Write a letter to express angry feelings.

4. **Blow off steam with physical and creative activity.** Your body and mind can become energized when you are angry. Physical activity reduces the tension in your body. Creative activity helps your mind relax.

5. **Talk with a responsible adult, such as your parents, your guardian, or a mentor.** They can help you understand why you are feeling angry. You can consider what you might do. You can discuss how to express your anger in a healthful way.

Keep the Lines of Communication Open at Home

- Do not talk back to your parents or guardian.
- Do not say or do anything you will regret later.
- Express your feelings with I-messages.

What Can I Do If I Feel Insecure?

To be **insecure** is to feel uncertain or to lack confidence. Everyone feels insecure at times. Some teens say they feel insecure when they are expected to give a speech in front of the class. Some teens say they feel insecure when they meet new people. Have you ever felt insecure? How do you respond when you feel insecure? Are you able to "carry on" or function well even though you do not feel confident? Or, do you fall apart? You can learn to work through feelings of insecurity.

How to Carry On When You Feel Insecure

Suppose you know a person who always puts you down. You feel insecure and threatened when this person is around.

1. **Develop positive self-talk.** Tell yourself, "I am not going to let this person get to me."

2. **Pretend you have a coat of armor surrounding you that will protect you from danger.** Visualize a coat of armor that covers you and protects you from what this person says and does.

3. **Visualize your fears as arrows that bounce off your coat of armor.** Visualize this person's put-downs as arrows. The put-downs are directed at you, but they bounce off your coat of armor. The put-downs might hurt, but they cannot get inside, rip you apart, and cause you to bleed.

4. **Stay focused on what you must say or do, not on your fears.** Choose an appropriate response. Respond to the person with an I-message or ignore what the person has said.

5. **Discuss the source of your insecurity with a responsible adult or friend, and ask for that person's opinion.** Go over the situation later. Discuss ways to be more confident.

How Can I Avoid Addictions?

Self-esteem is a person's feelings about his or her worth. Self-esteem can be positive or negative. You develop positive self-esteem by making responsible decisions that result in responsible actions. As a result, you respect yourself and earn the respect of others. You have good feelings about yourself. But, suppose you often choose wrong actions. You do not respect yourself or earn the respect of others. As a result, you have negative self-esteem.

There are no short cuts to gaining self-respect and good feelings about yourself. It takes hard work and self-discipline. Yet, some people take short cuts. They try instant gratification. **Instant gratification** is choosing an immediate reward regardless of the possible harmful effects.

Suppose a teen wants to feel good. The best way for the teen to feel good is to choose responsible actions and work hard. (S)he might do homework and help with family chores. (S)he might give up doing what (s)he would like to do at a given time. This teen has learned that self-discipline and hard work will pay off.

But, suppose a teen wants to feel good right now. For this teen, what might happen in the future is not as important as feeling good right now. This teen might focus on getting an "instant fix"—an immediate way to forget troubles. This is the way teens develop addictions. An **addiction** is the compelling need to continue a behavior even if it is harmful. The addiction begins to substitute for better ways to cope and to feel good. For example, drug addiction is the compelling need to use harmful drugs. A teen who suffers from drug addiction uses drugs to cope or just to feel good. But harmful drugs will never provide lasting good feelings. So, the teen continues to use harmful drugs to try to get the "instant fix."

Feel Good About Yourself

- Develop positive self-esteem by choosing responsible actions.

- Avoid "instant fixes" as a way to feel good. A high from drug use, shopping, or gambling will not last. "Instant fixes" usually have serious consequences.

Denial: What You Don't Know Can Hurt You

Have you ever heard the saying, "What you don't know can't hurt you?" This saying deserves a careful look. Consider what you know about addictions. Suppose a teen has a family member who has gambling addiction. The teen might be in denial. **Denial** is refusing to admit there is a problem. The teen might convince himself or herself that there is no problem. Someone might ask the teen about the family member's gambling. The teen might say, "No way. (S)he does not place bets!" It is painful for the teen to admit that there is a problem.

A teen might think it is OK to say, "What you don't know can't hurt you." WRONG. Without help, the family member with gambling addiction will continue to gamble. The teen who is in a state of denial may develop codependence. **Codependence** is a mental disorder in which a person denies feelings and copes in harmful ways. The teen might deny angry feelings about the gambling. The teen might not bring friends home in order to keep the gambling a secret. These kinds of behaviors are not healthful. The teen causes himself or herself more pain in this way. It would be better to own up to the problems. Talking to a responsible adult would be useful in arranging to get help.

Addictions

- Drug addiction is the compelling need to use harmful drugs.
- Shopping addiction is the compelling need to shop.
- Relationship addiction is the compelling need to be with another person.
- Television addiction is the compelling need to watch TV.
- Gambling addiction is the compelling need to gamble.

Activity

Phobia Bingo

Life Skill: I will choose behaviors that promote a healthy mind.

Materials: paper, pen or pencil, computer (optional)

Directions: A **phobia** is an excessive fear of an object, situation, or person. A person with a phobia may panic when near the object, situation, or person. Most phobias are related to past experiences. A mental health expert can help a person overcome a phobia. Follow the steps below to study ten common phobias.

1. **Make a Phobia Bingo (FEAR) Card.** Copy the FEAR Card on a separate sheet of paper. Optional: Using a computer, design a FEAR Card and print it out.

2. **Print the name of each of the phobias below in one of the spaces on the FEAR Card.** (You must use two phobias twice.)

3. **Study the definitions for each of the ten phobias.**

4. **Play Phobia Bingo.** Do not look at your book. Your teacher will give the definition of a phobia. If the name of the correct phobia is on your FEAR Card, make an X through it. Then your teacher will give another definition for a phobia. The winner of Phobia Bingo is the first student to have four Xs across or down on the FEAR Card.

Using a separate sheet of paper, write the name and definition of each phobia that appears on your FEAR Card. Check your answers in the textbook.

aerophobia	fear of flying
agoraphobia	fear of being in open spaces
algophobia	fear of pain
arachnophobia	fear of spiders
claustrophobia	fear of closed spaces
hematophobia	fear of the sight of blood
hydrophobia	fear of water
nyctophobia	fear of darkness
pyrophobia	fear of fire
xenophobia	fear of strangers

F	E	A	R
			Free Space
		Free Space	
	Free Space		
Free Space			

Review

Vocabulary Words

Write a separate sentence using each vocabulary word listed on page 30.

Health Content

1. What are six positive personality traits? **page 31**

2. What are four ways to communicate effectively? Explain each. **pages 32–33**

3. How can you stay in control of yourself when you get really angry? **page 34**

4. How can you carry on when you feel insecure? **page 35**

5. How can you feel good about yourself without turning to an "instant fix" or an addiction? **page 36**

The Responsible Decision-Making Model™

A group of teens is watching a World Series game together. One teen says, "We could make money on this game. Let's pool our money. I know a bookie I can call." Answer the following questions on a separate sheet of paper. Write "Does not apply" if a question does not apply to this situation.

1. Is it healthful to call a bookie and bet on the game? Why or why not?

2. Is it safe to call a bookie and bet on the game? Why or why not?

3. Is it legal to call a bookie and bet on the game? Why or why not?

4. Will you show respect for yourself if you call a bookie and bet on the game? Why or why not?

5. Will your parents or guardian approve if you call a bookie and bet on the game? Why or why not?

6. Will you demonstrate good character if you call a bookie and bet on the game? Why or why not?

What is the responsible decision to make in this situation?

Health Literacy

Effective Communication

Write a script for a TV public service announcement (PSA) explaining television addiction and why it is harmful.

Critical Thinking

What does a person who has shopping addiction have in common with a person who has gambling addiction?

How to Manage Stress and Be Resilient

Life Skills

- ◆ **I will follow a plan to manage stress.**
- ◆ **I will be resilient during difficult times.**

Vocabulary

stress

stressor

general adaptation syndrome (GAS)

adrenaline

depression

anti-depressant

beta-endorphins

suicide

suicide prevention strategies

resilient

Think of all the areas of your life that have changed and are still changing. The subjects you study at school change and become more difficult each year. Friends change. Change always requires adjustment. And, change can cause stress that affects your entire body. Do you adjust well to challenges and changes in your life? Do you make necessary adjustments and handle stress with confidence? Do you talk over your responses to change and stress with your parents or guardian? Do you take the opportunity to learn from mistakes?

The Lesson Objectives

- Explain what happens inside your body when you get stressed out—the three stages of the GAS.
- Make a plan to manage your stress.
- List actions to help you feel better if you get depressed.
- Identify suicide prevention strategies.
- Discuss what it means to be resilient.

What Happens Inside My Body If I Get Stressed Out?

Stress is the body's reaction to the demands of daily living. A **stressor** is a cause of stress. When you experience stress, your entire body responds. The **general adaptation syndrome (GAS)** is a series of changes that occur in the body when stress occurs. The GAS occurs in three stages.

Stage 1: An alarm goes off.

Your body responds to the stressor by secreting adrenaline into your bloodstream. **Adrenaline** (uh·DRE·nuhl·uhn) is a hormone that prepares the body for quick action. The following changes occur:

- Pupils dilate
- Heart rate increases
- Hearing sharpens
- Blood pressure increases
- Saliva decreases
- Digestion slows
- Blood flow to muscles increases
- Muscles tighten

Stage 2: The alarm is shut off.

The extra energy you feel allows you to respond to the stressor. Your stress is relieved. Your body stops secreting adrenaline. The following changes occur:

- Pupils constrict
- Heart rate decreases to normal
- Hearing is normal
- Blood pressure decreases to normal
- Saliva increases
- Digestion returns to normal
- Blood flow to muscles returns to normal
- Muscles relax

Stage 3: The alarm keeps ringing and ringing and ringing...

Suppose you do not respond to the stressor or your stress continues. Then the alarm does not shut off. Your body continues to secrete adrenaline. This causes wear and tear on your body. Your risk of becoming ill or having an accident increases.

What Can I Do If I Get Stressed Out?

If you get stressed out, take action. Deal with stressors and protect your health.

How to Deal with Stressors

Get away from the stressor if it is appropriate or possible.
- Example: Do not stay in a room where people are smoking.

Work through the stressor.
- Example: Use I-messages to discuss a disagreement with a friend.

Make a responsible decision and use resistance skills to stick to it.
- Example: Say NO if you are pressured by peers to drink alcohol.

Talk to a responsible adult, such as your parents or guardian.
- Example: Ask a parent how you might raise a low grade in a school subject.

How to Protect Your Health

Get vigorous exercise.
- Why: Exercise uses up the extra energy created by body changes.

Get plenty of rest and sleep.
- Why: Too much stress can exhaust you and cause you to become ill.

Eat foods and drink beverages that contain vitamin C.
- Why: Vitamin C keeps the immune system strong.

Spend time with family members and friends (or a pet) who comfort you.
- Why: Encouragement and support from others also help keep the immune system strong.

Warning: Too Much Stress Is Hazardous to Health

Stress can:
- cause psychosomatic diseases, such as headaches and ulcers;
- aggravate existing conditions, such as asthma and allergies;
- suppress your immune system, increasing your risk of disease;
- affect your concentration, causing higher accident rates.

Activity

Health Behavior Contract

Copy the health behavior contract on a separate sheet of paper.

DO NOT WRITE IN THIS BOOK.

Name:_____ **Date:**_____

Life Skill: I will follow a plan to manage stress.

Effect on My Health: If I manage my stress, I will be less likely to develop psychosomatic diseases such as ulcers. I will not aggravate any existing health conditions. I will help keep my immune system strong and resist diseases. I will be able to concentrate on what I am doing. I will not be as likely to have an accident.

My Plan: I will deal with stressors in an appropriate way. I will get away from stressors or work through them. I will make responsible decisions about stressful situations. If I feel stressed, I will talk to my parents or guardian. I will protect my health by exercising and getting plenty of rest and sleep. I will eat foods and drink beverages that contain vitamin C. I will spend time with family and friends. I will keep a journal for a week. I will staple my journal to this health behavior contract. Each day I will record stressors I experience. Then I will write one way I dealt with the stressor. I also will write one way I protected my health as a result.

My Calendar	M	T	W	Th	F	S	S

How My Plan Worked: (Complete after one week) _____

_____

_____

What Can I Do If I Feel Depressed?

Have you ever felt down in the dumps? **Depression** is the feeling of being sad, unhappy, or discouraged. Depression can be triggered by changes over which a teen has no control. For example, a teen might feel sad if parents get divorced or if the family must move. Depression also can be triggered by actions over which a teen has control. Harmful drug use is a leading cause of depression in teens.

There are other causes of depression. A teen who sets standards that cannot be reached might become very discouraged. A teen who spends most of his or her time with one other teen might become unhappy and depressed if the relationship ends.

Signs of depression include:

- A very sad expression
- A lack of desire to do anything
- Withdrawal from family and friends
- Feelings of rejection
- Sleep problems
- Sloppy appearance
- Change in appetite
- Thoughts of suicide

If you feel depressed, there are ways you can help yourself feel better.

1. **Examine the cause of your depression.** Can you do anything about the cause? Do you need more time to make an adjustment?

2. **Talk to your parents or guardian.** They can suggest ways to deal with the cause of your depression. They can decide if you need counseling or medical help. A physician might recommend an anti-depressant. An **anti-depressant** is a drug that corrects chemical imbalances in the brain that cause depression.

3. **Spend time with friends and family who support you.** Force yourself to keep social commitments. Try to have fun. Call friends. Stay connected.

4. **Exercise vigorously.** Vigorous exercise causes the release of beta-endorphins. **Beta-endorphins** (BAY·tuh·en·DOR·fuhnz) are substances produced in the brain that create a feeling of well-being.

5. **Pay attention to your health habits.** Dress neatly. Do not sleep too little or too much. Do not starve yourself or stuff yourself.

6. **DO NOT DRINK ALCOHOL OR USE OTHER HARMFUL DRUGS.**

What Are Suicide Prevention Strategies?

Suicide is the intentional taking of one's own life. **Suicide prevention strategies** are ways to help prevent a person from attempting or committing suicide.

1. Look for the following warning signs if someone is depressed:
   - making a direct statement about death, such as "No one would miss me if I were dead."
   - talking about a method of suicide, such as using a gun or taking an overdose;
   - having a close friend or relative who attempted or committed suicide;
   - giving away possessions;
   - using alcohol or other harmful drugs;
   - talking about getting even with others;
   - running away;
   - showing the signs of depression listed on page 44.

2. Listen without giving advice.

3. Take any suicide threat seriously.

4. Do not promise to keep the suicide threat a secret.

5. Call a parent, a guardian, or another responsible adult right away.

6. Stay with the person until a responsible adult arrives.

What Does It Mean to Be Resilient?

Throughout life, everyone has disappointments. Someone you care about might let you down. You might not make a team or get a job you want. You might feel out of control. But remember that tough times usually do not last. Keep going. Good times usually will return. Focus on being resilient. To be **resilient** (ri·ZIL·yuhnt) is to bounce back and learn from misfortune or change.

Activity

What's Awesome/What's Not

Life Skill: I will be resilient during difficult times.

Materials: paper, pen or pencil

Directions: Design a What's Awesome/What's Not chart. Include one health content fact for each of the following: stress, depression, and resiliency. The following is an example.

Health Content	What's Awesome	What's Not
Stress	Drinking orange juice if stressed	Drinking alcohol if stressed
Depression	Spending time with family if depressed	Withdrawing if depressed
Resiliency	Learning from mistakes	Ignoring mistakes

Vocabulary Words

Write a separate sentence using each vocabulary word listed on page 40.

Health Content

1. What happens during the three stages of the GAS? **page 41**

2. What are eight actions you can take if you get stressed out? **page 42**

3. What are six ways to feel better if you feel depressed? **page 44**

4. What are six suicide prevention strategies? **page 45**

5. What does it mean to be resilient? **page 46**

The Responsible Decision-Making Model™

A classmate of yours confides in you that his parents are divorcing. He asks you to have a few beers with him to "drown his sorrows." Answer the following questions on a separate sheet of paper. Write "Does not apply" if a question does not apply to this situation.

1. Is it healthful to drink beer with your classmate? Why or why not?

2. Is it safe to drink beer with your classmate? Why or why not?

3. Is it legal to drink beer with your classmate? Why or why not?

4. Will you show respect for yourself if you drink beer with your classmate? Why or why not?

5. Will your parents or guardian approve if you drink beer with your classmate? Why or why not?

6. Will you demonstrate good character if you drink beer with your classmate? Why or why not?

What is the responsible decision to make in this situation?

Health Literacy

Critical Thinking

Why would it be important not to keep it a secret if you suspect a person is thinking about suicide?

Responsible Citizenship

Make a list of three responsible adults (in addition to your parents or guardian) whom you could ask for help during tough times. Share the list with your parents or guardian.

Unit 1 Review

Health Content

Prepare for the Unit Test. Review your answers for each Lesson Review in this unit. Then write answers to each of the following questions:

1. What are the ranges of health conditions between premature death and optimal health? **Lesson 1 page 6**

2. Why might a person who is 70 years old have better health status than a person who is 55 years old? **Lesson 1 pages 6–7**

3. What are the six steps in *The Responsible Decision-Making Model™*? **Lesson 2 page 18**

4. How can you decide in advance that a decision will be a wrong one? **Lesson 2 page 18**

5. What are three examples of character values? **Lesson 3 page 23**

6. What can you do if someone dares you to do something unsafe or illegal? **Lesson 3 page 26**

7. Why is having knowledge on different topics a positive personality trait? **Lesson 4 page 31**

8. How is an I-message different from a you-message? **Lesson 4 pages 32–33**

9. Why might you eat foods and drink beverages that contain vitamin C during stressful times? **Lesson 5 page 42**

10. How can vigorous exercise be helpful if you are depressed? **Lesson 5 page 44**

Health Behavior Contract

Make a health behavior contract for one of the life skills in this unit. Review your health behavior contract with your parents or guardian.

Vocabulary Words

Number a sheet of paper from 1–10. Select the correct vocabulary word and write it next to the corresponding number. DO NOT WRITE IN THIS BOOK.

stress	self-respect
character	addiction
health status	dare
life skill	personality
risk	resilient

1. To be _____ is to bounce back and learn from misfortune or change. **Lesson 5**

2. _____ is the condition of a person's health. **Lesson 1**

3. _____ is a person's use of self-control to act on responsible values. **Lesson 3**

4. An _____ is the compelling need to continue a behavior even if it is harmful. **Lesson 4**

5. A _____ is a healthful action that is learned and practiced for a lifetime. **Lesson 1**

6. _____ is a person's unique blend of traits. **Lesson 4**

7. A _____ is a request to do something as a test of courage. **Lesson 2**

8. _____ is the body's reaction to the demands of daily living. **Lesson 5**

9. _____ is a high regard for oneself because one behaves in responsible ways. **Lesson 3**

10. A _____ is a chance that a person takes that has an unknown outcome. **Lesson 2**

The Responsible Decision-Making Model™

You are walking to school and you are late. There is a short cut you could take to save time. However, you would need to walk through property that has a "No Trespassing" sign posted. Answer the following questions on a separate sheet of paper. Write "Does not apply" if a question does not apply to this situation.

1. Is it healthful for you to take the short cut? Why or why not?

2. Is it safe for you to take the short cut? Why or why not?

3. Is it legal for you to take the short cut? Why or why not?

4. Will you keep your self-respect if you take the short cut? Why or why not?

5. Will your parents or guardian approve if you take the short cut? Why or why not?

6. Will you demonstrate good character if you take the short cut? Why or why not?

What is the responsible decision to make in this situation?

Health Literacy

Effective Communication

Write a slogan for a bumper sticker. The slogan should make a statement about the importance of having good character.

Self-Directed Learning

Review the television programs that will be aired in your community during the next week. Make a list of five programs that might stimulate your thinking. Give reasons for your selections.

Critical Thinking

Write a short essay to explain why you should take responsibility for your own health.

Responsible Citizenship

Offer to help another family member complete a chore.

Multicultural Health

Vitamin C helps keep you healthy. Make a list of three other countries. What foods containing vitamin C are available in these countries?

Family Involvement

Ask your parents or guardian to discuss your family's guidelines with you. What are ten family guidelines they consider important? Ask them to share reasons why they are so important.

UNIT 2
Family and Social Health

PRACTICE
HEALTH STANDARD 5
Use Conflict Resolution Skills

Practice this standard at the end of this unit.

Situation: A friend is telling lies about another friend of yours, and that is upsetting to you. Pair up with a classmate who will role play the friend.

1. **Remain calm.** Take some quiet time to think about how you want to handle this situation.

2. **Discuss the ground rules with the other person.** Tell the person who is telling lies that you want to speak with him or her.

3. **Describe the conflict.** Explain that (s)he is telling lies about your friend. Using an I-message, tell how you feel.

4. **Brainstorm a list of possible solutions.**

5. **Use the six questions from The Responsible Decision-Making Model™ to evaluate each possible solution before agreeing to one.** Use the six questions on page 63 to evaluate each possible solution.

6. **Agree on a solution.**

7. **Ask a trusted adult for help if you cannot agree on a solution.**

How to Be a Responsible Family Member

Life Skills

- ◆ I will develop healthful family relationships.
- ◆ I will work to improve difficult family relationships.
- ◆ I will make healthful adjustments to family changes.

Vocabulary

relationship
family guidelines
authority figure
healthful relationship
dysfunctional relationship
drug dependence
perfectionism
workaholism
abuse
physical abuse
emotional abuse
neglect
sexual abuse
violence
domestic violence
abandonment
codependence
recovery program

You have many different relationships right now. You will have more in the future. A **relationship** is a connection a person has with another person. The quality of your relationships will influence your health and happiness. So, it is important for you to know how to connect with other people. The best place to learn and practice relationship skills is within your family. That is why you must work on having healthful family relationships.

The Lesson Objectives

- Discuss reasons why you should follow family guidelines.
- Discuss actions that can help you develop healthful family relationships.
- Explain steps that can be taken to improve dysfunctional family relationships.
- Discuss adjustments that can be made if you experience family changes.
- Discuss ways parents' divorce can affect a teen's future relationships.

Why Do I Need to Follow Family Guidelines?

Do your homework before you watch TV.

Don't watch television shows that contain violent scenes.

Remember your curfew! Don't be late!

Don't have friends over when we're not home.

Do the comments above sound familiar? Most parents and guardians expect their teens to follow family guidelines. **Family guidelines** are rules a family makes to help members live in a responsible way. Your parents or guardian are in charge of your home. They are your authority figures. An **authority figure** is a person who has the power and right to apply rules and laws. Society expects your parents or guardian to protect you and teach you to be responsible. Following family guidelines prepares you for adulthood, keeps you protected, and shows you are responsible. Someday, you likely will be an authority figure. For example, you might be a parent or guardian, a school principal, or a police officer. You will be expected to know how to set guidelines and help others to follow them.

But, what if you feel like rebelling? To rebel is to resist authority. Have you ever felt like rebelling against your parents or guardian? Have you ever tested their limits? Have you ever broken one of their guidelines? Have you ever said, "I don't want anyone telling me what to do?" During your teen years, you are gaining experience in making your own decisions. Your parents or guardian are there to help you gain this experience. They are available to support you if you make mistakes. These are the reasons why their guidelines are so important. They care about you and your future. They want you to become a responsible adult.

Suppose your parents or guardian do not have family guidelines. Suppose they let you do just about anything you want to do. Chances are, you would experience some very serious consequences. You also might feel neglected.

Family Guidelines:

- protect you from harm;
- teach you responsibility;
- help you prepare to be an authority figure.

What Actions Can I Take to Develop Healthful Family Relationships?

A **healthful relationship** is a relationship that promotes mutual respect and responsible behavior. You can develop healthful family relationships by practicing the following actions.

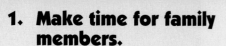

1. Make time for family members.

Make a priority of spending time with members of your family. Set aside time each day to talk. Listen to family members and share feelings with them. Plan activities you can enjoy as a family.

2. Respect the right to privacy.

Allow other family members the right to have time alone. For example, a family member might retreat to a bedroom to be alone. Recognize that other family members might need to be together without you sometimes. For example, your parents need time to talk alone. If you are in a stepfamily, you may want time alone with your parent or stepparent. Family members also might want to be by themselves with their friends. Remember that family members need privacy when talking on the phone.

3. Share the phone, the computer, the TV, the bathroom.

Remember, several members of your family share the same resources. Be fair about who goes first or who gets to choose. Do not "hog" the phone, computer, TV, or bathroom. Agree to reasonable limits and stick to them. Take turns making some choices, such as which TV show to watch. Be cheerful when it is a family member's turn to make a choice you would rather make yourself.

4. Complete chores.

A chore is a small job or task that helps the family. Doing dishes, shoveling snow, cutting grass, and childsitting are common family chores. Be dependable and complete the chores expected of you without being reminded. Volunteer to help other family members with their chores. Family relationships require everyone to pitch in and help.

5. Spend money within the limits of your family's budget.

Your family's income is the amount of money your family receives on a regular basis from different sources. Your family's fixed expenses cannot exceed your family's income. Fixed expenses are what is required for your family to live. Fixed expenses might include rent or mortgage payments, utility bills, car payments, and groceries. Your family makes plans if money is left after fixed expenses are paid. Some money might be put into savings. Some is spent. Respect your family's budget. Never spend more than you are told you can spend. Think of ways you can help with the family budget. You might earn spending money by childsitting, mowing grass, or helping with other tasks for neighbors.

6. Take care of your belongings and those of other family members.

"Don't lose your jacket." "Keep your feet off the furniture." "What do you mean you loaned your sweater to a friend and the friend lost it?" "Why did you take my shirt without asking me?" Sound familiar? Your belongings and those of other family members have an economic value. When you take care of your belongings, they do not need to be replaced unnecessarily. Belongings also might have a sentimental value. No doubt there are special belongings in your home that cannot be replaced. And just as you have special personal belongings, so does each member of your family. Always ask permission before you use something that is not yours.

7. Show appreciation.

Never let an act of kindness go unrecognized. For example, one or both of your parents might have a demanding job to help with expenses. One or both of your parents might cook dinners for you. A brother, sister, stepbrother, or stepsister might help you with a task. A family member might listen and try to help you with a difficult situation. Say thanks.

8. Never use put-downs.

Family members need a place to "let their hair down" and to feel safe. You can help make your home emotionally safe for everyone in your family. Support each other. Do not use put-downs. Use I-messages to share feelings when you are angry or upset with another member of your family. This will help develop trust within your family.

How Can Dysfunctional Family Relationships Be Improved?

Some teens live in families in which family members do not show respect for each other. If a family member chooses irresponsible behavior, his or her relationships with other family members might become dysfunctional. Teens who have dysfunctional family relationships can take four steps.

Step 2:
Recognize causes of dysfunctional family relationships.

1. **Drug Dependence** Drug dependence is the compelling need to take a drug even though it harms the body, mind, and relationships. Drug dependence also is called chemical dependence.

2. **Other Addictions** An addiction is a compelling need to continue a behavior even if it is harmful. People with shopping, television, relationship, or gambling addictions can ruin family relationships. **Perfectionism** is the compelling need to be accurate. **Workaholism** is the compelling need to work. Addictions can ruin family relationships.

3. **Abuse** Abuse is the harmful treatment of another person. There are four kinds of abuse. **Physical abuse** is harmful treatment that results in physical injury to the victim. **Emotional abuse** is "putting down" another person and making the person feel worthless. **Neglect** is failure to provide proper care and guidance. **Sexual abuse** is sexual contact that is forced on a person.

4. **Violence** Violence is the use of physical force to injure, damage, or destroy oneself, others, or property. **Domestic violence** is violence that occurs within a family. Domestic violence can include physical abuse and sexual abuse.

5. **Abandonment** Abandonment is removing oneself from those whose care is one's responsibility. Parents or guardians who abandon their children are not available for them. Their absence is painful to the other family members.

Step 1:
Know the difference between a dysfunctional relationship and a healthful relationship.

A **dysfunctional relationship** is a relationship that *does not* promote mutual respect and responsible behavior. A healthful relationship is a relationship that promotes mutual respect and responsible behavior.

Step 3:
Recognize the warning signs of codependence.

It is painful for the entire family when a family member abuses drugs, has other addictions, is violent, is abusive, or is totally unavailable. Teens in these kinds of situations might respond by:

- denying their feelings about what is happening;
- covering up what is happening;
- becoming over-responsible in hopes things will change;
- copying the disrespectful and irresponsible behavior;
- becoming a people pleaser;
- feeling alone and afraid;
- trying to control other people;
- withdrawing from other people;
- trying to fix other people's problems;
- fearing abandonment in all relationships.

These are all characteristics of codependence. **Codependence** is a mental disorder in which a person denies feelings and copes in harmful ways.

Step 4:
Get help.

- Keep a journal in which you record what is happening. Include specifics, such as the date, time, exact behavior of the family member(s), and how the behavior affected you.

- Talk to a responsible adult family member. Select another adult if there is no adult family member with whom you can speak about the situation. Be honest about what is happening and how you feel about it.

- Be aware of recovery programs that are available. A **recovery program** is a group that supports members as they change their behavior to become responsible. There are recovery programs for family member(s) who have an addiction or who are abusive or violent. Gamblers Anonymous and Alcoholics Anonymous are examples. There also are recovery programs for friends and family members of people who have addictions. Al-Anon and Alateen are examples.

How Can I Adjust to Family Changes?

A family moves to a new neighborhood.

A grandparent moves in.

An uncle is very ill in the hospital.

A baby is born.

A parent loses a job.

Parents divorce.

A divorced parent begins to date.

A parent remarries.

A stepparent disciplines children in the family.

Stepbrother(s) and stepsister(s) join the family.

A foster child comes to live with a family.

A family member commits a crime and goes to jail.

Suppose you were asked to brainstorm a list of possible ways a family might change. Would you list any of the changes that are identified on this page? Did you identify other changes? Your family might change in ways over which you have little or no control. You might look forward to a change. For example, a parent might get a new job that pays more. The extra money allows your family to take a vacation. On the other hand, you might be disappointed or discouraged by a change. For example, teens whose parents separate may feel sad.

Make Adjustments to Changes

- **Discuss family changes with your parents or guardian.** Ask questions so that you know what you might expect in the future.

- **Express your feelings in healthful ways.** Use I-messages. Write your feelings in a journal and share them with a trusted adult. Do not act in wrong ways if you are angry or frustrated.

- **Do not use alcohol or other drugs to cope with painful feelings.**

- **Be patient and optimistic.** Take things one day at a time. Remember, it takes time to work through a period of change.

- **Protect your health.** When changes occur, good or bad, extra demands are placed on you. If you neglect your health, you can become ill. Get plenty of exercise, rest, and sleep. Eat a healthful diet. Include vitamin C to help your immune system. Plan to have some fun by enjoying activities with family and friends.

How Can Parents' Divorce Affect a Teen's Future Relationships?

At the present time, nearly one child in three experiences parents' divorce before the age of 18. Teens whose parents divorce often feel insecure because they do not have an intact family structure. They feel vulnerable and fearful. It might be difficult for them to concentrate.

Divorced fathers usually do not have custody of their teens. Many divorced fathers have little or no contact with their teens. The lack of a continuous relationship takes a toll. One-third of teens whose parents divorce experience a decline in their grades. Teens whose parents divorce have higher rates of depression, inappropriate sexual behavior, and drug abuse. In general, teens whose parents divorce have two traits in common:

- **A fear of rejection and betrayal**
- **A worry that they will always lose people they love**

These traits can affect future relationships. Females whose parents are divorced often fear they will be abandoned in other relationships. As a result, they might often want to have a back-up relationship. This is the reason why they might have more than one boyfriend at a time. They also might date older males, because they might think older males are less likely to break off relationships. Unfortunately, the fear of being alone might cause these females to stay in dysfunctional relationships.

Males whose parents are divorced often have difficulty feeling secure or trusting females. They often hold back their feelings. They might fear rejection and overreact to the slightest threat. They might break off relationships before females can break them off. These males invest a lot of energy in hiding their feelings. They might protect themselves by getting so involved in sports or work that they have little time for relationships.

To Prepare for Future Relationships, Teens Whose Parents Have Divorced Must:

- **overcome feelings of rejection or abandonment;**
- **learn to trust other people;**
- **share their feelings;**
- **examine how they relate to the opposite sex;**
- **get help if they have dysfunctional relationships.**

Activity

Welcome Wagon

Life Skill: I will make healthful adjustments to family changes.

Materials: construction paper, lined paper, scissors, colored markers

Directions: Teens and their families might move to a new home after parents divorce or change jobs, or for other reasons. Teens who move to a new community must make adjustments to their new environment. Some communities offer welcome wagon packages to new families. A welcome wagon package includes information that a new family can use to learn about the community. Follow the steps below to create a welcome wagon package for a family who has just moved to your community.

1. **Design a map of sites in your community in which teens would be interested.** For example, you might include youth centers, sports fields, movie theaters, restaurants, and schools.

2. **Create a list of places and activities in which a teen who is new to the community might meet other teens.**

3. **Make a "Top Five List of Favorite Places" in your community.** Include five places where you enjoy spending time.

4. **Write a brief letter welcoming the teen and his or her family to the community.** Include in your letter a summary of the contents of your welcome wagon package.

5. **If possible, share your welcome wagon package with a new student in your school or a new family in your community.**

Vocabulary Words

Write a separate sentence using each vocabulary word listed on page 52.

Health Content

1. What are three reasons you should follow family guidelines? **page 53**

2. What are eight actions that can help you develop healthful family relationships? **pages 54–55**

3. What are four steps that can be taken to improve dysfunctional family relationships? Explain each step. **pages 56–57**

4. What adjustments can you make if you experience family changes? **page 58**

5. How can parents' divorce affect a teen's future relationships? **page 59**

Health Literacy

Critical Thinking

On a separate sheet of paper, write a paragraph explaining why it is wrong to talk back to your parents or guardian if they ground you for disobeying their rules.

Responsible Citizenship

Make a list of the authority figures with whom you have contact. Over which area of your life does each person you listed have authority? Show respect for these adults.

The Responsible Decision-Making Model™

You have permission to stay over at your friend's house Friday night. Your parents or guardian have said you must be in by curfew. Your friend wants to stay out later. Your friend suggests calling your parents or guardian from his or her home at curfew and then going out again. Then your parents or guardian would not know you stayed out past your curfew. Answer the following questions on a separate sheet of paper. Write "Does not apply" if a question does not apply to this situation.

1. Is it healthful to call your parents or guardian and then go out again? Why or why not?

2. Is it safe to call your parents or guardian and then go out again? Why or why not?

3. Is it legal to call your parents or guardian and then go out again? Why or why not?

4. Will you maintain your self-respect if you call your parents or guardian and then go out again? Why or why not?

5. Will your parents or guardian approve if you call them and then go out again? Why or why not?

6. Will you demonstrate good character if you call your parents or guardian and then go out again? Why or why not?

What is the responsible decision to make in this situation?

What would you say to your friend in this situation?

How to Resolve Conflict

Life Skill ◆ **I will use conflict resolution skills.**

Vocabulary

conflict
conflict resolution skills
conflict style
button pusher
time bomb
sulker
silent treatment
mediator

Throughout your life, you will have conflicts. A **conflict** is a disagreement. Some conflicts are internal. For example, you might want to go to a movie, but you know you need to study for a test. Knowing how to resolve internal conflicts helps you be at peace with yourself. Other conflicts involve the people with whom you interact. For example, you might disagree with your brother about which TV program to watch. There are at least three reasons why you need to learn to resolve conflict in healthful ways. You will be less likely to develop diseases due to stress. You will have better relationships. You will decrease your risk of injury from violence.

The Lesson Objectives

- Identify three reasons why you need to learn to resolve conflict in healthful ways.

- Explain how to use conflict resolution skills.

- Identify the six questions from *The Responsible Decision-Making Model™* that you can use to evaluate possible solutions to conflict.

- Explain how to deal with people who use harmful conflict styles.

- Explain how an adult mediator can help teens resolve conflicts.

How Do I Use Conflict Resolution Skills?

Conflict resolution skills are steps that can be taken to settle a disagreement in a responsible way. Consider the following steps as you work with another person to resolve a conflict.

1. Remain calm.
2. Discuss the ground rules with the other person.
   - Do not blame.
   - Do not use put-downs.
   - Do not interrupt.
   - Do not use threats.
3. Describe the conflict.
   - Tell what *you* think happened.
   - Be honest about what you have said or done to cause the conflict.
   - Use I-messages to express your feelings about the conflict.
   - Allow the other person to describe what *(s)he* thinks happened.
   - Listen without interrupting.
   - Respond to the other person's feelings.
4. Brainstorm a list of possible solutions.

5. Use the six questions from *The Responsible Decision-Making Model™* to evaluate each possible solution before agreeing to one.
   - Will the solution lead to actions that are healthful?
   - Will the solution lead to actions that are safe?
   - Will the solution lead to actions that are legal?
   - Will the solution lead to actions that show respect for you and others?
   - Will the solution lead to actions that follow the guidelines of responsible adults, such as your parents or guardian?
   - Will the solution lead to actions that demonstrate good character?
6. Agree on a solution.
   - Keep your word and follow the solution on which you agreed.
7. Ask a trusted adult for help if you cannot agree on a solution.

Work It Out.
Work It Out.
Work It Out.
Work It Out.
Work It Out.

How Can I Deal with People Who Use Harmful Conflict Styles?

A **conflict style** is the particular way a person responds to conflict. It is easiest to deal with people who use a healthful conflict style that includes conflict resolution skills. But, what can you do when you have a conflict with someone who uses a harmful conflict style? One thing you don't want to do is to lower your standards and respond in a harmful way.

How to Deal with a Person Who Is a Button Pusher

A **button pusher** is a person who pushes the "hot button" of another person to cause trouble. For example, you might be very sensitive about your grade in math. The button pusher keeps referring to the sensitive issue. The button pusher wants a response from you. This is his or her way of taking control. The button pusher wants you to lose control and say or do something foolish or wrong.

- **Use conflict resolution skills to settle disagreements.** Remember, you must stick to your plan to use these skills regardless of what another person does.

- **Reassure yourself and stay in control.** For example, you might think, "I am not going to let him or her get to me."

- **Express your feelings using an I-message.** For example, you might say to the button pusher, "When you talk about my math grade, I believe you are trying to upset me and I get very angry."

- **Set limits if the behavior does not stop.** Tell the button pusher you will avoid him or her if the behavior continues. Avoid the button pusher if you must.

How to Deal with a Person Who Is a Time Bomb

A **time bomb** is a person who has a quick temper and is ready to explode without warning. The slightest threat can set off a time bomb. As a result, you often are unprepared for his or her actions. A time bomb is at risk for harming you and others. A time bomb also can self-destruct.

- **Use conflict resolution skills to settle disagreements.** Remember, you must stick to your plan to use these skills regardless of what another person does.

- **Get the help of a trusted adult.** A time bomb needs help, and you are not the person to give it.

- **Protect yourself from harm.** Get away from the person at the slightest display of temper.

How to Deal with a Person Who Is a Sulker

A **sulker** is a person who uses the silent treatment. The **silent treatment** is ignoring or indirectly fighting with a person with whom one has a disagreement. Sulkers want to get even. They usually are hurt by something that has happened or that has been said. They want to respond by doing something hurtful. If you ask them what is wrong, they probably will mutter "nothing." They do not take responsibility for settling disagreements. They want you to figure out the problem. If you do not, they will continue to punish you with the silent treatment.

- **Use conflict resolution skills to settle disagreements.** Remember, you must stick to your plan to use these skills regardless of what another person does.

- **Use an I-message to confront the behavior of the person.** "When I receive the silent treatment from you, I do not always know why. I get frustrated."

- **Set limits and refuse to respond to a sulker.** Explain that both of you need to take responsibility for disagreements. Indicate that this time you asked what was wrong to try to settle the disagreement. Explain that in the future you do not expect to get the silent treatment. If you do not set limits, the person will continue to use the silent treatment.

How Does an Adult Mediator Help Teens Resolve Conflicts?

Suppose you are unable to resolve a conflict with someone. You and the other person can agree on an adult to serve as a mediator. A **mediator** is a responsible adult who helps people resolve conflicts. The mediator will meet with you and the other person and set ground rules. The mediator will ask both of you to tell what happened. You will not be allowed to use put-downs or to show disrespect for each other.

The mediator will help you brainstorm possible solutions to your conflict. Together, you will evaluate each solution using the six questions from *The Responsible Decision-Making Model*™. The mediator will ask you to sign a written agreement. Then the mediator will set a date for a follow-up meeting. At this meeting, you will review how well the agreement is working.

Activity

Mediator Wanted: Only Adults Need Apply

Life Skill: I will use conflict resolution skills.

Materials: paper, pen or pencil, computer (optional)

Directions: Write an ad titled "Mediator Wanted: Only Adults Need Apply" for the classified section of a newspaper or magazine. State what the mediator will be expected to do. Include three personal characteristics you believe a mediator should have. Share your ad with your classmates. Your teacher will make a list of all the personal characteristics students mentioned in their ads.

Vocabulary Words

Write a separate sentence using each vocabulary word listed on page 62.

Health Content

1. What are three reasons why you need to learn to resolve conflict in healthful ways? **page 62**

2. What are the seven steps to follow when using conflict resolution skills? **page 63**

3. What are the six questions from *The Responsible Decision-Making Model™* you can use to evaluate possible solutions to conflict? **page 63**

4. How can you deal with a person who is a button pusher? A person who is a time bomb? A person who is a sulker? **pages 64–65**

5. How does an adult mediator help teens resolve conflicts? **page 66**

The Responsible Decision-Making Model™

You get into a disagreement with a classmate who has a quick temper. The classmate shoves you against your locker. Other classmates standing nearby encourage you to fight back and punch your classmate. Answer the following questions on a separate sheet of paper. Write "Does not apply" if a question does not apply to this situation.

1. Is it healthful to fight back and punch your classmate? Why or why not?

2. Is it safe to fight back and punch your classmate? Why or why not?

3. Is it legal to fight back and punch your classmate? Why or why not?

4. Will you show respect for your classmate if you fight back and punch him or her? Why or why not?

5. Will your parents or guardian approve if you fight back and punch your classmate? Why or why not?

6. Will you demonstrate good character if you fight back and punch your classmate? Why or why not?

What is the responsible decision to make in this situation?

Health Literacy

Effective Communication

Suppose a friend gives you the silent treatment after you forget to return her telephone call. What might you say to your friend? What if she continues to give you the silent treatment?

Responsible Citizenship

Make a list of five adults who you believe would be excellent mediators for teen conflicts. Share your list with your parents or guardian. Explain why you selected the five adults.

How to Develop Healthful Relationships

* I will develop healthful relationships.
* I will develop skills to prepare for dating.
* I will recognize harmful relationships.

Vocabulary

healthful relationship
dysfunctional relationship
personal reflection
to be respected
to be popular
one-sided relationship
abusive relationship
controlling relationship
codependent relationship
dating

Having healthful relationships has a positive influence on your health status. A **healthful relationship** is a relationship that promotes mutual respect and responsible behavior. A **dysfunctional relationship** is a relationship that *does not* promote mutual respect and responsible behavior. Dysfunctional relationships can be described as "sick" relationships. "Sick" relationships can cause a decline in a person's health status. Never take your relationships for granted. Take time to evaluate how your relationships are affecting you. Make changes when necessary.

The Lesson Objectives

* Discuss reasons why you need to plan time to be alone.
* Explain why it is more important to be respected than it is to be popular.
* Give examples of "sick" relationships and tell what to do about them.
* List and explain the DOs and DON'Ts for dating.
* Discuss information your parents or guardian will need *before* giving you approval to have a date.

Why Do I Need to Plan Time to Be Alone?

When you look in a mirror, you see a reflection of yourself. This reflection helps you assess your physical appearance. You might like some aspects of what you see. Perhaps you like the way you smile. Or, you might decide to make some changes. For example, you might comb your hair differently or change your shirt.

There is another kind of reflection that helps you to see yourself clearly. **Personal reflection** is serious or careful thought about oneself. You need to plan time to be alone for personal reflection. You can give careful thought to the kind of person you are and want to be. You can think seriously about the events that are occurring in your life and how you feel about those events. You can give careful thought to the kinds of relationships you have. Remember, you might not find time to be alone unless you plan it ahead of time.

There is another reason you need to plan time to be alone. Time alone gives you the opportunity to "stop and smell the roses." You can think about your accomplishments. You can take time to appreciate your surroundings.

Finally, you need to plan time to be alone to develop and enjoy hobbies. Hobbies can help you express and develop another side of your personality. Being involved in hobbies can help reduce stress in your life.

Be a Friend to Yourself—Plan Time

- For personal reflection
- To "stop and smell the roses"
- For hobbies

Why Is It More Important to Be Respected Than to Be Popular?

To be respected is to be held in high regard by others because one behaves in responsible ways. **To be popular** is to be liked by others. A person might:

- **be respected and be popular;**
- **be respected and not be popular;**
- **not be respected and be popular.**

Wow! What does all of this mean? And, why is it important? Many teens feel pressure to be popular. Suppose there were a popularity contest at your school. Every student would list the ten students (s)he liked the best. The ten students receiving the most votes would win. How important would it be to you to be one of the winners of such a contest? You probably would like to be a contest winner.

But, let's look at this popularity contest more closely. Suppose some votes were for students who wore nice clothes. Suppose some votes were for students who were good-looking. Suppose some votes were for students who were really good at sports. Students who had nice clothes, an attractive appearance, and athletic ability would get the most votes. If you did not fit this description, you could not win the popularity contest. Yet, you might have many desirable traits. For example, you might be trustworthy, loyal, and honest. These are more desirable traits because they say something about your character.

Let's look again at what it takes to be popular. Suppose you are with a group of teens at a party. You did not know that there would be alcohol at the party or that there would be no adult supervision. When you realize this, you call your parents or guardian to come pick you up. The next day you learn that several of the teens who were at the party do not want to hang out with you anymore. You are no longer popular with *this* group of teens. They know you will not drink alcohol. They know you will leave a party if alcohol is served. However, other teens who behave in responsible ways will respect you. They know you have good character.

Popularity vs. Respect

If you are respected by others, they have high regard for you because you behave in responsible ways. If you are popular with others, they like you. They might like you because you behave in responsible ways. They might like you because you go along with their wrong actions. They might like you because you have things, such as clothes or jewelry, that others do not have. You might want to be respected and be popular. But, this is not always possible. Never behave in wrong ways so that you will be liked. If you do, you are paying too high a price for being popular.

Instead, earn the respect of peers and adults who behave in responsible ways. Concentrate on being liked and respected for having good character. Develop healthful friendships that involve mutual respect and promote responsible behavior.

What Can Be Done About "Sick" Relationships?

Have you ever heard someone say, "He makes me sick" or "She makes me sick?" Dysfunctional, or sick, relationships can affect your health status. If you do not feel at ease around a person, changes can occur in your body that make you more likely to become ill. In other words, feeling "dis-ease" can lead to disease. Sick relationships can cause you to develop headaches, ulcers, and other changes in your health status. Take a moment to do a relationship checkup. Some kinds of "sick" relationships are described on this page and the next page.

One-Sided Relationships

Do you know anyone who has to have his or her way all the time? Do you know anyone who always allows others to have their own way? These two people might form a one-sided relationship with each other. A **one-sided relationship** is a relationship in which one person does most of the taking and the other person does most of the giving. Remember that in a healthful relationship, there is *mutual* respect. It is not healthful to be a taker most of the time. Nor is it healthful to always place the needs of others ahead of your own. Both the giver and the taker must take responsibility for the "sickness" in the relationship. Each person must focus on changing his or her *own* behavior.

Abusive Relationships

An **abusive relationship** is a relationship in which one person harms another person with cruel words or actions and the other person endures this behavior. The person who endures the abuse usually lacks self-respect. There usually is a pattern of abuse. A pattern of abuse means the abuse is repeated again and again. Both the abuser and the person abused must take responsibility for the "sickness" in the relationship. Each person must focus on changing his or her *own* behavior.

Controlling Relationships

A **controlling relationship** is a relationship in which one person has the power and the other person gives up all power. The controlling person usually is very possessive. This person demands constant attention. (S)he usually does not want the other person to spend time with others. The controlling person monopolizes the other person's time. As a result, the other person does not spend as much time as (s)he should with family and friends. (S)he might become afraid of what the controller will do if (s)he does not do what the controller wants. The person who is controlled also must be concerned about personal safety. Male controllers have been known to harm their girlfriends. Both the controller and the other person must take responsibility for the "sickness" in the relationship. Each person must focus on changing his or her *own* behavior.

Codependent Relationships

A **codependent relationship** is a relationship in which one person acts in wrong ways and the other person, the enabler, denies or supports the wrong actions. For example, one person might drink heavily, lie, gamble, or have an eating disorder. The enabler might deny that the other person drinks. The enabler might lie about it. The enabler might give the other person money to gamble. The enabler might praise the other person for starving himself or herself and losing weight. Both the enabler and the other person must take responsibility for the "sickness" in the relationship. Each person must focus on changing his or her *own* behavior.

What to Do About "Sick" Relationships

- Take responsibility for your own behavior.
- Do not focus on changing someone else.
- Talk to a responsible adult.
- Do not put your personal safety at risk.

What Are DOs and DON'Ts for Dating?

Dating is having social plans with another person. Some teens refer to dating as "going out" or "hanging out." Teens may go out in groups or in couples. Many teens have concerns about their dating skills. Some common dating concerns are discussed in *The DOs and DON'Ts for Dating*.

The DOs and DON'Ts for Dating

My parents won't let me date. They say I can go out only with a group of friends. But this guy who I have been dying to have notice me asked me to sneak out and meet him. What should I do?

DO follow your parents' or guardian's guidelines for dating. Your parents or guardian do not set rules to embarrass you. They set rules because they care about you and want to protect you. Tell a potential date that you follow the guidelines set by your parents or guardian. If a person encourages you to break these guidelines, then you know (s)he is the wrong person for you to date. Do not date a person who will not respect your parents' or guardian's guidelines.

My friend told me that a girl in our class is going to ask me to a dance. I don't want to go to the dance with her. So far, I have managed to avoid her. What should I say if she asks me?

DO respect the feelings of a person who asks you out on a date. You can't—and shouldn't—hide forever. Be polite and do not hurt her feelings. Thank her for asking you out. Tell her you are flattered she asked you but that you are not interested in going. Do not be dishonest. For example, do not say you have other plans if you do not. Be friendly when you see the girl again.

I went on a date with an older guy. He brought me flowers and took me out to dinner. Then he pressured me to be sexually active. He said I "owed" him for all of the money he had spent on me. I said NO and called my parents to come pick me up right away. Should I feel guilty for not being a "good" date?

DO call your parents or guardian if you are on a date and need help. If a date pressures you to behave in wrong ways, make the call immediately and leave the situation. You should never feel guilty for saying NO when someone pressures you to do something wrong. Never give in to pressure to be sexually active. Do not date this person again.

A really cute guy asked me if I would meet him at a party this weekend. The person throwing the party is really into "partying." Is it OK to go to the party if I don't drink?

DON'T go on a date where teens will be drinking or using other drugs. Being around teens who are drinking or using drugs is risky, even if you are not drinking. Ask the really cute guy if he would be interested in doing something else with you and your friends. Discuss with your parents or guardian ideas for appropriate places you might go with this person.

This girl has been calling me on the phone. She writes my name all over her notebooks and dedicates songs to me on the radio. She asked me if we could date only each other. I like talking to her, but I'm not really ready for anything serious. What should I do?

DON'T rush into a steady relationship. Some teens always want to be in a serious relationship. They always want to have a boyfriend or girlfriend who helps them feel secure and needed. But dating different people has advantages. You are free to get to know many people and to enjoy their company. And don't worry if you don't feel ready to date. Many teens do not have their first date until they are in high school or even later.

I asked a girl out and she said NO. I thought I would die. I feel like such a loser.

DON'T consider yourself a success or failure based on your ability to get a date. Teens have dating ups and downs. If you are rejected when asking for a date, you are not a loser. Give yourself credit for trying. Get up your courage and ask someone else.

The other night my boyfriend got mad because I was talking to another guy. He pushed me up against a wall. He said he only did it because he loves me. He said seeing me with another guy just made him crazy. Should I pretend it never happened?

DON'T date someone who hits you, shoves you, hurts you, threatens you, or says cruel words to you. There is no excuse for this kind of behavior. A date should show respect for you at all times. Call a parent, guardian, or other responsible adult immediately if any of these actions occur. Leave the situation immediately. Do not continue seeing this person. Discuss what happened with your parent or guardian.

What Information Do My Parents Need Before I Get Approval for a Date?

Parents have different opinions about the appropriate age for dating. Review the Information to Discuss with a Parent or Guardian Before Going Out on a Date. You can use this list each time you would like to go out on a date.

Information to Discuss with a Parent or Guardian Before Going Out on a Date

1. Your date's name
2. Your date's age
3. Where your date attends school
4. The name(s) and phone number(s) of your date's parents or guardian
5. The time you will go out
6. The place(s) you will go
7. The time you are expected home
8. The transportation you will use
9. Where you can reach your parents or guardian if there is a problem
10. Who will pay for the date

Activity
A Mural of Responsible Dating

Life Skill: I will develop skills to prepare for dating.

Materials: paper, colored paper, butcher paper or poster board

Directions: There are expected standards for you and your date to follow. For example, neither you nor your date should drink alcohol or use other drugs. Neither you nor your date should be sexually active. Follow the steps below to contribute to "A Mural of Responsible Dating."

1. On a separate sheet of paper, write ten safety tips for teens who date. For example, your list might include: "Never get into a car if the driver has been drinking alcohol or using other drugs," or "Always get permission from a parent or guardian before changing plans."

2. Select the five safety tips you consider to be most important for teens.

3. Your teacher will hang a sheet of butcher paper or poster board on the wall as a mural. Your teacher will title the mural "A Mural of Responsible Dating."

4. Use colored markers to write on the mural the five safety tips you selected. Write in large letters so that students can view the tips from anywhere in the classroom.

Review

Vocabulary Words

Write a separate sentence using each vocabulary word listed on page 68.

Health Content

1. What are three reasons why you need to plan time to be alone? **page 69**

2. Why is it more important to be respected than it is to be popular? **pages 70–71**

3. What are four kinds of "sick" relationships? What can be done about "sick" relationships? **pages 72–73**

4. What are three DOs and four DON'Ts for dating? Explain each. **pages 74–75**

5. What information do you need to give your parents or guardian to get approval for a date? **page 76**

The Responsible Decision-Making Model™

An older teen you know has a steady boyfriend. She tells you her boyfriend gets very angry and threatens her whenever she speaks to another guy. She says she is afraid of what he might do. Answer the following questions on a separate sheet of paper. Write "Does not apply" if a question does not apply to this situation.

1. Is it healthful for your friend to be in the relationship? Why or why not?

2. Is it safe for your friend to be in the relationship? Why or why not?

3. Is it legal for your friend to be in the relationship? Why or why not?

4. Will your friend show respect for herself if she stays in the relationship? Why or why not?

5. Will your friend's parents or guardian approve if your friend stays in the relationship? Why or why not?

6. Will your friend demonstrate good character if she stays in the relationship? Why or why not?

What is the responsible decision for your friend to make?

Health Literacy

Self-Directed Learning

Make a list of five hobbies you might enjoy doing alone. Set aside time to do one of these hobbies in the next week.

Critical Thinking

Write reasons why it is important to follow guidelines for dating set by your parents or guardian.

What to Know About Abstinence

Life Skill

◆ **I will practice abstinence.**

During your teen years, you will make many choices. One of the most responsible choices you can make is to practice abstinence. **Abstinence** is choosing not to be sexually active. Responsible adults, such as your parents or guardian, expect you to practice abstinence because they want to protect you.

The Lesson Objectives

- Discuss the benefits of a monogamous traditional marriage.

- Use *The Responsible Decision-Making Model™* to explain why abstinence is the expected standard for teens.

- Identify the harmful consequences that can result from having babies outside of marriage.

- Explain how abstinence reduces your risk of becoming infected with HIV and STDs.

- Identify *The Top Ten List of Reasons to Practice Abstinence™.*

- Explain how to stick to limits for expressing affection.

- Identify ten behaviors that indicate respect in a relationship.

- Outline resistance skills you can use if you are pressured to be sexually active.

- Explain how a drug-free lifestyle supports your decision to practice abstinence.

- Identify guidelines to use to choose entertainment that supports your decision to practice abstinence.

Vocabulary

abstinence

monogamous traditional marriage

commitment

self-sufficient

prenatal care

premature birth

low birth weight

toxemia of pregnancy

sexually transmitted disease (STD)

genital warts

genital herpes

human immunodeficiency virus (HIV)

Acquired Immune Deficiency Syndrome (AIDS)

hormone

sexual feelings

affection

resistance skills

drug-free lifestyle

drug slipping

media

What Are the Benefits of a Monogamous Traditional Marriage

A **monogamous** (muh·NAW·guh·muhs) **traditional marriage** is a marriage in which a husband and wife have sex *only with each other*. Having sex with someone is very intimate. Keeping sex within marriage makes sex even more intimate and special. Monogamous traditional marriage:

1. **Preserves the marriage tradition in society.** The institution of marriage provides a structure for the ways a family lives in society.

2. **Protects the marriage commitment.** A commitment is a pledge or promise to do something. A husband and wife make a commitment to each other when they marry. The commitment to have sex *only with one's marriage partner* strengthens one's marriage.

3. **Helps prevent divorce.** Marriage is a choice. If a husband or wife has sex outside of marriage, this affects the "glue" that helps a couple stick together through tough times. A marriage partner's having sex outside of marriage is a leading cause of divorce.

4. **Provides a home in which parents raise children together.** Children benefit from living with both parents. If parents are loving and committed, children feel secure and learn by watching them.

5. **Provides emotional security and trust.** Each marriage partner has agreed to "be there" for the other person at all times.

6. **Helps protect marriage partners from infection with STDs and HIV.** Married couples who are faithful to each other reduce the risk of infecting one another with STDs and HIV.

Why Is Abstinence the Expected Standard for Teens?

The Responsible Decision-Making Model™ can be used to explain why abstinence is the expected standard for teens.

Practicing Abstinence Protects Health

- You reduce the risk of becoming infected with HIV and developing AIDS.
- You reduce the risk of becoming infected with sexually transmitted diseases (STDs).
- You will not become a teenage parent.

Practicing Abstinence Protects Safety

- You reduce the risk of violence that is associated with teen parenthood.

Practicing Abstinence Follows Laws

- You avoid being in situations in which you can be prosecuted for having sex with a minor.
- You avoid sexual behavior for which you can be prosecuted for date rape.

Practicing Abstinence Shows Respect for Self and Others

- You maintain a good reputation because you are responsible.

Practicing Abstinence Follows the Guidelines of Parents and of Other Responsible Adults

- You avoid having conflicts with your parents or guardian because you follow their guidelines.

Practicing Abstinence Demonstrates Good Character

- You are self-disciplined and can delay gratification in order to uphold your values. Delaying gratification is waiting to have sex until a person is older, married, and able to handle the responsibilities of parenthood.

What Are the Harmful Consequences That Can Result from Having Babies Outside of Marriage?

It is risky to become a parent before you are in your 20s, married, and self-sufficient. To be **self-sufficient** is to have the skills and financial resources to take care of oneself. Consider the following risks of being a teen parent.

Babies born to teen parents face risks. Most pregnant teens did not plan to be pregnant. Many are not careful about health habits, such as smoking or drinking. These habits affect the health of the developing baby. Most teens do not get early prenatal care. **Prenatal care** is care that is given to a mother-to-be and her developing baby before birth. As a result, teen pregnancy often results in premature birth. A **premature birth** is the birth of a baby before it is fully developed. If a baby is born too early, the baby can have a low birth weight. A **low birth weight** is a weight at birth that is less than 5.5 pounds (2.5 kilograms). This is a major cause of infant death and mental retardation. Also, babies born to teens are more likely to be abused by their parents. They are less likely to get medical and dental care as small children.

Teen mothers face risks. Teen females are in their normal growth spurt. Pregnant teens have many additional demands on their bodies. The extra demands of pregnancy can result in health problems. **Toxemia of pregnancy** is a disorder of pregnancy that causes high blood pressure, tissue swelling, and protein in the urine. Pregnant teens and teen mothers often drop out of school and do not meet their career goals. They might not have the time or money to enjoy the social activities that their friends enjoy. They are likely to live in poverty. Out of frustration, they sometimes abuse their babies.

Teen fathers face risks.
Teen fathers must pay child support. They might drop out of school and have to change career plans. Many teen fathers lack contact with their children. Teen fathers also risk abusing their babies.

Society faces risks. The costs of teen pregnancies and births are very high. Taxpayers might pay the health care costs for teen mothers and their babies. They might also pay the costs of caring for children who live in poverty. And, society pays a social cost for which it is difficult to determine a dollar amount— the unhappiness and frustration that usually affect teen parents.

How Does Abstinence Reduce My Risk of Becoming Infected with HIV and Other STDs?

A risk behavior is an action that threatens your health. Teens who are sexually active are choosing a risk behavior. They are at risk for becoming infected with an STD. An STD or **sexually transmitted disease** is a disease caused by pathogens that are transmitted from an infected person to an uninfected person during intimate sexual contact. Genital warts and genital herpes are STDs. **Genital warts** is an STD caused by a virus that produces wart-like growths on the sex organs. **Genital herpes** is an STD caused by a virus that produces cold sores and blisters on the sex organs or in the mouth. There is no cure for genital warts or genital herpes. There are other STDs. You will learn more about STDs in Lesson 32. **One way to keep from becoming infected with STDs is to practice abstinence.**

Sexually active teens also are at risk for becoming infected with HIV. HIV or **human immunodeficiency virus** is a pathogen that destroys infection-fighting T cells in the body. HIV is an STD. People who are infected with HIV have HIV in some of their body fluids. During sexual contact, HIV from an infected person may enter the body of an uninfected person through exposed blood vessels in small cuts or tiny cracks in skin or mucous membranes. A person who is infected with HIV can develop AIDS. AIDS or **Acquired Immune Deficiency Syndrome** is a condition that results when infection with HIV causes a breakdown of the body's ability to fight other infections. There is no cure for HIV. You will learn more about HIV and AIDS in Lesson 33. **One way to keep from becoming infected with HIV and developing AIDS is to practice abstinence.**

What Is The Top Ten List of Reasons to Practice Abstinence™?

1. I want to follow family guidelines.
2. I want to respect myself.
3. I want to respect others.
4. I want to have a good reputation.
5. I do not want to feel guilty.
6. I am not ready for marriage.
7. I do not want to risk pregnancy.
8. I am not ready to be a parent.
9. I do not want to be infected with an STD.
10. I do not want to be infected with HIV.

You need to be self-sufficient before you marry and become a parent.

How Can I Stick to Limits for Expressing Affection?

Throughout your life, your body secretes hormones. A **hormone** is a chemical messenger that is released into the bloodstream and regulates body activities. Certain hormones secreted during the teen years cause your body to change and become more like the body of an adult. Hormones also influence your feelings. You begin to have sexual feelings. **Sexual feelings** are feelings that result from an attraction to another person. It is OK to have sexual feelings, but it is not OK to be sexually active. So, how do you keep sexual feelings under control so that you can stick to your decision to practice abstinence? You must set limits for expressing affection. **Affection** is a fond or tender feeling for another person.

Think Ahead

- Talk to your parents or guardian about the age at which they will approve of your dating.
- Consider how you will set limits and stick to them.

1. Limit your expressions of affection to hand-holding, hugging, and casual kissing to keep your brain in control of your decisions and actions.

2. Tell a person your limits before expressing affection.

3. Do not date someone who does not respect your limits.

4. Avoid drinking alcohol and using other drugs that dull your brain and interfere with wise judgment.

5. Do not date someone who drinks alcohol or uses other drugs that dull the brain and interfere with wise judgment.

What Are Ten Behaviors That Help Me Know If I Am Getting the Respect I Deserve?

If you respect a person, you have a high regard for the person. One way to support your decision to practice abstinence is to spend time only with teens who respect you. Use the following list to check whether or not you are getting the respect you deserve.

A person who respects me:

- Builds me up
- Shows interest in what I say and do
- Encourages me to do my best in school
- Makes responsible decisions
- Encourages me to make responsible decisions
- Practices a drug-free lifestyle
- Is nonviolent
- Obeys laws
- Has a healthful attitude about members of both sexes
- Practices abstinence

A person who does NOT respect me:

- Puts me down
- Shows interest only in himself or herself
- Does not encourage me to do my best in school
- Makes wrong decisions
- Encourages me to make wrong decisions
- Misuses or abuses drugs
- Is violent
- Breaks laws
- Has a negative attitude about members of one or both sexes
- Pressures me to be sexually active

How Can I Resist Pressure to Be Sexually Active?

Use resistance skills if you are pressured to be sexually active. **Resistance skills** are skills that are used to say NO to an action or to leave a situation.

1. **Be confident and say, "NO, I do not want to be sexually active."**

2. **Give reasons why you practice abstinence.**
   - I want to follow family guidelines.
   - I want to respect myself.
   - I want to respect others.
   - I want to have a good reputation.
   - I do not want to feel guilty.
   - I am not ready for marriage.
   - I do not want to risk pregnancy.
   - I am not ready to be a parent.
   - I do not want to be infected with an STD.
   - I do not want to be infected with HIV.

3. **Repeat your reasons for practicing abstinence.** Be doubly sure to get your message across. Choose one reason and repeat it several times.
   - I want to follow family guidelines.
   - I want to follow family guidelines.
   - I want to follow family guidelines.

4. **Do not send a mixed message.** Never lead someone on or tease in a sexual way.

5. **Avoid situations in which there might be pressure to be sexually active.** Do not go to the bedroom of a member of the opposite sex, or to parties that are not supervised by adults.

6. **Break off a relationship when someone does not respect your limits.**

7. **Influence others to practice abstinence.**

How Does a Drug-Free Lifestyle Support My Decision to Practice Abstinence?

A **drug-free lifestyle** is a lifestyle in which a person does not misuse or abuse drugs. Alcohol and other harmful drugs affect the part of your brain that controls judgment. Suppose you drink alcohol or use another harmful drug. Your ability to make responsible decisions can be affected. Here are reasons why alcohol and other drugs do *not* mix with abstinence.

1. Teens who use drugs might not stick to their decision to practice abstinence.

2. Teens who use drugs increase their risk for having a pregnancy outside of marriage.

3. Teens who use drugs are at increased risk for becoming infected with HIV and other STDs.

4. Teens who use drugs increase their risk for being in situations in which rape occurs.

5. Teens who are around people who are using drugs are at risk for drug slipping.

6. Teens who are drug-dependent might exchange sex for drugs or for money to buy drugs.

7. Teens who are involved in injection drug use might share a needle that has infected blood on it.

Protect Yourself Against Drug Slipping

Drug slipping is placing a drug into someone's food or beverage without that person's knowledge. Hang out with friends who choose a drug-free lifestyle. Do not get into situations where teens are drinking or using drugs.

What Guidelines Can I Use to Choose Entertainment That Supports My Decision to Practice Abstinence?

You might watch TV, watch a videotape, or go to a movie. You might read a book, listen to recorded music, or access the Internet. If you do, you are using media. **Media** are the various forms of mass communication. One purpose of media is to entertain. To get and keep your attention, media can be very dramatic and exaggerated. How many teens do you know who live like the teens you see on some TV shows or in some movies?

Suppose you do not choose carefully what you listen to, watch, or read. You might develop faulty thinking. Faulty thinking is a thought process in which a person ignores or denies facts or believes false information. For example, after watching some TV shows, you might believe teen sex is OK. This is an example of faulty thinking. Use the guidelines on the right for choosing entertainment to protect yourself against faulty thinking.

1. Entertainment should be approved for your age group.
2. Entertainment should be approved by your parents or guardian.
3. Entertainment should not show harmful drug use as acceptable behavior.
4. Entertainment should not lead you to believe sex outside of marriage is acceptable behavior.
5. Entertainment should not show violence against people or property.

Activity
A Totally Awesome® Teen Television Program

Life Skill: I will practice abstinence.

Materials: paper, pen or pencil

Directions: Your teacher will divide the class into groups of five students. Each group should create its own teen television program. Make up a name for the program. Select popular teen actors and actresses that you would want to have star in your program. Write a screenplay for one episode of the show. The plot must encourage teens to practice abstinence.

Vocabulary Words

Write a separate sentence using each vocabulary word listed on page 78.

Health Content

1. What are six benefits of monogamous traditional marriage? **page 79**

2. How does practicing abstinence protect health? Protect safety? Follow laws? Show respect for self and others? Follow the guidelines of parents and other responsible adults? Demonstrate good character? **page 80**

3. What are the harmful consequences that can result from having babies outside of marriage? **page 81**

4. How does abstinence reduce the risk of becoming infected with HIV? Other STDs? **page 82**

5. What is *The Top Ten List of Reasons to Practice Abstinence™*? **page 83**

6. What are five ways to stick to limits for expressing affection? **page 84**

7. What are ten behaviors of a person who respects you? **page 85**

8. What are resistance skills you can use if you are pressured to be sexually active? **page 86**

9. Why is it risky to use drugs when you want to practice abstinence? **page 87**

10. What are five guidelines for choosing entertainment that supports your decision to practice abstinence? **page 88**

The Responsible Decision-Making Model™

An older teen pressures you to have sex. Answer the following questions on a separate sheet of paper. Write "Does not apply" if a question does not apply to this situation.

1. Is it healthful to be sexually active? Why or why not?

2. Is it safe to be sexually active? Why or why not?

3. Is it legal to be sexually active? Why or why not?

4. Will you show respect for yourself if you are sexually active? Why or why not?

5. Will your parents or guardian approve if you are sexually active? Why or why not?

6. Will you demonstrate good character if you are sexually active? Why or why not?

What is the responsible decision to make in this situation?

How might you use resistance skills to reinforce your decision to practice abstinence?

Health Literacy

Effective Communication

A classmate of yours tells dirty jokes. Write an I-message to share your uncomfortable feelings with his or her behavior.

Responsible Citizenship

Design a greeting card for a married couple who will celebrate a golden (50th) anniversary. Include a message that indicates at least one way committed marriage benefits society.

What to Know About Marriage and Parenthood

Life Skills

- ◆ I will develop skills to prepare for marriage.
- ◆ I will develop skills to prepare for parenthood.

Vocabulary

career

marriage

self-sufficient

monogamous traditional marriage

mentor

A **career** is the work that a person prepares for and does through life. Suppose you want to have a career as a physician, teacher, architect, auto mechanic, or professional athlete. You begin to prepare for one of these careers by taking certain courses in school. Have you ever thought of marriage and parenthood as careers? Both marriage and parenthood require hard work and skills that last a lifetime. You are not ready to marry and become a parent right now. But, you can learn about these two important careers.

The Lesson Objectives

- Discuss factors that help make a marriage last.
- Explain why teens who feel unloved are more at risk for teen marriage and/or teen parenthood.
- Identify responsibilities of parents.

What Is the "Glue" That Keeps a Marriage Together?

Marriage is a legal commitment a man and woman make to love and care for one another. Before a couple marries, the couple might consider the factors—the "glue"—that keeps a marriage together. The five factors follow.

Both partners are mature adults who are self-sufficient. To be **self-sufficient** is to have the skills and financial resources to take care of oneself.

Each partner respects the other partner. Mutual respect is very important in marriage. Partners show respect by resolving conflict in healthful ways. Both partners behave in responsible ways. They are never violent or abusive.

Each partner considers the other partner a best friend. Every survey and poll done on success in marriage mentions the importance of friendship. Partners must like being with each other. They need to have interests in common.

Each partner is committed to being married to the other partner. Partners must honestly mean "I do" when they say "I do." Marriage requires work and effort.

Each partner agrees to have sex only with the other partner. A **monogamous** (muh·NAW·guh·muhs) **traditional marriage** is a marriage in which a husband and wife have sex *only with each other*. Having sex with someone is very intimate and special. In marriage, this intimacy strengthens the bond. Having sex outside the marriage breaks the trust that married partners share.

Why Are Teens Who Feel Unloved More at Risk for Teen Marriage and Parenthood?

Teens who have difficult life experiences while growing up might feel unloved. They are more at risk for teen marriage and parenthood than are other teens. Perhaps their parents divorced, and they had little or no contact with one parent. Perhaps a parent abandoned them. Perhaps they never knew one or both of their parents. Perhaps they were abused by one or both parents. Perhaps there were addictions, such as to drugs or gambling, in the family.

Teens can overcome the emptiness that can result from such difficult life experiences. However, it takes hard work. These teens must have their needs for love and recognition met in healthful ways. They might get the love that was missing from other family members who are able to give it. They might develop a relationship with a mentor. A **mentor** is a responsible person who guides another person. They might choose to have counseling. With help and hard work, these teens recover. They learn to trust others. They learn that they are lovable and capable of loving others.

Some teens do not recover from difficult life experiences. They feel an emptiness that they want to fill. They desperately want to be loved. They might go "looking for love in all the wrong places." They might become sexually active. They confuse having sex with being loved. They might marry to hang on to a boyfriend or girlfriend. They might have a baby because they think the baby will help them feel loved. But, these actions do not fill up their empty feelings. These actions only create additional, difficult life experiences for teens.

Faulty Thinking

"He'll never leave me if I have his baby."

WRONG! Most teen females who become pregnant do not marry the fathers of their babies. And, teen fathers usually do not stick around to develop loving relationships. The teen females feel even more rejected than they did before they became pregnant. They have fewer opportunities to get involved in social activities. Other guys might not want to date teen females who have babies.

"I'll have a baby to love me."

WRONG! Choosing to be a parent means choosing to meet the needs of a baby. This means feedings at midnight, changing diapers, and comforting a baby who is fussy. A parent must meet the needs of a baby. A baby cannot be expected to meet the needs of a parent.

"I'll be the center of attention."

WRONG! Teens who are pregnant, married, or are parents might get attention at first. Other teens might be interested in seeing the baby for a while. But, this attention does not last. Other teens will be too busy with school and social activities to pay attention to married teens and teen parents.

"I'll have someone to take care of me."

WRONG! Teens who are neglected by their families might desperately want someone to marry them and take care of them. They believe this person will do all the little things that no one has ever done for them. They are very needy. If they marry, they might feel loved for a short time, but then they need more and more attention to feel loved. They drain the energy from a partner. When the partner stops giving, they feel unloved again. Teen marriages usually end in divorce.

Activity
The Baby Owner's Manual

Life Skill: I will develop skills to prepare for parenthood.

Materials: paper, pen or pencil, or computer

Directions: Suppose someone handed you a baby. Would you know how to care for the baby? Would you need to read a book or have someone tell you what to do? Follow the directions for creating *The Baby Owner's Manual.*

1. Make a creative cover for *The Baby Owner's Manual.*

2. Design a table of contents that includes three chapters.

3. List three points that should be included in Chapter 1.

4. List five points that should be included in Chapter 3.

5. Share your work with your teacher and your classmates.

The Baby Owner's Manual

Chapter 1. Parenthood Is an Awesome Responsibility

Chapter 2. Ten Responsibilities of Parenting a Baby
- Furnishing a Baby's Room
- Diapering a Baby
- Feeding a Baby
- Clothing a Baby
- Bathing a Baby
- Caring for a Baby Who Is Fussy
- Caring for a Baby Who Is Sick or Injured
- Playing with a Baby
- Preparing a Baby for Sleep
- Choosing a Childsitter and Getting Child Care

Chapter 3. Why Teens Are Not Ready for Parenthood

Review

Vocabulary Words

Write a separate sentence using each vocabulary word listed on page 90.

Health Content

1. What are five factors that help keep a marriage together? **page 91**

2. How can teens overcome the emptiness that might result from feeling unloved while growing up? **page 92**

3. What is meant by the saying, "looking for love in all the wrong places?" **page 92**

4. Why are teens who feel unloved at risk for teen marriage and parenthood? **page 92**

5. What are ten responsibilities that a baby's parents have? **page 94**

The Responsible Decision-Making Model™

You pick up a magazine and read the latest news on your favorite male actor. The actor is married, but he is dating the star female actor in his latest movie. Examine the actor's behavior. Answer the following questions on a separate sheet of paper. Write "Does not apply" if a question does not apply to this situation.

1. Is it healthful for the married male actor to date the female actor? Why or why not?

2. Is it safe for the married male actor to date the female actor? Why or why not?

3. Is it legal for the married male actor to date the female actor? Why or why not?

4. Does the married male actor show respect for himself? For his wife? For the female actor? Why or why not?

5. Does the married male actor follow the guidelines of responsible adults? Why or why not?

6. Does the married male actor demonstrate good character? Why or why not?

What are the benefits of a monogamous traditional marriage?

Health Literacy

Effective Communication

Design a poster that illustrates one of the five factors that keep a marriage together. Design your poster on a computer or use various art materials. Write the factor you selected on the poster.

Self-Directed Learning

Find a current magazine written for parents. Read two articles in the magazine. For each article, make a list of five things you did not know before you read the article.

Health Content

Prepare for the Unit Test. Review your answers for each Lesson Review in this unit. Then write answers to each of the following questions.

1. What are five causes of dysfunctional family relationships? **Lesson 6 pages 56**

2. What are the warning signs of codependence? **Lesson 6 page 57**

3. Why do you need to set limits and refuse to respond to a sulker? **Lesson 7 page 65**

4. What might you do if you and another person cannot resolve a conflict? **Lesson 7 page 66**

5. What is the difference between a healthful relationship and a dysfunctional relationship? **Lesson 8 page 68**

6. What happens in a codependent relationship? **Lesson 8 page 73**

7. What risks do babies born to teen parents face? **Lesson 9 page 81**

8. What are three STDs for which there is no cure? **Lesson 9 page 82**

9. What are ten behaviors of a person who does not respect you? **Lesson 9 page 85**

10. Why is it faulty thinking for a female to believe, "I'll have a baby to love me?" **Lesson 10 page 93**

11. Why is it faulty thinking for a female to believe, "He'll never leave me if I have his baby?" **Lesson 10 page 93**

Health Behavior Contract

Make a health behavior contract for one of the life skills in this unit. Review your health behavior contract with your parents or guardian.

Vocabulary Words

Number a sheet of paper from 1–10. Select the correct vocabulary word and write it next to the corresponding number. DO NOT WRITE IN THIS BOOK.

to be popular	personal reflection
authority figure	abstinence
self-sufficient	mentor
mediator	drug slipping
conflict	dysfunctional relationship

1. An _____ is a person who has the power and right to apply rules and laws. **Lesson 6**

2. _____ is choosing not to be sexually active. **Lesson 9**

3. _____ is to be liked by others. **Lesson 8**

4. _____ is placing a drug into someone's food or beverage without that person's knowledge. **Lesson 9**

5. A _____ is a disagreement. **Lesson 7**

6. A _____ is a responsible person who guides another person. **Lesson 10**

7. _____ is serious or careful thought about oneself. **Lesson 8**

8. A _____ is a relationship that *does not* promote mutual respect and responsible behavior. **Lesson 6**

9. To be _____ is to have the skills and financial resources to take care of oneself. **Lesson 10**

10. A _____ is a responsible adult who helps people resolve conflicts. **Lesson 7**

The Responsible Decision-Making Model™

Your favorite actress is in a movie that is not approved for your age group. A friend suggests that you buy a ticket for a different movie. Then you can sneak into the other movie. Answer the following questions on a separate sheet of paper. Write "Does not apply" if a question does not apply to this situation.

1. Is it healthful to sneak into the movie that is not approved for your age group? Why or why not?

2. Is it safe to sneak into the movie that is not approved for your age group? Why or why not?

3. Is it legal to sneak into the movie that is not approved for your age group? Why or why not?

4. Will you show respect for yourself if you sneak into the movie that is not approved for your age group? Why or why not?

5. Will your parents or guardian approve if you sneak into the movie that is not approved for your age group? Why or why not?

6. Will you demonstrate good character if you sneak into the movie that is not approved for your age group? Why or why not?

What is the responsible decision to make in this situation?

Health Literacy

Effective Communication

Make a picture to illustrate the following conflict styles: button pusher, time bomb, sulker. Share your illustration with the class.

Self-Directed Learning

Select a magazine written for parents. Read one of the articles. Write a two-page paper that discusses five reasons why you are not ready to be a parent right now.

Critical Thinking

Refer to *The Top Ten List of Reasons to Practice Abstinence™* on page 83. Write a paragraph that explains the number one reason why you think you should practice abstinence. Tell why.

Responsible Citizenship

Some people who are elderly do not have family members who live nearby. Get permission from a parent or guardian. Volunteer to help a person who is elderly with a task such as grocery shopping.

Multicultural Health

In your school or community library, find a book that discusses teens who live in another country or culture. Write a one-page paper explaining a dating custom or guideline that differs from the customs with which you are familiar.

Family Involvement

Make a list of ten resources your family must share. For example, you might include the phone, the TV, the bathroom. Discuss ways to share these resources with your family.

UNIT 3
Growth and Development

PRACTICE

HEALTH STANDARD 1 Comprehend Health Facts

Practice this standard at the end of this unit.

1. **Study and learn health facts.** Review the information on page 107. Focus on the information about the relationship between exposure to the sun and malignant melanoma.

2. **Ask questions if you do not comprehend health facts.** Write a question about malignant melanoma. Find the answer using the Internet or by conducting research in the library.

3. **Answer questions to show you comprehend health facts.** Write an answer to this question: How could you tell the difference between malignant melanoma and other kinds of skin cancers?

4. **Use health facts to practice life skills.** Suppose you want to practice this life skill: *I will keep my body systems healthy.* Tell some ways you can protect your skin from damage.

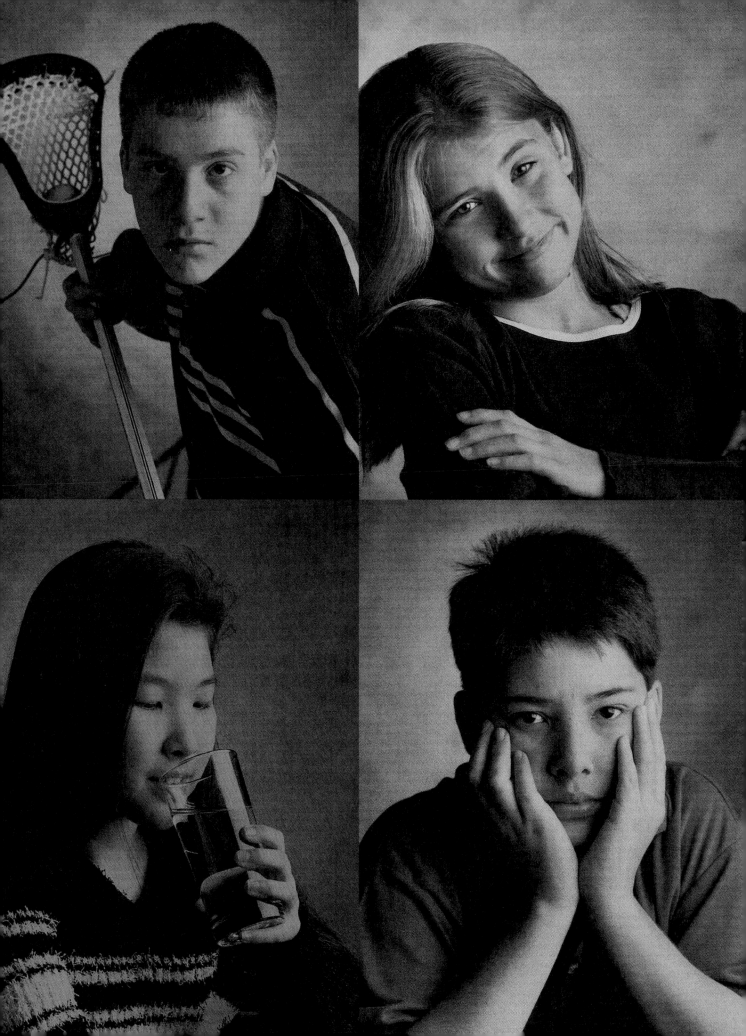

How to Take Care of Your Body

Life Skill

◆ **I will keep my body systems healthy.**

An owner's manual tells the new owner of an automobile how to take care of it. What if you could get an owner's manual that would tell you how to take care of your body? This lesson includes *The Body Systems Owner's Manual.* Follow the directions it contains to keep your body in top condition.

The Lesson Objectives

- Discuss ways to protect your brain and spinal cord.
- Discuss ways to keep your heart muscle strong and your arteries clear.
- Discuss ways to keep your lungs clear.
- Discuss ways to stand tall and keep your bones strong.
- Discuss ways to keep your muscles strong and flexible.
- Discuss ways to protect your skin.
- Discuss ways to improve digestion.
- Discuss ways to replace water lost from sweat and urination.
- Discuss ways to check on your physical growth and development.
- Discuss ways to keep your immune system strong.

Vocabulary*

nervous system

circulatory system

respiratory system

skeletal system

muscular system

integumentary system

digestive system

urinary system

endocrine system

immune system

*A complete listing of vocabulary words appears on page 112.

The Body Systems Owner's Manual

The Nervous System
The Circulatory System
The Respiratory System
The Skeletal System
The Muscular System
The Integumentary System
The Digestive System
The Urinary System
The Endocrine System
The Immune System

How Can I Protect My Brain and Spinal Cord?

The Nervous System

The **nervous system** is the body system for communication and control. The parts of the nervous system include the brain, spinal cord, and spinal nerves.

- The **brain** is the organ that is the control center for the body.

- The **cerebrum** (suh·REE·bruhm) is the part of the brain that controls the ability to reason and to make judgments.

- The **cerebellum** (ser·uh·BEL·uhm) is the part of the brain that controls how muscles work together.

- The **brain stem** is the part of the brain that controls the functions of inner organs.

- The **medulla** (muh·DUH·luh) is the part of the brain that controls involuntary actions, such as heart rate and breathing.

- The **spinal cord** is a thick band of nerve cells through which messages enter and leave the brain.

- **Spinal nerves** are nerves that branch from the spinal cord and convey messages to and from the spinal cord.

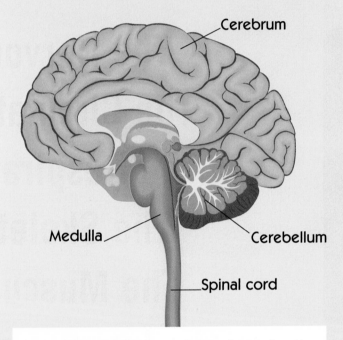

Cerebrum

Medulla

Cerebellum

Spinal cord

Alcohol and other depressant drugs slow the functions of the nervous system. Using these drugs is risky. If you use drugs, you are not able to think clearly. Your muscles do not work together as they should. You are more likely to have accidents. Depressant drugs can affect the medulla, and death can result.

- **Use a safety restraint system when riding in an automobile.**
- **Wear a safety helmet for sports when appropriate.**
- **Follow safety rules.**

- **Do not use alcohol or other harmful drugs.**
- **Do not ingest or breathe in poisons.**

How Can I Keep My Heart Muscle Strong and My Arteries Clear?

The Circulatory System

The **circulatory system** is the body system that transports oxygen, food, and waste products throughout the body. The circulatory system consists of blood, blood vessels, and the heart.

- The **heart** is a muscular organ that pumps blood to the body.
- An **artery** (AR·tuh·ree) is a blood vessel that carries blood away from the heart.
- A **vein** (VAYN) is a blood vessel that returns blood to the heart.
- A **capillary** (KA·puh·lehr·ee) is a tiny blood vessel that connects arteries and veins.

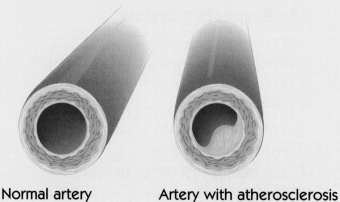

Normal artery   Artery with atherosclerosis

Atherosclerosis (A·thuh·ROH·skluh·ROH·suhs) is a disease in which fat deposits on artery walls. This reduces blood flow through the arteries. Blood pressure in the arteries must increase to deliver blood to body cells.

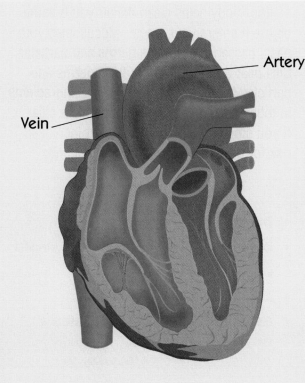

Artery

Vein

- **Exercise each day.**
- **Limit your intake of fatty foods.**
- **Do not smoke or breathe in second-hand smoke.**
- **Maintain a healthful weight.**
- **Follow a plan to manage stress.**

How Can I Keep My Lungs Clear?

The Respiratory System

The **respiratory system** is the body system that provides the body with oxygen and removes waste carbon dioxide from the body.

- The **cilia** (SI·lee·uh) are tiny hairs that line the air passages.

- The **trachea** (TRAY·kee·uh) is the windpipe through which air travels to the lungs.

- The **bronchial** (BRAHN·kee·uhl) **tubes** are two short tubes through which air enters the lungs.

- The **lungs** are two organs that supply the blood with oxygen and rid the blood of carbon dioxide.

- The **alveoli** (al·vee·OH·ly) are small air sacs in the lungs through which oxygen enters the blood and carbon dioxide leaves the blood.

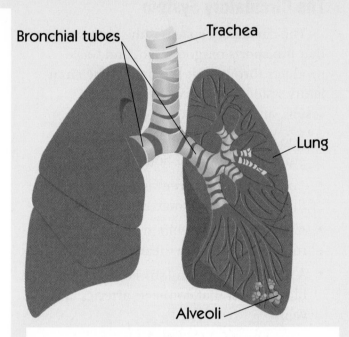

Bronchial tubes · Trachea · Lung · Alveoli

Your body helps clean the air you breathe before it enters your lungs. Mucus lines your nasal passages and traps germs and particles. Cilia beat back and forth to keep germs and particles from entering your lungs. Ingredients in tobacco smoke and alcohol paralyze cilia. If you smoke and drink, you are at increased risk for developing respiratory infections.

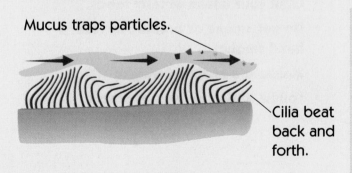

Mucus traps particles.

Cilia beat back and forth.

- **Do not smoke.**
- **Do not breathe in secondhand smoke.**
- **Do not inhale toxic fumes.**
- **Avoid breathing polluted air.**
- **Get medical help if you develop a respiratory infection.**

How Can I Stand Tall and Keep My Bones Strong?

The Skeletal System

The **skeletal system** is the body system that consists of bones that provide a support framework. This body system protects inner organs and, together with muscles, provides movement.

- A **joint** is a point at which two bones meet.
- **Cartilage** (KAHR·tuhl·ij) is soft material at the ends of bones that keeps them from rubbing together.
- The **vertebral column** or backbone is a column of bones that encloses, supports, and protects the spinal cord.
- **Ligaments** are tough bands of tissue that attach bones together at joints.

- **Engage in weight-bearing exercise to make bones dense and strong.**
- **Eat foods and drink beverages that contain vitamin D and calcium.**
- **Use correct posture.**
- **Wear comfortable shoes.**
- **Be screened for scoliosis.**

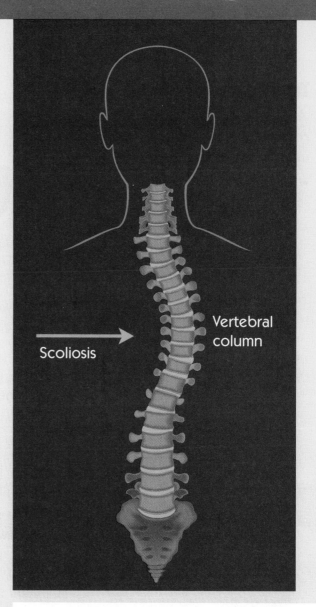

Scoliosis

Vertebral column

Scoliosis (skoh·lee·OH·sis) is an S-shaped curvature of the spine. This condition can lead to permanent disfigurement if not treated. You might be screened for scoliosis at school. If you have curvature, you will be referred to a physician. An X-ray will be taken. A body brace or cast might be used to reduce the curvature.

How Can I Keep My Muscles Strong and Flexible?

The Muscular System

The **muscular system** is the body system composed of skeletal muscles that provide motion and maintain posture.

- **Voluntary muscles** are muscles that can be controlled.
- **Tendons** (TEN·duhnz) are tough tissue fibers that connect muscles to bones.

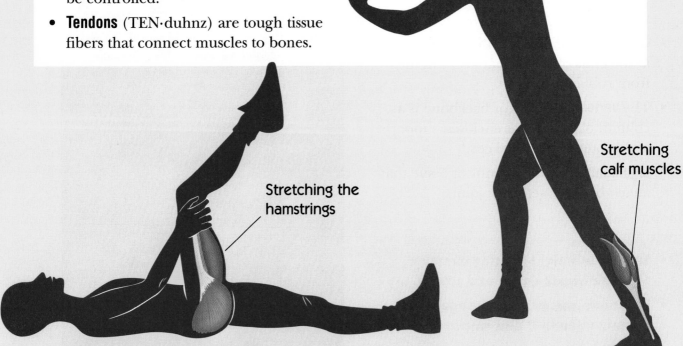

Stretching the hamstrings

Stretching calf muscles

- **Choose exercises for different muscle groups.**
- **Do static stretching.**
- **Warm up before exercising.**
- **Lift objects by bending your knees and keeping your back straight.**
- **Eat foods with protein for muscle growth.**

Flexibility is the ability to bend and move the joints through a full range of motion. Flexibility helps prevent injuries to muscles and joints. It helps reduce the risk of accidents, such as falls. You can improve flexibility with static stretching. **Static stretching** is stretching the muscle to a point where it pulls, and then holding the stretch for 15–30 seconds.

How Can I Protect My Skin?

The Integumentary System

The **integumentary** (in·teh·gyuh·MEN·tuh·ree) **system** is the body system that covers and protects the body. Skin, hair, nails, and glands in the skin are parts of this body system.

- **Sweat glands** are glands in skin that help maintain a healthful body temperature.
- **Melanin** (ME·luh·nuhn) is a substance that protects skin and gives it color.
- A **birthmark** is an area of discolored skin present from birth.
- A **mole** is a small dark skin growth that develops from melanin.

Almost everyone has moles. Moles usually develop in childhood or adolescence. They vary in size. They can be flat or raised and be smooth or rough. They can have hairs growing from them. Moles usually are dark brown or black. You might consider a mole a blemish or a beauty mark depending on its location or appearance. If a mole is unattractive or if clothing rubs it, it can be removed by a physician. Most moles are harmless. However, some moles develop into malignant melanoma. **Malignant melanoma** (muh·LIG·nuhnt ME·luh·NOH·muh) is a serious form of skin cancer. Exposure to ultraviolet radiation increases the risk of malignant melanoma.

- **Avoid overexposure to the sun.**
- **Wear a sunscreen with a sun protection factor (SPF) of at least 15.**
- **Do not use tanning booths or lamps.**
- **Check your body often for changes in moles, freckles, or skin.**
- **Bathe or shower each day to remove germs, dirt, and oil from the skin.**

Malignant melanoma   Normal mole

The **ABCD**s of melanoma:
Asymmetrical shape
Border irregularity
Color differences
Diameter larger than a pencil eraser

How Can I Improve Digestion?

The Digestive System

The **digestive system** is the body system that breaks down food so that it can be used by the body.

- The **salivary** (SA·luh·vehr·ee) **glands** are glands that produce saliva to soften foods.

- The **esophagus** (i·SAH·fuh·guhs) is a tube through which food passes from the mouth to the stomach.

- The **stomach** is the organ that releases digestive juices to break down food.

- The **small intestine** is the organ in which most digestion takes place, and in which digested food is absorbed into the blood.

- The **pancreas** (PAN·kree·uhs) is a gland that secretes juices that breakdown some foods and secretes insulin, which regulates blood sugar.

- The **liver** is a gland that produces bile to break down fats.

- The **large intestine** is the organ in which undigested food is stored until it leaves the body. The large intestine also is called the colon.

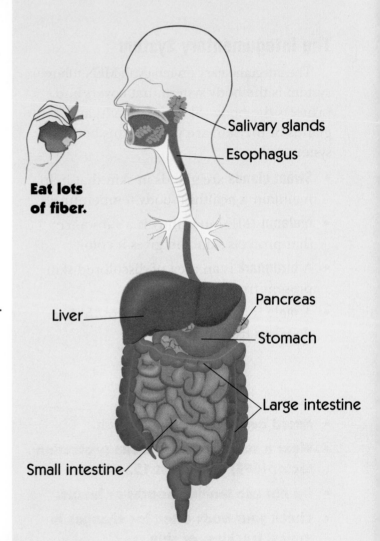

Eat lots of fiber.

Salivary glands
Esophagus
Liver
Pancreas
Stomach
Large intestine
Small intestine

- **Take small bites of food.**
- **Chew your food thoroughly.**
- **Do not gulp down your food.**
- **Eat foods rich in fiber.**
- **Exercise regularly.**

Fiber is the part of grains and plant foods that cannot be digested. Wheat bread, bran cereal, rice, and oats contain fiber. Fruits and vegetables contain fiber. Eating lots of fiber helps you have a daily bowel movement. Getting plenty of exercise also helps you have a daily bowel movement. Daily bowel movements help prevent colon cancer.

How Can I Replace Water Lost from Sweat and Urination?

The Urinary System

The **urinary system** is the body system that removes liquid wastes from the body.

- The **kidneys** are organs through which blood circulates as wastes are filtered.
- The **urinary bladder** is a muscular organ that stores urine.
- **Urine** is liquid waste that collects in the urinary bladder.
- The **urethra** (yu·REE·thruh) is a narrow tube through which urine and semen pass out of the body.

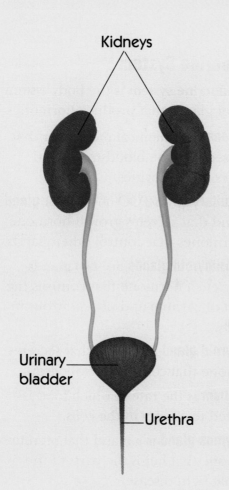

Kidneys

Urinary bladder

Urethra

- **Drink six to eight glasses of water each day.**
- **Eat fresh fruits and vegetables.**

1 2 3 4 5 6

What Are Ways I Can Check on My Physical Growth and Development?

The Endocrine System

The **endocrine system** is the body system made up of glands that produce hormones.

- A **hormone** is a chemical messenger that is released into the bloodstream and regulates body activities.

- The **pituitary** (puh·TOO·uh·TER·ee) **gland** is a gland that secretes growth hormone and hormones that control other glands.

- The **parathyroid glands** are two glands that secrete a hormone that controls the amount of calcium and phosphorous in the body.

- The **thyroid gland** is a gland that secretes a hormone that controls metabolism.

- **Metabolism** is the rate at which food is converted to energy in the cells.

- The **thymus gland** is a gland that secretes a hormone that helps the parts of the body that fight disease.

- The **adrenal** (uh·DREE·nuhl) **glands** are glands that secrete a hormone that helps the body react to emergency situations.

- The **pancreas** is a gland that secretes juices that break down some foods and secretes insulin, which regulates blood sugar.

- The **testes** are two glands that produce testosterone and sperm cells. Testosterone is a hormone that produces male secondary sex characteristics.

- The **ovaries** are two glands that produce estrogen and ova. Estrogen is a hormone that produces female secondary sex characteristics and affects menstruation. Ova are female reproductive cells.

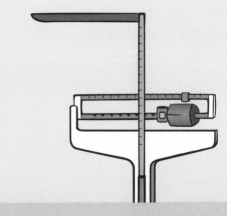

- **Have regular medical checkups.**
- **Ask your parent or guardian and physician questions about your growth and development.**

How Can I Keep My Immune System Strong?

The Immune System

The **immune system** is the body system that removes harmful organisms from the blood and fights pathogens.

- A **helper T cell** is a white blood cell that signals B cells to produce antibodies.

- A **B cell** is a white blood cell that produces antibodies.

- An **antibody** is a special protein in blood that helps fight infection.

- A **macrophage** (MAK·roh·fahj) is a white blood cell that surrounds and destroys pathogens.

- **Lymph** is a clear liquid that surrounds body cells and circulates in lymph vessels.

- A **lymph node** is a structure that filters and destroys pathogens.

- The **spleen** is an organ that filters foreign matter from the blood and lymph.

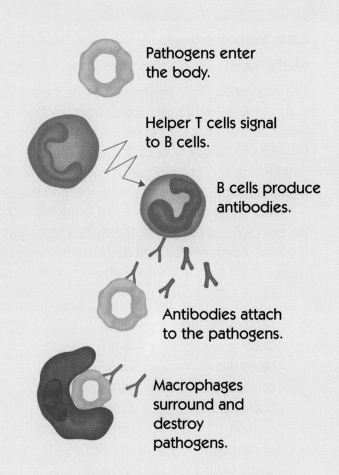

Pathogens enter the body.

Helper T cells signal to B cells.

B cells produce antibodies.

Antibodies attach to the pathogens.

Macrophages surround and destroy pathogens.

- **Do not use tobacco products.**
- **Do not drink alcohol.**
- **Get plenty of rest and sleep.**
- **Get the required immunizations.**
- **Consume foods and beverages that contain vitamin C.**

Suppose pathogens enter the body. Helper T cells send a signal to B cells. B cells produce antibodies. Antibodies attach to the pathogens. This makes it easier for the macrophages to surround and destroy pathogens. Digested pathogens enter lymph. They are destroyed in the lymph nodes and removed by the spleen.

Activity

Body Systems Vocabulary Concentration

Life Skill: I will keep my body systems healthy.

Materials: 22–24 index cards for each group of students, pen or pencil

Directions: Your teacher will divide the class into six groups. Your teacher will assign each group 11 or 12 vocabulary words from the following list. Each group will make two sets of concentration cards. Print each of the vocabulary words on a separate index card. Then print the definition for each vocabulary word on a different index card. You will have one word or definition per card. Shuffle both sets of index cards together and lay them out in rows, face down. Each student will take a turn turning over two cards, attempting to match the vocabulary word with the correct definition. If the two cards match, the student keeps the two cards and attempts to make another match. If the two cards do not match, the student loses his or her turn. The next student attempts to make a match. Continue play until all the cards have been claimed. The player with the most cards is the winner of the round. Then switch cards with another group, and play again. Continue playing with different sets of cards until your teacher tells you to stop.

nervous system	lungs	malignant melanoma	parathyroid glands
brain	alveoli	digestive system	thyroid gland
cerebrum	skeletal system	salivary glands	metabolism
cerebellum	joint	esophagus	thymus gland
brain stem	cartilage	stomach	adrenal glands
medulla	vertebral column	small intestine	testes
spinal cord	ligaments	pancreas	ovaries
spinal nerves	scoliosis	liver	immune system
circulatory system	muscular system	large intestine	helper T cell
heart	voluntary muscles	fiber	B cell
artery	tendons	urinary system	antibody
vein	flexibility	kidneys	macrophage
capillary	static stretching	urinary bladder	lymph
atherosclerosis	integumentary system	urine	lymph node
respiratory system	sweat glands	urethra	spleen
cilia	melanin	endocrine system	
trachea	birthmark	hormone	
bronchial tubes	mole	pituitary gland	

Vocabulary Words

Write a separate sentence using each vocabulary word listed on page 100.

Health Content

1. What are five ways to protect your brain and spinal cord? **page 102**

2. What are five ways to keep your heart muscle strong and your arteries clear? **page 103**

3. What are five ways to keep your lungs clear? **page 104**

4. What are five ways to stand tall and keep bones strong? **page 105**

5. What are five ways to keep your muscles strong and flexible? **page 106**

6. What are five ways to protect your skin? **page 107**

7. What are five ways to improve digestion? **page 108**

8. What are two ways to replace water lost from sweat and urination? **page 109**

9. What are two ways to check on your physical growth and development? **page 110**

10. What are five ways to keep your immune system strong? **page 111**

The Responsible Decision-Making Model™

You are playing on a summer softball team. A teammate thinks it is cool to use chewing tobacco and offers you a wad. Review ways tobacco affects the body systems. Answer the following questions on a separate sheet of paper. Write "Does not apply" if a question does not apply to this situation.

1. Is it healthful to chew tobacco? Why or why not?

2. Is it safe to chew tobacco? Why or why not?

3. Is it legal to chew tobacco? Why or why not?

4. Will you show respect for yourself if you chew tobacco? Why or why not?

5. Will your parents or guardian approve if you chew tobacco? Why or why not?

6. Will you demonstrate good character if you chew tobacco? Why or why not?

What is the responsible decision to make in this situation?

How would you respond to your teammate?

Health Literacy

Effective Communication

You are a book cover designer. Select a body system discussed in Lesson 11. Design a cover for a book about that body system. Include a paragraph describing ways to take care of the body system you selected. Share your book cover with your classmates.

What to Know About Puberty

Life Skills

- ◆ I will achieve the developmental tasks of adolescence.
- ◆ I will recognize habits that protect female reproductive health.
- ◆ I will recognize habits that protect male reproductive health.

You have had many periods of growth. Think about how you looked a year ago. Perhaps you are taller now, or your shoe size has changed, or you have noticed other changes. **Puberty** is the period of growth when secondary sex characteristics appear. **Secondary sex characteristics** are physical and emotional changes that occur in puberty. Although these changes make your body capable of producing offspring, you are not ready to be a parent right now. Other changes still have to occur.

The Lesson Objectives

- Discuss what to do if mood swings occur during puberty.
- Identify the female secondary sex characteristics.
- Explain what occurs during the menstrual cycle.
- Discuss habits a female can practice to protect reproductive health.
- Identify the male secondary sex characteristics.
- Discuss habits a male can practice to protect reproductive health.
- Identify eight developmental tasks you should work on right now.
- List and give the definition for each of the male and female reproductive organs.

Vocabulary

puberty

secondary sex characteristics

mood swings

estrogen

female reproductive system

menstrual cycle

ovulation

menstruation

toxic shock syndrome (TSS)

breast self-examination (BSE)

Pap smear

testosterone

male reproductive system

ejaculation

semen

circumcision

smegma

testicular self-examination (TSE)

developmental task

sex role

What Should I Do If I Have Mood Swings?

Have you ever felt OK and then suddenly felt like crying? Have you ever felt good about a friendship and suddenly felt insecure? Do you sometimes experience rapid emotional changes? Do these changes confuse you?

Hormones are chemical messengers that are released into the bloodstream. Hormones cause changes in both males and females during puberty. These hormones also cause emotional changes. **Mood swings** are emotional ups and downs caused by changing hormone levels. Part of becoming more like an adult is learning how to handle emotional ups and downs. Remember, you are accountable for the way you express your emotions. When you recognize that you are experiencing a mood swing, use the following questions before acting out.

1. **What emotion am I experiencing?**
2. **Why am I experiencing this emotion?**
3. **How might I express this emotion in a healthful way?**
   - Do I need to talk to my parent, my guardian, or another caring adult?
   - Would writing in a journal be helpful?
   - Would it be helpful to spend time alone and sort out my emotions?
   - Could I express my emotions in a creative way, such as by writing a poem or making a drawing?
   - Would it be helpful to blow off steam by exercising?
   - What I-message might I use to express my emotions?

What Are Female Secondary Sex Characteristics?

During puberty, the female body secretes the hormone estrogen. **Estrogen** is a hormone that produces female secondary sex characteristics and affects menstruation.

Female Secondary Sex Characteristics

- Increase in height
- Increase in perspiration
- Growth of underarm hair
- Growth of pubic hair
- Increase in breast size
- Widening of hips
- Increase in size of reproductive organs
- Beginning of menstruation
- Formation of mature ova

The Female Reproductive System

The **female reproductive system** consists of the organs in the female body that are involved in producing offspring. The internal female reproductive organs are the ovaries, Fallopian tubes, uterus, and vagina.

- The **ovaries** are two glands that produce estrogen and ova. Ova are female reproductive cells. They also are called eggs.

- A **Fallopian** (fuh·LOH·pee·uhn) **tube** is a four-inch-(ten-centimeter-) long tube through which ova move from an ovary to the uterus. A female has two Fallopian tubes—one near each ovary.

- The **uterus** (YOO·tuh·ruhs) is a muscular organ that receives and supports a fertilized ovum during pregnancy.

- The **cervix** is the lower part of the uterus that connects to the vagina.

- The **vagina** is a muscular tube that connects the uterus with the outside of the body. The vagina serves as the birth canal and the passageway for the menstrual flow.

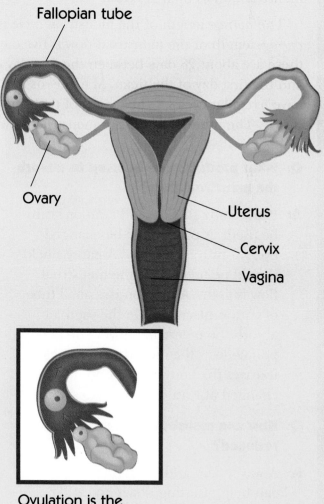

Fallopian tube

Ovary

Uterus

Cervix

Vagina

Ovulation is the release of a mature ovum from an ovary.

What Occurs During the Menstrual Cycle?

The **menstrual cycle** is a monthly series of changes that involves ovulation, changes in the uterine lining, and menstruation. **Ovulation** (ahv·yuh·LAY·shuhn) is the release of a mature ovum from an ovary. A mature ovum is released every month from an ovary. **Menstruation** (men·stroo·WAY·shuhn) is the period during which the menstrual flow leaves the body. The menstrual flow is made up of the unfertilized ovum and the lining of the uterus. Females often refer to menstruation as their "period."

The *average* length of the menstrual cycle is 28 days. The *average* length of the menstrual flow is five days. This means there are about 28 days between the first day of one period and the first day of the next. Many teens and adult females have irregular cycles. The length of their menstrual cycle varies. The number of days of menstrual flow also varies.

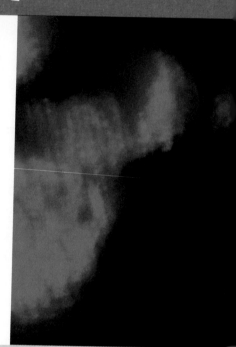

Q: What products can be used to absorb the menstrual flow?

A: Pads, panty shields, and tampons can be used. A pad should be changed every four to six hours. A panty shield should be used when the menstrual flow is light. A tampon is a small tube of cotton placed inside the vagina to absorb the menstrual flow. The tampon collects the menstrual flow before it leaves the body. A tampon must be changed at least every four to six hours.

Q: How can menstrual cramps be reduced?

A: A warm bath and moderate exercise can help. Cutting down on caffeine and sodium helps, too. A female should check with her parents or guardian and physician about medications to relieve pain.

Q: What is toxic shock syndrome?

A: Toxic shock syndrome (TSS) is a severe illness resulting from toxins secreted by *Staphylococcus* (sta·fuhloh·KAH·kuhs) bacteria. Females who use super-absorbent tampons during their periods are at increased risk for TSS. TSS is the reason females should change tampons often, and should use the lowest-absorbency tampon that meets their needs. Symptoms of TSS are similar to those of the flu: high fever, vomiting, diarrhea, fainting, and skin rash. Prompt medical attention is needed.

What Habits Can a Teen Female Practice to Protect Her Reproductive Health?

- **Practice abstinence from sex.** Practicing abstinence prevents infection with HIV and other STDs. Practicing abstinence prevents pregnancy outside of marriage.

- **Keep track of the menstrual cycle on a calendar.** Keep track of the number of days in each cycle. Keep track of the number of days of the menstrual flow. Make note of menstrual cramps or mood swings. A female should share the calendar with her parents or guardian and physician.

- **Practice habits to reduce the chance of menstrual cramps.** Limit the amount of caffeine and sodium in the diet. Exercise regularly.

- **Perform BSE each month.** A breast self-examination (BSE) is a monthly check for lumps and changes in the breasts. BSE should be performed each month after the menstrual flow has stopped.

- **Have regular medical checkups.** A physician can examine a female and discuss body changes. The physician can speak with the teen's parents or guardian about when she should have a pelvic exam and Pap smear. A **Pap smear** is a screening test for cancer of the cervix.

- **Get medical attention for signs of infection or missed periods.** A discharge from the vagina, lumps, sores, or rashes require medical attention. These are symptoms of some STDs. Missed periods can indicate that a female is pregnant.

What Are Male Secondary Sex Characteristics?

During puberty, the male body secretes the hormone testosterone. **Testosterone** is a hormone that produces male secondary sex characteristics.

Male Secondary Sex Characteristics

- Increase in height
- Increase in perspiration
- Growth of underarm hair
- Growth of pubic hair
- Broader shoulders
- Deepened voice
- Increase in muscle mass
- Increase in size of reproductive organs
- Formation of sperm

The Male Reproductive System

The **male reproductive system** consists of the organs in the male body that are involved in producing offspring.

- The **penis** is the male sex organ used for reproduction and urination.

- The **scrotum** is a sac-like pouch that holds the testes and helps regulate their temperature.

- The **testes** are two glands that produce testosterone and sperm cells.

- The **epididymis** (e·puh·DI·duh·muhs) is a structure on the top of the testes where sperm mature.

- The **vas deferens** (VAS DE·fuh·ruhnz) is one of two long, thin tubes that act as passageways for sperm and that store sperm.

- The **seminal vesicles** (SE·muh·nuhl VE·si·kuhls) are two small glands that secrete a fluid rich in sugar that nourishes and helps sperm move.

- The **prostate gland** is a gland that produces fluid that helps keep sperm alive.

- The **Cowper's glands** are two small glands that secrete a clear fluid into the urethra.

- The **urethra** (yu·REE·thruh) is a narrow tube through which urine and semen pass out of the body.

Ejaculation is the passage of semen from the penis. Ejaculation is the result of a series of muscular contractions. **Semen** is a mixture of sperm and fluids from the seminal vesicles, prostate gland, and Cowper's glands.

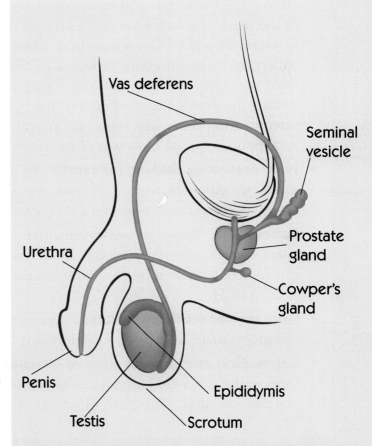

What Habits Can a Teen Male Practice to Protect His Reproductive Health?

- **Practice abstinence from sex.** Practicing abstinence prevents infection with HIV and other STDs.

- **Bathe or shower daily.** Keep your reproductive organs clean. The foreskin is a piece of skin that covers the end of the penis. **Circumcision** is the surgical removal of the foreskin. In a male who is not circumcised, smegma can collect under the foreskin. **Smegma** (SMEG·muh) is dead skin and secretions that collect under the foreskin. Pulling the foreskin back when washing the penis keeps smegma from collecting. This cuts down on infection and reduces the risk of cancer of the penis.

- **Wear protective clothing for sports.** An athletic supporter should be worn to support the penis and testes. A protective cup prevents injuries to these organs.

- **Perform TSE.** Testicular self-examination (TSE) is a check for lumps or tenderness in the testes. Testicular cancer is one of the most common cancers among males ages 15 to 34.

- **Have regular medical checkups.** A physician can examine a male and answer any questions he has.

- **Get medical attention for signs of infection.** Lumps, sores, rashes, or a discharge from the penis require medical attention. These are symptoms of some STDs.

Say NO!

What Tasks Do I Need to Master to Become a Responsible Adult?

You have developed from childhood into adolescence. Your next step will be to develop into a responsible adult. A **developmental task** is a task that a person must master at a given age. Copy the following contract on a separate sheet of paper. The contract includes eight developmental tasks you should work on right now.

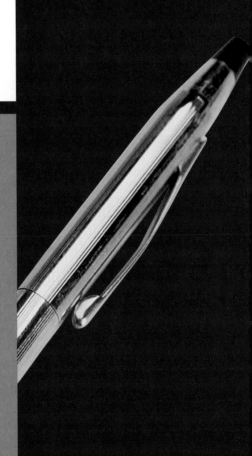

A Contract for Working to Become a Responsible Adult

1. I will develop friendships with members of both sexes.

2. I will accept that I am male or female.

3. I will choose behaviors that show I respect my body.

4. I will work on skills that I will need to become independent from my parents or guardian.

5. I will work on skills that I will need if I decide to marry and become a parent when I am an adult.

6. I will work on skills that will help me get a job and support myself.

7. I will develop a set of values to guide my behavior.

8. I will cooperate with others to make the world a better place.

Activity

A Collage of Femaleness or Maleness

Life Skill: I will achieve the developmental tasks of adolescence.

Materials: poster board, scissors, glue, old magazines

Directions: The developmental task you are working on in this activity is *I will accept that I am male or female.* Follow the directions below and create a collage. A collage is an artistic display in which materials are glued onto a surface.

1. **Females Only:** Cut out words from magazines that you think describe femaleness. For example, you might cut out the words "awesome," "intelligent," and "caring."

2. **Males Only:** Cut out words from magazines that you think describe maleness. For example, you might cut out the words "sensitive," "compassionate," and "strong."

3. **Glue your words on a poster board.** Create a unique design.

4. **Share your completed collage with classmates.** Explain why you selected the words that you did.

Sex role is the way a person acts and his or her feelings and attitudes about being male or female. Your sex role influences what you expect of yourself. Your sex role influences how you behave. Respect both males and females. Recognize and appreciate ways males and females are alike and different.

Vocabulary Words

Write a separate sentence using each vocabulary word listed on page 114.

Health Content

1. What should you do if you have mood swings? **page 115**

2. What are the female secondary sex characteristics? **page 116**

3. List and give the definition for each of the internal female reproductive organs. **page 117**

4. What occurs during the menstrual cycle? **page 118**

5. What are the symptoms of toxic shock syndrome? **page 118**

6. What are six habits a female can practice to protect her reproductive health? **page 119**

7. What are the male secondary sex characteristics? **page 120**

8. List and give the definition for each of the male reproductive organs. **page 121**

9. What are six habits a male can practice to protect his reproductive health? **page 122**

10. What are eight tasks to work on to become a responsible adult? **page 123**

The Responsible Decision-Making Model™

Your sister is having her menstrual period. She suddenly develops a fever of 102°F and has flu-like symptoms. Your parents or guardian are not home. She says, "Don't bother to call them. They'll be back in several hours." Answer the following questions on a separate sheet of paper. Write "Does not apply" if a question does not apply to this situation.

1. Is it healthful for your sister if you do not call your parents or guardian? Why or why not?

2. Is it safe for your sister if you do not call your parents or guardian? Why or why not?

3. Is it legal for your sister if you do not call your parents or guardian? Why or why not?

4. Will you show respect for your sister if you do not call your parents or guardian? Why or why not?

5. Will your parents or guardian expect you to call them right away? Why or why not?

6. Will you demonstrate good character if you do not call your parents or guardian? Why or why not?

What is the responsible decision to make in this situation?

Health Literacy

Critical Thinking

A developmental task you can work on right now is *I will develop friendships with members of both sexes.* How might you work on this developmental task?

What to Know About Pregnancy and Childbirth

Life Skills

- ◆ I will learn about pregnancy and childbirth.
- ◆ I will provide responsible care for infants and children.
- ◆ I will practice abstinence to avoid teen pregnancy and parenthood.

Vocabulary

ovulation

conception

placenta

umbilical cord

amniotic sac

pregnancy

miscarriage

premature birth

low birth weight

fetal alcohol syndrome (FAS)

prenatal care

infertile

labor

childbirth

bonding

childsitter

Think about how long a school year lasts. It lasts approximately nine months. Do you know that it also takes nine months for a baby to develop and grow before it is ready to be born? During that nine months, the behaviors of both parents affect the health of the baby. This is an important reason for teens to avoid teen pregnancy and parenthood by practicing abstinence. WAIT— until you are older, married, and ready to be a parent.

The Lesson Objectives

- Explain what happens in the first week after conception.
- Explain ways a mother-to-be's behaviors can affect the health of her baby.
- Explain ways a male's behavior can affect the health of his baby.
- Explain what happens during labor and childbirth.
- Explain how parents can bond with their baby.
- Identify skills needed to be a childsitter.
- Discuss reasons to practice abstinence and avoid teen pregnancy and parenthood.

What Happens in the First Week After Conception?

Ovulation (ahv·yuh·LAY·shuhn) is the release of a mature ovum from an ovary. An ovum is a female reproductive cell. An ovum also is called an egg. After ovulation, the ovum enters one of the Fallopian tubes. Conception usually takes place in the Fallopian tube. **Conception** is the union of a sperm and an ovum. Conception also is called fertilization.

The fertilized ovum begins to divide right away as it moves through a Fallopian tube to the uterus. The outer cells of the fertilized ovum form the placenta. The **placenta** is a structure that attaches the ovum to the inner wall of the uterus. The **umbilical** (uhm·BI·li·kuhl) **cord** is a rope-like structure that connects the placenta to the developing baby. There are blood vessels in the umbilical cord. The mother's blood containing oxygen and nutrients flows through the cord to the baby. Waste materials from the baby flow through the cord to the mother. The mother's blood and the baby's blood do not mix.

The **amniotic** (am·nee·AH·tik) **sac** is a pouch filled with fluid that surrounds a developing baby. This fluid cushions the developing baby and protects the baby from injury.

Why an Early Pregnancy Test Is Needed

A female who thinks she might be pregnant should have a pregnancy test. The test should be confirmed by a physician. A female should avoid risk behaviors even before she confirms she is pregnant. Suppose a female doesn't know she is pregnant, and she smokes and drinks alcohol. Perhaps she takes aspirin and drinks a large amount of caffeine. These behaviors can affect the developing baby.

How Can a Mother-to-Be's Behaviors Affect the Health of Her Baby?

Pregnancy is the time period between conception and birth. Within the first week of pregnancy, the mother-to-be and baby are connected by the umbilical cord. If the mother-to-be chooses harmful behaviors, they can affect her developing baby.

- **Smoking cigarettes.** Nicotine is a harmful stimulant drug in cigarettes. A mother-to-be who smokes might have a miscarriage or experience a premature birth. A **miscarriage** is a natural early ending of a pregnancy. A **premature birth** is the birth of a baby before it is fully developed. The baby might have a low birth weight. A **low birth weight** is a weight at birth of less than 5.5 pounds (2.5 kilograms). Low birth weight babies are more likely to have physical and mental problems.

- **Using crack or cocaine.** A mother-to-be who uses crack or cocaine is likely to experience a miscarriage or premature birth. A baby who is born addicted to crack or cocaine is likely to have brain damage and other birth defects.

- **Drinking alcoholic beverages.** Alcohol is a depressant drug. Alcohol can enter the baby's bloodstream from the mother's blood. **Fetal alcohol syndrome (FAS)** is the presence of birth defects in a baby born to a mother who drank alcohol during pregnancy. Babies born with FAS might be mentally retarded and have heart disease. They might have defects in their joints, arms, and legs.

- **Inhaling chemicals and secondhand smoke.** Any gases, drugs, and chemicals that the mother-to-be inhales get into her developing baby's blood. If she inhales glue, the harmful fumes affect the baby. If she inhales smoke from someone else's cigarette, the smoke affects the baby. If she inhales pesticides, the baby feels the effects of the harmful chemicals.

When a Mother-to-Be Is Infected with HIV or Other STDs

Suppose the mother-to-be is infected with HIV or other STDs. HIV and the pathogens causing other STDs can get into the bloodstream of her developing baby. Then the baby will be infected. Most babies who develop AIDS die within the first few years of life.

Why Prenatal Care Is Important

Prenatal care is care that is given to a mother-to-be and her developing baby before birth. A physician will examine the mother-to-be and help her outline a plan for a healthful pregnancy. The physician will advise her about the following:

- Proper nutrition
- Appropriate exercise
- Avoiding alcohol, tobacco, and other drug use
- Avoiding and limiting certain over-the-counter and prescription drugs
- Where to learn more about childbirth and child care
- When to get physical examinations

Touring the Hospital

Mothers- and fathers-to-be might tour the hospital where their baby will be born. Touring the hospital helps them prepare for the birth of their baby. They learn what to expect. They can ask questions about what will happen during the birth of their baby. They can get to know the hospital staff who will take care of the mother and baby.

During a tour, the mother- and father-to-be might view a video about the maternity center at the hospital. A hospital employee will take them on a tour of the maternity center. A maternity center is the place in the hospital where babies are born and cared for. The couple might tour the delivery room where the baby will be born. They might visit another room called the recovery room, where the mother will recover after the birth of the baby. Some hospitals have viewing rooms so that family members and friends can see the baby.

The baby could need intensive care if the baby is premature or has other medical problems. The intensive care unit (ICU) at a hospital has special equipment for babies who are premature or who have medical problems.

How Can a Male's Behavior Affect the Health of His Baby?

A male's choice of behaviors can affect the quality of the sperm he produces. Suppose he has been exposed to pesticides and other toxic substances. He might not produce healthy sperm. He might be infertile. To be **infertile** is to be incapable of producing offspring.

Suppose he does father a child. The quality of his sperm might be affected by chronic exposure to solvents, paints, and pesticides. His baby is at an increased risk for miscarriage, stillbirth, and some childhood cancers. Stillbirth is the birth of a dead baby.

Suppose a male drinks alcohol, smokes, or uses other drugs around the time of conception. These habits also affect the quality of the sperm he produces. Suppose a father-to-be smokes cigarettes or cigars around the mother-to-be. She will breathe in the chemicals, drugs, and gases. They will enter the baby's bloodstream. The developing baby's health will be affected.

Childbirth Classes for Fathers-to-Be

Childbirth preparation classes help both the mother- and father-to-be know what to expect in the last months of pregnancy and during labor and childbirth. They help a mother and father bond and become a team. Childbirth classes are considered an important part of prenatal care.

In childbirth classes, fathers might learn about the following:

- The stages of labor and childbirth
- The emotional needs of the mother
- Good nutrition for the mother and the baby
- Exercise for the mother and the baby
- Relaxation and breathing exercises that help the mother
- How to prepare to bring the baby home

A Developing Baby Deserves the Gift of Good Health from BOTH Parents

- Both parents should practice healthful habits before trying to conceive a baby.
- A mother-to-be should practice healthful habits during pregnancy.
- A father-to-be should practice healthful habits around his pregnant wife.

- Practice abstinence.
- Wait until you are older and married to have a baby.

What Happens During Labor and Childbirth?

Labor is a series of stages that result in the birth of a baby. **Childbirth** is the process by which the baby moves from the uterus out of the mother's body. The amniotic sac can break before or after labor begins, causing fluid to be released from the vagina. Muscular contractions of the uterus force the baby toward the cervix.

Stage 1

The lower part of the uterus, the cervix, dilates or widens enough for the baby to pass through. This stage can last from two hours to an entire day.

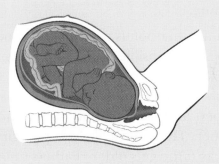

Stage 2

The baby passes into the birth canal, the vagina. The baby passes out of the birth canal and begins to breathe on its own. The umbilical cord is cut.

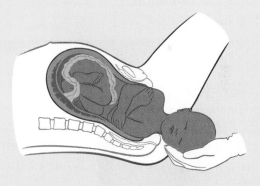

Stage 3

The placenta passes out of the birth canal. If this does not occur, the physician removes the placenta.

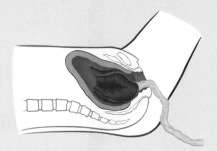

How Do Parents Bond with Their Baby?

Bonding is a process in which two people develop feelings of closeness for each other. Bonding between each parent and the baby begins shortly after birth. Soft touches, gently spoken words, and physical closeness help a baby bond with his or her parents. Smiling at the baby and responding to the baby's needs also promote bonding. When parents make an effort to bond with their baby, the baby's emotional needs are met. The baby feels secure and trusting.

When a father bonds with his baby, the likelihood that he will be a responsible parent increases. Research shows that a new father who gets involved with the baby's care right away is more likely to stay involved. A new father who diapers and plays with his baby is more likely to be a good father. He is more likely to participate in his child's activities as (s)he gets older. Fathers-to-be benefit from knowing about bonding. A baby needs both its mother and its father.

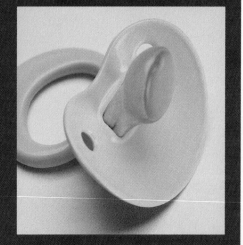

Preparing for the Baby at Home

It is important to prepare for the birth of the baby. But it is equally important to prepare for bringing the baby home. Right away the baby will need certain things. Some of the materials that the baby needs are:

- Clothing
- Sleepers
- Mittens
- Booties
- Hats
- Sweaters
- T-shirts
- Blankets

- Diapers (disposable or cloth) and diaper wipes
- Cradle or bassinet
- Crib
- Mattress pad
- Rubber sheets
- Bumper pads
- Infant car seat

- Bottles and formula
- Baby soap and shampoo and other toiletries
- Pacifier
- Bathtub
- Baby monitor
- Playpen
- Baby carrier

Activity
The Childsitter Certificate

Life Skill: I will provide responsible care for infants and children.

Materials: poster board, glue, paper, pen or pencil, markers, ribbon, etc.

Directions: Perhaps you have had a job as a childsitter. Or perhaps you are looking forward to being a childsitter. A **childsitter** is a person who provides care for someone else's children. A childsitter needs to be approved by the child's parents or legal guardian. Imagine you are a responsible adult who is teaching a course on childsitting. The teens taking the course will receive a Childsitter Certificate.

1. **Develop a pamphlet or flyer to advertise the course.** Explain the skills that teens taking the course will learn.

Skills to Be a Childsitter

How to Get Approval to Childsit

What Information to Get from the Child's Parents or Guardian

How to Make an Emergency Telephone Call

How to Give Basic First Aid

How to Take Care of Infants and Small Children

Which Activities Are Appropriate for Different Ages

2. **Create a Childsitter Certificate.** The certificate will be awarded to teens who complete the course.

3. **Plan what you will say to teens when they receive their Childsitter Certificates.** Motivate them to provide responsible care for infants and children.

4. **Have an imaginary graduation ceremony.** Call on one of your classmates to pretend (s)he is graduating from your course. Award the Childsitter Certificate to this classmate in front of the rest of the class.

What Are Reasons I Should Practice Abstinence and Avoid Teen Pregnancy and Parenthood?

1. **Babies born to teen parents are at risk for:**

- being born prematurely;
- having a low birth weight;
- not surviving the infant years;
- being mentally retarded;
- having birth defects;
- having little contact with their fathers;
- being abused;
- growing up in poverty.

2. **Teen mothers and fathers are at risk for:**

- dropping out of school;
- giving up career goals;
- living in poverty;
- getting divorced if they marry;
- abusing their children;
- having a limited social life;
- having health problems (teen mothers);
- making child support payments (teen fathers);
- lacking contact with their child (non-custodial parent).

3. **Society is at risk for:**

- increased medical care costs;
- having more families living in poverty;
- having a higher divorce rate;
- having more children raised without regular contact with two parents;
- having a higher incidence of violence.

Review

Vocabulary Words

Write a separate sentence using each vocabulary word listed on page 126.

Health Content

1. What happens in the first week after conception? **page 127**

2. Why should a female have a pregnancy test as soon as possible if she suspects she is pregnant? **page 127**

3. Why is it risky for a mother-to-be to smoke cigarettes? To use crack or cocaine? To drink alcoholic beverages? To inhale chemicals and secondhand smoke? **page 128**

4. How can a male's behavior affect the quality of the sperm he produces? **page 130**

5. What can happen if a father-to-be smokes cigarettes or cigars around the mother-to-be? **page 130**

6. What happens during labor and childbirth? **page 131**

7. How do parents bond with their baby? **page 132**

8. What effect does early bonding have on fathers? **page 132**

9. What are six skills to learn to be a childsitter? **page 133**

10. What are reasons you should practice abstinence and avoid teen pregnancy and parenthood? **page 134**

The Responsible Decision-Making Model™

Your aunt calls and tells you she is pregnant. She invites you and other relatives over for a celebration. One relative brings a gift of a bottle of champagne. Answer the following questions on a separate sheet of paper. Write "Does not apply" if a question does not apply to this situation.

1. Is it healthful for your aunt to drink alcohol during her pregnancy? Why or why not?

2. Is it safe for your aunt to drink alcohol during her pregnancy? Why or why not?

3. Is it legal for your aunt to drink alcohol during her pregnancy? Why or why not?

4. Will your aunt show respect for the developing baby if she drinks alcohol during her pregnancy? Why or why not?

5. Will your aunt's physician advise her to drink alcohol during her pregnancy? Why or why not?

6. Will your aunt demonstrate good character if she drinks alcohol during her pregnancy? Why or why not?

What is the responsible decision for your aunt to make in this situation?

Health Literacy

Responsible Citizenship

Design a warning label for a package of cigarettes. The warning should address the effects that smoking can have on sperm.

How to Age in a Healthful Way

Life Skills

- ◆ I will develop habits that promote healthful aging.
- ◆ I will develop my learning style.

Vocabulary

chronological age

biological age

osteoporosis

cataract

mental alertness

learning style

lifelong learning

stroke

caregiver

retirement community

nursing home

Chronological age is the number of years a person has lived. No matter what you do, you will be one year older each year. **Biological age** is a measure of how well a person's body parts function. The habits you choose right now influence your biological age. Suppose you choose healthful habits. Your biological age can be lower than your chronological age.

The Lesson Objectives

- Explain how a person's biological age can be lower than the person's chronological age.
- Discuss habits that help a person stay healthy into old age.
- Discuss ways to stay mentally alert into old age.
- Discuss different living arrangements available for older family members.
- Identify ways you can provide companionship for older family members.

How Can I Stay Healthy into Old Age?

Practice healthful habits right now to:

- protect your body parts;
- improve the function of your body parts;
- keep your biological age lower than your chronological age.

Throughout your life:

Participate in physical activity. Regular physical activity strengthens your heart muscle. Your heart will pump more blood with each beat. Your heart will beat less often and get more rest between beats. Regular physical activity helps keep fat from sticking to the inside lining of your arteries. Blood will flow more easily to your cells. Regular physical activity makes your bones denser and stronger.

Eat a healthful diet. You probably will not develop heart disease as a teen. But, you need to know that at your age, fat can begin to build up on the inner lining of your arteries. Limit the amount of fatty foods you eat. Make diet choices that help you build a strong body. For example, calcium makes your bones and teeth strong.

You can avoid conditions such as osteoporosis by getting the recommended amount of calcium. **Osteoporosis** (AHS·tee·oh·puh·ROH·suhs) is a disease in which the bones become thin and brittle. Your bones must support your body for a lifetime. And your teeth must last a lifetime.

Do not smoke or use other tobacco products. Some teens believe they can smoke or use other tobacco products now and easily quit later. Nicotine is a drug in tobacco that affects blood circulation. Use of tobacco products now increases the risk of heart disease and cancer later. The latest research shows that your health can be affected more than ten years after quitting tobacco use. Teens who have smoked or used tobacco products must quit right away. Teens who have never had the tobacco habit should not start.

Protect yourself from the sun. Ultraviolet (UV) radiation causes wrinkles and sun spots. It can cause skin cancer. The incidence of skin cancer is increasing. Stay out of the sun from 11 a.m. until 3 p.m. To protect yourself when in the sun, wear a hat, sunglasses, and sunscreen. The sunscreen should have a sun protection factor (SPF) of at least 15. Sunglasses should block all UV rays. Having too much sun in the eyes for a number of years increases the risk of cataracts when you are older. A **cataract** is a clouding of the lens of the eye, that affects vision.

Get regular checkups. Checkups provide you with information about your biological age. Your physician can use this information to help you make a plan to stay healthy into old age. For example, your blood pressure might be high. High blood pressure indicates that the heart and blood vessels are working too hard. If your blood pressure is high, your physician will help you make a plan to lower your blood pressure.

How Can I Stay Mentally Alert into Old Age?

The biological age of your mind might be even more important than that of your body. **Mental alertness** is the sharpness of the mind. If you are mentally alert, you remember facts. You understand what you read and hear. You are able to follow the conversation of others. How can you stay mentally alert into old age?

Develop your own learning style. **Learning style** is a person's way of gaining knowledge and skills. You have your own personal learning style. Perhaps you outline your home-work to remember important facts. Perhaps you learn best when you ask questions or participate in activities at school. Pay attention to how you learn best. Try to increase the amount you retain in a fixed period of time.

Develop the habit of lifelong learning. **Lifelong learning** is being involved in gaining knowledge and skills throughout life. Learn from places and activities outside of school. Watch educational programs on TV. Work difficult cross-word puzzles. Read magazines and newspapers. Exchange ideas with adults who challenge your thinking.

Participate in physical activity. Your brain cells need oxygen to function. Physical activity improves circulation. Blood will flow to your brain cells more easily. Physical activity decreases the risk of a stroke as you age. A **stroke** is a condition caused by a blocked or broken blood vessel in the brain. A stroke can cause cells in the brain to die.

Do not use harmful drugs. Keep as many brain cells as you can! Healthy brain cells are needed for you to be mentally alert. Alcohol and other harmful drugs kill brain cells. Avoid harmful drugs right now.

Activities to Help You Stay Mentally Alert

Learning new vocabulary words

Doing art projects

Discussing current events with others

Listening to news programs on the radio

Learning a new language

Watching educational television

Playing word games

Reading books, magazines, and newspapers

Using the computer

Doing crossword puzzles

Activity

Health Behavior Contract

Name:_____ **Date:**_____

Life Skill: I will develop habits that promote healthful aging.

Effect on My Health: Mental alertness is the sharpness of the mind. If I am mentally alert, I will remember facts. I will understand what I read and hear. I will be able to follow the conversation of others. I can develop habits right now that will help me stay mentally alert into old age.

My Plan: I will develop the habit of lifelong learning. I will choose an activity that promotes mental alertness. The activity I choose will be one I could continue throughout my life. The activity will be in addition to my assigned schoolwork. I will participate in this activity at least three days for the next week. On the calendar below, I will write down what I do, when, and for how long I do it.

	M	T	W	Th	F	S	S
My Calendar							

How My Plan Worked: (Complete after one week) _____

_____

_____

How Can I Respond to the Needs of Older Family Members?

Most people stay physically active and mentally alert beyond the age of 65. Their health status depends on their heredity, their habits, the medical care they receive, and the support they get from family and friends. You cannot change many things about the health status of older family members. But there are ways you can respond to their needs.

- Encourage older family members to practice healthful habits.
- Provide companionship.
- Be educated about available medical care, living arrangements, and caregiving.

What to Know About Living Arrangements

A **caregiver** is a person who provides care to someone who needs assistance. Perhaps you have an older family member who lives in his or her own home or lives with you. (S)he might need limited help. For example, (s)he might need help with chores, such as lawnmowing and grocery shopping. (S)he might need someone to drive him or her to appointments. (S)he might have a personal alert device to get help if (s)he has an emergency and cannot get to a phone.

Perhaps an older family member lives in a retirement community. A **retirement community** is a group of homes in which older people live. Residents might share a home or live by themselves. Many retirement communities provide medical care, transportation services, and social activities. Perhaps an older family member lives in a nursing home. A **nursing home** is a live-in facility that provides medical care, food, and social activities. An older family member needs your companionship and acts of kindness no matter where (s)he lives.

How to Provide Companionship

- Celebrate special occasions, such as birthdays and holidays.
- Keep in touch by phone.
- Agree to be a pen pal.
- Share school projects and daily activities.
- Share physical activities such as walks or golf.
- Take a pet when you visit.
- Make a scrapbook or tape interviews to preserve memories.

Review

Vocabulary Words

Write a separate sentence using each vocabulary word listed on page 136.

Health Content

1. How can your biological age be lower than your chronological age when you are older? **page 136**

2. What are five habits that will help you stay healthy into old age? How does each habit benefit you? **page 137**

3. What are four actions that will help you stay mentally alert into old age? **page 138**

4. What are different living arrangements to provide caregiving for older family members? **page 140**

5. What are seven ways that you can provide companionship for an older family member? **page 140**

Health Literacy

Responsible Citizenship

Pretend that you are the mayor in your community. An award is to be given to a senior citizen for community service. Select a senior citizen you believe is worthy of the award. Write a short speech to use when giving the award.

The Responsible Decision-Making Model™

Today is your grandmother's birthday. She has asked you to spend the evening with her. Your friends want you to go to a movie. They suggest that you tell her you have to go to the library to finish a report for tomorrow. That way, she won't know you chose the movie over being with her. Answer the following questions on a separate sheet of paper. Write "Does not apply" if a question does not apply to this situation.

1. Is it healthful to make up an excuse instead of being with your grandmother on her birthday? Why or why not?

2. Is it safe to make up an excuse instead of being with your grandmother on her birthday? Why or why not?

3. Is it legal to make up an excuse instead of being with your grandmother on her birthday? Why or why not?

4. Will you show respect for your grandmother if you make up an excuse instead of being with her on her birthday? Why or why not?

5. Will your parents or guardian approve if you make up an excuse instead of being with your grandmother on her birthday? Why or why not?

6. Will you demonstrate good character if you make up an excuse instead of being with your grandmother on her birthday? Why or why not?

What is the responsible decision to make in this situation?

How to Express Grief

Life Skill

♦ **I will share with my family my feelings about dying and death.**

Death is the end of life when vital organs no longer function. Sometimes you have time to prepare for the death of someone you know or love. For example, this person might have a terminal illness. A **terminal illness** is an illness that will result in death. At other times, you do not have time to prepare for the death of someone you know or love. For example, a person might have a sudden heart attack or die in an accident. When someone you know dies, you might experience grief. **Grief** is an emotional reaction to a loss or misfortune. To **grieve** is to express feelings of grief.

The Lesson Objectives

- Discuss ways you might respond if someone you know dies.
- Discuss healthful and harmful ways of grieving when someone close to you dies.
- Explain why out-of-order death is extra difficult.
- Identify five leading causes of death in teens.
- Explain why you might grieve when a well-known person dies.

Vocabulary

death

terminal illness

grief

grieve

shock

denial

tribute

out-of-order death

crisis intervention program

invincible

How Might I Respond If Someone I Know Dies?

You might have already known some people who have died. Perhaps you responded the same way in each instance. Perhaps you did not. Your responses might have surprised you. Responding in different ways to death is normal. It is important to be aware of how you respond to a person's death. Then you can make healthful adjustments to your loss. Consider the following responses you might have.

You might experience shock. **Shock** is a dangerous change in blood flow to the body. When you are in shock, you feel faint and nauseated. Perhaps you have seen someone on TV faint after learning about the death of another person. Medical attention is needed if a person experiences shock.

You might experience denial. **Denial** is refusing to admit there is a problem. Sometimes you can't deal with a death right away. To cope, you put it out of your mind. You do not face the reality that you will never see the person again. You also do not deal with the changes in your life that result from the person's death.

You might become angry. You did not want the person to die. You do not want to make adjustments to the loss. You might be angry at a physician who could not save the person's life. You might be angry at the driver of the car involved if it was an accident. You might even be angry at the person who died. After all, this person left you. You might believe life is being very unfair to you.

You might become depressed. It is difficult to lose someone close to you. You might be overcome by sadness. You might cry or need time alone. Doing schoolwork or other activities might be difficult for you. It might be difficult to get to sleep. It is best to talk to a parent, guardian, or counselor about your sad feelings.

You might experience changes in your health status. As you know, your emotions can affect your body functions. You might have headaches or stomachaches. You might feel less energetic than you usually do. When you are grieving, protect your health by taking extra-good care of yourself.

What Are Healthful and Harmful Ways I Can Express Grief?

It is difficult to experience the death of someone who has been close to you. Do not stuff your feelings inside and pretend nothing has happened. Do not express your feelings in ways that will be harmful to you or others. Work through your feelings of grief in healthful ways.

Grieving DOs and DON'Ts

Healthful DOs

1. Allow time to adjust to the loss you have experienced.

2. Share your grief with a parent, guardian, or other responsible adult.

3. Feel free to cry and to express your sadness.

4. Join a support group or obtain counseling if necessary.

5. Share your memories of the person with others.

6. Pay a tribute to the person. A **tribute** is something done to pay respect to someone. You might visit the person's grave, write a poem about the person, or make a charitable contribution in memory of the person.

Harmful DON'Ts

1. Don't use alcohol or other drugs to numb the pain you feel. Drugs, such as alcohol, are depressants. If you use drugs, you can become more depressed.

2. Do not become sexually active to feel close to another person. Putting yourself at risk for getting pregnant or getting someone pregnant is unwise. Putting yourself at risk for being infected with STDs, including HIV infection, is unwise. Clinging to a boyfriend or girlfriend will not substitute for the loss of someone else.

3. Do not express your anger with violence. Do not take revenge if the death was a wrongful death. There is a legal system to handle wrongful death. It is not appropriate to damage property or harm someone just because you feel out of control.

4. Do not consider a suicide attempt. Even if you miss the dead person very much, this is not the time for you to "join" him or her. You will get through your grief. Talk to an adult immediately if suicide crosses your mind.

Why Is Out-of-Order Death Extra Difficult?

An **out-of-order death** is the death of a person that occurs at an unexpected time in his or her life cycle. In a family, you expect the grandparents to die before the parents. You expect the parents to die before any of their children. It is especially difficult when death occurs in a different order. The surviving family members have additional feelings to work through as they grieve.

For example, suppose someone your age dies. Family members and friends would grieve. Later, they might think about what the teen would miss. (S)he would miss the high school prom. (S)he would not go to college or vocational school. (S)he would not marry and have children. Family members and friends would realize they would miss participating with the teen in these life events. They would feel cheated, too.

Sometimes there is a tragedy and several teens in a community die. This kind of situation can be overwhelming for people your age. It also is overwhelming for the adults in the community. There is so much to deal with at one time. The school or community might have a crisis intervention program. A **crisis intervention program** is a program in which a trained team of adults offers assistance to help people who experience severe difficulty. The program might include speakers and individual counseling. Support groups might be formed. A crisis program helps people work through their grief together.

Out-of-order death is disturbing. Suppose someone your age dies. Then death becomes more realistic to you. After all, if a teen dies in an automobile accident, you could too. Right? And if a teen has a terminal illness, you could too. Right? That is hard to face. Most teens believe they are invincible. To be **invincible** (in·VIN·suh·buhl) is to be incapable of being harmed. Teens are not invincible. However, most people do not die in their teens. Choose responsible behavior. Decide to make the most of each day by doing your best and treating others kindly.

Activity

PSA to Protect Teens

Life Skill: I will share with my family my feelings about dying and death.

Materials: paper, pen or pencil

Directions: A public service announcement (PSA) is a short announcement that gives important information to the community. Write a PSA that will provide information to teens about one of the leading causes of death.

1. **Choose one of the leading causes of death in teens listed below.**
   - **Accidents**
   - **Heart disease**
   - **Cancer**
   - **AIDS**
   - **Pneumonia and influenza**

2. **Use the library or Internet to research your choice.** Find facts about teen deaths resulting from the cause of death you chose. Include facts on ways teens can reduce their risk of death from that cause.

3. **Write a PSA.** The PSA should take 30 seconds to read. It should provide information on ways teens can reduce their risk of death from the cause you chose. Include five facts from your research.

Why Do People Grieve When a Person Who Is Well-Known Dies?

Most likely, you have seen the reactions of the public to the death of a well-known person. Perhaps you saw Princess Diana's funeral on television. Perhaps you listened to the news coverage regarding a politician's death. Or you might have read a story about the death of an actor, actress, or singer.

People often grieve the death of a person who is well-known. They grieve even though they might have had no personal contact with the person. They might grieve the loss of the contributions the person made. They know society will miss these contributions in the future.

They also might grieve their relationship with the person. Just because you have not met someone does not mean you cannot feel connected. For example, you might have a favorite singer. Perhaps you collect this singer's albums and listen to them often. You develop a feeling of closeness. Perhaps you watch a television show because of the stars in the show. It is normal to develop a feeling of closeness to them. You feel a loss if one of these people dies. You also feel sad for the other people who experience the loss. For example, most people feel sad for Prince William and Prince Harry. People know they will miss their mother, Princess Diana.

It also is normal to have other feelings when a person who is well-known dies. For example, you might feel angry. Suppose a singer you enjoyed overdoses on drugs. You might feel very angry that the singer would choose such wrong actions. You might feel let down.

Always work through feelings of grief. Suppose someone says, "Why does this bother you? You didn't even know the person." Remember, do not deny your feelings. When you feel grief, you must deal with it in a healthful way.

Vocabulary Words

Write a separate sentence using each vocabulary word listed on page 142.

Health Content

1. What are five ways you might respond if someone you know dies? **page 143**

2. What are six healthful ways to grieve if someone close to you dies? What are four harmful ways? **page 144**

3. Why is out-of-order death extra difficult? **page 145**

4. What are five leading causes of death in teens? **page 145**

5. Why might you grieve when a person who is well-known dies? **page 146**

Health Literacy

Self-Directed Learning

Research ways that the public has paid tribute to well-known people who have died. For example, a highway, library, or monument might have been named out of respect for a person.

The Responsible Decision-Making Model™

A teen in your school died in an automobile crash in which the driver was speeding. The driver is awaiting his trial. A classmate suggests slashing his tires. Answer the following questions on a separate sheet of paper. Write "Does not apply" if a question does not apply to this situation.

1. Is it healthful to slash the driver's tires? Why or why not?

2. Is it safe to slash the driver's tires? Why or why not?

3. Is it legal to slash the driver's tires? Why or why not?

4. Will you show respect for yourself if you slash the driver's tires? Why or why not?

5. Will your parents or guardian approve if you slash the driver's tires? Why or why not?

6. Will you demonstrate good character if you slash the driver's tires? Why or why not?

What is the responsible decision to make in this situation?

How might you express your anger in a healthful way?

Health Content

Prepare for the Unit Test. Review your answers for each Lesson Review in this unit. Then write answers to each of the following questions:

1. How do depressant drugs affect your nervous system? **Lesson 11 page 102**

2. How does the immune system respond when pathogens enter your body? **Lesson 11 page 111**

3. How can menstrual cramps be reduced? **Lesson 12 page 118**

4. Why should teen males perform TSE? **Lesson 12 page 122**

5. Why is it dangerous for a father-to-be to smoke around the mother-to-be? **Lesson 13 page 130**

6. What are the risks for a baby born to teen parents? **Lesson 13 page 134**

7. How does wearing sunglasses right now protect your eyes later? **Lesson 14 page 137**

8. How can you develop the habit of lifelong learning? **Lesson 14 page 138**

9. What are healthful ways to grieve? **Lesson 15 page 144**

10. Why might the out-of-order death of a friend be extra upsetting? **Lesson 15 page 145**

Health Behavior Contract

Make a health behavior contract for one of the life skills in this unit. Review your health behavior contract with your parents or guardian.

Vocabulary Words

Number a sheet of paper from 1–10. Select the correct vocabulary word and write it next to the corresponding number. DO NOT WRITE IN THIS BOOK.

toxic shock syndrome (TSS)	immune system
out-of-order death	cataract
scoliosis	tribute
learning style	circumcision
bonding	infertile

1. _____ is an S-shaped curvature of the spine. **Lesson 11**

2. _____ is the surgical removal of the foreskin. **Lesson 12**

3. The _____ is the body system that removes harmful organisms from the blood and fights pathogens. **Lesson 11**

4. A _____ is something done to pay respect to someone. **Lesson 15**

5. _____ is a process in which two people develop feelings of closeness for each other. **Lesson 13**

6. _____ is a severe illness resulting from toxins secreted by *Staphylococcus* bacteria. **Lesson 12**

7. _____ is a person's way of gaining knowledge and skills. **Lesson 14**

8. A _____ is a clouding of the lens of the eye, that affects vision. **Lesson 14**

9. An _____ is the death of a person that occurs at an unexpected time in his or her life cycle. **Lesson 15**

10. To be _____ is to be incapable of producing offspring. **Lesson 13**

The Responsible Decision-Making Model™

You are waiting to be seated in the non-smoking section of a restaurant. The married couple behind you also is waiting to be seated there. The manager announces that there is a table available in the smoking section. You decline, but the married couple behind you asks to be seated there. She is pregnant and tired of standing. Answer the following questions on a separate sheet of paper. Write "Does not apply" if a question does not apply to this situation.

1. Is it healthful for the pregnant wife to sit in the smoking section? Why or why not?

2. Is it safe for the pregnant wife to sit in the smoking section? Why or why not?

3. Is it legal for the pregnant wife to sit in the smoking section? Why or why not?

4. Will the pregnant wife show respect for her developing baby if she sits in the smoking section? Why or why not?

5. Would most responsible adults agree with her decision to sit in the smoking section? Why or why not?

6. Will the pregnant wife demonstrate good character if she sits in the smoking section? Why or why not?

What is the responsible decision to make in this situation?

Health Literacy

Effective Communication

Cover a shoebox or other box with paper. Your shoebox will represent the gifts of good health parents can give their children. Use a marker and write gifts on the paper covering the box. For example, you might write "attention" or "smoke-free home."

Self-Directed Learning

Lifelong learning is being involved in gaining knowledge and skills throughout life. Keep a journal for one week. Each day write down at least one new fact or skill you have learned.

Critical Thinking

Think of three well-known people who had an out-of-order death. Investigate the cause of their deaths.

Responsible Citizenship

Get permission from your parents or guardian. Contact a nursing home or rest home. Ask for the name of a person who does not receive visitors or mail. Design a card with a cheerful message to send to this person.

Multicultural Health

Many cultures insist that the eldest family members be given the highest respect. They value the wisdom that accompanies the aging process. Identify such a culture. Learn ways that the eldest family members are recognized.

Family Involvement

Suppose you are having visitors who have a toddler. Make a list of ways to "childproof" your home.

UNIT 4
Nutrition

PRACTICE

HEALTH STANDARD 4

Analyze Influences on Health

Practice this standard at the end of this unit.

1. **Identify people and things that might influence you.** Identify a commercial on TV that claims a certain food product is nutritionally sound.

2. **Evaluate the effects the influence might have on health.** Refer to the six classes of nutrients given on pages 154-155. Read the food label of the product. To what degree are the nutrients present in the product? Are the claims in the commercial accurate?

3. **Choose positive influences on health.** Suppose the TV commercial promoted a healthful food product. Have some of your friends watch the commercial. Get their opinions as to why the commercial is a positive influence.

4. **Protect yourself from negative influences on health.** If the commercial did not promote a healthful product, tell your friends why they should not be influenced by it. Let them know what alternatives they have.

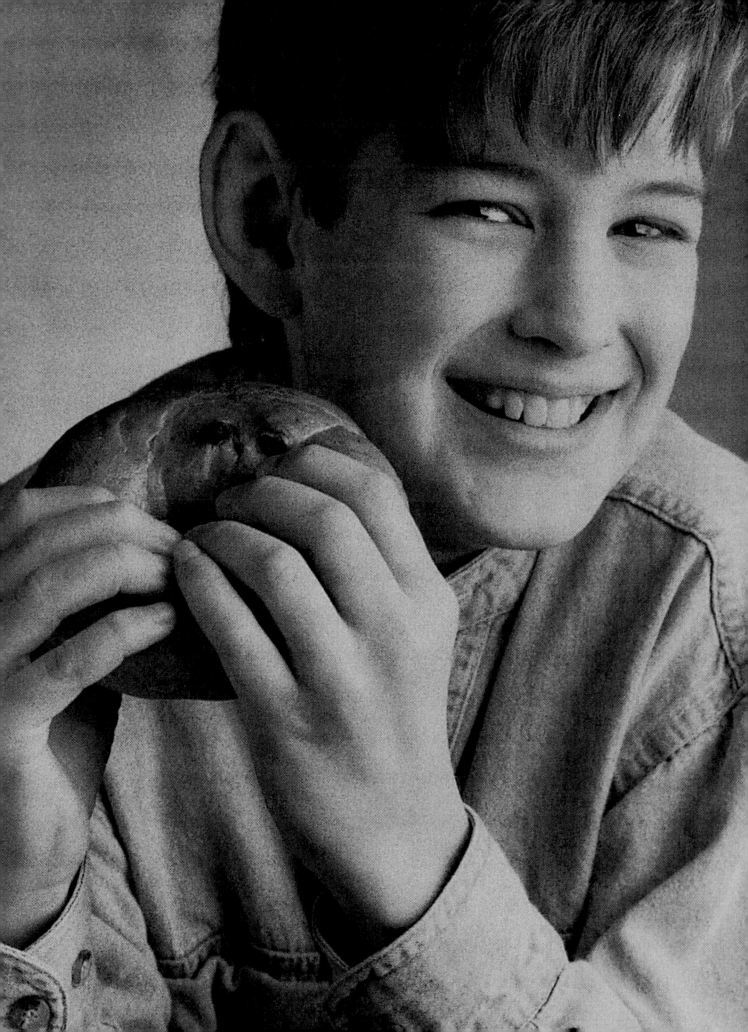

How to Follow the Dietary Guidelines

Life Skills

- ◆ I will follow the Dietary Guidelines.
- ◆ I will eat the recommended number of servings from the Food Guide Pyramid.
- ◆ I will plan a healthful diet that reduces the risk of disease.

One of the most important ways you can promote your health is to make healthful food choices. **Nutrition** is the study of what people eat and the effects of food on health. Diet refers to everything a person eats and drinks. The kinds of foods you choose affect your health. They affect your energy level and your risk of illness and disease.

The Lesson Objectives

- Identify sources of the six classes of nutrients.
- Explain why you should follow each of the seven Dietary Guidelines.
- Identify the number of servings you need each day from each group in the Food Guide Pyramid.
- Discuss diet choices that reduce your risk of developing premature heart disease.
- Discuss diet choices that reduce your risk of developing cancer.

Vocabulary

nutrition

nutrient

calorie

proteins

carbohydrates

starch

fiber

fats

saturated fat

unsaturated fat

vitamins

beta carotene

minerals

water

Dietary Guidelines

desirable weight

cholesterol

sodium

Food Guide Pyramid

food group

plaque

atherosclerosis

antioxidants

cruciferous vegetables

Why Is My Diet a Key to My Health Status?

"You are what you eat." This popular quote emphasizes the importance of nutrition. Your food and beverage choices affect your health. A **nutrient** is a substance in foods that:

- **builds, repairs, and maintains body tissues;**
- **helps with body processes;**
- **and provides energy.**

Energy is measured in calories. A **calorie** is a unit of energy produced by food and used by the body.

Nutrients in foods:

Promote shiny hair

Promote clear skin

Reduce the risk of disease

Help heal wounds

Help form bones

Reduce the risk of illness

Help form teeth

Help with waste removal

Help the body use energy

Prevent cell damage

Build cells

Promote strong nails

Provide energy

What Are the Six Classes of Nutrients?

There are six classes of nutrients.

Proteins

Proteins are nutrients that are needed for growth and repair of body cells. Proteins make up your muscles, skin, nails, and hair. You should obtain between 10 and 15 percent of your total daily calories from protein.

Spectacular Sources of Proteins:
chicken • fish • turkey • eggs • beef • milk • wheat germ • nuts • cheese • tofu • beans • pasta • peas • seeds • rice

Carbohydrates

Carbohydrates (KAHR·boh·HY·drayts) are nutrients that are the main source of energy for the body. Sugars, starches, and fiber are carbohydrates. **Starch** is a substance that is made in plants. **Fiber** is the part of grains and plant foods that cannot be digested.

Super Sources of Carbohydrates:
fruit • cereal • potatoes • vegetables • breads • rice • popcorn

Fats

Fats are nutrients that provide energy and help the body store vitamins. There are two types of fat. **Saturated fat** is a type of fat from dairy products, solid vegetable fat, and meat and poultry. **Unsaturated fat** is a type of fat obtained from plant products and fish. A gram of fat has more than twice as many calories as does a gram of protein or carbohydrates. This is why high-fat foods such as French fries and ice cream are considered more fattening than foods high in protein or carbohydrates. You should obtain no more than 30 percent of your daily calories from fat.

Substantial Sources of Fats:
oils • butter • margarine • nuts • egg yolks • cheese • fried foods • milk • ice cream • pastries • salad dressings

Vitamins

Vitamins are nutrients that help the body use carbohydrates, proteins, and fats. You need more vitamins during adolescence than you did as a child.

Some vitamins your body needs are:

Vitamin C: Vitamin C helps heart, cells, and muscles function. About eight ounces of orange juice will supply you with a day's worth of vitamin C.

> **Solid Sources of Vitamin C:**
> citrus fruits • strawberries • melons • tomatoes • broccoli • potatoes • green vegetables

B Vitamins: B vitamins are important for growth and nerve function.

> **Solid Sources of B Vitamins:**
> dairy products • meats • fish • poultry • whole-grain breads • eggs • vegetables • fruits • beans

Vitamin A: Vitamin A keeps eyes, skin, hair, teeth, and gums healthy. **Beta carotene** (BAY·tuh KEHR·uh·teen) is a substance found in food that is changed to vitamin A in the body. It is thought to play a role in fighting disease.

> **Solid Sources of Vitamin A:**
> eggs • butter • milk • cheese • green, orange, and yellow vegetables • liver • fruits

Vitamin D: Vitamin D is needed for healthy bones and teeth. Vitamin D is obtained from foods and sunlight.

> **Solid Sources of Vitamin D:**
> butter • milk • cheese • tuna • egg yolks

Vitamin E: Vitamin E helps form and maintain cells. It also helps your body maintain immunity against disease.

> **Solid Sources of Vitamin E:**
> green vegetables • wheat germ • nuts • vegetable oils • whole-grain cereals and breads

Minerals

Minerals are nutrients that are involved in many of the body's activities.

Iron: Iron is an essential part of hemoglobin (HEE·muh·GLOH·buhn), which is the red substance in blood. Hemoglobin carries oxygen to cells and carbon dioxide away from cells. Females need more iron when they begin menstruating.

> **Solid Sources of Iron:**
> lean red meats • fish • nuts • egg • liver • whole-grain cereals • dried peas and beans

Calcium: Calcium helps build bones and teeth. You need calcium for growth.

> **Solid Sources of Calcium:**
> milk • yogurt • cheese • tofu • sardines • soybeans • calcium-added orange juice • spinach • salmon

Zinc: Zinc helps with digestion and healing wounds.

> **Solid Sources of Zinc:**
> fish • poultry • meat • beans • peas • nuts

Potassium: Potassium keeps fluids balanced in cells.

> **Solid Sources of Potassium:**
> potatoes • spinach • winter squash • bananas • oranges • dry beans • milk • yogurt

Water

Water is a nutrient that makes up blood, helps digest food, helps with waste removal, regulates body temperature, and cushions bones and joints. You should drink at least six to eight glasses of water a day.

> **Secret Sources of Water**
> fruits • vegetables • soup • juice • frozen juice pops • sorbet

What Are the New Dietary Guidelines?

A Guide to the Guidelines

The new **Dietary Guidelines** are recommendations for diet choices for healthy Americans ages two or older.

1. **Aim for a healthful weight.** People who maintain a healthful weight help stay healthy now and later in life. Healthful foods eaten in the correct amounts help keep weight down.

    Why follow this guideline? Keeping weight down helps reduce the risk of developing heart disease and cancer.

2. **Be physically active each day.** Physical activity is a way to use up calories. Balancing your food intake with physical activity helps you maintain your desirable weight. **Desirable weight** is the weight that is most healthful for a person. Your desirable weight is the most healthful weight for your age, height, sex, and body frame.

    Why follow this guideline? Being over your desirable weight increases the risk of high blood pressure, heart disease, and stroke. It is also linked to diabetes, cancer, arthritis, breathing problems, and other illnesses.

3. **Follow the Food Guide Pyramid.** The Food Guide Pyramid will serve as a guide to making food selections that reduce your risk of disease and illness. It will help you maintain your desirable weight.

    Why follow this guideline? The healthier you are now and the better your food choices, the greater the chance that this will carry through adulthood.

4. **Choose a variety of grains daily, especially whole grains.** Grain products are low in fat and high in fiber. The high fiber helps you have regular bowel movements. **Why follow this guideline?** Grain products help reduce your risk of developing certain types of cancer.

5. **Choose a variety of fruits and vegetables daily.** Fruits and vegetables provide vitamins and minerals your body needs. **Why follow this guideline?** Fruits and vegetables help you reduce your risk of heart disease and cancer. They help you maintain a healthy cholesterol level.

6. **Keep food safe to eat**. Keep foods that need to be cool refrigerated. Cook foods thoroughly. **Why follow this guideline?** Foods that are prepared the correct way will prevent you from becoming ill.

7. **Choose a diet that is low in saturated fat and cholesterol and moderate in total fat.** Cholesterol is a fatty substance that is made by the body and is found in dairy products. Your diet should provide less than 10 percent of calories from fat. **Why follow this guideline?** A diet high in fat, saturated fat, and cholesterol increases the risk of being overweight. It increases the risk of heart disease and cancer.

8. **Choose beverages and foods to moderate your intake of sugars.** Sugars are carbohydrates. They are high in calories but contain few nutrients. **Why follow this guideline?** Eating or drinking too many foods with high sugar content increases the risk of being overweight and contributes to tooth decay.

9. **Choose and prepare foods with less salt.** Sodium is a mineral that is found in table salt and prepared foods. Most people consume almost twice as much sodium as they need daily. **Why follow this guideline?** A diet high in salt increases the risk of high blood pressure.

10. **Do not drink alcohol. (Adults who drink should do so in moderation.)** Children and teens should not drink alcohol. Alcohol is high in calories and does not contain any vitamins, minerals, or protein. **Why follow this guideline?** Drinking alcohol can increase the risk of stroke, heart disease, and certain cancers. It harms brain cells and body organs such as the liver and can cause high blood pressure.

How Do I Use the Food Guide Pyramid?

The **Food Guide Pyramid** is a guide that shows how many servings are needed from each food group each day. A **food group** is foods that contain similar nutrients. The numbers of servings you need depends on your age, sex, and activity level.

Milk, Yogurt, and Cheese Group

2 to 3 servings each day

Good sources of calcium and protein

One serving =

1 cup milk
or
1 1/2 ounces (42 grams) of natural cheese
or
2 ounces (56 grams) of processed cheese
or
1 cup of yogurt

Fats, Oils, and Sweets

Limit the amount of fats, oils, and sweets you eat.

Fats, oils, and sweets provide few vitamins and minerals and are high in sugars and fats.

Meat, Poultry, Fish, Dry Beans, Eggs, and Nuts Group

2 to 3 servings each day

Good sources of protein, B vitamins, iron, and zinc

One serving =

2 to 3 ounces (56 to 84 grams) of cooked lean meat, poultry, or fish
or
1/2 cup of dry beans
or
1 egg
or
2 tablespoons of peanut butter

Fruit Group

2 to 4 servings each day

Good sources of vitamins A and C, potassium, fiber, and carbohydrates

One serving =

1 medium apple, banana, or orange
or
1/2 cup chopped, cooked, or canned fruit
or
3/4 cup 100 percent fruit juice

Vegetable Group

3 to 5 servings each day

Good sources of vitamins A and C, minerals, carbohydrates and fiber

One serving =

1 cup raw, leafy vegetables
or
1/2 cup cooked or raw vegetables
or
3/4 cup vegetable juice

Bread, Cereal, Rice, and Pasta Group

6 to 11 servings each day

Good sources of vitamins, minerals, carbohydrates, fiber, iron, and vitamin B

One serving =

1 slice of bread
or
1 ounce (28 grams) of ready-to-eat cereal
or
1/2 cup cooked cereal, rice, or pasta

Activity

Health Behavior Contract

Copy the health behavior contract on a separate sheet of paper.

DO NOT WRITE IN THIS BOOK.

Name:_____ **Date:**_____

Life Skill: I will eat the recommended number of servings from the Food Guide Pyramid.

Effect on My Health: Eating the recommended number of servings from the Food Guide Pyramid will help me get the nutrients I need each day.

My Plan: I will eat six to eleven servings each day from the bread, cereal, rice, and pasta group. I will eat three to five servings each day from the vegetable group. I will eat two to four servings each day from the fruit group. I will eat two to three servings each day from the milk, yogurt, and cheese group. I will eat two to three servings each day from the meat, poultry, fish, dry beans, eggs, and nuts group. I will limit the amount of fats, oils, and sweets I eat. I will complete a chart listing the foods I eat for one week.

My Calendar	M	T	W	Th	F	S	S

How My Plan Worked: (Complete after one week) _____

_____

_____

How Do I Plan a Diet to Reduce My Risk of Premature Heart Disease?

Heart disease is a leading cause of death. You can reduce your risk of premature heart disease. You can make diet choices that help you maintain a normal blood cholesterol level, normal blood pressure, and healthful weight.

Limit fat intake.

Saturated fat raises blood cholesterol levels more than any other dietary source. Cholesterol is a fatty substance that is made by the body and is found in dairy products and animal products. Plaque can form in your blood vessels if your blood cholesterol level is high. **Plaque** is hardened deposits that form on the inner walls of blood vessels. Plaque deposits can result in atherosclerosis. **Atherosclerosis** (A·thuh·ROH·skluh·ROH·suhs) is a disease in which fat deposits on artery walls. It can cause heart attack and stroke.

Ways to Limit Fat in Your Diet

- Limit fried foods.
- Cut off fat from meat and poultry.
- Eat lean meats.
- Choose low-fat and fat-free dairy products.
- Eat low-fat desserts, such as frozen yogurt.
- Limit fatty snack foods.

Eat foods containing antioxidants.

A diet containing antioxidants might lower the risk of heart disease. **Antioxidants** are substances that protect cells from being damaged by oxidation. Antioxidants include vitamins A, C, and E and beta carotene.

Ways to Get Antioxidants

- Eat yellow and orange vegetables.
- Eat green vegetables, such as spinach.
- Eat whole-grain cereals and breads.
- Eat citrus fruits, such as oranges.

Limit sodium intake.

Sodium is a mineral found in table salt and processed foods. Too much sodium is linked to high blood pressure in some people.

Ways to Limit Sodium in Your Diet

- Choose foods labeled low in salt or salt-free.
- Choose fresh foods.
- Choose TV dinners and canned soups labeled low in salt or salt-free.
- Limit foods on which you can see salt, such as pretzels.
- Limit salt-cured foods, such as bacon.
- Do not add extra salt to foods.

How Do I Plan a Diet to Reduce My Risk of Cancer?

Cancer is a leading cause of death. However, many kinds of cancer can be prevented. Follow these diet suggestions to reduce your risk of cancer.

Limit the amount of fats in your diet. Eating foods high in fat might lead to being overweight. Being overweight is linked to cancers of the prostate, pancreas, breast, ovary, colon, and gallbladder.

Eat several servings of fruits and vegetables each day. Eating fruits and vegetables that contain antioxidants helps reduce the risk of developing cancers of the lung, gallbladder, and intestine. **Cruciferous** (kroo·SI·fuh·ruhs) **vegetables** are vegetables that belong to the cabbage family. Eating these vegetables helps reduce the risk of developing cancers of the stomach, colon, and lung. Some types of cruciferous vegetables are cauliflower, broccoli, kale, and brussels sprouts.

Eat foods rich in fiber. Fiber is the part of grains and plant foods that cannot be digested. Eating fiber reduces the risk of developing colon cancer.

Limit foods that are smoked, salt-cured, and nitrite-cured. This group of foods includes bacon, sausage, hot dogs, luncheon meats, and ham. Eating too many of these foods can increase the risk of developing cancers of the stomach and esophagus.

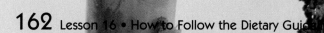

Review

Vocabulary Words

Write a separate sentence using each vocabulary word listed on page 152.

Health Content

1. What are three sources of proteins? Carbohydrates? Fats? Vitamins? Minerals? Water? **pages 154–155**

2. Identify five of the new Dietary Guidelines and give a fact about each. **pages 156-157**

3. How many servings from the bread, cereal, rice, and pasta group do you need each day? Vegetable group? Fruit group? Meat, poultry, fish, dry beans, eggs, and nuts group? Milk, yogurt, and cheese group? Fats, oils, and sweets? **pages 158–159**

4. What are three diet choices that reduce your risk of developing premature heart disease? **page 161**

5. What are four diet choices that reduce your risk of developing cancer? **page 162**

The Responsible Decision-Making Model™

Your friend eats potato chips and drinks soda pop for breakfast every day. Explain to your friend why (s)he should follow the Dietary Guidelines at breakfast. Answer the following questions on a separate sheet of paper. Write "Does not apply" if a question does not apply to this situation.

1. Is it healthful to eat potato chips and drink soda pop for breakfast? Why or why not?

2. Is it safe to eat potato chips and drink soda pop for breakfast? Why or why not?

3. Is it legal to eat potato chips and drink soda pop for breakfast? Why or why not?

4. Does your friend show respect for himself or herself if (s)he eats potato chips and drinks soda pop for breakfast? Why or why not?

5. Does your friend follow the guidelines of his or her parents or guardian if (s)he eats potato chips and drinks soda pop for breakfast? Why or why not?

6. Does your friend demonstrate good character if (s)he eats potato chips and drinks soda pop for breakfast? Why or why not?

What is the responsible decision to make in this situation?

Health Literacy

Effective Communication

Create a new recipe that follows the Dietary Guidelines. Design a recipe card that includes your recipe.

Critical Thinking

Make a list of your favorite snacks. Using the information from this lesson, determine whether the foods you listed are healthful.

How to Improve Your Eating Habits

Life Skills

- ◆ I will evaluate food labels.
- ◆ I will select foods that contain nutrients.
- ◆ I will develop healthful eating habits.
- ◆ I will follow the Dietary Guidelines when I go out to eat.

Vocabulary

eating habits

guideliner

grazer

gorger

garbage eater

food label

processed food

Nutrition Facts

Serving Size

Servings Per Container

Calories from Fat

Calories Listing

Percent Daily Value

doggie bag

fast food

metabolism

The food you eat each day is your source of energy. So your eating habits really determine your level of energy. **Eating habits** are a person's usual ways of eating. What are your favorite foods? Do you often munch on snacks? Do you often pig out? Do you get enough servings from the Food Guide Pyramid each day? Your answers to these questions provide clues to your eating habits.

The Lesson Objectives

- Describe different eating styles.
- List the information you can learn from reading a food label.
- Identify guidelines to follow when you "eat on the run."
- Explain how you can follow the Dietary Guidelines when you order foods from fast food restaurants.
- Plan a healthful breakfast menu.

Activity
Check Your Eating Style

Life Skill: I will develop healthful eating habits.

Materials: paper, pen or pencil; computer (optional)

Directions: Follow the steps below to prepare a survey on eating habits.

1. **Read the boxes that contain information about four different eating styles.**

2. **Prepare a survey to give to a classmate.** The survey will be a list of eight questions to help your classmate check his or her eating style. Include two questions on each of the four eating styles. Do not put your name on your survey. A sample question for each eating style appears below.

_____ **Do you pig out several times a week?** (If yes, gorger)

_____ **Do you eat small servings of veggies several times a day?** (If yes, grazer)

_____ **Do you limit the amount of salt you eat?** (If yes, guideliner)

_____ **Do you drink soda pop and have a doughnut for breakfast?** (If yes, garbage eater)

3. **Your teacher will collect your surveys.** Your teacher will distribute the surveys randomly to your class. Complete the survey you receive.

4. **Write a paragraph to summarize what you have learned about your eating style.** Do you need to improve your eating style?

What to Know About Eating Styles

Read each of the following descriptions. You might have one eating style. Or, you might have a combination of two eating styles. The best combination of styles is the guideliner and the grazer.

- The **guideliner** is a person who follows the Dietary Guidelines. (S)he eats the recommended number of servings from the Food Guide Pyramid.

- The **grazer** is a person who eats small portions of food several times a day.

- The **gorger** is a person who eats large portions of food at a time. The gorger takes seconds and thirds. The gorger "stuffs" himself or herself.

- The **garbage eater** is a person who mostly eats foods that are high in sugar, fat, and salt.

What Information Is Found on a Food Label?

A **food label** is a panel of nutrition information found on foods. A food label is required on all processed foods. A **processed food** is a food that has been specially treated or changed. An example of a food that is specially treated is cheese spread made from cheese. An example of a food that is changed is applesauce made from apples. You can read food labels to help you make healthful food selections.

Nutrition Facts is the title of the information panel that is required on most foods.

Serving Size is the listing of the amount of food that is considered a serving.

Servings Per Container is the listing of the number of servings in the container or package. The number can be deceiving. Suppose you drink a bottle of juice. You might glance at the label and see the number "90" next to the category "calories." So, you might think the bottle contains 90 calories. But check the servings per container. If the bottle contains two servings, you are actually consuming 180 calories.

Nutrition Facts

Serving Size 1/2 cup (114g)
Servings Per Container 4

Amount Per Serving

Calories 90	Calories from fat 30

	% Daily Value*
Total Fat 3g	**5%**
Saturated Fat 0g	**0%**
Cholesterol 0mg	**0%**
Sodium 300mg	**13%**
Total Carbohydrate 13g	**4%**
Dietary Fiber 3g	**12%**
Sugars 3g	
Protein 3g	

Vitamin A	80%	•	Vitamin C	60%
Calcium	4%	•	Iron	4%

*Percent Daily Values are based on a 2,000 calorie diet. Your daily values may be higher or lower depending on your calorie needs.

Total Fat	Less than	65g	80g
Sat Fat	Less than	20g	25g
Cholesterol	Less than	300mg	300mg
Sodium	Less than	2,400mg	2,400mg
Total Carbohydrate		300g	375g
Fiber		25g	30g

Calories per gram

Fat 9 • Carbohydrate 4 • Protein 4

Calories from Fat is the listing of the number of calories from fat in one serving of the food.

Calories Listing is the listing of the number of calories in one serving of the food.

Percent Daily Value is the portion of the daily amount of a nutrient provided by one serving of the food. Your goal is to eat 100 percent of the daily values of total carbohydrate, dietary fiber, vitamins, and minerals each day.

Health Claims You Might See on a Package of Food

Healthy = Low in total fat, low in saturated fat, and no more than 60 milligrams cholesterol per serving

Fat Free = Less than .5 grams of fat per serving

Low Fat = 3 grams of fat (or less) per serving

Lean = Less than 10 grams of fat, 4.5 grams of saturated fat, and no more than 95 milligrams of cholesterol per serving

Light or Lite = 1/2 fewer calories or no more than 1/2 the fat or sodium of the regular version

Cholesterol Free = Less than 2 milligrams of cholesterol and 2 grams of fat or less of saturated fat per serving

____ Free = No amount or only a very small amount of fat, saturated fat, cholesterol, sodium, sugar, and/or calories per serving

____ Less = At least 25 percent less of a nutrient or calories than the regular version

High = Supplies 20 percent or more of the Percent Daily Value of a particular nutrient per serving

How Can I Make Healthful Food Choices When I "Eat on the Run?"

You are "eating on the run" when you eat at places other than your table at home. When you "eat on the run," you might not have the opportunity to read food labels. You might not know the ingredients in the foods. How can you make healthful choices when you "eat on the run?"

Checklist for Making Healthful Food Choices When You "Eat on the Run"

1. Follow the Dietary Guidelines.

2. Obtain the correct number of servings from the Food Guide Pyramid.

3. Request a nutritional information brochure.

4. Ask the server any questions you have about the ingredients in the food.

5. Ask the server any questions you have about how the food is prepared.

6. Keep your portions moderate.

7. Request a doggie bag if portions are large. A **doggie bag** is a container of leftovers from a meal.

At the Movies

Rated N for NO WAY	Rated G for Good Choice
Popcorn smothered in butter and salt	Air-popped popcorn without butter or salt
Jumbo size popcorn	Small popcorn
Large size soda pop	Bottle of juice or sparkling water
Giant candy bar	Bag of dried fruit

At the Game

Limit the Choices	Winning Choices
Hot dog or sausage	Slice of cheese or veggie pizza
Nachos covered in cheesy sauce	Unsalted big pretzel with mustard
Peanuts	Unbuttered popcorn
Alcohol	Bottled juice or water

At the Party

Party Poopers	Party On...
Taco chips with nine-layer dip	Raw veggies
Potato chips and cheesy puffs	Whole-wheat crackers with low-fat cheese
Chicken wings	Low-fat ham chunks
Extra helpings of birthday cake	A small slice of birthday cake
Alcohol	Bottled juice or water

At the Food Court

Window Shopping	Stop and Shop
Double cheeseburger	Grilled chicken sandwich
Creamy potato bacon soup	Vegetable soup
Steak and cheese sandwich	Tortilla-wrap sandwich with fresh veggies
Sausage and pepperoni pizza	Veggie pizza
French fries with cheese	Unsalted big pretzel with salsa
Cinnamon pastry with icing	Fruit smoothie with low-fat yogurt
Chocolate chip cookies	Whole-wheat bagel topped with a thin layer of fruit spread

How Can I Follow the Dietary Guidelines When I Order Foods at Fast Food Restaurants?

Many teens enjoy eating at fast food restaurants. **Fast food** is food that can be served quickly. Fast foods are convenient. They often can be obtained at a drive-through window without even leaving the car. However, fast foods also can be high in calories, fat, and sodium.

Trendy and Tasty Tips for Following the Dietary Guidelines at the Drive-Through

Guideline 1: Eat a variety of foods. Ask to see a nutrition information brochure to check out nutrients in foods. Choose a balanced meal that gives you the servings you need from the Food Guide Pyramid.

Guideline 2: Balance the food you eat with physical activity—maintain or improve your weight. Maintain or improve your weight by eating foods in moderation and exercising regularly. Avoid super-size, jumbo, and extra-large items.

Guideline 3: Choose a diet low in fat, saturated fat, and cholesterol. Many fast food items are high in fat content. Choose foods that are grilled, baked, or steamed, instead of fried and breaded. Eat lean meats and poultry. Hold the mayo on sandwiches. Use a small amount of barbecue sauce, mustard, salsa, or ketchup instead. Pass up extra cheese. Limit use of high-fat items from the salad bars, such as pasta salads made with mayonnaise. Choose reduced-fat or fat-free salad dressings. Have low-fat yogurt sundaes and shakes for dessert instead of whole milk ice cream.

Guideline 4: Choose a diet with plenty of grain products, vegetables, and fruits. Order extra vegetables and fruits on sandwiches and as side dishes. Have a side salad or fruit cup instead of fries or chips. Load up on veggies at the salad bar. Choose whole-wheat or oat bran buns for sandwiches to get extra fiber.

Guideline 5: Choose a diet moderate in sugars. Drink water or 100 percent fruit juice instead of soda pop. Limit your intake of cakes, pies, and other sugary desserts. Watch for hidden sugar in salad dressings.

Guideline 6: Choose a diet moderate in salt and sodium. Many fast foods are high in sodium. For example, an order of French fries can have a day's supply of sodium, even without adding a packet of salt. Limit salt-cured and nitrite-cured foods such as bacon and ham. Eat only small amounts of ketchup and mustard. Don't add extra salt to food.

Guideline 7: Do not drink alcohol. It is illegal for teens to drink alcohol. It is illegal for minors to purchase alcohol. Do not purchase alcohol from drive-through places. Drinking alcohol is risky to your health.

May I Take Your Order?

Burgers

- A low-fat grilled chicken sandwich, no mayo or cheese
- A baked potato with fat-free sour cream and broccoli
- A side salad with veggies and fruit, with fat-free dressing
- A low-fat yogurt shake

Pizza

- Pizza with low-fat cheese and lots of veggies: broccoli, tomatoes, peppers, pineapple, and spinach
- A side salad with a variety of veggies, with fat-free dressing
- A large bottle of water

Deli

- A turkey wrap sandwich with extra veggies and low-fat dressing
- A bowl of vegetable and bean soup
- A low-fat frozen yogurt sundae with fresh fruit topping
- A carton of skim milk

Chinese

- An order of steamed fish with stir-fry vegetables, no salty soy sauce
- A side of brown rice
- A cup of low-fat won ton soup
- Skip the fatty eggroll!

Mexican

- A grilled chicken and vegetable fajita, extra lettuce and tomato, low-fat cheese
- A side of black beans, not refried
- A side of rice
- Skip the tortilla chips!

Rotisserie

- White meat chicken or turkey without the skin
- A baked sweet potato, no butter
- A side of steamed veggies
- A bottle of 100 percent fruit juice

What Options Do I Have for Getting a Healthful Breakfast?

You might have heard breakfast called "the most important meal of the day." Breakfast is important because eating gets your metabolism going. **Metabolism** is the rate at which food is converted to energy in the cells. Eating breakfast helps you have more energy during the day. It helps you feel more mentally alert.

It is important not to skip breakfast. Your body's blood sugar level can be low in the morning. Your body has not had food since the night before. If you skip breakfast, your blood sugar level might be too low. This will cause you to feel sluggish in the middle of the morning. Skipping breakfast does not help you lose weight. Most people who skip breakfast end up eating more throughout the day.

A healthful breakfast should include a source of protein for energy. Protein can help keep your blood sugar regulated throughout the morning. Avoid eating sugary foods, such as doughnuts or danishes, for breakfast. Avoid drinking soda pop for breakfast. These foods can cause a rise in your blood sugar level. Your blood sugar level will drop a short time later. You will end up being tired, irritable, and hungry again by the middle of the morning.

What's for Breakfast?

Who says breakfast needs to be "breakfast foods?" In fact, some "breakfast foods" are very high in fat, sugar, and salt. For example, croissants (kwah·SAHNTS), fried potatoes, and sausage are high in fat. Certain breakfast cereals and breakfast bars are high in sugar. Bacon and ham are high in salt. Certain TV-dinner style breakfasts are high in salt. Start your day off right with the foods on the right that contain protein, vitamins, and minerals.

- Cereals with no sugar added, in skim or low-fat milk, topped with bananas
- Egg-substitute omelet with vegetables
- Low-fat yogurt
- Whole-wheat toast and fruit spread
- Fresh fruit sprinkled with wheat germ
- Low-fat cottage cheese with fruit
- Celery spread with peanut butter
- Fresh fruit smoothies with wheat germ
- 100 percent orange, grapefruit, or cranberry juice with no sugar added
- Grilled fish
- Vegetable soup
- Veggie pizza
- Vegetables and egg substitute in a tortilla
- Fat-free cream cheese on a multi-grain bagel
- Tuna sandwich made with low-fat mayo

Vocabulary Words

Write a separate sentence using each vocabulary word listed on page 164.

Health Content

1. What are four eating styles? Which combination is the most healthful? **page 165**

2. What information can you learn from reading a food label? **pages 166–167**

3. What guidelines can you follow when you "eat on the run?" **pages 168–169**

4. How can you follow each of the Dietary Guidelines when eating at a fast food restaurant? **pages 170–171**

5. Plan a healthful breakfast for tomorrow. List the foods and beverages you would choose. **page 172**

The Responsible Decision-Making Model™

You are eating at a fast food restaurant. The menu offers several healthful options, but you really want a triple burger with everything on it. Answer the following questions on a separate sheet of paper. Write "Does not apply" if a question does not apply to this situation.

1. Is it healthful to order the triple burger? Why or why not?

2. Is it safe to order the triple burger? Why or why not?

3. Is it legal to order the triple burger? Why or why not?

4. Will you show respect for yourself if you order the triple burger? Why or why not?

5. Will you follow the guidelines of your parents or guardian if you order the triple burger? Why or why not?

6. Will you demonstrate good character if you order the triple burger? Why or why not?

What is the responsible decision to make in this situation?

Health Literacy

Responsible Citizenship

You are giving a party. Plan a healthful menu for your party. For each food on your menu, make a card listing the nutrition information. You might have to look at the label on your food, or on the packages of the ingredients if you made the food.

Self-Directed Learning

Request nutrition information lists from several places where you might "eat on the run," such as a fast food restaurant or movie theater. Identify the most healthful foods on each list. Write a one-page paper describing the most healthful foods at each place.

What to Know About Foodborne Illnesses

◆ **I will protect myself from foodborne illnesses.**

Vocabulary

foodborne illness

pathogen

Salmonellosis

Campylobacteriosis

E. coli 0157:H7

hemorrhagic colitis

food poisoning

cross contamination

Foodborne illnesses affect millions of people every year. A **foodborne illness** is an illness caused by consuming foods or beverages that have been contaminated with pathogens or toxins produced by pathogens. A **pathogen** is a germ that causes disease. A toxin is a poisonous substance. You cannot see pathogens or toxins in foods. Usually, you cannot smell or taste them either. Fortunately, almost all foodborne illnesses can be prevented.

The Lesson Objectives

- Identify different kinds of foodborne illnesses—causes, symptoms, and treatment.
- Identify ways to reduce your risk of getting a foodborne illness from the foods you eat at home.
- Identify ways to reduce your risk of getting a foodborne illness when you go out to eat.

What Are Foodborne Illnesses?

Salmonellosis (SAL·muh·ne·LOH·suhs) is a foodborne illness caused by consuming food contaminated by *Salmonella* (sal·muh·NE·luh) bacteria. **Campylobacteriosis** (KAM·pi·loh·bak·ter·ee·OH·sis) is a foodborne illness caused by consuming food contaminated by *Campylobacter* (kam·pi·loh·BAK·ter) bacteria. *Salmonella* and *Campylobacter* live in the intestines of animals. The bacteria enter the body when people consume contaminated meat, poultry, or eggs that are raw or undercooked. Symptoms of salmonellosis and campylobacteriosis include fever, cramps, diarrhea, and vomiting. Treatment is drinking plenty of fluids. Antibiotics are sometimes prescribed.

Escherichia coli (es·shuh·REE·shuh COH·ly) is a bacterium that lives in the intestines of humans and animals. Most strains are harmless. **E. coli O157:H7** is a strain of *E. coli* that can cause hemorrhagic colitis. **Hemorrhagic colitis** (HE·muh·RA·jik koh·LY·tuhs) is inflammation of the large intestine with pain and bloody diarrhea. Most infections with *E. coli* O157:H7 have come from eating contaminated ground beef that is undercooked or raw. Symptoms of foodborne illness with *E. coli* O157:H7 are bloody diarrhea and abdominal cramps. Treatment is drinking plenty of fluids. Some people have kidney failure and must be treated in an intensive care unit.

Food poisoning is a foodborne illness caused by toxins produced by pathogens. Staphylococcal (STA·fuh·loh·KAH·kuhl) food poisoning is an illness caused by *Staphylococcus* (STA·fuh·loh·KAH·kuhs) bacteria that are normally found on the skin. The bacteria on a person's hands can get into food. The bacteria can multiply when food that should be refrigerated is left at room temperature for several hours. The bacteria produce a toxin that causes illness. Symptoms include diarrhea and vomiting. Treatment is drinking plenty of fluids.

How Can I Reduce My Risk of Getting a Foodborne Illness from the Foods I Eat at Home?

Tips for Grocery Shopping

1. Do not buy cans with dents or bulges.
2. Do not buy cracked or dirty eggs.
3. Place raw meat and poultry in separate plastic bags before placing in your cart.
4. Buy milk that is pasteurized.
5. Pick up cold and frozen foods last. This decreases the chance they will warm to room temperature. Pathogens grow best at room temperature.

Tips for Refrigerating and Freezing Foods

1. Place cold and frozen foods in the refrigerator and freezer as soon as you get home from the store.
2. Do not let juices from raw meat be in contact with other foods. This might result in cross contamination. **Cross contamination** is the transfer of pathogens from a contaminated food or surface to another food.
3. Maintain refrigerator temperature between 34°F and 40°F.
4. Maintain freezer temperature at 0°F.
5. Thaw frozen food in the refrigerator or microwave.
6. Divide a large quantity of cooked food into shallow containers before placing it in the refrigerator. Hot or warm foods that are refrigerated in large quantities might take hours or days to chill. Bacteria might grow during this time.
7. Refrigerate leftovers promptly.
8. Eat or freeze leftovers within two days.

Tips

Tips

Tips for Preparing Meals

1. Wash your hands with soap and warm water for at least 20 seconds before preparing food.

2. Cover open sores or cuts on your hands with rubber or plastic gloves.

3. Do not prepare food for others if you have a cold, flu, or symptoms of a foodborne illness.

4. Do not taste a food with your finger or a utensil, and then put the finger or utensil back into the food. Germs in your mouth can get into the food.

5. Wash fruits and vegetables with water and scrub them with a brush.

6. Use paper towels instead of sponges to wipe up spills. Throw away paper towels after each use. Wash kitchen towels and aprons frequently.

7. Use an antibacterial cleaner or a bleach solution on surfaces after contact with raw meat, eggs, or poultry. Make a bleach solution by adding one tablespoon unscented chlorine bleach to one gallon water.

8. Cook meat until it is no longer red or pink.

Tips for Microwaving Foods

1. Cover food to allow steam to cook food all the way through. Do not use foam, plastic wraps, or containers, such as margarine tubs, not designed for microwave use. Chemicals in the containers might get into foods. Wax paper, oven cooking bags, white microwave paper towels, and glass lids are safe to use.

2. Cook meat and poultry immediately after thawing in the microwave.

3. Stir or rotate food once or twice during microwaving so that food cooks evenly.

4. Use a meat thermometer in several places to check that food is done.

5. Follow directions for standing times. Food continues to cook after the microwave has stopped.

How Can I Reduce My Risk of Getting a Foodborne Illness When I Go Out to Eat?

Tips

Tips for Eating at a Picnic

1. Carry food to the picnic site in a cooler with ice or ice packs.

2. Keep the cooler in the shade or shelter. Keep the lid closed except to take out or put in food.

3. Chill hot food if it will not be eaten within two hours. Reheat on the grill.

4. Do not use the same platter and utensils for raw and cooked meat and poultry.

5. Do not reuse marinade used on raw meat and poultry.

6. Cook meat and poultry thoroughly.

Tips for Ordering Food

1. Ask your server if the eggs in items such as chocolate mousse or Hollandaise sauce have been pasteurized or cooked.

2. Send undercooked meat or seafood back and request that it be cooked until done.

3. Eat meat or poultry that is thoroughly cooked.

4. Ask your server if you have questions about how the food was prepared.

Tips for Eating at a Buffet

1. Do not eat food that is supposed to be cold, such as pasta salad, if it is not on ice.

2. Do not eat food that is supposed to be hot, such as soup, if it is sitting at room temperature. Hot foods should be in a chafing dish or warming tray.

3. Ask your server if you have questions about how food was prepared.

4. Do not eat undercooked meat or poultry.

Top Four Food Handling Mistakes

1. **Improper handwashing.** Wash your hands after using the bathroom and before preparing food.

2. **Cross contamination.** Wash and sanitize surfaces after contact with raw meat, poultry, or eggs.

3. **Improper temperature holding.** Keep hot foods hot and cold foods cold. Do not allow them to sit at room temperature more than two hours.

4. **Improper cooling.** Divide a large quantity of food into shallow containers before placing it in the refrigerator.

Heat Pasteurization Is Cool

Pasteurization is heating food until dangerous pathogens are killed. Mayonnaise and cookie dough you buy at the store contain pasteurized eggs. Other pasteurized foods can include milk, eggnog, and cider.

Cook That Food!

The Food and Drug Administration advises that thoroughly cooking foods such as meat, poultry, eggs, and fish reduces the risk of food-borne illness. People with certain health conditions might be at higher risk if they eat these foods raw or undercooked.

Source: *Food Code.* 1997 Recommendations of the United States Public Health Service. Food and Drug Administration.

Activity

Food Safety Rap

Life Skill: I will protect myself from foodborne illnesses.

Materials: paper and pencil; handheld musical instruments, such as finger cymbals or tambourines; overhead transparency for each group

Directions: Complete the following activity to review ways to protect yourself from foodborne illnesses.

1. Following your teacher's instructions, form groups of three or four. Create a rap song that contains information about and tips for protecting yourself from foodborne illnesses. The rap should contain at least 12 lines. Your rap might begin something like this:

> Don't eat raw or undercooked meat.
> The cramps might knock you off your feet.
> Make sure you always sanitize,
> Or else you might get *E. coli.*

2. Write your rap on an overhead transparency.

3. Perform your rap for the class using handheld musical instruments.

4. Show the overhead transparency and have the class join in with your group.

Review

Vocabulary Words

Write a separate sentence using each vocabulary word listed on page 174.

Health Content

1. What are four foodborne illnesses? What are the causes, symptoms, and treatments for each of these? **page 175**

2. What are five tips for grocery shopping to help you reduce your risk of getting a foodborne illness? **page 176**

3. What are eight tips for refrigerating and freezing foods to help you reduce your risk of getting a foodborne illness? **page 176**

4. What are eight tips for preparing meals to help you reduce your risk of getting a foodborne illness? **page 177**

5. What are four tips when ordering out to help you reduce your risk of getting a foodborne illness? **page 178**

The Responsible Decision-Making Model™

You go to a picnic. The meat tray is not on ice. You ask how long the meat tray has been sitting out. You find out it has been out for about four hours. Answer the following questions on a separate sheet of paper. Write "Does not apply" if a question does not apply to this situation.

1. Is it healthful to eat the meat? Why or why not?

2. Is it safe to eat the meat? Why or why not?

3. Is it legal to eat the meat? Why or why not?

4. Will you show respect for yourself if you eat the meat? Why or why not?

5. Will your parents or guardian approve if you eat the meat? Why or why not?

6. Will you demonstrate good character if you eat the meat? Why or why not?

What is the responsible decision to make in this situation?

Health Literacy

Responsible Citizenship

Make a list of food safety practices that you have not been following. Write a plan to put these practices into action. Post the list in the kitchen to remind you and your family to follow food safety practices.

Effective Communication

Design a poster that illustrates a food safety practice. Write the food safety practice on the poster. Display the poster in the cafeteria or hallway where other students can learn from it.

How to Maintain Your Desirable Weight

Life Skill

◆ **I will maintain a desirable weight and body composition.**

Vocabulary

body composition

desirable weight

weight management

calorie

fad diet

pigging out

eating trigger

self-control

overweight

obesity

Your body is made up of two kinds of tissue—fat and lean. **Body composition** is the percentage of fat tissue and lean tissue in the body. When you maintain your desirable weight, your body is more likely to be lean. **Desirable weight** is the weight that is most healthful for a person. Your desirable weight is determined by your age, sex, height, and body frame. You need a plan to reach and maintain your desirable weight and body composition. **Weight management** is a plan used to have a healthful weight. It includes what you eat and your daily activities.

The Lesson Objectives

- Explain how to maintain a desirable weight.
- Discuss steps you can take so you do not pig out.
- Identify why it is risky to be overweight.

How Can I Maintain My Desirable Weight?

Being at your desirable weight and having a healthful body composition helps you look and feel your best. Your risk of diseases and illnesses also is reduced. Maintaining your desirable weight involves balancing calories. A **calorie** is a unit of energy produced by food and used by the body. You take in calories when you eat. You use up calories through daily activity and physical activity. Your body uses more calories when you are physically active than when you are not active. The number of calories you eat compared to the number of calories your body uses determines if you lose, maintain, or gain weight.

There are two kinds of body tissue—fat tissue and lean tissue. Keeping the amount of fat tissue low is healthful. Regular physical activity decreases the amount of fat tissue and increases the amount of lean tissue.

How to Maintain Weight

- Ask a health professional to help you determine your desirable weight.
- Keep track of the number of calories you eat each day.
- Keep track of the number of calories you use up each day.
- **The number of calories you eat and the number of calories you use up through daily activity and physical activity should be in balance.**

How to Lose Weight

- Discuss any plan to lose weight with your parent or guardian.
- Always check with a physician or dietitian before going on a diet because you are growing rapidly. Ask a physician or other health professional to help you determine your desirable weight. Discuss a time frame in which to lose weight safely. Losing one to two pounds per week often is recommended.
- Avoid fad diets. Most people who lose weight quickly do not keep the weight off. A **fad diet** is a quick weight-loss diet that is popular. Fad diets and diet pills can be dangerous.
- Do not use risky behaviors to lose weight. Do not skip meals, vomit, or use diet pills or laxatives.
- Participate in physical activities.
- Eat a healthful breakfast.
- Limit high-fat foods and eat smaller portions.
- Drink water before meals.
- Limit fats, oils, and sweets.
- Eat extra servings from the fruit and vegetable groups.

How to Gain Weight

- Ask a health professional to help you determine your desirable weight. Discuss a time frame in which to gain weight safely.
- Eat extra servings from the bread, cereal, rice, and pasta group.
- Eat extra servings of low-fat foods from the milk, yogurt, and cheese group.
- Eat a healthful breakfast.
- Eat extra healthful snacks.
- Participate in physical activities that develop muscle.

How Can I Keep from Pigging Out?

Everybody "pigs out" sometimes. **Pigging out** is stuffing oneself with a large amount of food. Pigging out once in a while is not harmful. However, pigging out can become a harmful habit. Pigging out increases your risk of being overweight. And, people who pig out often make a habit of pigging out on junk foods, such as chips or chocolate. You will not get the nutrients you need for optimal health if you pig out and fill up on junk food.

Know Your Eating Triggers

An **eating trigger** is something that causes a person to feel the urge to eat. An eating trigger might be a situation, an emotion, a TV commercial, or a type of food. Review the statements in the circles. Each one identifies an example of an eating trigger.

Eating Triggers

"I am a major choco-holic. I can polish off a whole chocolate cake myself."
(Trigger: Chocolate)

"I hate to have slices of pizza left over."
(Trigger: Pizza)

"I'm so stuffed. But I can't pass up dessert!"
(Trigger: Dessert)

"I have no plans for Saturday night. I'm going to order a pizza and gorge."
(Trigger: Being home without plans on a weekend night)

"I am so depressed. I need a hot fudge sundae."
(Trigger: Depression)

"The purpose of holidays is to pig out."
(Trigger: Holidays)

"I am so stressed out. Time to break into the tortilla chips."
(Trigger: Stress)

"I have my period. I need chocolate."
(Trigger: Menstruation)

Steps You Can Take to Keep from Pigging Out

1. **Use self-control.** **Self-control** is the degree to which a person regulates his or her own behavior. Most teens know that eating an entire bag of cookies at one time is not a healthful behavior. If you have self-control, you are able to eat one or two cookies and leave the rest. You stuff yourself with cookies if you do not have self-control.

2. **Recognize your eating triggers.** Make a list of your eating triggers and prepare ahead of time. Suppose you eat when you are stressed. Use stress management skills as a healthful way to cope. Participate in physical activity or call a friend instead of eating.

3. **Avoid or plan ahead for situations that tempt you.** If you always pig out at parties, eat a small healthful snack ahead of time. Stay away from the tables with the munchies. Or, hang out by the veggie tray.

4. **Don't skip meals.** You will be hungry and eat more later.

5. **Don't wait until you feel starved to eat.** You will feel so hungry you might end up overeating.

6. **Drink a glass of water before you eat.** The water will help you feel full.

7. **Don't order extra-large, jumbo, or giant portions.** Eating food in moderate portions is part of a healthful diet.

8. **Practice leaving a small amount of food on your plate.** Do not eat food simply because it is available. Stop eating when you feel full.

9. **Don't put much food on your plate.** Serve yourself small portions of food. Do not go back for seconds.

10. **Don't use food as a reward.** Reward yourself with an activity you enjoy, or spend time with friends instead.

Remember, fat-free and low-fat does not always mean low calorie. These foods also can be high in sugar and salt. You can still gain weight from eating fat-free and low-fat foods if you are not careful about portions.

Activity

Chow Chart

Life Skill: I will maintain a desirable weight and body composition.

Materials: paper, pen or pencil

Directions: Review the chart below. The chart identifies foods that help satisfy a food craving for sweets. The items in the left-hand column are items that are healthful choices to satisfy a sweet tooth. The items in the right-hand column are items that are not healthful choices to satisfy a sweet tooth. Copy the design of the chart on a separate sheet of paper. Make your own chart of fried foods. Include healthful choices that might satisfy a craving for fried food. Include at least five examples in each column. Title your chart.

Satisfy Your Sweet Tooth

Try...	NOT
Low-fat chocolate yogurt pop	Chocolate ice cream
Fruit juice bar	Milk shake
Chocolate rice cake	Candy bar
A few fat-free chocolate cookies	A whole bag of fat-free chocolate cookies
Cocoa with skim milk	Soda pop

Why Is It Risky to Be Overweight?

Overweight is a weight above a person's desirable weight. Getting on a scale or comparing your weight to a chart does not indicate if you are overweight. Some teens who weigh more than others have a larger body frame. Other teens have more muscle, which adds weight. A physician can help you determine if you have a healthful weight.

Obesity is a weight more than 20 percent over desirable body weight. People who are obese usually lack energy. Being overweight or obese as a teen can be risky to health. Seventy-five percent of obese teens stay obese as adults.

Being overweight or obese increases the risk of:

- **Premature heart disease**
- **High blood pressure**
- **Certain types of cancer**
- **Diabetes**
- **Stroke**

Body composition is the percentage of fat tissue and lean tissue in the body. Fat tissue decreases and lean tissue increases as a person becomes physically fit. A healthful percentage of body fat for teen males is about 11 to 17 percent. A healthful percentage of body fat for teen females is about 16 to 24 percent. The scale is not always the best indicator of physical fitness. Since muscle weighs more than fat, you could have a high weight, but have a healthful body composition. Or, you could have a healthful weight, but have too much fat tissue. Ask your physician or dietitian to measure your percent body fat. Participate in physical activity to decrease body fat and to increase your amount of lean tissue.

People carry their weight in different areas of their bodies. People who carry their body fat in the upper half of the body, such as the stomach or waist, have what is called an "apple" shape. People who carry their weight in the bottom half, such as the buttocks, hips, and thighs, have what is called a "pear" shape. People who have an apple shape are more at risk for diseases associated with obesity.

Vocabulary Words

Write a separate sentence using each vocabulary word listed on page 182.

Health Content

1. How can you maintain your ideal weight? Lose weight? Gain weight? **page 183**

2. Why is it important to be at your desirable weight and have a healthful body composition? **page 183**

3. What are ten steps you can take to keep from pigging out? **page 185**

4. How can you satisfy a craving for sweets? **page 185**

5. Why is it risky to be overweight or obese? How can you develop a healthful body composition? **page 186**

The Responsible Decision-Making Model™

Your friend suggests you try the latest fad diet. "I lost ten pounds in one week," (s)he says. Answer the following questions on a separate sheet of paper. Write "Does not apply" if a question does not apply to this situation.

1. Is it healthful to try the fad diet? Why or why not?

2. Is it safe to try the fad diet? Why or why not?

3. Is it legal to try the fad diet? Why or why not?

4. Will you show respect for yourself if you try the fad diet? Why or why not?

5. Will you follow the guidelines of your parents or guardian if you try the fad diet? Why or why not?

6. Will you demonstrate good character if you try the fad diet? Why or why not?

What is the responsible decision to make in this situation?

Health Literacy

Critical Thinking

Keep an eating trigger journal for one day. List each time you wanted to eat something when you were not hungry. Describe what you were doing at the time. List any specific foods you craved. If you found yourself responding to eating triggers, make a plan to eat only when you are hungry.

Responsible Citizenship

Interview a health care professional about ways to maintain a healthful weight. Write a speech including the information you learned in the interview. Present the speech in front of the class.

How to Recognize Eating Disorders

Life Skill

◆ I will develop skills to prevent eating disorders.

Vocabulary

body image

anabolic steroids

eating disorder

binge eating disorder

bulimia nervosa

laxative

diuretic

anorexia nervosa

relapse

enabler

Body image is the feeling a person has about his or her appearance. Teens with a positive body image are comfortable with the way they look. Teens who have a negative body image are not comfortable with the way they look. These teens compare themselves to others. They place great emphasis on their appearance. They have difficulty accepting the body changes that come with adolescence. Having a positive body image is essential for your good health.

The Lesson Objectives

• Discuss the pressures teens face to have a perfect body.

• Identify reasons it is important to have a positive body image.

• Discuss the symptoms and risks of binge eating disorder, bulimia nervosa, and anorexia nervosa.

• Discuss treatment options for teens who have an eating disorder.

How Do I Resist the Pressures to Have a Perfect Body?

Think about the actors, actresses, models, and professional athletes whom you see in the movies and on TV. Actors and actresses usually are very attractive. Models often are very tall and slender. Professional athletes usually are very physically fit. They all have special talents.

It is OK to want to be recognized for your special talents and for your appearance. But you need to set your own standards rather than comparing yourself to others. What talents do you have and how can you develop them? How can you look your best? Teens who have a healthful body image try to look their best. They work out and eat healthful foods. If they need to lose weight, they lose weight slowly. If they want to build muscle, they follow a weight training plan. They do not choose behaviors that might harm them in order to look their best.

Teens who have a negative body image are at risk for choosing behaviors that would harm them. They might be tempted to purchase products they see in ads. They might be tempted to starve themselves to lose weight. They might be tempted to try a fad diet that does not contain the nutrients they need.

Some teens are tempted to use anabolic steroids. **Anabolic steroids** are drugs that are used to increase muscle size and strength. But, steroids can harm health. These drugs will be discussed further in Lesson 30. Some teens might take diet pills or smoke tobacco to help control their weight.

Some teens become frustrated and starve and then pig out. These teens are at risk for developing an eating disorder. An **eating disorder** is an emotional disorder in which a person chooses harmful eating patterns. To resist pressures to have a perfect body:

- **Do not set unrealistic standards for your appearance.**
- **Do not compare yourself to others.**
- **Do not be influenced by ads that say you will look a certain way if you buy a certain product or eat a special food.**
- **Use resistance skills and say NO if you are pressured to use anabolic steroids.**
- **Use resistance skills and say NO if you are pressured to try a harmful fad diet.**
- **Do not use your weight as an excuse for avoiding social or physical activities.**
- **Discuss your appearance with your parents or guardian, physician, or other trusted adult.**

Messages That Might Indicate a Teen Has a Negative Body Image

"I want to look like a super model; I'm going to starve myself."

"I have to lose weight to fit into my new dress for the school dance."

"I'll go on a fad diet to lose 10 pounds the week before cheerleading tryouts."

"I've got to make weight for the wrestling match."

"If I get bigger muscles, maybe she'll notice me."

"I need to bulk up so I'll make more tackles."

"I'm tired of being called skinny; I'm gonna beef up."

"I'll starve myself to look good in my bikini."

"If I lose 20 pounds, maybe he'll look at me."

Don't give in to pressures to have the perfect body.

Activity

It's in to Be...Healthful

Life Skill: I will develop skills to prevent eating disorders.

Materials: paper, pens, and colored markers or computer

Directions: If you look at teen magazines, you likely will see articles about being thin. These articles have titles such as "Five Ways to Fight Fat" and "Ten Ways to Fit into Your Bathing Suit This Summer!" The message is: It is "in to be thin." You will create a page for a class teen magazine. Your page will include an article and illustrations. Your page will emphasize ways teens can resist pressure to have a perfect body.

1. Write a one-page article about ways teens can resist pressure to have a perfect body.
Be creative with your article. For example, you might write a mock interview with a celebrity who resists pressure to have harmful eating habits to maintain a perfect body.

2. Give your article a clever title.
For example, you might title your article, "Twenty Things to Do Besides Complain About Your Body."

3. Design a page of a teen magazine. Include your article on the page. You might choose to design the page by drawing illustrations, cutting out photographs from old magazines, or using the computer.

4. Share your magazine page with your classmates. Compile your articles to make a class teen magazine. Brainstorm a title for the magazine with your classmates. Work with your classmates to create a cover for the magazine.

5. Share your class magazine with students in another class.

What Are Eating Disorders?

An eating disorder is an emotional disorder in which a person chooses harmful eating patterns. There are different kinds of eating disorders. Most people who have eating disorders first developed them as teens. There are behaviors that indicate a teen is at risk for developing an eating disorder.

- **The teen has a negative body image.**
- **The teen constantly compares himself or herself to others.**
- **The teen eats food when (s)he is depressed, lonely, stressed, or angry.**
- **The teen wears baggy clothes to hide his or her body.**
- **The teen feels uncomfortable with his or her peers.**
- **The teen frequently worries about his or her appearance.**

Binge Eating Disorder

Binge eating disorder is an eating disorder in which a person frequently stuffs himself or herself with food. People with this disorder eat beyond the point of being full. This disorder also is known as compulsive overeating. Teens with this disorder eat to cope with emotions. They stuff themselves when they are depressed, angry, lonely, or bored. They lose control of their eating. They hide the amount of food they eat from others. They often are depressed. They try to follow a diet but are unable to stick to it.

Binge eating disorder is a common cause of obesity. People realize these teens are overweight. However, they do not realize that they have an eating disorder. Teens with binge eating disorder are at risk for the diseases and disorders that are associated with being overweight:

- **Premature heart disease**
- **Diabetes**
- **High blood pressure**
- **Certain types of cancer**

Bulimia Nervosa

Bulimia nervosa (boo·LEE·mee·uh nehr·VOH·suh) is an eating disorder in which a person stuffs himself or herself and then rids the body of food. It is commonly called bulimia. Teens with bulimia binge eat. Then they vomit or take laxatives and diuretics to try to rid their body of the food. A **laxative** is a drug that helps a person have a bowel movement. A **diuretic** (DY·yuh·RE·tik) is a drug that increases the amount of urine the body excretes. Teens with bulimia eat to try to cope with their feelings. They worry about their weight and feel guilty about eating. They try to get rid of the food they eat, usually by vomiting.

Teens with bulimia might be at a healthful weight. However, they are unable to control their behavior. Some teens hide their behavior. They might excuse themselves to go to the bathroom after a meal. Some teens do not hide their bulimia. They become friends with other teens with bulimia and plan their binges together.

Teens with bulimia risk:

- Dental problems from the acid in vomit
- Swollen cheeks and face
- Sore gums
- Dry and brittle hair
- Heartburn
- Irregular bowel movements
- Increase in blood pressure
- Stomach cramps and rupture
- Rupture of the esophagus
- Damage to kidneys, colon, and heart

Anorexia Nervosa

Anorexia nervosa (a·nuh·REK·see·uh nehr·VOH·suh) is an eating disorder in which a person starves himself or herself and has a low body weight. It is commonly called anorexia. Females develop anorexia more frequently than males. People with anorexia weigh 15 percent or more below their desirable weight. Teens with anorexia are obsessed with their weight. They starve themselves to be thin. They use diet pills, laxatives, and exercise to lose more weight. They think they are fat even when they are extremely underweight. They do not recognize that they have an eating disorder. Teens who have anorexia are at risk for making suicide attempts.

Teens with anorexia risk:

- Malnutrition
- Damage to the kidneys, heart, and other body organs
- Irregular heart rate
- Stomach pain and constipation
- Weakness and fatigue
- Hair loss or dull hair
- Dull and yellow skin
- Growth of excess body hair
- Absence of menstruation in females

What Are Treatment Options for Teens Who Have an Eating Disorder?

Eating disorders are most successfully treated when they are diagnosed early. Teens who have an eating disorder need treatment. Some teens deny that they have an eating disorder. They might not want to get treatment. They might fear that other people are trying to make them "fat." These teens might promise to stop the harmful behavior. But, the behavior likely will continue until the teen gets professional help.

A physical examination is needed to determine any health problems. A hospital stay might be needed. The teen needs counseling to understand and cope with the disorder. Health professionals can help the teen find healthful ways to cope with feelings. Even with professional help, relapses might occur. A **relapse** is a return to harmful behavior. The relapses are likely to occur during stressful times. A teen with an eating disorder can avoid relapses by working with his or her parents or guardian and health professionals to maintain healthful eating habits.

Family members and friends of a teen who has an eating disorder might need help, too. A family member or friend of the teen might be an enabler. An **enabler** is a person who supports the harmful behavior of another person. The enabler might deny that anything is wrong. For example, (s)he might say the teen's eating habits are just fine. (S)he might make excuses for a person who has an eating disorder. For example, an enabler might say the teen likely has an upset stomach that causes the teen to throw up. Or, the enabler might participate in the harmful eating behavior. For example, two friends might make plans to binge at lunch and vomit after class. Such an enabler also would need professional help. People who are enablers need to obtain counseling. Enablers need help changing their behavior.

Vocabulary Words

Write a separate sentence using each vocabulary word listed on page 188.

Health Content

1. Why is it risky to have a negative body image? **page 189**

2. What are seven ways to resist pressure to choose harmful behaviors to develop a perfect body? **page 189**

3. What are the symptoms and risks of binge eating disorder? **page 192**

4. What are the symptoms and risks of bulimia nervosa? **page 193**

5. What are the symptoms and risks of anorexia nervosa? **page 193**

The Responsible Decision-Making Model™

At lunch each day, your friend eats a lot of food. One day, you see your friend throwing up in the bathroom after lunch. "Don't tell anyone," she says. "I do it every day so I can stay thin." Decide whether to keep your friend's secret. Answer the following questions on a separate sheet of paper. Write "Does not apply" if a question does not apply to this situation.

1. Is it healthful to keep your friend's secret? Why or why not?

2. Is it safe to keep your friend's secret? Why or why not?

3. Is it legal to keep your friend's secret? Why or why not?

4. Will you show respect for your friend if you keep her secret? Why or why not?

5. Will you follow the guidelines of your parents or guardian if you keep your friend's secret? Why or why not?

6. Will you demonstrate good character if you keep your friend's secret? Why or why not?

What is the responsible decision to make in this situation?

Health Literacy

Effective Communication

Design a flyer listing signs of eating disorders. Your flyer should encourage teens who have these signs or who recognize them in someone else to tell a responsible adult. Explain that teens with eating disorders need professional help.

Self-Directed Learning

Go to your school or community library and find books on eating disorders. Write a bibliography listing at least five books on eating disorders. Include each book's title, author, publisher, and date and place of publication.

Unit 4 Review

Health Content

Prepare for the Unit Test. Review your answers for each Lesson Review in this unit. Then write answers to each of the following questions:

1. Why do you need to eat plenty of grain products? **Lesson 16 page 157**

2. What are some examples of cruciferous vegetables? **Lesson 16 page 162**

3. How can you eat a diet low in fat when you eat at a fast food restaurant? **Lesson 17 page 170**

4. Why do you need to eat a source of protein for breakfast? **Lesson 17 page 172**

5. Why should hamburger be cooked thoroughly before you eat it? **Lesson 18 page 175**

6. Why should you divide a large quantity of cooked food into shallow containers before you place it in a refrigerator? **Lesson 18 page 176**

7. Why is pigging out a harmful habit? **Lesson 19 page 184**

8. What is a healthful percentage of body fat for females? For males? **Lesson 19 page 186**

9. What behaviors indicate a teen might be at risk for developing an eating disorder? **Lesson 20 page 192**

10. What are some ways that an enabler might support the harmful behavior of a person who has an eating disorder? **Lesson 20 page 194**

Health Behavior Contract

Make a health behavior contract for one of the life skills in this unit. Review your health behavior contract with your parents or guardian.

Vocabulary Words

Number a sheet of paper from 1–10. Select the correct vocabulary word and write it next to the corresponding number. DO NOT WRITE IN THIS BOOK.

metabolism	cruciferous vegetables
eating trigger	*E. coli* 0157:H7
antioxidants	processed food
body image	eating disorder
hemorrhagic colitis	pigging out

1. _____ are substances that protect cells from being damaged by oxidation. **Lesson 16**

2. A _____ is a food that has been specially treated or changed. **Lesson 17**

3. _____ is the feeling a person has about his or her appearance. **Lesson 20**

4. _____ are vegetables that belong to the cabbage family. **Lesson 16**

5. _____ is a strain of *E. coli* that can cause hemorrhagic colitis. **Lesson 18**

6. _____ is the rate at which food is converted to energy in the cells. **Lesson 17**

7. _____ is stuffing oneself with a large amount of food. **Lesson 19**

8. An _____ is an emotional disorder in which a person chooses harmful eating patterns. **Lesson 20**

9. _____ is inflammation of the large intestine with pain and bloody diarrhea. **Lesson 18**

10. An _____ is something that causes a person to feel the urge to eat. **Lesson 19**

The Responsible Decision-Making Model™

A friend of yours wants to be a top-notch wrestler. He shares his training plan with you. He is going to wear a rubber suit to lose body water. Then he is going to starve himself and bulk up with steroids. He asks you to keep his training plan a secret. Answer the following questions on a separate sheet of paper. Write "Does not apply" if a question does not apply to this situation.

1. Is your friend's training plan healthful? Why or why not?

2. Is your friend's training plan safe? Why or why not?

3. Is your friend's training plan legal? Why or why not?

4. Will your friend show respect for himself if he follows his training plan? Why or why not?

5. Would your friend's parents or guardian and coach approve of his training plan? Why or why not?

6. Will your friend demonstrate good character if he follows his training plan? Why or why not?

What is the responsible decision to make in this situation?

Health Literacy
Effective Communication

Refer to page 165. Design a symbol for: a guideliner, a grazer, a gorger, and a garbage eater. List the days of the week on a sheet of paper. At the end of each day, select one or more of the symbols to describe your eating style for the day. Place the appropriate symbol(s) next to that day of the week.

Self-Directed Learning

List all of the foods and beverages you consume in one day. Obtain a book that indicates the number of calories in foods and beverages. Calculate the number of calories you consume for one day.

Critical Thinking

What are your eating triggers? What do these eating triggers tell you about yourself?

Responsible Citizenship

Suppose you were put in charge of a school campaign to reduce the pressure on teens to have a perfect body. Write a paper in which you describe at least three things you would do.

Multicultural Health

Select a specific ethnic group. Design a Food Guide Pyramid. Fill the Pyramid with ethnic foods that belong to the different food groups.

Family Involvement

Browse through cookbooks to find low-fat, low-salt recipes. Ask permission from your parents or guardian to prepare a recipe for your family.

UNIT 5
Personal Health and Physical Activity

PRACTICE

HEALTH STANDARD 3

Make a Health Behavior Contract

Practice this standard at the end of this unit.

1. **Tell the life skill you want to practice.** Use the life skill: *I will participate in physical activity.*

2. **Write a few statements describing how the life skill will affect your health.** Tell how physical activity can improve your health. Refer to the health facts on pages 220–221.

3. **Design a specific plan to practice the life skill and a** way to record your progress in making the life skill a habit. Choose one of the physical activities described on pages 222–223, or a different activity. Design a plan to do this activity for a two-week period.

4. **Describe the results you got when you tried the plan.** After doing the activity for two weeks, describe the results you got.

Why You Need Regular Examinations

Life Skills

♦ I will have regular examinations.
♦ I will follow a dental health plan.

Vocabulary

health history
physical examination
vaccine
antibody
audiologist
hearing loss
noise pollution
visual acuity
ophthalmologist
optometrist
myopia
hyperopia
astigmatism
orthodontist
malocclusion
braces
flossing
dental plaque
retainer

Regular physical examinations are important for three reasons. First, they provide a continuing record of your health status. Second, regular physical examinations can identify health problems that might be just starting. Treatments could be recommended and started. Third, regular physical examinations give a health care professional a chance to discuss your health habits with you. You can discuss ways to improve your health by changing any harmful health habits.

The Lesson Objectives

- Describe three parts of a physical examination.
- Identify six vaccines and tell why and when they are recommended.
- Explain five ways hearing loss is corrected.
- Discuss three ways problems with visual acuity are corrected.
- Describe three ways crooked teeth can be straightened.

What Should I Expect During a Physical Examination?

A physical examination has three parts:

1. The physician will obtain a health history. A **health history** is recorded information about a person's past and present health status. Health status is the condition of a person's health. The physician might ask you about the following:

- **Past illnesses**
- **Allergies and drug sensitivities**
- **Health habits**
- **Health facts about family members**
- **Current symptoms of illness**

2. The physician will perform a physical examination. A **physical examination** is a series of tests that measure health status. The physician might do the following:

- **Measure your height, weight, pulse rate, and blood pressure**
- **Look at parts of your body for signs of illness, such as a rash**
- **Feel parts of your body to check for signs of illness, such as any swelling**
- **Use instruments to check your eyes, eardrums, mouth, and throat**

3. The physician will conduct diagnostic tests as necessary. A diagnostic test is a procedure that uses special instruments, machines, or laboratory methods to examine body fluids, tissues, or body functions. The following tests might be performed as part of a physical examination.

- **Laboratory tests on urine**
- **Laboratory tests on blood**
- **X-rays**

The physician might perform additional tests if you have signs or symptoms of illness.

What Vaccines Do I Need?

Your physician will advise you on the vaccines you need. Vaccines protect you from certain diseases. You can get vaccinated at your physician's office, local health department, or community clinic. A **vaccine** is a substance containing dead or weakened pathogens that is introduced into the body to prevent a disease. You become immune to the disease.

Suppose a pathogen enters your body for the first time. Your body will make antibodies to the pathogen. An **antibody** is a special protein in blood that helps fight infection. A vaccine works by stimulating production of antibodies. You want to get the vaccine for a disease before you become infected with the pathogens. The antibodies already are present when the pathogen enters your body. You are able to fight off the disease without becoming ill.

Vaccine/Disease Prevented

	Age Vaccine Given
Hepatitis B • Hepatitis B can cause scarring and cancer of the liver.	Birth, 2 months, 6 months OR three doses at 11–12 years if not given as an infant
DTP • **D**iphtheria can cause difficult breathing and paralysis. • **T**etanus can cause severe muscle spasms that can lead to death. • **P**ertussis can cause difficult breathing and severe cough.	2 months, 4 months, 6 months, 12–18 months, 4–6 years, 11–12 years (DT only)
Hib • *Haemophilus influenza* type **b** can cause brain infection, ear infection, and pneumonia.	2 months, 4 months, 6 months, 12–18 months
OPV (Oral Polio Vaccine) • Polio can cause severe muscle pain and paralysis.	2 months, 4 months, 6–18 months, 4–6 years
MMR • **M**easles can cause hearing loss, brain infection, and pneumonia. • **M**umps can cause painful salivary glands and hearing loss. • **R**ubella can cause heart disease, blindness, and hearing loss in unborn children.	12–18 months, 11–12 years
Varicella (chickenpox) • Chickenpox causes skin sores, fever, and can be severe in teens and adults.	12–18 months OR 11–12 years if not vaccinated or have not had chickenpox

Problems with visual acuity can be corrected with eyeglasses, contact lenses, or surgery. Myopia, hyperopia, and astigmatism can be corrected with eyeglasses. Prescribed lenses bend the light so that it focuses correctly on the retina. Bifocals are prescribed lenses that correct for both close and distant vision.

Myopia can be corrected with surgery. Radial keratotomy (kehr·uh·TOT·uh·mee) is a type of surgery that changes the curve of the cornea. Photorefractive keratectomy (kehr·uh·TEHK·tuh·mee) is laser surgery that reshapes the cornea.

Myopia, hyperopia, and astigmatism also can be corrected with contact lenses. A contact lens is a small lens placed directly on the cornea. Two of the most widely used contact lenses are rigid and soft. Rigid contact lenses are gas permeable and made of inflexible or slightly inflexible plastic. Soft contact lenses are made of a gel-like plastic that absorb water from the eye and become soft. Both rigid and soft lenses allow oxygen to pass through to the cornea.

Tips for Wear and Care of Contact Lenses

1. Do not use saliva or tap water to wet your lenses. Use only approved solutions.

2. Use a fresh solution every time you disinfect your lenses.

3. Clean your contact lenses regularly.

4. Keep aerosols and creams out of your eyes.

5. Wear make-up that is approved for wearers of contact lenses.

6. Wear protective eyewear when participating in sports.

7. Get regular eye examinations.

How Are Crooked Teeth Straightened?

Straight, even teeth can help make your whole face attractive. Knowing that you have an attractive smile can promote positive self-esteem. More important, straight, even teeth are needed for good health. You will be able to chew your food correctly; your teeth will not wear down as easily; your teeth will be easier to clean; and you will be able to breathe more easily.

You need regular examinations by a dentist to detect crooked teeth. Your dentist might refer you to an orthodontist. An **orthodontist** (AWR·thu·DAHN·tist) is a dentist who specializes in detecting and treating malocclusion. **Malocclusion** (MA·luh·KLOO·zhuhn) is an abnormal fitting together of teeth when the jaws are closed. Most people with malocclusion have inherited problems such as crowding of teeth. Malocclusion can be caused by other factors such as thumb sucking.

Malocclusion can be corrected in three ways: removing teeth, applying braces, or applying orthodontic headgear. Many teens with malocclusion wear braces. **Braces** are devices that are cemented or bonded to the teeth and wired together to bring the teeth into correct alignment. Your orthodontist might include rubber bands, or elastics, as part of your treatment. Rubber bands help move teeth into their proper position. Orthodontic headgear is a device that pushes teeth into their correct position or prevents them from moving into an incorrect position.

Tips for Wear and Care of Braces

1. **Brush and floss your teeth after every meal.** Flossing is the removal of dental plaque and bits of food from between the teeth using a string-like material called floss. **Dental plaque** is an invisible, sticky film of bacteria on teeth, especially near the gum line.

2. **Change rubber bands routinely, as directed by your orthodontist.** This will decrease the chance they will snap inside your mouth.

3. **Wear rubber bands as instructed by your orthodontist.** You will have to wear your braces longer if you do not wear rubber bands when you are told to do so.

4. **Chew gum only if your orthodontist approves.** Gum can get caught in your braces and pull them off.

5. **Do not eat hard, sticky, or crunchy food.** These foods can pull or knock off your braces. Check with your orthodontist if you are unsure whether to eat a certain food.

6. **Wear a mouthguard if you play sports.** Getting hit in the mouth can be very painful and cause injury.

A retainer is usually worn after braces are removed. A **retainer** is a plastic device with wires that keeps the teeth from moving back to their original places. Total treatment time with braces and a retainer is usually one to three years.

Tips for Wear and Care of Your Retainer

1. **Wear your retainer as instructed by your orthodontist.**

2. **Keep your retainer clean.**

3. **Do not place your retainer in hot water or near heat.**

4. **Write your name and phone number on the case in which you carry your retainer so it can be returned if you lose it.**

Activity

Health Behavior Contract

Copy the health behavior contract on a separate sheet of paper.

DO NOT WRITE IN THIS BOOK.

Name: _____ **Date:** _____

Life Skill: I will follow a dental health plan.

Effect on My Health: Dental plaque builds and continues to harden on teeth. It must be removed by a dental health professional. I can help prevent dental plaque buildup by following a dental plan.

My Plan: My plan will include:
• Brushing and flossing my teeth after each meal
• Having regular cleanings by a dental hygienist
• Having a dental checkup every six months in which my dentist checks for malocclusion and cavities
I will write down the date and time for my next dental appointment.
I have to get my teeth cleaned and checked _____.
I will make a star on the chart for each time I brush my teeth each day.
I will make a check on the chart for each time I floss my teeth each day.

My Calendar	M	T	W	Th	F	S	S

How My Plan Worked: (Complete after one week) _____
_____
_____

Vocabulary Words

Write a separate sentence using each vocabulary word listed on page 200.

Health Content

1. What are three parts of a physical examination? **page 201**

2. What are six vaccines? What illnesses do they prevent? **page 202**

3. What are five electronic devices that help correct hearing loss? **page 203**

4. What are three ways to correct problems with visual acuity? **pages 204–205**

5. What are three ways to straighten crooked teeth? **pages 206–207**

Health Literacy

Self-Directed Learning

Check the library or the Internet to find out about new technologies to correct hearing loss. Write a summary of your findings and present your summary to the class.

Critical Thinking

An adult family member has symptoms of illness that worry you. This person has not had a physical examination in several years. What reasons can you give this family member to persuade him or her to have a physical examination?

The Responsible Decision-Making Model™

You and a friend go to a fair. Both of you wear braces. Your friend wants to eat a caramel apple. You tell her eating a caramel apple can damage her braces. Your friend says, "You're being a bore. It's fun to break the rules once in a while. Besides, I'll brush my teeth for an extra long time tonight." Answer the following questions on a separate sheet of paper. Write "Does not apply" if a question does not apply to this situation.

1. Is it healthful to eat a caramel apple while wearing braces? Why or why not?

2. Is it safe to eat a caramel apple while wearing braces? Why or why not?

3. Is it legal to eat a caramel apple while wearing braces? Why or why not?

4. Will you show respect for yourself if you eat a caramel apple while wearing braces? Why or why not?

5. Will your parents or guardian and ortho-dontist approve if you eat a caramel apple while wearing braces? Why or why not?

6. Will you demonstrate good character if you eat a caramel apple while wearing braces? Why or why not?

What is the responsible decision to make in this situation?

How to Be Well-Groomed

Life Skills

- ◆ I will be well-groomed.
- ◆ I will get adequate rest and sleep.

Your grooming habits affect your health. **Grooming** is taking care of the body and having a neat appearance. Good grooming habits help you reduce the risk of infection from pathogens. Good grooming habits help you develop self-respect. **Self-respect** is a high regard for oneself because one behaves in responsible ways. When you are well-groomed, other teens will notice that you respect yourself. They will find you more attractive.

The Lesson Objectives

- Use questions to evaluate ads for grooming products.
- Identify grooming products for your hair and nails.
- Discuss ways to care for your skin.
- Explain what you can do if you have acne.
- Explain how to get a good night's sleep.

Vocabulary

grooming
self-respect
grooming product
advertisement
media
target audience
media literacy
dandruff
lice
cuticle
artificial nails
hangnail
sunscreen
acne
sebum
dermatologist
perspiration
deodorant
antiperspirant
insomnia

How Can I Evaluate Ads for Grooming Products?

A **grooming product** is an item that helps a person have a neat appearance and that keeps the body clean. How do you determine which grooming products you use? An **advertisement,** or ad, is a paid announcement about a product or service. Ads for grooming products are placed in many forms of media. **Media** are the various forms of mass communication. Media include television, radio, magazines, newspapers, the Internet, and billboards.

Advertisers want to influence people to buy their products. A **target audience** is the group of people for whom a message was created. Advertisers recognize that teens spend large amounts of money on grooming products. Teens are the target audience for many ads for grooming products. The ads are placed where teens will see or hear them, such as in teen magazines, on TV, and on radio. Ads show people whom teens might admire, such as attractive teens, actresses, actors, and professional athletes. The ads include words that would appeal to teens. The ads include places teens would enjoy, such as a party or a beach.

The purpose of ads is to convince you to buy a product. Information in ads might be misleading. For example, ads might claim that a product gives instant results or that it changes your appearance. Ads might try to sell more than just a product. For example, ads might try to convince you that your life will be better if you use the product. You need to evaluate ads before purchasing grooming products. You need to develop media literacy. **Media literacy** is the ability to recognize and evaluate the messages in media.

Activity

Media Literacy

Life Skill: I will be well-groomed.

Materials: magazines or newspapers

Directions: Follow the steps below to help you recognize and evaluate the messages in an ad for a grooming product.

1. **Find an ad for a grooming product that targets teens.**

2. **Evaluate the ad by answering the Questions to Evaluate Ads for Grooming Products.**

Questions to Evaluate Ads for Grooming Products

- What kind of grooming product is being advertised?
- Where did the ad appear?
- What is the purpose of the message?
- How does the ad target teens?
- Who will profit if teens are influenced by the message?
- What information is missing from the message? Why?
- Would you buy this product? Why or why not?

3. **Write a summary of your findings. Attach your ad to the summary.**

What Are Ways I Can Care for My Hair and Nails?

Hair Care

Shampoo is a mild detergent for the hair.

Conditioner is a product that coats, smooths, and detangles hair.

A curling iron is a device that heats up and is used to curl hair. Overuse of curling irons can cause hair to burn or break. Be careful to keep a curling iron away from your head to avoid burning the scalp. If you use a curling iron, keep it on a low setting.

Dandruff is a condition in which dead skin is shed from the scalp and becomes visible. Mild dandruff can be treated with a dandruff shampoo and thorough rinsing. Teens with persistent dandruff should consult a dermatologist.

Use a brush and comb gently to avoid hair breakage. Brushing and combing hair when it is wet can pull out hair. Sharing combs and brushes with others increases the risk of head lice. **Lice** are insects that attach to the skin and cause itching and swelling.

A hair dryer is a device that blows air and is used to dry hair. Use hair dryers on cool, warm, or low settings. Hair dryers used on high settings can be hot enough to burn the scalp.

Hairspray is a substance that is sprayed on hair to keep it in place. Do not inhale hairspray or spray it too close to your face. Hairspray can irritate the lungs and eyes. Overuse of hairspray can cause flaking of the scalp. This might look like dandruff.

Hair color is a product that changes the color of hair. Follow the instructions for using hair color. Hair color contains chemicals that can damage hair, skin, and scalp. Hair color does not necessarily turn out as promised on the package. Ask your parent or guardian for permission before using hair color.

Barrettes, scrunchies, headbands, and pony twists are items to hold hair in place. They can damage hair if used improperly. Do not fasten them too tightly or hair might break or the root might be damaged. Wearing hair pulled too tightly can cause headaches.

Nail polish is a product that coats nails to provide color and shine. Nail polishes contain identical ingredients. Frequent use of nail polish can make nails dry and weak. Dark nail polish colors can discolor nails.

Cuticle remover is a product that removes the nail cuticle. The **cuticle** is the non-living skin that surrounds and protects the nails. Cuticle remover can destroy your cuticles. Do not trim cuticles.

A permanent wave, or perm, is a product that produces curls. A perm contains chemicals that can irritate the skin and eyes. Perms can dry hair and cause splitting. Your hair might react differently to a perm than another person's hair. Ask your parent or guardian for permission before using a perm.

A razor is a device with a blade used for shaving hair. Improper use of a razor can irritate the skin and cause cuts. Ask your parent or guardian before using a razor. Check with a physician before shaving hair from a mole.

Artificial nails are products used to make nails longer or more attractive. Examples are wraps, gels, and tips. Always ask permission of a parent or guardian before using these products. Be cautious if you use these products. A fungus infection or allergic reaction sometimes occurs.

Nail clippers are devices used to trim nails. Fingernails and toenails should be trimmed regularly. Trim nails straight and close to the skin. Picking, biting, or tearing at nails can cause infection. Nail clippers also can be used to remove hangnails. A **hangnail** is a piece of skin torn near the fingernail. A hangnail should be trimmed and covered until it heals. Picking at hangnails can cause infection.

Hair and Nail Products

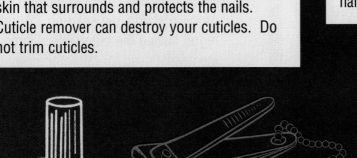

What Are Ways I Can Care for My Skin?

Your skin protects you from infection and helps regulate your body temperature. Your skin protects you from harmful ultraviolet rays. The nerve endings in skin alert you to pain, heat, and cold.

Seven Ways to Care for the Skin

1. **Wear a sunscreen daily.** A sunscreen is a product that protects the skin from the sun's rays. Most of your exposure to the sun's rays comes from daily exposure, not tanning. Your face and hands are the most exposed areas of your body. Wear a sunscreen with a sun protection factor (SPF) of 15 or higher each day to reduce the risk of skin cancer.

2. **Do not use too many skin products.** Gels, scrubs, beads, sprays, washes, lotions...there are now entire stores devoted to body care products. These products contain many chemicals. The chemicals in one product when combined with chemicals in another product might cause a harmful reaction. Your skin might become irritated, itchy, or red if you use too many different products.

3. **Do not share skin products through which you might spread infection.** You can share shampoo because you are only sharing a container. However, do not share items such as roll-on deodorant or lipstick.

4. **Eat a healthful diet.** Eat foods that contain vitamin A, such as milk and green vegetables. Foods with vitamin A can help you have healthy skin and nails. Drink plenty of water for healthy skin.

5. **Get enough sleep.** Lack of sleep can cause you to look tired and have bags under your eyes.

6. **Avoid skin products that cause irritation or itching.** You might be sensitive to ingredients in some skin products. Stop using a skin product immediately if your skin becomes irritated or itchy. Contact a physician if the skin irritation continues.

7. **Do not get tattoos or have your body pierced.** Getting a tattoo can cause infection and scarring. You might regret having the tattoo later. Suppose the needle used for tattooing or body piercing was previously used on an HIV infected person. You can become infected with HIV.

What to Know About Acne

Acne is a skin disorder in which pores in the skin are clogged with oil. Acne can range from mild to severe. Acne is related to the hormones that are secreted during puberty. These hormones stimulate the glands of the skin to produce sebum. **Sebum** (SEE·buhm) is a fatty substance secreted by the skin. Sebum interacts with bacteria to cause acne.

What to Do When You Have Acne

Most treatments for acne need time to be effective. If you have mild acne, use a mild soap to cleanse the face two times a day. More frequent cleaning can dry the skin around the acne. A physician can recommend an over-the-counter medication to apply. Do not squeeze or pick acne. Squeezing and picking can cause scars and infection. Do not use oil-based or heavy cosmetics. Limit time in the sun to reduce perspiration. If you have severe acne or a skin infection, check with a dermatologist. A **dermatologist** is a physician who specializes in the care of the skin.

Five Things That Make Acne Worse

- Stress
- Sun exposure
- Anabolic steroids
- Behaviors such as popping and picking acne pimples
- Oily and heavy cosmetics

Keep skin clean to avoid body odor. **Perspiration** is a mixture of water, salt, and waste products. Perspiration combines with dirt, oil, and bacteria on the skin to produce body odor. Bathing daily and wearing clean clothes help reduce body odor. A common place for body odor is under the arms. A **deodorant** is a product that reduces body odor and perspiration. An **antiperspirant** is a product used to reduce the amount of perspiration. Foot odor can be reduced by washing feet often and drying feet well. Wear clean socks. Alternate wearing different pairs of shoes. This allows shoes to dry before you wear them again.

How Can I Get a Good Night's Sleep?

Consider a day when you did not get enough sleep the night before. You might have difficulty getting out of bed in the morning. You might not think clearly during the day. You might doze off during class. You might be irritable and tired.

Getting a good night's sleep is important to your health. Your ability to resist disease weakens when you do not get enough sleep. Your risk of illness increases. Most teens need about eight hours of sleep. A teen who frequently has difficulty getting sleep might have insomnia. **Insomnia** is a condition in which a person has difficulty falling asleep or staying asleep.

Ways to Get a Good Night's Sleep

1. **Have a comfortable place to sleep.** Sleep in a dark room. Limit outside noises by wearing ear plugs and shutting the door. Keep room temperature between 64 and 70 degrees.

2. **Have a nightly routine before going to bed.** Read or listen to relaxing music. Try to go to bed and wake up at the same time each day. Try to get the same amount of sleep each night. Don't try to catch up on missed sleep by sleeping in on the weekends.

3. **Limit naps to less than one half-hour.** Naps that last longer keep you from getting to sleep at night.

4. **Do not drink caffeine in the evening.** Caffeine is a stimulant and can keep you awake. Be aware of sources of caffeine, such as hot chocolate and some pain relievers.

5. **Do not eat large meals or spicy foods before bedtime.** Large meals and spicy foods can cause stomach upset.

6. **Drink milk before bedtime.**

7. **Do not use tobacco products.** Nicotine in tobacco products is a stimulant and can cause shallow sleeping and restlessness.

8. **Participate in vigorous physical activity during the day rather than close to bedtime.**

Vocabulary Words

Write a separate sentence using each vocabulary word listed on page 210.

Health Content

1. What questions can you use to evaluate ads for grooming products? **page 211**

2. What are ten grooming products for your hair and nails? **pages 212–213**

3. What are seven ways to care for your skin? **page 214**

4. What can you take to treat acne? **page 215**

5. What are eight ways to get a good night's sleep? **page 216**

Health Literacy

Effective Communication

Design a magazine advertisement for a grooming product in this lesson. Use the Questions to Evaluate Ads for Grooming Products on page 211 to evaluate your ad.

The Responsible Decision-Making Model™

You read an ad for a new acne product on the Internet. The ad promises that your acne will be cured overnight. You have a major zit. School pictures will be taken later this week, and you do not want the zit to show. Should you buy and use this acne product? Answer the following questions on a separate sheet of paper. Write "Does not apply" if a question does not apply to this situation.

1. Is it healthful to buy and use this acne product? Why or why not?

2. Is it safe to buy and use this acne product? Why or why not?

3. Is it legal to buy and use this acne product? Why or why not?

4. Will you show respect for yourself if you buy and use this acne product? Why or why not?

5. Will your parents or guardian approve if you buy and use this acne product? Why or why not?

6. Will you demonstrate good character if you buy and use this acne product? Why or why not?

What is the responsible decision to make in this situation?

Why You Need Physical Activity

Life Skill

◆ **I will participate in regular physical activity.**

Vocabulary

physical activity

regular physical activity

physical fitness

health-related fitness

muscular strength

muscular endurance

flexibility

cardiorespiratory endurance

healthful body composition

life expectancy

premature death

cardiovascular diseases

stroke volume

high density lipoproteins (HDLs)

diabetes

beta-endorphins

Would you choose to have a trimmer body? How about more energy? Or a healthy heart? Regular exercise will benefit your health in many different ways. If you start now, you will develop skills that you can practice and enjoy throughout your life. There are many physical activities that you can choose that will benefit your health now and later.

The Lesson Objectives

- Write a summary statement of the findings of *Physical Activity: A Report of the Surgeon General.*
- Identify the five kinds of health-related fitness.
- Discuss ways regular physical activity can improve your health.
- Identify physical activities you can choose to develop health-related fitness.

What Are Physical Activity and Physical Fitness?

Physical activity is body movement produced by muscles and bones that requires energy. **Regular physical activity** is physical activity that is performed on most days of the week. Consider the following summary statement.

Regular physical activity improves the health and well-being of people.

Physical Activity: A Report of the Surgeon General.

Physical fitness is the condition of the body that results from regular physical activity. **Health-related fitness** is the ability of the heart, lungs, muscles, and joints to perform well. There are five kinds of health-related fitness.

- **Muscular strength** is the ability to lift, pull, push, kick, and throw with force.

- **Muscular endurance** is the ability to use muscles for an extended period of time.

- **Flexibility** is the ability to bend and move the joints through a full range of motion.

- **Cardiorespiratory endurance** is the ability to do activities that require oxygen for extended periods of time.

- **Healthful body composition** is having a high ratio of lean tissue to fat tissue in the body.

How Can Regular Physical Activity Improve My Health?

1. **I can reduce my risk of premature death.**
   Life expectancy is the number of years a person can expect to live. **Premature death** is death that occurs before a person reaches his or her life expectancy. Regular physical activity right now will help you live longer. You also will have a healthier lifestyle.

2. **I can reduce my risk of cardiovascular diseases.**
   Cardiovascular diseases are diseases of the heart and blood vessels. Regular physical activity strengthens your heart muscle. This increases stroke volume. **Stroke volume** is the amount of blood the heart pumps with each beat. A strong heart does not have to beat as often to supply your body with blood carrying oxygen. Regular physical activity also increases HDLs. HDLs or **high density lipoproteins** (ly·poh·PROH·teens) are substances in blood that carry cholesterol to the liver for breakdown and excretion. When cholesterol is excreted, it does not stay in your blood and stick to your artery walls.

3. **I can reduce my risk of developing diabetes.**
   Diabetes (DY·uh·BEE·teez) is a disease in which the body produces little or no insulin or cannot use insulin. NIDDM is a type of diabetes in which a person's body produces insulin, but cannot use it. A main cause of NIDDM is being overweight. Regular physical activity helps you control your weight.

4. **I can reduce my risk of developing high blood pressure.** When fat deposits on your artery walls, your blood pressure must increase so blood can be pumped throughout your body. Regular physical activity helps keep fat from collecting on your artery walls.

5. **I can reduce my risk of developing colon cancer.** Regular physical activity helps speed the movement of waste through your colon. This helps you have a bowel movement. Daily bowel movements reduce your risk of developing colon cancer.

6. **I can reduce my risk of feeling depressed or anxious.** Regular physical activity causes your body to produce higher levels of beta-endorphins. **Beta-endorphins** (BAY·tuh·en·DOR·fuhnz) are substances produced in the brain that create a feeling of well-being. These substances help reduce feelings of depression. Regular physical activity also helps you blow off steam. You are less likely to feel anxious.

7. **I can control my weight.** Regular physical activity causes you to use energy. You are able to eat more when you work out more. You can maintain a healthful weight.

8. **I can have a healthful body composition.** Regular physical activity affects your body composition. You reduce the amount of fat in your abdominal area. You increase lean tissue, or muscle. As a result, you have a leaner appearance.

9. **I can have feelings of accomplishment.** The routine of regular physical activity increases self-discipline. Completing a workout gives you a feeling of accomplishment. You improve your self-respect when you work out regularly.

What Physical Activities Can I Choose to Develop Health-Related Fitness?

Basketball

Basketball is a game in which players toss an inflated ball through a raised basket. Usually, two teams of five players play on a court. They must bounce the ball with their hands while moving, and they score points by shooting the ball through the basket. "Pick-up" games of basketball can be played on a smaller court with different numbers of players. Playing basketball improves cardiorespiratory endurance, muscular endurance, and body composition.

In-Line Skating

In-line skating is a sport in which participants move over asphalt, concrete, or other hard surfaces wearing skates with four wheels lined up in a row. In-line skating is similar to ice skating. You need skates, a helmet, and knee and elbow pads. You should carry a water bottle. People also play hockey on in-line skates. In-line skating improves cardiorespiratory endurance, muscular strength and endurance, and body composition.

Martial Arts

Martial arts are methods of self-defense and combat. Martial arts include karate, tae kwon do (TY·KWAHN·DOH), judo, tai chi (TY·CHEE), and kickboxing. Martial arts training involves stretching, running, practicing, and sparring, as well as learning psychological and emotional preparations. Martial arts require special clothing, but little other equipment. Different martial arts improve different areas of fitness, including cardiorespiratory endurance, muscular strength and endurance, flexibility, and body composition.

Rock Climbing and Wall Climbing

Rock climbing is scaling rocks or cliffs. Wall climbing is climbing walls that are designed to resemble rocks or cliffs. You need special equipment to climb, including ropes, harnesses, and helmets and other protective equipment. Climbing improves muscular strength, muscular endurance, and body composition.

Cycling and Mountain Biking

Cycling is riding a bicycle on streets and roads. Mountain biking is riding an all-terrain bicycle, or mountain bike, on mountains or off-road trails. Road bicycles can be ridden only on smooth surfaces. You need a bicycle and a helmet to cycle or mountain bike. You need additional protective gear for mountain biking. You should carry a water bottle. Cycling and mountain biking improve cardiorespiratory endurance, muscular endurance and strength, and body composition.

Aerobics

Aerobics is an exercise program that involves dance steps and other movements done to music. Aerobics might include step aerobics using a low step, exercises using weights, boxing moves, low-impact exercises, dance steps, exercises in a pool (water aerobics), or combinations of these. You need exercise shoes and exercise clothing to do aerobics. You should have a water bottle or water fountain nearby. For water aerobics, you need a swimsuit and a towel. Depending on the activity, aerobics improves muscular endurance, cardiorespiratory endurance, body composition, and flexibility.

Walking and Hiking

Walking is moving on foot at a slow pace. Hiking is walking through forests, fields, mountains, or other terrain. Hiking usually is more strenuous than walking. If you carry small hand weights, your walks will be more challenging. You need comfortable shoes to walk or hike. You should carry a water bottle. For hiking, you might want hiking boots, depending on the terrain. Walking and hiking improve cardiorespiratory endurance, muscular endurance, and body composition.

Lacrosse

Lacrosse is a fast-paced team sport in which players use a lacrosse stick to shoot, pass, catch, or carry a ball. A lacrosse team has 10 to 12 players. The object of lacrosse is to score points by maneuvering the ball into a goal. Only the goalie may touch the ball with his or her hands. Lacrosse usually is played outdoors in the fall or spring. You need a ball, lacrosse stick, stick head, helmet, gloves, a mouthguard, and other protective gear to play lacrosse. You need additional equipment if you are the goalie. Playing lacrosse improves muscular endurance, cardiorespiratory endurance, and body composition.

Snowboarding

Snowboarding is a sport that involves gliding down a snow-covered hill or mountain on a single board. You need a snowboard, a helmet, boots, and cold-weather clothing to snowboard. Snow-boarding improves muscular strength and endurance, cardiorespiratory endurance, body composition, and flexibility.

Activity

Physical Activity Map

Life Skill: I will participate in regular physical activity.

Materials: large sheet of poster board, paper, pencil, markers

Directions: Follow the directions below to discover physical activities in which you might participate.

1. **Draw an outline of the state or country in which you live on the poster board.** Make your outline as large as you can.

2. **List ten physical activities in which you might participate in the state or country in which you live.** Write your list on a sheet of paper. You might need to do some research if you are unable to list at least ten physical activities.

3. **Design a symbol to represent each physical activity on your list.** Draw the symbol next to the physical activity. For example, you might have listed "tennis." Next to the word "tennis" you might draw a tennis racket.

4. **Draw the ten symbols inside the outline of the state or country you drew on the poster board.** The poster you have completed is your Physical Activity Map. Share your Physical Activity Map with classmates.

Vocabulary Words

Write a separate sentence using each vocabulary word listed on page 218.

Health Content

1. Write a summary statement of the findings in *Physical Activity: A Report of the Surgeon General.* **page 219**

2. What are the five kinds of health-related fitness? **page 219**

3. What are nine ways physical activity can improve your health? **pages 220–221**

4. What are three physical activities that improve muscular strength and endurance? That improve flexibility? **pages 222–224**

5. What are three physical activities that improve cardiorespiratory endurance? That improve body composition? **pages 222–224**

The Responsible Decision-Making Model™

Your sister has borrowed in-line skates from a friend. She suggests that you try them, too. However, you do not have a helmet. Answer the following questions on a separate sheet of paper. Write "Does not apply" if a question does not apply to this situation.

1. Is it healthful to in-line skate without a helmet? Why or why not?

2. Is it safe to in-line skate without a helmet? Why or why not?

3. Is it legal to in-line skate without a helmet? Why or why not?

4. Will you show respect for yourself if you in-line skate without a helmet? Why or why not?

5. Will you follow the guidelines of your parents or guardian if you in-line skate without a helmet? Why or why not?

6. Will you demonstrate good character if you in-line skate without a helmet? Why or why not?

What is the responsible decision to make in this situation?

Health Literacy

Self-Directed Learning

Find a book in your school or community library about a sport that is unfamiliar to you. Read the book. Then, write a one-page paper about the sport.

Responsible Citizenship

Some sporting events, such as the Special Olympics, are designed for people with disabilities. Volunteer to help at such a sporting event.

How to Develop Fitness

Life Skills

- ◆ I will develop and maintain health-related fitness.
- ◆ I will develop and maintain skill-related fitness.
- ◆ I will follow a physical fitness plan.

Physical fitness is the condition of the body that results from regular physical activity. There are two areas of physical fitness. **Health-related fitness** is the ability of the heart, lungs, muscles, and joints to perform well. **Skill-related fitness** is the ability to perform well in sports and physical activities. Being physically fit means that you have the energy and ability to meet your everyday responsibilities and tasks.

The Lesson Objectives

- Explain how to develop flexibility.
- Explain how to develop muscular strength and muscular endurance.
- Explain how to develop cardiorespiratory endurance and a healthful body composition.
- Develop a physical fitness plan.
- Identify fitness skills you can use when you participate in sports and physical activities.

Vocabulary

physical fitness

health-related fitness

skill-related fitness

flexibility

static stretching

muscular strength

muscular endurance

resistance exercise

repetitions

cardiorespiratory endurance

healthful body composition

aerobic exercise

target heart rate

maximum heart rate

warm-up

cool-down

fitness skills

agility

balance

coordination

reaction time

speed

power

How Can I Develop Flexibility?

Flexibility is the ability to bend and move the joints through a full range of motion. When you are flexible, you can reach, bend, and stretch more easily. You are less likely to injure your muscles and joints. Regular stretching helps you reduce tension. You feel less stressed. Inactivity reduces your flexibility.

A Plan for Flexibility

- Perform stretching exercises two to three times a week.
- Choose from a variety of exercises that involve static stretching. **Static stretching** is stretching the muscle to a point where it pulls, and then holding the stretch for 15–30 seconds.
- Repeat each stretching exercise three to five times.
- Include exercises to stretch the muscles that work each of the major joints in the body.
- Continue your stretching routine for 15 to 30 minutes.

A Test to Measure Lower Back and Hamstring Flexibility

V-Sit Reach or Sit and Reach Mark a line on the floor. Sit on the floor with your feet five or six inches (12.5 or 15 centimeters) apart directly behind the line. Clasp your thumbs so that your hands are together, palms down. Lean forward. Place your hands on the measuring line between your feet. With a partner holding your legs straight, reach as far forward as you can. Your score is the number of inches you can reach beyond the line. Write your score on a sheet of paper.

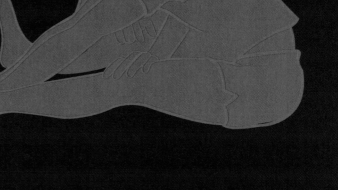

How Can I Develop Muscular Strength and Muscular Endurance?

Muscular strength is the ability to lift, pull, push, kick, and throw with force. When you have muscular strength, you can do heavy work. You can lift heavy objects. You can enjoy sports which require strength. You are less likely to injure your muscles. **Muscular endurance** is the ability to use muscles for an extended period of time. You are able to last longer when you play sports and games that require strength.

Resistance exercises help develop muscular strength and muscular endurance. A **resistance exercise** is an exercise in which a force acts against muscles. To get resistance, you can lift your own weight, lift free weights, or work with weights on a machine. **Repetitions** are the number of times an exercise is performed. A heavy weight and a low number of repetitions (1–5) helps you build muscular strength. A lighter weight and a higher number of repetitions (20–25) helps you build muscular endurance.

A Plan for Muscular Strength and Muscular Endurance

- **Develop a training program with the supervision of an adult.**
- **Train with weights two to four days a week.**
- **Schedule a day of rest between your workouts.**
- **Choose from a variety of resistance exercises. Use your own body for resistance by doing: pull-ups, push-ups, or sit-ups. Use free weights or a weight machine to do bench presses, leg presses, leg curls, or pull-downs.**
- **Keep a record of the amount of resistance and the number of repetitions you do.**
- **Begin with a weight you can move easily for 8–12 repetitions.**
- **Add more weights until you can do three sets of 10–12 repetitions.**

A Test to Measure Upper Body Strength and Endurance

Pull-Ups Grasp a bar with an overhand grip. You might need to be lifted into this position. Your feet should not touch the floor. Your legs should be straight. Begin by hanging with your arms straight. Pull your body up with a steady movement until your chin is over the bar. Then extend back down. Do as many pull-ups as you can. There is no time limit. Your score is the number of repetitions you complete. Write your score on a sheet of paper.

A Test to Measure Leg Strength and Endurance

Shuttle Run Place two blocks of wood or similar objects behind a line. The start position should be 30 feet from this line. Someone will give a "Ready, Go!" signal. Run to the blocks, pick one up. Bring it back and place it behind the starting line. Then run and pick up the second block. Bring it back across the starting line. Record your time. Write your fastest time on a sheet of paper.

A Test to Measure Abdominal Strength and Endurance

Curl-Ups Sit on the floor with your knees bent. Your feet should be about 12 inches from your buttocks. Place your hands on opposite shoulders. Keep your arms close to your chest. A partner should hold your feet and count each curl-up. Raise your trunk up to touch your elbows to your thighs. A complete curl-up is counted each time you lie back and touch your shoulders to the floor. The goal is to do as many curl-ups as you can in one minute. Your score is the number of repetitions you complete in one minute. Write your score on a sheet of paper.

How Can I Develop Cardiorespiratory Endurance and a Healthful Body Composition?

Cardiorespiratory endurance is the ability to do activities that require oxygen for extended periods of time. Suppose you have cardiorespiratory endurance. You do not get out of breath when you work out or play sports and games. Your heart muscle is strong and can deliver more oxygen to cells each time it beats. A **healthful body composition** is having a high ratio of lean tissue to fat tissue in the body. Your body has a lean and firm appearance.

Aerobic exercises help you develop these two kinds of health-related fitness. An **aerobic exercise** is one in which large amounts of oxygen are used for an extended time. Running for twenty minutes at a steady pace without stopping is an aerobic exercise. Aerobic exercises help you in another way. Aerobic exercises burn extra calories and help you maintain your weight.

A Plan for Cardiorespiratory Endurance and a Healthful Body Composition

- Participate in aerobic exercises three to five days a week. Start with three days and work up to five days.

- Choose from a variety of aerobic exercises: bicycling, cross-country skiing, in-line skating, fast walking, running, jumping rope, or swimming.

- Perform the exercise at your target heart rate. **Target heart rate** is a heart rate of 75 percent of a person's maximum heart rate. **Maximum heart rate** is 220 beats per minute minus a person's age.

- Maintain a steady pace for 20 minutes or more.

How to Calculate My Target Heart Rate

Copy the following equation on a separate sheet of paper.
DO NOT WRITE IN THIS BOOK.

220 – _____ (my age) = _____ (my maximum heart rate)

.75 X _____ (my maximum heart rate) = _____ (my target heart rate)

A Test for Cardiorespiratory Endurance

One-Mile Walk and Run Test Do this test on a track. Four laps on most tracks is a mile. Walk part of the way if you cannot run the entire mile. Stop if you feel dizzy or sick. Time yourself, or have a partner time you. At the end, cool down for a few minutes. Your score is the time it took you to run or walk the mile. Write your time on a sheet of paper.

Can You Meet the President's Challenge?

Compare your scores from the fitness tests in this lesson to the scores in the chart below. You qualify for The Presidential Physical Fitness Award if you scored at or above the scores listed for your age and sex on all five events.

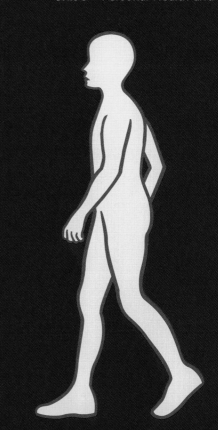

The Presidential Physical Fitness Award

Qualifying Standards

boys

Age	V-Sit Reach (inches)	or Sit and Reach (centimeters)	Pull-Ups	Curl-Ups (timed one minute)	Shuttle Run (seconds)	One-Mile Run (minutes/seconds)
11	+4.0	31	6	47	10.0	7:32
12	+4.0	31	7	50	9.8	7:11
13	+3.5	33	7	53	9.5	6:50
14	+4.5	36	10	56	9.1	6:26

girls

Age	V-Sit Reach (inches)	or Sit and Reach (centimeters)	Pull-Ups	Curl-Ups (timed one minute)	Shuttle Run (seconds)	One-Mile Run (minutes/seconds)
11	+6.5	34	3	42	10.5	9:02
12	+7.0	36	2	45	10.4	8:23
13	+7.5	38	2	46	10.2	8:13
14	+8.5	40	2	47	10.1	7:59

What Should I Include in My Physical Fitness Plan?

You can make a physical fitness plan. You need to plan regular workouts. Your workouts should include exercises for each of the five kinds of health-related fitness. When you work out, always remember to warm up and cool down. A **warm-up** is three to five minutes of easy physical activity to prepare the muscles for more work. A **cool-down** is five to ten minutes of reduced physical activity after a workout. You can reduce the risk of being injured by warming up and cooling down.

Get organized today. Make a health behavior contract like the one on page 233. Decide which days of the week you will have workouts to develop the different kinds of health-related fitness. Remember, you must include:

- **warm-up exercises (before each workout);**
- **static stretching exercises to develop flexibility (2–3 days a week);**
- **resistance exercises to develop muscular strength and muscular endurance (2–4 days a week);**
- **aerobic exercises to develop cardiorespiratory endurance and a healthful body composition (3–5 days a week);**
- **cool-down exercises (after each workout).**

Be realistic. Your workouts must fit into a schedule that allows you time for schoolwork and family responsibilities. Be certain the equipment and facilities you need are available for the exercises you choose. If not, choose other exercises. Ask friends or family members to workout with you. They can encourage you to keep your commitment to exercise. Think of ways to stay motivated. For example, you might keep your health behavior contract on your mirror where you will see it. Make frequent checks of your physical fitness. Use the tests in this lesson. Compare your scores to the qualifying standards set by The President's Council on Physical Fitness on page 231.

Activity

Health Behavior Contract

Name:_____ **Date:**_____

Life Skill: I will follow a physical fitness plan.

Effect on My Health: If I have health-related fitness, I will be able to lift, pull, push, kick, and throw with force. I will be able to use my muscles without tiring. I will be able to bend and move easily. I will be able to do activities for extended periods of time. I will have a lean body.

My Plan: I will use the calendar to plan these workouts:

- Static stretching exercises on 2–3 days

- Resistance exercises on 2–4 days

- Aerobic exercises on 3–5 days

I will plan to warm up for three to five minutes before each workout. I will plan to cool down for five to ten minutes after each workout. I will follow my plan for a week. I will make a star by each workout I complete. If I do not complete a scheduled workout, I will write the reason why.

My Calendar	M	T	W	Th	F	S	S

How My Plan Worked: (Complete after one week) _____
_____
_____

What Fitness Skills Do I Need to Participate in Sports and Physical Activities?

Fitness skills are skills that can be used in sports and physical activities. There are six fitness skills.

- **Agility** is the ability to move quickly and easily. You need agility to change directions when you play soccer.

- **Balance** is the ability to keep from falling. You need balance for in-line skating.

- **Coordination** is the ability to use body parts and senses together for movement. You need coordination to hit a tennis ball. You keep your eyes on the ball while you swing the racket with your arm.

- **Reaction time** is the time it takes to move after a person hears, sees, feels, or touches a stimulus. You need a fast reaction time if you are swimming in a race and want a quick start when the starting signal is given.

- **Speed** is the ability to move quickly. You need speed to run the bases if you play baseball.

- **Power** is the ability to combine strength and speed. You need power to throw a football twenty yards.

Fitness Skills

Agility   Coordination   Speed

Balance   Reaction Time   Power

Vocabulary Words

Write a separate sentence using each vocabulary word listed on page 226.

Health Content

1. How can you develop flexibility? **page 227**

2. How can you develop muscular strength and muscular endurance? **pages 228–229**

3. How can you develop cardiorespiratory endurance and a healthful body composition? **pages 230–231**

4. What should you include in a physical fitness plan? **page 232**

5. What are six fitness skills you need to participate in sports and physical activities? **page 234**

Health Literacy

Effective Communication

Research exercises that fit each of the five exercise categories on page 232. Design a poster that shows or describes how to do an exercise for one category. Display your poster in your classroom.

Critical Thinking

Why is it important to do a warm-up before a workout? a cool-down after a workout?

The Responsible Decision-Making Model™

Your parent or guardian has given you permission to begin a program using weights at a gym. A qualified person is available to help design a program for you. (S)he tells you how much weight to use and how many repetitions to do. But, you want to get fit right away. You want to ignore his or her advice and lift extra weight. Should you ignore his or her advice and lift extra weight right away? Answer the following questions on a separate sheet of paper. Write "Does not apply" if a question does not apply to this situation.

1. Is it healthful to lift extra weight? Why or why not?

2. Is it safe to lift extra weight? Why or why not?

3. Is it legal to lift extra weight? Why or why not?

4. Will you show respect for yourself if you lift extra weight? Why or why not?

5. Will you follow the guidelines of the person who helped you design your program if you lift extra weight? Why or why not?

6. Will you demonstrate good character if you lift extra weight? Why or why not?

What is the responsible decision to make in this situation?

How to Prevent Injuries During Physical Activity

Life Skills

◆ I will prevent physical activity-related injuries and illnesses.

◆ I will be a responsible spectator and participant in sports.

It is possible to reduce the risk of being injured when you are being physically active. Thinking ahead and taking some simple precautions can help prevent some injuries before they happen. This applies to both sports participants and sports spectators. A **sports participant** is a person who plays sports. A **sports spectator,** or **fan,** is a person who watches and supports sports. When you choose responsible behavior, you protect yourself and others. You demonstrate good character.

The Lesson Objectives

- Explain what is included in a sports physical.
- Discuss ways to reduce the risk of being injured during physical activity.
- Discuss common physical activity-related injuries.
- Identify ways to demonstrate good character if you participate in sports.
- Follow a spectator code of conduct.

Vocabulary

sports participant
sports spectator
fan
sports physical
warm-up
cool-down
training zone
overload
training threshold
training ceiling
RICE Treatment
sprain
tennis elbow
fracture
muscle cramp
runner's knee
shin splint
exercise-induced asthma (EIA)
character
self-control
self-respect
bookie
anabolic steroids
referee
code of conduct

What Is Included in a Sports Physical?

You need to have a sports physical before you participate in a sport. A **sports physical** is a physical examination to determine a person's health status before participation. A sports physical can help determine if a teen has any physical limitations that might affect the teen's ability to participate in a particular sport.

Your physician will examine your medical records. (S)he will examine your muscles, joints, and bones. (S)he will ask about any injuries, major illnesses, or surgery you have had. The physician will evaluate your cardiorespiratory fitness. (S)he will ask if you have experienced any shortness of breath, fainting, loss of consciousness, or chest pain while participating in physical activity. (S)he will ask if you have allergies or asthma. The physician will ask if you are taking any medication or are under the care of another physician. (S)he might recommend further testing. (S)he then will determine if you can safely participate in the sport. If you can participate in the sport, the physician will sign a form provided by your school. A sample form appears below.

Student Participation and Physical Exam Card

Student's Name	last	first	middle

Birth Date	Sex	Grade

City

School

Place of Birth

Student's Address	street	city	zip

Parent(s) Name

Address (if different from student)	street	city	zip

Home Telephone No.

Family Physician's Name	address	phone #

Athlete's History (Circle Yes or No)
1. Has this athlete ever had hospitalization, surgery, injury, or serious medical illness? Yes No
2. Is this athlete now under the care of a physician or taking any medication? Yes No
3. Have you ever recommended or do you feel that there should be limits placed on participation in competitive sports? Yes No
4. Does this athlete have any known allergies to medications? Yes No
5. Does this athlete wear glasses or contact lenses? Give date of last eye exam if "yes." Yes No
6. Has this athlete ever blacked out or lost consciousness during physical activity? Yes No
   If yes, please specify:

We consent to the participation of the student in the athletic program of his or her school including practice sessions and travel to and from athletic contests. We also agree to emergency medical treatment as deemed necessary by the physicians designated by school authorities.

Physician Signature	Date

Parent Signature	Date

How Can I Reduce My Risk of Being Injured During Physical Activity?

You can reduce your risk of being injured when you participate in physical activities by following these guidelines.

1. **Have a sports physical.** A physician will examine you and determine any physical limitations you might have that would affect your ability to participate.

2. **Have appropriate adult supervision.** An adult can monitor the activities for safety.

3. **Follow safety rules.** Rules are developed by experts to protect you from injury.

4. **Review basic first aid procedures.** Be prepared in case of an injury.

5. **Wear appropriate clothing and shoes.** Wear clothing appropriate for the physical activity. Dress for the weather.

6. **Use appropriate equipment.** Use equipment that is appropriate for your size and skill level. Get instructions on the use of the equipment.

7. **Warm up and cool down.** A **warm-up** is three to five minutes of easy physical activity to prepare the muscles for more work. A **cool-down** is five to ten minutes of reduced physical activity after a workout. A cool-down allows the heart rate to slow down gradually after the activity.

8. **Do not compete beyond your ability level.** You can be injured if you compete against teens who are "out of your league."

9. **Do not continue playing when you suspect you have an injury.** Avoid playing if you are in pain.

10. **Stay in the training zone.**

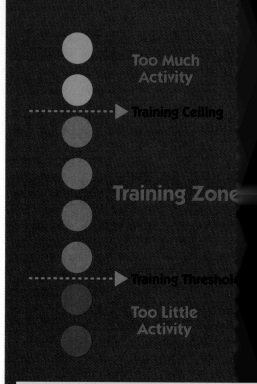

Too Much Activity

Training Ceiling

Training Zone

Training Threshold

Too Little Activity

The **training zone** is the range of activity required to obtain fitness benefits. This range of activity includes overload. **Overload** is including exercise beyond what a person usually does to obtain added benefits. The **training threshold** is the minimum amount of overload required to obtain fitness benefits. Workouts below the training threshold do not provide fitness benefits. The **training ceiling** is the maximum amount of overload required to obtain fitness benefits without risking injury or illness. Workouts that go beyond the training ceiling are risky to health.

What Are Common Physical Activity-Related Injuries?

You may need to obtain medical attention if you are injured during physical activity. One common treatment for these injuries is the RICE Treatment. The **RICE Treatment** is a technique for treating injuries that involves rest, ice, compression, and elevation. The RICE Treatment is discussed on page 494. Review the following common physical activity-related injuries.

Common Physical Activity-Related Injuries

1. A **sprain** is an injury to the ligaments, tendons, and soft tissue around a joint caused by undue stretching. Signs of a sprain include pain, soreness, and swelling. Treatment for sprains includes the RICE Treatment and medical help.

2. **Tennis elbow** is damage to the tendons that move the wrist, and causes pain to the elbow and forearm. Tennis elbow commonly occurs from swinging a tennis racket, pitching a baseball, throwing a javelin, and carrying a suitcase. Symptoms include pain in the elbow and forearm. Treatment includes strengthening exercises and avoiding the sport that caused injury.

3. A **fracture** is a break or crack in a bone. Signs of a fracture include pain, swelling, loss of movement, and deformity. Treatment for fractures is discussed on page 493.

4. A **muscle cramp** is a sudden tightening of a muscle. Symptoms include sharp pains. Treatment includes drinking fluids and gently massaging the muscles that cramp.

5. **Runner's knee** is a condition in which the kneecap rubs against the thighbone. Symptoms include pain and swelling on the underside of the kneecap. Treatment includes resting, avoiding running, doing strengthening exercises, and using shoe inserts.

6. A **shin splint** is a condition in which the muscles along the lower leg or shin are damaged. Shin splints commonly occur during running or aerobic exercise. Symptoms include pain along the front and outside of the shin. Treatment includes avoiding exercise while the injury heals, stretching, and possible surgery.

Exercise-induced asthma (EIA) is a condition in which vigorous physical activity causes a person to have asthma attacks. Symptoms include wheezing, difficulty breathing, chest pain, and fatigue. A physician can help teens with asthma develop an appropriate physical activity plan. Treatment can include taking medication and limiting certain types of exercise.

How Can I Demonstrate Good Character If I Participate in Sports?

A sports participant is a person who plays sports. You can demonstrate good character when you participate in sports. **Character** is a person's use of self-control to act on responsible values. **Self-control** is the degree to which a person regulates his or her own behavior. Let's look at ways you can demonstrate that you have good character.

1. **Play by the rules.** Rules were made to protect your safety and the safety of other participants.

2. **Be honest.** Do not cheat. You risk getting a reputation as being a cheat. Others will not want to participate in sports with you. When you are honest, you maintain self-respect. **Self-respect** is a high regard for oneself because one behaves in responsible ways.

3. **Be committed to your teammates.** Show up for practices and games on time. Help teammates play at their best. Thank them for helping you. Congratulate them when they play well.

4. **Do not gamble.** Do not place bets on games. It is illegal for minors to use a bookie. A **bookie** is a person who takes bets and gets a percentage of the money. People who gamble might develop gambling addiction.

5. **Follow school guidelines for participation.** Do not drink alcohol. Do not smoke or use other tobacco products. Follow safety guidelines when traveling to a game on a bus or by car. Check on your school policy for additional guidelines.

6. **Do not use drugs to enhance performance.**
Do not use painkillers to help you "play through the pain." Consult a physician before using any painkillers. Do not use anabolic steroids. **Anabolic steroids** are drugs that are used to increase muscle size and strength. Teens might believe taking these drugs will improve performance and build muscles. It is illegal to use anabolic steroids without the supervision of a physician. It is illegal for a person who is not a physician to sell steroids or to give them to a minor.

7. **Do not choose wrong actions to maintain eligibility to play sports.** Do not cheat on tests to make grades. Do not take water pills to change weight for wrestling or gymnastics. Do not choose harmful eating habits, such as starving, vomiting, following fad diets, or skipping meals.

8. **Show respect for your coach.** Respect your coach's decisions. Your coach's job is to help you play at your best and stay safe. Follow your coach's rules and safety guidelines. Tell a parent or guardian immediately if your coach chooses wrong actions or encourages you to choose wrong actions.

9. **Show respect for the referees.** A **referee** is an official who enforces rules in a sports event. Respect the decisions of the referees. Do not yell or use foul language when talking to a referee.

10. **Have a healthful attitude about winning and losing.** Say words of encouragement to your opponents if you win. Do not put down your opponents. Congratulate your opponent(s) if you lose. Do not become upset or angry if you lose.

Activity

Spectator Code of Conduct

Life Skill: I will be a responsible spectator and participant in sports.

Materials: paper, pen or pencil, or computer

Directions: Follow the steps below to create a cheer based on *The Spectator Code of Conduct*.

1. **Review *The Spectator Code of Conduct* on the right.** A sports spectator is a person who watches and supports sports. A sports spectator should demonstrate good character when watching a sporting event. Sports spectators should follow a code of conduct. A **code of conduct** is the expected standard of behavior. When you follow a code of conduct, you follow rules and safety guidelines. You do not participate in illegal behavior.

2. **Write a cheer to support the fans who follow *The Spectator Code of Conduct*.** The cheer should include at least five facts from the code of conduct.

3. **Perform your cheer for the class.**

The Spectator Code of Conduct

1. I will recognize that I represent my school when I attend sports events.
2. I will not make rude remarks about players on my team or the opposing team.
3. I will not make rude remarks about the coaches or referees.
4. I will not try to interrupt the game by making noise or throwing things.
5. I will not start or participate in any fights.
6. I will keep my emotions under control.
7. I will not use swear words.
8. I will not use alcohol or other drugs before, during, or after a game.
9. I will support my team by showing up to games, being a cheerleader, or being a member of the pep squad.
10. I will support my team when it loses as well as when it wins.
11. I will not damage property at an opposing team's school.
12. I will not bet on sports events.

Vocabulary Words

Write a separate sentence using each vocabulary word listed on page 236.

Health Content

1. What is included in a sports physical? **page 237**

2. What are ten ways to reduce the risk of being injured during physical activity? **page 238**

3. What are six common physical activity-related injuries? What are the symptoms and treatment for each of these? **page 239**

4. What are ten ways to demonstrate good character if you participate in sports? **pages 240–241**

5. What are 12 guidelines that are included in *The Spectator Code of Conduct?* **page 242**

Health Literacy

Responsible Citizenship

Obtain your school guidelines for participating in sports. Write a paragraph about these guidelines. Include the consequences you face if you disobey the guidelines.

The Responsible Decision-Making Model™

Tryouts for a school athletic team are after school. Students who try out must have a sports physical and have a sports physical form signed by their physician. You forgot to get your sports physical, but you are in good condition. Your friend tells you to forge the physician's signature on the form so that you can try out. Answer the following questions on a separate sheet of paper. Write "Does not apply" if a question does not apply to this situation.

1. Is it healthful to try out for the team without obtaining a physician's permission? Why or why not?

2. Is it safe to try out for the team without obtaining a physician's permission? Why or why not?

3. Is it legal to try out for the team without obtaining a physician's permission? Why or why not?

4. Will you show respect for yourself if you try out for the team without obtaining a physician's permission? Why or why not?

5. Will your parents or guardian approve if you try out for the team without obtaining a physician's permission? Why or why not?

6. Will you demonstrate good character if you try out for the team without obtaining a physician's permission? Why or why not?

What is the responsible decision to make in this situation?

Health Content

Prepare for the Unit Test. Review your answers for each Lesson Review in this unit. Then write answers to each of the following questions:

1. What are the common causes of hearing loss? **Lesson 21 page 203**

2. What is the usual total treatment time if you have braces and a retainer? **Lesson 21 page 207**

3. What are five ways you can keep acne from getting worse? **Lesson 22 page 215**

4. How much sleep do you need? **Lesson 22 page 216**

5. Why does exercise help if you feel anxious or depressed? **Lesson 23 page 221**

6. What health-related fitness benefits can you get from walking? **Lesson 23 page 223**

7. What is the correct way for you to perform static stretching? **Lesson 24 page 227**

8. Why do you need to have cardiorespiratory endurance? **Lesson 24 page 230**

9. What might be included in a sports physical? **Lesson 25 page 237**

10. What might happen if you work out beyond the training ceiling? **Lesson 25 page 238**

Health Behavior Contract

Make a health behavior contract for one of the life skills in this unit. Review your health behavior contract with your parents or guardian.

Vocabulary Words

Number a sheet of paper from 1–10. Select the correct vocabulary word and write it next to the corresponding number. DO NOT WRITE IN THIS BOOK.

acne	sports physical
resistance exercise	insomnia
cool-down	runner's knee
vaccine	malocclusion
stroke volume	high density lipoproteins (HDLs)

1. _____ is an abnormal fitting together of teeth when the jaws are closed. **Lesson 21**

2. _____ are substances in blood that carry cholesterol to the liver for breakdown and excretion. **Lesson 23**

3. _____ is a skin disorder in which pores in the skin are clogged with oil. **Lesson 22**

4. A _____ is a physical examination to determine a person's health status before participation. **Lesson 25**

5. _____ is a condition in which a person has difficulty falling asleep or staying asleep. **Lesson 22**

6. _____ is a condition in which the kneecap rubs against the thighbone. **Lesson 25**

7. A _____ is five to ten minutes of reduced physical activity after a workout. **Lesson 24**

8. A _____ is a substance containing dead or weakened pathogens that is introduced into the body to prevent a disease. **Lesson 21**

9. _____ is the amount of blood the heart pumps with each beat. **Lesson 23**

10. A _____ is an exercise in which a force acts against muscles. **Lesson 24**

The Responsible Decision-Making Model™

Tonight is the final soccer game of the season. You have an injury. Your parents or guardian take you to a physician and stay in the waiting room. Your physician diagnoses a shin splint and advises you not to play in the game. Your parents or guardian did not hear this advice. You consider taking several painkillers and playing anyway. Answer the following questions on a separate sheet of paper. Write "Does not apply" if a question does not apply to this situation.

1. Is it healthful for you to ignore the advice of your physician? Why or why not?

2. Is it safe for you to ignore the advice of your physician? Why or why not?

3. Is it legal (does it follow school guidelines for sports participation) if you ignore the advice of your physician? Why or why not?

4. Will you show respect for your physician if you ignore his or her advice? Why or why not?

5. Will your parents or guardian approve if you ignore the advice of your physician? Why or why not?

6. Will you demonstrate good character if you ignore the advice of your physician? Why or why not?

What is the responsible decision to make in this situation?

Health Literacy

Effective Communication

Imagine that you are a coach for one of the sports teams offered at your school. Write a short speech to give at the first team meeting. Emphasize ways to demonstrate good character during sports participation. Refer to pages 240–241 in Lesson 25.

Self-Directed Learning

Obtain permission from your parents or guardian to visit a workout facility in your community. List the kinds of equipment available at the facility. Next to each piece of equipment you list, identify the fitness benefit you might get from its use.

Critical Thinking

Prepare a pamphlet on training to be given for people who are beginning to use a fitness facility. Illustrate the training zone. Explain the risks of too much overload and not enough overload.

Responsible Citizenship

Suppose you or a friend has a physical disability. Identify the physical disability. Then make a list of three physical activities in which you could participate together.

Multicultural Health

Investigate your favorite Olympic sport. What countries participate in this sport? What facilities for training are available in these countries?

Family Involvement

Design a Top Ten List of Physical Activities in Which Our Family Can Participate Together. Have other family members help you rank order the physical activities.

UNIT 6
Alcohol, Tobacco, and Other Drugs

PRACTICE

HEALTH STANDARD 6

Make Responsible Decisions

Practice this standard at the end of this unit.

Situation: You are at a friend's home and your friend wants you to try smoking a cigarette.

1. **Describe the situation that requires a decision.**

2. **List possible decisions you might make.**

3. **Share the list of possible decisions with a trusted adult.** Write the name of a trusted adult with whom you could share the list.

4. **Evaluate the consequences of each decision.** Suppose you choose to smoke the cigarette. Ask yourself the following questions. Will this decision result in actions that:

• are healthful?
• are safe?
• are legal?
• show respect for myself and others?
• follow the guidelines of responsible adults, such as my parents or guardian?
• demonstrate good character?

5. **Decide which decision is responsible and most appropriate.** Write what you will decide.

6. **Act on your decision and evaluate the results.**

What to Know About Drugs

Life Skills

- ◆ I will follow guidelines for the safe use of prescription and OTC drugs.
- ◆ I will not misuse or abuse drugs.
- ◆ I will be aware of resources for the treatment of drug misuse and abuse.

A **drug** is a substance other than food that changes the way the body or mind functions. A **prescription drug** is a medicine that can be legally obtained only with a prescription. An **over-the-counter drug** or OTC drug is a drug that can be purchased from a legal source without a prescription. It is very important that you follow guidelines for responsible drug use.

The Lesson Objectives

- Explain the difference between responsible drug use and wrong drug use.
- Discuss six kinds of drugs.
- Identify guidelines for the responsible use of prescription drugs.
- Identify guidelines for the responsible use of OTC drugs.
- Discuss signs that a teen misuses or abuses drugs.
- Discuss treatment and recovery for people who abuse drugs and their families.

Vocabulary

drug

prescription drug

over-the-counter (OTC) drug

responsible drug use

drug misuse

drug abuse

illegal drug use

prescription

pharmacist

side effect

tamper-resistant package

indication for use

drug dependence

physical dependence

tolerance

withdrawal symptoms

psychological dependence

overdose

denial

formal intervention

outpatient care

inpatient care

What Is Responsible Drug Use?

You probably have taken a prescription drug for an illness, such as flu. You might have used an OTC drug, such as aspirin. **Responsible drug use** is the correct use of legal drugs to promote health and well-being. Both prescription drugs and OTC drugs are legal drugs. The term "drug use" commonly refers to wrong drug use. Wrong drug use includes the following:

- **Drug misuse** is the incorrect use of a prescription or OTC drug.
- **Drug abuse** is the intentional use of a drug when no medical or health reasons exist.
- **Illegal drug use** is the wrong use, possession, manufacture, or sale of controlled drugs, and the use, possession, manufacture, or sale of illegal drugs.

Different Kinds of Legal Drugs

Analgesics

Analgesics are drugs that relieve minor to moderate pain.

Cold remedies

Cold remedies are drugs that relieve cold symptoms.

Antitussives

Antitussives are drugs that relieve coughing.

Sedative hypnotics

Sedative hypnotics are a group of drugs that slow down the nervous system.

Antacids

Antacids are drugs that relieve indigestion.

Antibiotics

Antibiotics are drugs that treat infections caused by bacteria.

What Are Guidelines for the Responsible Use of Prescription Drugs?

A prescription drug is a medicine that can be legally obtained only with a prescription. A **prescription** is a written order from a licensed health professional. A **pharmacist** is a health professional who is licensed to prepare and sell prescription drugs.

Perhaps you have taken prescription drugs when you were ill or recovering from surgery. For example, you might have taken penicillin for an infection. Some prescription drugs are taken for chronic health conditions. For example, anti-asthmatic drugs help with breathing. Teens who have asthma might have to carry an inhaler to dispense the drug. Amphetamines might be prescribed by a physician for teens with Attention Deficit Disorder.

Both misuse and abuse of prescription drugs are risky. Suppose a teen takes a prescription drug after the expiration date on the label has passed. The teen can become ill from the effects of the drug. Suppose a teen takes a friend's anti-asthmatic drug. The teen can develop an irregular heartbeat.

Guidelines for the Responsible Use of Prescription Drugs

1. Follow the directions for use given by your physician. Your physician will tell you when and how often to take the drug. You might need to take the drug with meals or with water. Pay attention to any warnings about side effects that might cause injury. A **side effect** is an unwanted body change. If a side effect of a drug is drowsiness, for example, do not play contact sports or operate machinery such as a lawn mower.

2. Contact your physician if you experience any unexpected side effects of a drug.

3. Do not stop taking the drug because you start to feel better.

4. Ask a physician before taking more than one drug at a time.

5. Follow the directions for storing the drug.

6. Keep prescription drugs out of the reach of children.

7. Do not take prescription drugs that appear to have been tampered with.

8. Do not take a drug prescribed for another person.

9. Do not use prescription drugs past the expiration date on the label.

10. Flush down the toilet prescription drugs that no longer are needed.

What Are Guidelines for the Responsible Use of OTC Drugs?

An over-the-counter (OTC) drug is a drug that can be purchased from a legal source without a prescription. OTC drugs are taken to relieve symptoms of an illness. OTC drugs can be purchased in stores. OTC drugs include cold medications, antacids, and aspirin. A physician or pharmacist can recommend an appropriate OTC drug if you have questions.

Both misuse and abuse of OTC drugs can be risky. Suppose a teen who is trying to stay awake at night takes more than the recommended dose of an OTC caffeine pill. The teen might develop a headache and stomachache. OTC drugs can be abused. Suppose a teen who is trying to lose weight takes laxatives for a period of time. This teen can develop digestive problems and colon damage.

Guidelines for the Responsible Use of OTC Drugs

1. Obtain permission from a parent or guardian before using an OTC drug.

2. Ask a pharmacist or physician if you have questions about the use of an OTC drug.

3. Do not take an OTC drug if the package has been opened or is broken. All OTC drugs are placed in tamper-resistant packaging. A **tamper-resistant package** is a package that is sealed for safety.

4. Use an OTC drug only for its indication for use. **Indication for use** is a symptom or condition for which an OTC drug should be used.

5. Follow the directions for use on the label. Pay attention to any warnings.

6. Do not participate in activities in which you can be injured if drowsiness is a side effect of the drug. For example, do not ride a bicycle, play a contact sport such as football, or operate machinery while using the OTC drug.

7. Stop using an OTC drug if you experience any unexpected side effects, and contact a physician.

8. Do not take more than one OTC drug at a time without telling a physician.

9. Do not take more than the recommended dose.

10. Do not use old OTC drugs. Check the expiration date. OTC drugs can become harmful or ineffective over periods of time.

What Are Signs That a Teen Is Misusing or Abusing Drugs?

Read through the list of Twenty Warning Signs of Teen Drug Misuse and Abuse. These signs are serious. Drug misuse and abuse can lead to drug dependence. **Drug dependence** is the compelling need to take a drug even though it harms the body, mind, and relationships. Drug dependence also is known as drug addiction and being "hooked" on drugs.

Physical dependence is repeated drug use that causes tolerance. **Tolerance** is a condition in which the body becomes used to a substance. Suppose a person has developed tolerance to a drug. The person needs more and more of the drug to get the same feeling. A person who has a physical dependence on a drug might experience withdrawal symptoms. **Withdrawal symptoms** are unpleasant reactions experienced when drug use is stopped. Withdrawal symptoms can include nausea, vomiting, fatigue, stomach cramps, depression, shaking, and thoughts of suicide. **Psychological dependence** is a desire for a drug for emotional reasons. For example, a person might feel the need to smoke a cigarette when (s)he is stressed.

Twenty Warning Signs of Teen Drug Misuse and Abuse

1. Lying about using drugs
2. Hanging out with people who use drugs
3. Giving up friends who do not use drugs
4. Having glassy eyes and slurred speech
5. Having a runny nose
6. Having shaky hands
7. Having bloodshot eyes
8. Having changes in weight and appetite
9. Acting sluggish
10. Acting jittery
11. Skipping grooming
12. Wearing drug-related clothing
13. Having mood swings
14. Keeping secrets from family members
15. Getting poor grades in school
16. Getting into trouble
17. Skipping school
18. Joining a gang
19. Requesting money without explanation
20. Showing no interest in activities

Activity

Special Report: Drug Misuse and Abuse Is Risky to Health

Life Skill: I will not misuse or abuse drugs.

Materials: paper, pen or pencil, newspapers or magazines, or Internet access

Directions: Review the list of possible consequences of using drugs. Remember that using drugs is risky. Even trying a drug just one time is risky.

Possible Consequences of Drug Misuse and Abuse

Overdose To **overdose** is to take an excess amount. A drug overdose can cause illness and death. A drug overdose can occur the first time a drug is taken.

Difficult relationships Drugs change the way people act and think. People who use drugs might behave in cruel ways to friends and family members.

Violence and crime Most murders and abuse occur when people are under the influence of drugs. People who are under the influence of drugs are more likely to steal and damage property. Most people who have committed suicide were under the influence of drugs.

Accidents Drugs affect judgment and coordination. People cannot think clearly when they are under the influence of drugs. Most fatal motor vehicle accidents involve a driver who is under the influence of drugs.

HIV and STDs Teens who use drugs often do not make responsible decisions about their sexual behavior. They might have sex and become infected with HIV or other STDs.

Drug dependence People who use drugs even one time can become drug-dependent. People who are drug-dependent focus their energy on obtaining and using drugs.

1. **Select one of the consequences of drug misuse and abuse.**

2. **Pretend you are a newspaper reporter.** You are asked to cover a late-breaking story. A teen has used drugs and experienced the consequence you selected. Your job is to interview a family member of the teen. The family member requested the interview to warn other teens that drug misuse and abuse is risky.

3. **Write a pretend interview with the family member.** Include at least three reasons why it is risky for teens to misuse or abuse drugs.

What Are Treatment Options for People Who Abuse Drugs and Their Families?

Most people who abuse drugs do not seek treatment on their own. They often are in denial. **Denial** is refusing to admit there is a problem. Family members or friends might need to help them get treatment.

Formal intervention is an action by people who want a person to get treatment for a problem. A trained counselor can help family members and friends confront the person. Together they can discuss the person's harmful actions and discuss why they want the person to get treatment. They can make plans for the person to enter treatment. Family members usually need counseling, too.

There are many treatment options for a person who abuses drugs. A teen who wants to get help for drug abuse should talk to a parent, guardian, school counselor, or teacher. The adult will help the teen find appropriate treatment options. **Outpatient care** is treatment that does not require overnight stay at a facility. **Inpatient care** is treatment that requires overnight stay at a facility. After treatment, a person who has abused drugs might get involved in a recovery program. Some examples include Alateen, Alcoholics Anonymous, and Narcotics Anonymous.

Do You Misuse or Abuse Drugs?

1. Do you take large amounts of a drug for no medical reason?

2. Have you taken a drug for a longer period of time than it was prescribed?

3. Have you developed tolerance to a drug?

4. Do you experience withdrawal symptoms when you stop using a drug you are taking?

5. Have you tried to stop using a drug with no success?

6. Do you spend time trying to get a drug that is not prescribed for you?

7. Do you spend most of your time planning future drug use?

8. Do you spend lots of time recovering from a hangover or other effects of a drug?

9. Do you give up activities, such as school clubs or sports, to make it easier to use drugs?

10. Do you continue to use a drug even though it is causing you problems?

You are misusing or abusing drugs if you answered "yes" to any of these questions. You might be drug-dependent if you answered "yes" to three or more of these questions. You need to obtain treatment.

Adapted from the *Diagnostic and Statistical Manual of Mental Health Disorders*, 4th Edition. American Psychiatric Association. Washington, D.C. 1994. p. 181.

Vocabulary Words

Write a separate sentence using each vocabulary word listed on page 248.

Health Content

1. What is the difference between responsible drug use and wrong drug use? **page 249**

2. What are ten guidelines for the responsible use of prescription drugs? **page 250**

3. What are ten guidelines for the responsible use of OTC drugs? **page 251**

4. What are 20 warning signs that a teen is misusing or abusing drugs? **page 252**

5. What are treatment options for people who abuse drugs and their families? **page 254**

The Responsible Decision-Making Model™

You have a terrible headache. Your father has been prescribed painkillers while he is recovering from surgery. You consider taking one for your headache. Answer the following questions on a separate sheet of paper. Write "Does not apply" if a question does not apply to this situation.

1. Is it healthful to take your father's prescription painkillers? Why or why not?

2. Is it safe to take your father's prescription painkillers? Why or why not?

3. Is it legal to take your father's prescription painkillers? Why or why not?

4. Will you show respect for yourself and others if you take your father's prescription painkillers? Why or why not?

5. Will your parents or guardian approve if you take your father's prescription painkillers? Why or why not?

6. Will you demonstrate good character if you take your father's prescription painkillers? Why or why not?

What is the responsible decision to make in this situation?

Health Literacy

Critical Thinking

Why might a person who is drug-dependent become angry during a formal intervention? Why is it important for this person to receive treatment even if (s)he resists?

Responsible Citizenship

Write a 30-second PSA for the radio to inform parents or guardians of signs that their teens might be using drugs. If possible, tape the PSA. Obtain permission to submit the PSA to a local radio station.

How to Resist Drug Misuse and Abuse and Protect Society

Life Skills

- ◆ I will choose a drug-free lifestyle to reduce my risk of violence and accidents.
- ◆ I will choose a drug-free lifestyle to reduce my risk of HIV, STDs, and unwanted pregnancy.
- ◆ I will practice protective factors that help me stay away from drugs.
- ◆ I will use resistance skills if I am pressured to misuse or abuse drugs.

Vocabulary

drug trafficking

rape

drug slipping

injection drug use

protective factor

self-respect

resistance skills

resilient

drug-free role model

enabler

codependence

honest talk

Harmful drug use increases the risk of violence and accidents and is a threat to society. Teens involved in harmful drug use can get a criminal record for choosing illegal behavior. They can become infected with HIV and other STDs. Teens who become pregnant often are under the influence of drugs when they decide to have sex. Protect yourself and society by resisting drug misuse and abuse.

The Lesson Objectives

- Explain why harmful drug use increases the risk of accidents and violence.
- Identify ways to prevent drug slipping.
- Explain why harmful drug use increases the risk of HIV, STDs, and unwanted pregnancy.
- Discuss protective factors that will help you stay away from drugs.
- Outline resistance skills you can use if you are pressured to use drugs.
- Discuss ways you can keep from being an enabler.

The term "drug use" in this lesson refers to drug misuse and abuse.

Why Does Drug Use Increase the Risk of Accidents and Violence?

Warning: Teens who use drugs are at higher risk of being injured or killed in an accident than are other teens.

Drugs change the way people think and behave. Teens who use drugs do not think clearly. Drugs dull the senses and affect coordination. Suppose a teen drinks alcohol. This teen ordinarily might know that swimming across a lake after drinking is risky. However, the alcohol affects the teen's thinking. The teen might think that other people might be affected by alcohol but that (s)he can swim across the lake. The teen drowns.

Drugs affect judgment. Teens who use drugs do not use good judgment or make responsible decisions. They take risks they would not usually take. Suppose a teen who has been using drugs is dared by other teens to take a risky action. This teen might take the dare and be injured.

Using drugs increases the risk of injury or death from:

- **Motor vehicle accidents**
- **Pedestrian accidents**
- **Boating accidents**
- **Drowning**
- **Fires**
- **Falls**

Warning: Teens who use drugs are at higher risk of being involved in violence than are other teens.

A crime is a violation of the law. Drug use is illegal. Teens who use drugs are committing a crime. Under the influence of drugs, some teens commit additional crimes. This happens because some drugs can cause teens to become aggressive and violent. Other drugs cause teens to become depressed. Teens who use these drugs are at increased risk for attempting suicide. Teens who are drug-dependent might steal or harm others to obtain the drugs they need.

Drug trafficking is the illegal production, distribution, sales, and purchase of drugs. People involved in drug trafficking are at very high risk of being involved in violence. People who are involved in drug trafficking often carry weapons to protect their territory and their drugs. Teens who use drugs increase their risk of being around people involved in drug trafficking.

Using drugs increases the risk of being involved in:

- **Murder**
- **Suicide**
- **Theft**
- **Abuse**
- **Rape**

Why Does Drug Use Increase the Risk of Rape?

Rape is the threatened or actual use of physical force to get someone to have sex without giving consent. Rape is illegal. Rape is a form of violence. Teens who use drugs are at increased risk of being raped or raping someone.

Teens who use drugs take risks they usually would not take. For example, a teen female might accept a ride with a male she does not know and risk being raped. Teens who have been using drugs become aggressive. For example, a teen male might not control his behavior and might force a female to have sex when she has said NO.

Suppose you do not use drugs, but the people around you do. You are at increased risk for drug slipping. **Drug slipping** is placing a drug into someone's food or beverage without that person's knowledge. Drug slipping is illegal. Suppose a person slips a drug into a teen's drink and the teen dies from the effects of the drug. The person who slipped the drug can be charged with homicide. There are certain drugs that are known as "date rape drugs." These drugs include "roofies," GHB, and "ecstasy." These drugs cause sleepiness and some memory loss. A teen male might slip such a drug into a female's drink and commit rape after she passes out.

Teens who have been slipped a drug might feel dizzy, sleepy, or "out of it." Teens who think they have been slipped a drug should call a parent, guardian, or other trusted adult immediately. They should call 911 and be taken to an emergency room immediately. They should bring a sample of the food or beverage with them for the police.

Ways to Protect Yourself from Drug Slipping

1. Always keep your food and beverage in sight.
2. Serve your own food or beverage when possible.
3. Don't accept a drink in an open container from someone you do not know.
4. Avoid situations where there is teen drug use.
5. Call your parent or guardian immediately if you suspect drug use.

Why Does Drug Use Increase the Risk of HIV, STDs, and Unwanted Pregnancy?

Teens who use drugs are at increased risk of becoming infected with HIV and pathogens that cause other STDs. They are at increased risk of becoming pregnant or getting someone pregnant.

Teens who use drugs might have faulty thinking. For example, they might not stick to the decision they made to practice abstinence. Teens who have sex often are under the influence at the time. They risk becoming infected with HIV and other STDs. They might get pregnant or get someone pregnant. More than half of all teens who become pregnant report they had been drinking before they had sex.

Teens who use drugs are at increased risk for rape. Under the influence of drugs, a teen can be raped and risks becoming pregnant. The person who commits the rape risks becoming infected with HIV and other STDs. The person who is raped risks becoming infected with HIV and other STDs.

Teens who inject drugs might share a needle with infected blood on it. **Injection drug use** is drug use that involves injecting drugs into the body. A needle or a syringe is used to inject the drugs. Suppose a needle or syringe has been used by a teen who is infected with HIV. Droplets of blood infected with HIV will get on the needle. If other teens use that needle, droplets of infected blood will enter their bodies. They will become infected with HIV. For example, teammates might share a needle to inject steroids. If one teammate is infected with HIV, other teammates who use the same needle can become infected with HIV.

The term "drug use" in this lesson refers to drug misuse and abuse.

What Protective Factors Will Help Me Stay Away from Drugs?

A **protective factor** is something that increases the chance of a positive outcome. There are protective factors to help you avoid drugs. Make a decision to work on gaining as many protective factors as possible.

The term "drug use" in this lesson refers to drug misuse and abuse.

Ten Protective Factors to Help You Stay Away from Drugs

1. **Having self-respect** Self-respect is a high regard for oneself because one behaves in responsible ways. Teens who respect themselves make responsible decisions. They take care of their health and protect their safety by avoiding drugs.

2. **Using resistance skills** Resistance skills are skills that are used to say NO to an action or to leave a situation. Teens who use resistance skills do not give in to pressure to use drugs.

3. **Having friends who do not misuse or abuse drugs** Teens whose friends do not use drugs experience less pressure to try drugs.

4. **Being resilient** To be **resilient** (ri·ZIL·yuhnt) is to bounce back and learn from misfortune or change. A teen who is resilient does not turn to harmful behaviors, such as drug use, to try to make a difficult situation better.

5. **Having healthful family relationships** Teens who are close to family members are encouraged and have the support to make responsible decisions about drug use.

6. **Having social skills** Teens who have social skills have the ability to make and keep friends. They do not believe the only way they can "fit in" is to use drugs.

7. **Having goals** Teens who have set goals for themselves know that drug use will interfere with their plans. They avoid drugs to achieve their goals.

8. **Having stress management skills** Teens who manage their stress in healthful ways know that drug use would add stress to their lives. They do not turn to drugs when they are stressed out.

9. **Having anger management skills** Teens who manage their anger in healthful ways know that drugs can make them more angry and even violent. They do not turn to drugs when they are angry.

10. **Being involved in school activities and physical activities** Teens who are involved in school activities and physical activities have less free time. They do not have time to become bored and turn to drugs. They know they might get kicked out of school activities or off of sports teams if they use drugs.

Activity

Health Behavior Contract

Copy the health behavior contract on a separate sheet of paper.

DO NOT WRITE IN THIS BOOK.

Name:_____ **Date:**_____

Life Skill: I will practice protective factors that help me stay away from drugs.

Effect on My Health: Using drugs is harmful to health. Drug use puts me at risk for violence and accidents. Drug use puts me at risk for becoming infected with HIV and other STDs. Drug use harms relationships. It is illegal for me to use drugs.

My Plan: One protective factor for drug use is "Being involved in school activities and physical activities." I will identify one new way I can practice this protective factor. For example, I might select a new after-school sports team to join. Or I might work out before school. I will complete a calendar for two weeks. On my calendar I will write down the school and physical activities in which I participated.

My Calendar	M	T	W	Th	F	S	S

How My Plan Worked: (Complete after one week)_____

_____

_____

How Can I Resist Pressure to Use Drugs?

Teens who use drugs might pressure you to try drugs. They do not care about your health or your safety. Their reasons are selfish. Use resistance skills if you are pressured to use drugs.

The term "drug use" in this lesson refers to drug misuse and abuse.

Why Teens Might Pressure You to Use Drugs

1. **They want support for their wrong actions.** They think that if you use drugs with them their behavior will not seem as wrong. If they get in trouble, they know they will not be alone. You will get in trouble, too.

2. **They know drugs affect judgment.** Teens who pressure you to use drugs might want you to take risks they know you would not normally take. For example, a teen male might pressure a teen female to drink alcohol and have sex. He knows drinking alcohol can affect her decision to stick to abstinence.

3. **They want to make money in an illegal way.** Teens who use drugs might sell drugs to other teens. The more teens they convince to use drugs, the more money they make. Teens who sell drugs know that it is easy to get hooked on drugs. They often target younger teens. They know that the younger teens look up to them and might give in to the pressure.

Ways Teens Pressure Other Teens to Use Drugs

You might face peer pressure to use drugs. Teens who pressure you to use drugs use pressure tactics such as the following.

PRESSURE TACTICS

How do you know if you don't try?

Don't miss out on the fun.

You look stressed out. It will make you relax. Don't be a baby.

Use Resistance Skills If You Are Pressured to Use Drugs

1. **Say NO to drug use with confidence.** Look directly at the person to whom you are speaking. Say NO in a firm voice. Be confident because you are being responsible.

2. **Give reasons for saying NO to drug use.** Say that drug use is illegal, harmful, and unsafe.

3. **Be certain your behavior matches your words.** Do not do anything that shows you approve of drug use.
   - Do not pretend to sip a beer.
   - Do not pretend to try a drug.
   - Do not hold drugs for someone else.
   - Do not wear clothing with drug-related items on them.

4. **Avoid being in situations where there will be drug use.** Do not attend parties where there is teen drug use. Leave a situation immediately if there is teen drug use.

5. **Avoid being with peers who use drugs.** Choose friends who do not use drugs. They will not pressure you to use drugs.

6. **Abide by laws.** Remember that teen drug use is illegal. Teens who use drugs can be arrested.

7. **Influence others to make responsible decisions rather than wrong decisions.** Be a drug-free role model. A **drug-free role model** is a person who does not misuse or abuse drugs and encourages others to be drug-free.

Having a bad day? This will take your pain away.

Don't make a big deal over nothing. Just take it.

It's not like one time will kill you.

PRESSURE TACTICS

You won't get hooked if you are in control of yourself.

Hey, come join us. We're going out for a smoke.

This will give you courage to go talk to her.

Don't make trouble for the rest of us. Do you want to lose your friends?

How Can I Keep from Being an Enabler?

An **enabler** is a person who supports the harmful behavior of another person. People who are enablers often have codependence. **Codependence** is a mental disorder in which a person denies feelings and copes in harmful ways. Teens who have family members or friends who misuse or abuse drugs might be enablers. They might support the harmful drug use of another person.

Four Ways an Enabler Supports Harmful Drug Use

1. **An enabler denies the person's harmful drug use.** For example, an enabler might make excuses for a parent who misses a school event because of drug use.

2. **An enabler covers up for the person's harmful drug use.** For example, an enabler might clean up and hide empty bottles after a sibling has passed out from drinking.

3. **An enabler makes excuses for the person's harmful drug use.** For example, an enabler might tell siblings that a parent is stressed out and drugs are helping to ease the stress.

4. **An enabler encourages the person's harmful drug use.** For example, an enabler might offer a cigarette to a person who is hooked on nicotine.

Four Ways to Keep from Being an Enabler

1. **Use honest talk to confront a person about wrong behavior. Honest talk** is the open sharing of feelings. Do not hide your feelings about a person's wrong behavior. Be honest even if the person will become angry or upset.

2. **Do not take responsibility for another person's problems.** You are not responsible for another person's wrong behavior. For example, it is faulty thinking to believe, "My mom takes drugs because I make her stressed." You cannot control another person's actions.

3. **Do not try to "rescue" another person.** Do not try to fix another person's problems. If another person thinks you will come to his or her rescue, the person will not change his or her behavior. Obtain professional help if you constantly try to rescue others.

4. **Obtain professional help.** Get professional help for the person who misuses or abuses drugs. Remember, you are NOT a therapist or a physician. A family member or friend who misuses or abuses drugs needs medical help and counseling.

Vocabulary Words

Write a separate sentence using each vocabulary word listed on page 256.

Health Content

1. Why does drug use increase the risk of accidents and violence? Of rape? **pages 257–258**

2. Why does drug use increase the risk of HIV, STDs, and unwanted pregnancy? **page 259**

3. What protective factors can help you stay away from drugs? **page 260**

4. How can you resist pressure to use drugs? **pages 262–263**

5. How can you keep from being an enabler? **page 264**

The Responsible Decision-Making Model™

Your neighbor who is in high school invites you over to hang out with his friends. He introduces you around and tells his friends you are "cool." One of his friends offers you a beer. Should you accept the beer? Answer the following questions on a separate sheet of paper. Write "Does not apply" if a question does not apply to this situation.

1. Is it healthful to accept the beer? Why or why not?

2. Is it safe to accept the beer? Why or why not?

3. Is it legal to accept the beer? Why or why not?

4. Will you show respect for yourself and others if you accept the beer? Why or why not?

5. Will you follow the guidelines of your parents or guardian if you accept the beer? Why or why not?

6. Will you demonstrate good character if you accept the beer? Why or why not?

What is the responsible decision to make in this situation?

Health Literacy

Responsible Citizenship

Suppose your friend has accepted a date from an older teen. (S)he says (s)he is nervous. She plans to drink alcohol before the date to relax. Write a brief essay explaining why using drugs increases the risk of HIV, STDs, and unwanted pregnancy.

Self-Directed Learning

At your school or community library, look up information about the dangers of drug slipping. Design a poster that includes the information you found and emphasizes ways to protect against drug slipping.

How to Resist Pressure to Use Tobacco

Life Skill

◆ I will avoid tobacco use and secondhand smoke.

Tobacco use is the leading preventable cause of premature death in the United States. Yet, 3,000 children and teens begin smoking every day. **Tobacco** is a plant that contains nicotine. **Smokeless tobacco** is tobacco that is chewed. According to the Centers for Disease Control and Prevention (CDC), more people die each year from smoking-related causes than die from motor vehicle accidents, drugs, STDs, and homicides combined.

The Lesson Objectives

• Explain why it is risky to use tobacco even one time.

• Discuss the reasons why you should avoid smoking.

• Discuss the reasons why you should avoid breathing second-hand smoke.

• Identify ways you can avoid breathing secondhand smoke.

• Discuss reasons why you should avoid the use of smokeless tobacco.

• Outline resistance skills you can use if you are pressured to use tobacco products.

• Evaluate ways the media promote the use of tobacco products.

• Identify places that offer tobacco cessation programs.

Vocabulary

tobacco

smokeless tobacco

nicotine

drug dependence

tar

carbon monoxide

cilia

emphysema

fetal smoking syndrome

secondhand smoke

sidestream smoke

carcinogen

sudden infant death syndrome (SIDS)

snuff

nicotine patch

tobacco cessation program

Why Is It Risky to Use Tobacco Even One Time?

Tobacco products contain nicotine and thousands of other substances. **Nicotine** is an addictive stimulant drug found in tobacco. When a person smokes a cigarette, (s)he inhales nicotine. When a person chews smokeless tobacco, nicotine enters the bloodstream through the lining of the mouth. Within seconds, the nicotine enters the brain and produces a "high." It increases heart rate and blood pressure.

A teen who uses tobacco can become addicted or drug-dependent right away. **Drug dependence** is the compelling need to take a drug even though it harms the body, mind, and relationships. People who are addicted or dependent on nicotine feel a craving for more nicotine. They are obsessed with having their next cigarette or smokeless tobacco "chew." They have withdrawal symptoms if they try to quit. Withdrawal symptoms include headaches, mood swings, drowsiness, restlessness, and short temper. Many teens do not realize they are addicted until they try to quit. Teens who are addicted to nicotine need help if they want to quit using tobacco products.

Nicotine is as addictive as alcohol and cocaine.

The FDA regulation states that it is prohibited to sell cigarettes and smokeless tobacco to people under the age of 18. Retail stores are required to examine the identification of any customer under the age of 27 who wishes to buy cigarettes, loose cigarette tobacco, or smokeless tobacco. *Food and Drug Administration Talk Papers, T9740.*

Why Should
I Avoid Smoking?

Each time a person smokes a cigarette, more than 400 poisonous substances enter his or her body. Cigarettes contain many harmful chemicals in addition to nicotine. **Tar** is a sticky fluid that is formed when tobacco is burned. Tar accumulates in the lungs. **Carbon monoxide** is an odorless, colorless, poisonous gas. Carbon monoxide reduces the amount of oxygen in the blood and increases the heart rate.

Ingredients in tobacco smoke can paralyze cilia. **Cilia** (SI·lee·uh) are tiny hairs that line the air passages. Cilia cannot filter out dirt and germs if they are damaged by tobacco smoke. The lungs of teens who smoke do not grow to full size. These teens have shortness of breath and fits of wheezing and coughing.

Health risks associated with smoking include:

- **Cancer** Smoking increases the risk of lung cancer and cancer of the mouth, esophagus (i·SAH·fuh·guhs), larynx (LAR·inks), kidneys, and bladder.

- **Emphysema** Emphysema (EMP·fuh·ZEE·muh) is a condition in which the air sacs in the lungs become damaged. People who have emphysema have difficulty breathing. Breathing becomes very painful.

- **Heart disease** Tobacco use increases the heart rate and causes plaque to stick to artery walls. This increases the risk of atherosclerosis (A·thuh·ROH·skluh·ROH·suhs), a disease in which fat deposits on artery walls.

- **Stroke** Nicotine causes an increase in blood pressure. This increases the risk of a stroke, which is caused by a broken blood vessel in the brain.

- **Frequent colds**
- **Smoker's cough**
- **Ulcers**
- **Cavities**
- **Bronchitis**
- **Dulled sense of smell and taste**
- **Worsened allergies**
- **Headaches**
- **Osteoporosis**
- **Worsened asthma**
(AHS·tee·oh·puh·ROH·suhs)

YUCK! Teens who smoke have bad breath, yellow teeth, and yellow fingernails. They have runny noses, scratchy throats, and dull skin and hair. Their clothes and hair smell like smoke.

Fetal smoking syndrome is the presence of birth defects in a baby born to a mother who smokes cigarettes during her pregnancy. A mother-to-be who smokes increases her risk of having a premature birth and a baby who has a low birth weight.

WARNING: Cigar Use Harms Health
According to a study by the CDC, one in four teens ages 14 to 19 smoked at least one cigar in the past year. Teens who believe cigar smoking is harmless are wrong. One cigar contains more nicotine and 15 times as much tobacco as one cigarette. Cigar use can cause cancer of the lungs, mouth, and larynx.

Why Should I Avoid Breathing Secondhand Smoke?

Secondhand smoke is sidestream smoke and smoke that a person exhales while smoking. **Sidestream smoke** is smoke that is given off by a burning cigarette, pipe, or cigar. Secondhand smoke also is called environmental tobacco smoke.

The Environmental Protection Agency (EPA) has classified secondhand smoke as a class A carcinogen. A **carcinogen** (kar·SI·nuh·juhn) is a substance that causes cancer. Sitting in a nonsmoking space reduces your risk of breathing secondhand smoke. *However, you still inhale secondhand smoke if you sit in a nonsmoking section near the smoking section.*

Breathing secondhand smoke causes your heart rate and blood pressure to increase. Breathing secondhand smoke increases your risk of developing:

- **Lung cancer**
- **Colds**
- **Chronic cough**
- **Worsened asthma**
- **Sore throats**
- **Ear infections**
- **Pneumonia**
- **Reddened, watery eyes**

Current studies are investigating secondhand smoke as a cause of sudden infant death syndrome. **Sudden infant death syndrome (SIDS)** is the sudden, unexpected death of a seemingly healthy infant.

Ways to Avoid Breathing Secondhand Smoke

- Avoid being around people who are smoking.
- Ask people who are smoking around you to stop. Be assertive.
- Select restaurants and other places that have nonsmoking policies.
- Sit in nonsmoking sections as far away from the smoking section as possible.
- Encourage teens who smoke to quit.
- Encourage your family to have a "no smoking" policy in your home and automobile(s).

Why Should I Avoid the Use of Smokeless Tobacco?

Smokeless tobacco is tobacco that is chewed. A person who chews tobacco places a wad near the cheek or between the lower lip and gums. (S)he chews the wad and spits out the excess tobacco juice. **Snuff** is a tobacco product that is placed between the cheek and gums. A small amount, called a pinch, is held between the lip or cheek and gums. Manufacturers of smokeless tobacco try to make it more appealing by adding flavoring, such as cherry or mint. Some baseball players and rodeo stars use smokeless tobacco. However, most athletes and rodeo stars do not.

Myth: Using smokeless tobacco is less dangerous than smoking cigarettes or cigars. Using smokeless tobacco can be deadly. Nicotine in smokeless tobacco is an addictive drug. Nicotine increases heart rate and blood pressure. This increases the risk of heart disease and stroke. The ingredients in smokeless tobacco increase the risk of several cancers. Teens who use smokeless tobacco can develop oral cancer right away. And smokeless tobacco is costly. One pack costs approximately $3 to $3.50.

The FDA regulation states that it is prohibited to sell smokeless tobacco to people under the age of 18. *Food and Drug Administration Talk Papers, T9740.*

Risks Associated with Smokeless Tobacco

- Bad breath
- Black and hairy tongue
- Permanently stained teeth
- Tooth loss
- Ground down teeth
- Cavities in teeth
- Ulcers on the gums
- Cancer of the gums
- Cancer of the tongue
- Increased heart rate
- Increased blood pressure
- Heart disease

Quit NOW if you use smokeless tobacco.

How Can I Resist Pressure to Use Tobacco?

1. **Say NO to tobacco use with confidence.** Look directly at the person to whom you are speaking. Say NO in a firm voice. Be confident, because you are being responsible.

2. **Give reasons for saying NO to tobacco use.** Say:
   - **NO.** I want to protect my health.
   - **NO.** I do not want people who are near me to inhale secondhand smoke.
   - **NO.** I want to obey my parents or guardian.
   - **NO.** I do not want to get kicked off an athletic team.
   - **NO.** I do not want to waste money.
   - **NO.** I do not want to be addicted to nicotine.
   - **NO.** I do not want yellow teeth and yellow fingernails.
   - **NO.** I do not want my clothes and hair to smell like smoke.

3. **Be certain your behavior matches your words.** Do not do anything that shows you approve of tobacco use.
   - Do not pretend to puff a cigarette.
   - Do not pretend to chew or dip tobacco.
   - Do not keep cigarettes for someone else.
   - Do not wear clothing with tobacco-related logos or brand names.

4. **Avoid being in situations where you will inhale secondhand smoke.** Secondhand smoke is harmful to your health. If possible, leave a situation where there is tobacco use. Sit in nonsmoking sections of restaurants and public places.

5. **Avoid being with teens who use tobacco and pressure you to use tobacco.** Choose friends who do not use tobacco. They will not pressure you to smoke cigarettes or use smokeless tobacco.

6. **Resist pressure to do anything illegal.** Do not purchase tobacco. The FDA bans sales of cigarettes and smokeless tobacco to people under the age of 18.

7. **Influence others to make responsible decisions about tobacco use.** Educate others about the risks of tobacco use. Encourage other teens to avoid tobacco use or to quit if they use tobacco.

How Do the Media Promote the Use of Tobacco Products?

You probably have seen movies and TV shows in which the characters smoke cigarettes. You probably have seen pictures in magazines of actors and actresses puffing on cigars and cigarettes. You probably have seen baseball players chew and spit smokeless tobacco. You might think that if *they* do it, using smokeless tobacco must be cool. You might think that if the media show it, using smokeless tobacco must be glamorous. WRONG. Some teens copy the behavior of celebrities. They copy their hairstyles, clothing, and language. Teens who copy the behavior of celebrities who use tobacco are making a wrong decision. Remember, most athletes and celebrities DO NOT use tobacco products.

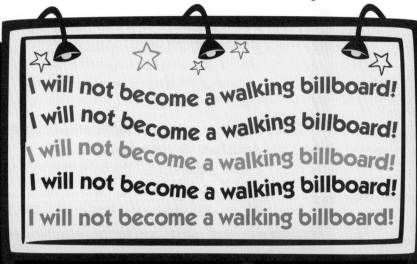

I will not become a walking billboard!
I will not become a walking billboard!
I will not become a walking billboard!
I will not become a walking billboard!
I will not become a walking billboard!

Don't Be a Walking Billboard

Tobacco companies offer promotions that appeal to teens. For example, a tobacco company might offer a catalog with items such as watches and sportswear. A person can send in a certain number of labels from packs of cigarettes and obtain these "free" items. But are these items really free? Each pack of cigarettes that carries the label costs money. And consider the costs of smoking on your health. Do not become a walking billboard for a tobacco company. Do not wear clothing with logos and brand names of tobacco companies. Do not order promotional items from tobacco companies.

1. **Media might ignore the health risks or consequences of using tobacco products.** Some characters in TV shows, movies, and music videos smoke cigarettes or cigars. These characters do not suffer harmful consequences from smoking. In real life, teens who smoke become addicted and are at increased risk for diseases and illnesses. Characters on TV shows who smoke have white teeth, healthy skin, and clean nails. In real life, teens who smoke have yellow teeth, dull skin, and yellow fingernails.

2. **Media sometimes display the brand names and logos of tobacco products.** Manufacturers of tobacco products pay movie producers to show their products. They want teens to notice their brand name and logo and purchase their products. They pay for name recognition for their products. They want teens to think that using their products is the "in" thing to do.

3. **Media might show celebrities using tobacco products as part of their everyday lives.** Some celebrities are photographed smoking. Their picture is published with their interview. Some celebrities smoke cigarettes while they are interviewed on TV. Some models are smoking cigarettes in the ads in fashion magazines. These celebrities send the message that it is glamorous to use tobacco products. Teens might think, "If a celebrity I admire uses tobacco, I should too." Teens who believe this have faulty thinking. Most celebrities do not use tobacco.

4. **Media might include advertisements that try to convince you that you will be a certain way if you use tobacco products.** For example, a very rugged male might be smoking cigarettes in an ad. The message is...you will be perceived as masculine and rugged if you smoke. A slender sexy female might be smoking in an ad. The message is...you will be perceived as being sexy and desirable if you smoke. But, the fact is...you can be masculine, feminine, and attractive without using tobacco.

Activity

Resources for Quitting Tobacco Use Q & A

Life Skill: I will avoid tobacco use and secondhand smoke.

Materials: paper, pen or pencil, computer (optional)

Directions: You will work with your classmates to compile a booklet of community resources to quit tobacco use.

1. Read the questions and answers below.

Q: Help! I didn't even know I was addicted to tobacco until I tried to quit. How can I quit?

A: The first step you should take is to talk to a physician. A physician can recommend a safe plan to quit using tobacco.

Q: My cousin wears a nicotine patch to help her quit. Should I borrow it to help me quit?

A: A **nicotine patch** is a skin patch that releases nicotine into the bloodstream. Only use a nicotine patch or nicotine gum with a physician's supervision. Some of these products can cause side effects. Side effects can include nausea, insomnia, itching, and swelling.

Q: What community agencies offer tobacco cessation programs?

A: A **tobacco cessation program** is a program to help a person quit smoking or using tobacco products. Tobacco cessation programs are offered by the American Cancer Society, the American Lung Association, and the American Heart Association.

2. Locate places in your community that offer tobacco cessation programs. Your school counselor might offer a tobacco cessation program. Agencies such as the ones just listed provide tobacco cessation programs. Your local hospital or health department might offer a tobacco cessation program. A physician or nurse can give you more information about tobacco cessation programs.

3. Get permission from a parent or guardian to contact a place that offers a tobacco cessation program. Contact the place and ask for information about the program it offers. Then, write a brief description of the program. Include: the name of the place offering the program; a description of the program; the number of sessions; the cost; how to enroll.

4. Create a "Guide to Tobacco Cessation Programs." Combine the description you wrote into a booklet with the descriptions your classmates wrote.

Vocabulary Words

Write a separate sentence using each vocabulary word listed on page 266.

Health Content

1. Why is it risky to use tobacco even one time? **page 267**

2. What are 14 health risks associated with smoking? **page 268**

3. How can a mother-to-be's smoking affect her unborn baby? **page 268**

4. What are eight health risks associated with breathing secondhand smoke? **page 269**

5. What are six ways to avoid breathing secondhand smoke? **page 269**

6. What are 12 reasons why you should avoid the use of smokeless tobacco? **page 270**

7. How can you resist pressure to use tobacco? **page 271**

8. What are four ways the media promote the use of tobacco products? **page 273**

9. Why should people who want to quit smoking get advice from their physician? **page 274**

10. What community agencies offer tobacco cessation programs? **page 274**

The Responsible Decision-Making Model™

You play on the baseball team. Your teammate gives you a wad of chewing tobacco. He tells you that you have to learn how to chew in order to make it to the big leagues. Answer the following questions on a separate sheet of paper. Write "Does not apply" if a question does not apply to this situation.

1. Is it healthful to chew tobacco? Why or why not?

2. Is it safe to chew tobacco? Why or why not?

3. Is it legal to chew tobacco? Why or why not?

4. Will you show respect for yourself if you chew tobacco? Why or why not?

5. Will your parents or guardian approve if you chew tobacco? Why or why not?

6. Will you demonstrate good character if you chew tobacco? Why or why not?

What is the responsible decision to make in this situation?

Health Literacy

Effective Communication

Some tobacco companies offer products with their brand name and logo on them. Some teens purchase cigarettes and save labels to get a product, such as a watch. The design of the watch promotes tobacco use. Wearing one of these watches promotes tobacco use. Design a watch that promotes being tobacco-free.

How to Resist Pressure to Use Alcohol

Life Skill ◆ **I will not drink alcohol.**

Alcohol is a depressant drug found in some beverages. Depressant drugs slow down the nervous system. Alcohol also is an addictive drug. Teens should not drink alcohol. It is illegal for teens to drink alcohol. It is important that you know how to resist pressure to drink alcohol.

The Lesson Objectives

- Explain why there is no such thing as "responsible teen drinking."
- Explain how drinking can harm your body.
- Explain how drinking can harm your mind.
- Explain how drinking can affect your decision to practice abstinence.
- Discuss ways the media promote drinking.
- Outline resistance skills you can use if you are pressured to drink alcohol.
- Discuss alcoholism and its effects on families.

Vocabulary

alcohol

intoxication

hangover

cirrhosis

fetal alcohol syndrome (FAS)

blackout

psychological dependence

glamorize

cyberbar

alcoholism

denial

honest talk

I-message

Why Is There No Such Thing As "Responsible Teen Drinking"?

You might have seen advertisements for alcohol on TV or in magazines. These ads send the following message: Drinking alcohol is OK if you drink "responsibly." Review *The Responsible Decision-Making Model*™ to learn why there is no such thing as responsible teen drinking.

1. **Is it healthful for you to drink alcohol? NO.** You will learn the harmful effects of alcohol on the mind and body later in this lesson.

2. **Is it safe for you to drink alcohol? NO.** You will learn reasons alcohol increases the risk of accidents and violence later in this lesson.

3. **Is it legal for you to drink alcohol? NO.** IT IS ILLEGAL FOR YOU TO DRINK ALCOHOL.

4. **Do you show respect for yourself if you drink alcohol? NO.** Choosing actions that harm health and are unsafe and illegal does not show respect for yourself.

5. **Does drinking alcohol follow the guidelines of responsible adults? NO.** Responsible adults know that it is illegal for you to drink alcohol.

6. **Does drinking alcohol demonstrate good character? NO.** It is wrong to choose actions that harm health and are unsafe and illegal.

It is illegal for minors to drink alcohol. A minor is a person who is under the legal age. It is illegal for minors to have alcohol in their possession. It is illegal for minors to purchase alcohol. It is illegal for a person who is over the legal age to sell alcohol to a minor.

Q: Does drinking cause a person to have problems or do problems cause a person to drink? Let's look at both scenarios.

Drinking can cause a person to have problems: Suppose a teen female experiments with alcohol. She thinks drinking is cool and continues drinking. She begins to miss school and her grades drop. She gets into fights with family members and friends while she is drinking. She is caught drinking and is arrested. Her drinking causes her to have problems.

Problems do NOT cause a person to drink: A person makes this wrong choice. Suppose a teen male is depressed. His parents are getting a divorce. He is having difficulty in school. Someone tells him alcohol will help cheer him up. He starts drinking to cope with his problems. His problems did not cause him to drink. He chose to drink to deal with problems. Now his problems will be greater.

A: Drinking causes problems. And, drinking to deal with problems makes problems worse. Protect yourself from problems and DO NOT DRINK. Do not use problems as an excuse for drinking. Always deal with your problems in a responsible way. DO NOT DRINK to cope.

How Can Drinking Harm My Body?

When a person drinks alcohol, the alcohol goes directly into the bloodstream. Alcohol circulates in the bloodstream. It affects every body organ.

1. **Intoxication** **Intoxication** is the condition of being drunk. Intoxication can cause loss of control of the body, a coma, and death.

2. **Hangover** A **hangover** is the aftereffect of using alcohol. A hangover usually occurs several hours after a person becomes intoxicated. Hangover symptoms include headaches, nausea, tiredness, vomiting, and shaking.

3. **Cardiovascular diseases** Alcohol damages the organs of the cardiovascular system. People who drink alcohol are at increased risk for developing high blood pressure, heart disease, and stroke.

4. **Nerve damage** Alcohol can destroy nerve cells. People who drink alcohol can lose control of their legs and arms. They might have "the shakes."

5. **Malnutrition** People who drink often might substitute drinking for eating healthful foods. Then they do not get the vitamins and minerals they need for optimal health. Alcohol interferes with the body's ability to use the vitamins in food.

6. **Obesity** Alcohol is high in calories. Drinking can cause weight gain. Being overweight is a risk factor for many diseases and illnesses.

7. **Cirrhosis** The liver processes most alcohol in the body. **Cirrhosis** (suh·ROH·suhs) is a disease of the liver in which cells are damaged. Cirrhosis can cause liver failure and death.

8. **Cancer** People who drink alcohol are at increased risk for cancers of the liver, larynx, mouth, esophagus, stomach, and pancreas.

9. **Kidney failure** Alcohol increases the flow of urine which can cause overuse of the kidneys. People who drink alcohol are at increased risk for kidney failure.

10. **Brain damage** Alcohol depresses the central nervous system. Alcohol use can cause short-term memory loss. Alcohol can permanently destroy brain cells. People who often drink too much are at risk of developing dementia. Dementia is a general decline in all areas of mental functioning.

11. **Digestive problems** Alcohol can irritate the stomach lining and cause vomiting, nausea, and ulcers.

12. **Reproductive system** Alcohol can affect the size of the testes in males. Alcohol can affect the amount of body and facial hair. In females, alcohol can delay the menstrual cycle and affect breast development.

13. **Respiratory illnesses** Alcohol depresses the immune system. The body's ability to fight infection is decreased. People who drink alcohol are more likely to develop colds, flu, and pneumonia.

14. **Fatigue** Alcohol interferes with sleep. A person who drinks alcohol can wake up tired even after a full night's sleep.

Alcohol Increases the Risk of Premature Death

Alcohol is linked to the leading causes of accidental deaths— motor vehicle accidents, falls, drownings, and fires. Studies show that alcohol has been related to almost two-thirds of homicides. Many people who have attempted suicide were drinking at the time. Alcohol use also is associated with many rapes, domestic violence, and child neglect.

A Risky Combination

The FDA has proposed requiring that certain OTC painkillers carry warnings against their combined use with alcohol. A combination of alcohol and aspirin, ibuprofen, and other common painkillers can cause stomach bleeding. A combination of alcohol and products containing acetaminophen (uh·SEE·tuh·MI·nuh·fuhn) can cause liver damage.

Drinking and Pregnancy

Females who drink alcohol during pregnancy put their developing baby at risk. Females risk having a miscarriage or a stillbirth. Their baby might be born with fetal alcohol syndrome. Fetal alcohol syndrome (FAS) is the presence of birth defects in a baby born to a mother who drank alcohol during pregnancy. A baby with FAS might have small eyes, a small jaw, heart defects, and mental retardation. All alcoholic beverages must have a warning label: According to the Surgeon General, females should not drink alcoholic beverages during pregnancy because of the risk of birth defects.

How Can Drinking Harm My Mind?

Ways Drinking Can Harm Your Mind

1. **Drinking interferes with your thinking.** It is difficult to use *The Responsible Decision-Making Model™* if you are under the influence of alcohol. You might make decisions that risk your safety. You might do or say things you might not normally do. You might give in to negative peer pressure.

2. **Drinking causes aggressive behavior.** You are more likely to be angry and violent if you are under the influence of alcohol. You are at increased risk for getting into fights with others.

3. **Drinking makes emotions stronger.** Your emotions are more intense if you are under the influence of alcohol. You might have mood swings. You might become very depressed or anxious. You are at increased risk for making a suicide attempt.

4. **Drinking affects memory.** Your memory is affected if you are under the influence of alcohol. You might have blackouts. A **blackout** is a period in which a person cannot remember what has happened. You might not be able to remember what was said or done after the alcohol took effect.

5. **Drinking affects coordination.** Your coordination is affected if you are under the influence of alcohol. You might not be able to stand or walk.

6. **Drinking causes psychological dependence.** **Psychological dependence** is a desire for a drug for emotional reasons. If you drink alcohol, you might develop a craving for alcohol. You might continue to drink alcohol even though it causes problems for you.

I Will Not Drink Alcohol

I Will Not Drink Alcohol

I Will Not Drink Alcohol

I Will Not Drink Alcohol

I Will Not Drink Alcohol

How Can Drinking Affect My Decision to Practice Abstinence?

You are working to become a responsible adult. One of the ways to prove you are responsible is to be accountable for your actions. If you drink, you will have difficulty being accountable. Drinking will change the way you think and act. Drinking will affect your judgment. Consider this fact. Most teens who are sexually active were under the influence of alcohol when they first decided to have sex. Most of these teens had planned to practice abstinence. But drinking affected their behavior. Consider the following scenarios.

Suppose a teen male drinks alcohol while on a date. This teen male had set limits for expressing affection. But drinking affects his judgment. The alcohol makes his emotions stronger. His sexual feelings increase. He has sex. He has placed himself at risk for the consequences of having sex. He might become infected with HIV and other STDs. He might get a female pregnant. He has broken the guidelines of responsible adults. He might get a bad reputation and lose the respect of other teens.

Suppose a teen female drinks alcohol. She has sex with a teen male. The next day she tells her friends, "I only had sex with him because I was drinking." Drinking alcohol cannot be used to excuse wrong behavior. This teen is stuck with the consequences. She might have become infected with HIV and other STDs. She might have gotten pregnant. She has broken the guidelines of responsible adults. She might get a bad reputation and lose the respect of other teens.

I Will Practice Abstinence

I Will Practice Abstinence

I Will Practice Abstinence

You cannot make clear decisions about sex if you drink. Suppose you decide to have sex. You will regret this decision. You and your partner would risk unwanted pregnancy and infection with HIV and other STDs. Do not drink alcohol. Stick to your decision to practice abstinence.

How Do the Media Promote Drinking?

The media often glamorize drinking. To **glamorize** is to associate something with desirable qualities. The media associate drinking with attractiveness and popularity. They want to convince you that you will be attractive, popular, and "cool" if you drink.

How do the media try to convince you to drink?

1. **Media might lead you to believe that there are no health risks or consequences associated with drinking alcohol.** Some characters on TV shows, in movies, and in music videos drink alcohol. These characters might be shown as having fun. Other characters might behave as if the behavior of the people who are drinking is funny. They show no harmful consequences of this behavior. In real life, teens who drink alcohol become addicted. They get diseases and illnesses. Some characters on TV shows do become addicted to alcohol. However, many of these characters recover by the next episode. In real life, teens who are addicted to alcohol need long-term treatment.

2. **Media sometimes display the brand names and logos of alcohol companies.** Alcohol companies pay movie producers to show their products in the movies. Alcohol companies might sponsor events teens watch on TV, such as concerts and athletic contests. They want teens to notice the brand names and logos and to purchase their products. They want teens to think drinking their brand of alcohol is the "in" thing to do.

3. **Media sometimes show celebrities drinking alcohol as part of their everyday lives.** Photos of celebrities drinking alcohol sometimes are published in magazines. These media send the message that alcohol use is glamorous. Teens might think, "If a celebrity whom I admire drinks, I should too." Teens who believe this have faulty thinking.

4. **Media might include advertisements that try to convince you that you will be a certain way if you drink.** For example, a beer ad might show a group of guys playing football or climbing a mountain. The message is...you'll be one of the guys if you drink. A wine ad might show a couple sipping a glass of wine. The message is...you need to drink to be romantic. But the fact is...you can be one of the guys or enjoy the company of the opposite sex without drinking.

ID Required: The Cyberbar

A **cyberbar** is a Web site in which people pretend they are at a bar. Companies that sell alcohol sponsor cyberbars on their Web sites. The cyberbars have video games, chat rooms, and offer prizes with the logos and brand names of the alcohol product. Cyberbars are not appropriate for teens.

Activity

ohol Ads: The Hidden Mes

l: I will not drink alcohol.

s: paper, pen or pencil, old magazines or newspapers

ns: Media literacy is the ability to recognize and evaluate the messages in me helps you develop media literacy.

1. **Find an ad for alcohol products in a magazine or newspaper.** Write the answers to the following questions about the ad.

- **What is being advertised?**
- **Where did the ad appear?**
- **What is the purpose of the message?**
- **How does the ad encourage people to purchase alcohol?**
- **If there are people in the ad, what desirable qualities do they have?**
- **What desirable qualities does the scenery or background have?**
- **Who will profit if teens are influenced by the message?**

2. **Write five statements that explain what this ad does not tell you.** Ads for alcohol do not tell you everything you need to know about alcohol use. Suppose your ad shows people playing volleyball and drinking wine coolers. You might write, "Alcohol affects coordination. People who drink alcohol might not be able to play sports well."

3. **Consider five ways the ad could be changed to reflect the reality of alcohol use.** Write a summary of these changes. For example, you might write, "One of the people in the ad has passed out and needs to go to the hospital."

4. **Attach your changes to the ad.** Discuss your changes with your classmates.

How Can I Resist Pressure to Drink?

You can use resistance skills if you are pressured to drink alcohol.

1. **Say NO to drinking alcohol with confidence.** Look directly at the person to whom you are speaking. Say NO in a firm voice. Be confident, because you are being responsible.

2. **Give reasons for saying NO to drinking alcohol.** Say:
    - "I want to have a healthy body."
    - "I want to avoid addiction."
    - "I want to stay in control of my thinking."
    - "It is illegal for me to drink alcohol."
    - "I want to keep my promise to practice abstinence."

3. **Be certain your behavior matches your words.** Do not do anything that suggests you approve of drinking alcohol.
    - Do not pretend to sip a beer.
    - Remember that even having a beer in your possession is illegal.
    - Do not hang out with teens who are drinking alcohol.
    - Join a group committed to stopping alcohol abuse, such as Students Against Drunk Driving.
    - Do not help teens purchase alcohol.
    - Do not wear clothing with alcohol-related logos or brand names.

4. **Avoid being in situations where teens will be drinking alcohol.** Do not attend parties where teens will be drinking. Do not go into bars. Do not go with teens to purchase beer.

5. **Avoid being with teens who will pressure you to drink alcohol.** Choose friends who do not drink alcohol. They will not pressure you to drink alcohol.

6. **Resist pressure to do anything illegal.** It is illegal for teens to drink alcohol. It is illegal to use a fake ID to purchase alcohol. It is illegal to use a fake ID to enter a bar. You could be arrested for these actions.

7. **Influence other teens to resist pressure to drink.** Educate others about the risks of alcohol use. Encourage other teens to avoid alcohol use or to stop drinking.

What Is Alcoholism?

Alcoholism (AL·kuh·HAW·LI·zuhm) is a disease in which there is dependence on alcohol.

Warning Signs of Alcoholism

1. **Drinking too much or too often** People who have alcoholism have different habits. They might drink every day or drink large amounts occasionally. They might drink when they are alone. They might drink to relax or to sleep. They might gulp drinks and get drunk on purpose. They might have frequent hangovers and blackouts.

2. **Being in denial** People who have alcoholism might be in denial. **Denial** is refusing to admit there is a problem.

3. **Developing tolerance** People who have alcoholism need increasingly more alcohol to produce the same effects.

4. **Having withdrawal symptoms** Withdrawal symptoms are unpleasant reactions experienced when drug use is stopped. Withdrawal symptoms include hands that shake, increased blood pressure, nausea, diarrhea, insomnia, depression, hallucinations, and seizures.

5. **Having health problems** People who have alcoholism are sick more often. They might show signs of liver damage as well as damage to other parts of the body.

6. **Being obsessed with alcohol** People who have alcoholism look forward to their next drink. They choose activities where they know alcohol will be available. They become upset if alcohol is not available.

7. **Having difficult relationships** People who have alcoholism have problems with family members and friends.

Treatment Is Available for People Who Abuse Alcohol

Your community offers resources for people who abuse alcohol. Discuss treatment options with a school counselor, teacher, or other responsible adult. Many schools and hospitals offer programs for people who abuse alcohol. There also are programs for the families and friends of people who abuse alcohol. Alcoholics Anonymous is a recovery program for people with alcoholism. Alateen is a program for teens whose family members or friends have alcoholism.

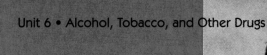

Research Update
Teen Drinking and Alcoholism

The National Institute on Alcohol Abuse and Alcoholism (NIAAA) warns against teen drinking. The findings of a study released in 1998 are alarming.

- **A 13-year-old who has no family history of alcohol abuse has a 28 percent chance of developing alcoholism if (s)he drinks.**

- **A 13-year-old who has a family history of alcohol abuse has a 58 percent chance of developing alcoholism if (s)he drinks.**

- **Teens who drink before they are fifteen are twice as likely to abuse alcohol as those who do not drink until the legal age.**

- **Teens who drink before they are fifteen are four times as likely to develop alcoholism as those who do not drink until the legal age.**

Teens who drink are much more likely to choose other risky behaviors. They are more likely to be sexually active. They are more likely to become pregnant. They are more likely to become infected with HIV and other STDs. They also are more likely to experience violence, depression, and suicide.

Drive-Through to an Arrest

It is illegal for minors to purchase alcohol. Some communities have drive-through stores where alcohol can be purchased. Teens might believe it is easier to buy alcohol at a drive-through because they do not check IDs. These teens are wrong. Police officers often check drive-through stores that sell alcohol. They check for teens who use a fake ID. These teens are arrested.

How Are Families Affected by Drinking and Alcoholism?

The entire family is affected when a family member has alcoholism. Alcoholism is a leading cause of the following problems.

Family violence Alcohol causes aggressive feelings. More than half of all acts of family violence involve alcohol use. People who have alcoholism are more likely to seriously injure or kill family members.

Child abuse People who have alcoholism often neglect their children. They are more likely to abuse their children. Their children often have to care for themselves because they cannot rely on a parent with alcoholism.

Divorce Alcoholism is a leading cause of divorce. People who drink alcohol might not be able to control their emotions. They are less likely to solve problems without fighting. They are less likely to remain sexually faithful to their partner.

Suicide Alcohol can cause depression. People who are depressed are more at risk for making a suicide attempt. Many people who have attempted suicide were under the influence of alcohol at the time.

Job loss People who have alcoholism have difficulties at work. They miss work, are late to work, or drink during work. They might be fired for their behavior. Job loss is very stressful for family members.

Illness and premature death People who have alcoholism are more likely to become ill and die at a young age.

Children of parents who have alcoholism might:

- blame themselves for their parents' drinking;
- take care of themselves rather than relying on their parents;
- take care of their parents;
- take care of their brothers and sisters;
- be ashamed to bring friends home in case a parent has been drinking;
- be people pleasers;
- feel alone and vulnerable;
- copy their parents' behavior and abuse alcohol and other drugs;
- be enablers.

Children who have a biological parent or grandparent who has alcoholism are at increased risk for developing alcoholism.

Activity

Honest Talk

Life Skill: I will not drink alcohol.

Materials: paper, pen or pencil

Directions: Suppose you have a friend who abuses alcohol. You want to let your friend know how you feel. You want your friend to get the help (s)he needs. You can use honest talk. **Honest talk** is the open sharing of feelings. You cannot accept responsibility for your friend's behavior. You cannot "rescue" your friend. However, you can try to help your friend recognize the problem and get help. Using honest talk shows respect for your friend. It shows you care for your friend and are responsible.

1. **Review the tips below for using honest talk.**

- **Discuss your plan with a responsible adult.** You might choose to talk to a parent or guardian, school counselor, or physician. Discuss what to do if your friend denies a problem or becomes angry.

- **Make a list of names of responsible adults to whom your friend might speak.** Ask a school counselor or physician about places where your friend can get treatment. You might ask your parents or guardian for permission to go with your friend to get help.

- **Choose the right time to talk.** Talk to your friend when (s)he has not been drinking. Choose a time when you will not be rushed. You might choose to have a responsible adult with you.

- **Speak in a caring tone.** Tell your friend you value your friendship with him or her.

- **Use I-messages to express your feelings.** An **I-message** is a statement or message that contains a reference to a specific behavior or event, the effect of the behavior or event, and the feelings that result. Examples of I-messages you might use are:

- *"I cannot invite you to parties because I don't know if you have been drinking, and that makes me sad."*

- *"I know that drinking is harmful behavior, and I am worried about you."*

- *"I cannot trust you when you lie about drinking. This makes me stressed out."*

2. **Write five I-messages you might say to use honest talk with a friend who abuses alcohol.**

3. **Exchange the I-messages you have written with a classmate. Read them aloud.**

Vocabulary Words

Write a separate sentence using each vocabulary word listed on page 276.

Health Content

1. Why is there no such thing as "responsible teen drinking"? **page 277**

2. How can drinking harm your body? **pages 278–279**

3. Why is it dangerous for a person to drink and take aspirin? **page 279**

4. How can drinking affect your mind? **page 280**

5. How can drinking affect your decision to practice abstinence? **page 281**

6. What are four ways the media promote drinking? **page 282**

7. How can you resist pressure to drink? **page 284**

8. What is alcoholism? **page 285**

9. How does alcoholism affect families? **page 287**

10. Why does a friend use honest talk if (s)he cares about someone who has signs of a drinking problem? **page 288**

The Responsible Decision-Making Model™

Your friend hands you a wine cooler. She tells you it is OK to drink it because it has only a small amount of alcohol in it. Answer the following questions on a separate sheet of paper. Write "Does not apply" if a question does not apply to this situation.

1. Is it healthful to drink the wine cooler? Why or why not?

2. Is it safe to drink the wine cooler? Why or why not?

3. Is it legal to drink the wine cooler? Why or why not?

4. Will you show respect for yourself if you drink the wine cooler? Why or why not?

5. Will your parents or guardian approve if you drink the wine cooler? Why or why not?

6. Will you demonstrate good character if you drink the wine cooler? Why or why not?

What is the responsible decision to make in this situation?

Health Literacy

Critical Thinking

Suppose you have a younger sibling who tells you (s)he is going to drink alcohol at a sleepover. (S)he says it will be safe since she will be at someone's house. How would you respond to your sibling?

How to Resist Pressure to Be Involved in Illegal Drug Use

Life Skill

◆ **I will not be involved in illegal drug use.**

A **controlled drug** is a drug for which possession, manufacture, and sale is regulated by law. A prescription is required for a controlled drug. A prescription sleeping tablet is an example of a controlled drug. An **illegal drug** is a drug for which possession, manufacture, and sale is against the law. Heroin and crack are illegal drugs. **Illegal drug use** is:

- the wrong use, possession, manufacture, or sale of controlled drugs;

- and the use, possession, manufacture, or sale of illegal drugs.

The Lesson Objectives

- Discuss reasons why the illegal use of the following drugs is dangerous: marijuana, cocaine and crack, methamphetamine, LSD, MDMA, roofies, heroin, PCP, inhalants, anabolic steroids.

- Explain why drug mixing can cause injury, illness, and death.

- State reasons you will not be involved in illegal drug use.

- Outline resistance skills you can use to resist pressure to be involved in illegal drug use.

Vocabulary

controlled drug

illegal drug

illegal drug use

THC

amotivational syndrome

cocaine

crack

euphoria

methamphetamine

LSD

rave

ecstasy

MDMA

designer drug

herbal ecstasy

flunitrazepam

drug slipping

heroin

PCP

inhalant

anabolic steroids

roid rage

drug mixing

Why Is It Risky to Use Marijuana?

Marijuana is a drug that affects mood and impairs short-term memory. The legal status of marijuana varies from state to state. It is illegal in some states. It is a controlled drug in other states. Marijuana is smoked in cigarettes, cigars, and pipes. Marijuana cigarettes are called joints. Marijuana also is added to food. Marijuana contains THC. **THC** is a compound that produces changes in a person's mind and body. THC is available with a prescription. It is used medically to relieve nausea and vomiting that can occur with chemotherapy for cancer. Marijuana sold today contains more THC than in the past. This makes marijuana more dangerous than in past decades.

grass
ganja
chronic
tea
skunk

Marijuana misuse and abuse harms health. Users begin to experience the effects of marijuana within minutes of smoking it. A user's pulse rate might increase dramatically. Blood vessels in the cornea dilate and cause red eyes. The user's throat and mouth become dry. Coordination and speech become difficult. Long-term use can lead to bronchitis and lung cancer. In males, marijuana use can delay puberty and decrease sperm production. In females, it can affect the menstrual cycle. It can harm unborn and nursing babies. Marijuana has been reported to cause tolerance. Tolerance is a condition in which the body becomes used to a substance.

Marijuana changes behavior. Users feel relaxed. They have a sense that things are unreal. They experience short-term memory loss. At high doses, marijuana causes hallucinations, feelings of paranoia, and panic attacks. Paranoia (PAR·uh·NOY·uh) is an inappropriate feeling of extreme fear or distrust of others. Long-term use can lead to amotivational syndrome. **Amotivational syndrome** is a loss of ambition and motivation. Teens with amotivational syndrome lose interest in daily activities. They stop setting goals. They no longer plan for the future. They do not care about their relationships with family and friends. They do not believe anything is fun, exciting, or worth working for.

Marijuana use is unsafe. Because marijuana affects coordination, the user cannot maintain body balance and is at increased risk of falling. Marijuana slows reaction time and affects visual perception. Users do not react quickly to dangers. They do not see well. They have poor judgment. They are at increased risk of injuries if they are using equipment or machinery.

mary jane
pot
catnip
weed reefer

Why Is It Risky to Use Cocaine and Crack?

Cocaine is a stimulant made from leaves of the coca bush. Cocaine is a controlled drug. It is prescribed medically as an anesthetic. It is controlled because its wrong use is dangerous. If snorted, cocaine reaches the brain in minutes. If injected or smoked, it reaches the brain in seconds. Freebasing is inhaling purified cocaine that is heated with a match or lighter. **Crack** is an illegal drug that is a smokable form of cocaine. It reaches the brain in seconds.

Cocaine and crack use harm health.
Cocaine and crack are stimulants. They cause blood vessels to narrow. This increases heart rate, blood pressure, and respiration. As a result, the risk of heart attack and stroke is increased. Cocaine and crack stimulate the brain. They depress the appetite and cause a person to feel "wired." Users experience euphoria. **Euphoria** (yoo·FOHR·ee·uh) is a feeling of intense happiness and well-being. Euphoria describes the "high" produced by some drugs, such as cocaine. But what goes up must come down. The higher the high, the lower the low that follows. Users can slide into a depression or "crash." They experience a let-down feeling, dullness, tenseness, and edginess. They want to escape the crash and get high again. The desire for euphoria makes cocaine and crack highly addictive.

Daily and occasional users experience personality changes. They become "coked out." They are confused, anxious, and short-tempered. They do not think clearly. Many have hallucinations. A common hallucination is the feeling that "coke bugs" are crawling under the skin.

Users might have runny noses and burns and sores in their noses from cocaine. They often have sore throats and hoarseness. They experience shortness of breath, cold sweats, and tremors. Long-term use can damage the liver. Users who share a needle to inject cocaine are at risk for infection with HIV and viral hepatitis. Users who exchange sex for drugs increase their risk of infection with HIV even more.

Even a small amount of cocaine can cause sudden death. A user might suddenly have seizures and a high fever. Then the user might stop breathing and die.

Cocaine and crack use are unsafe. Users can become very depressed and are at risk for suicide. They have an increased risk of motor vehicle accidents, suicides, burns, and falls. They can become aggressive and violent and cause harm to themselves and others.

Why Is It Risky to Use Methamphetamine?

Methamphetamine (ME·tham·FE·tuh·MEEN) or meth is a stimulant that can produce short-lived euphoria, followed by depression. Meth is a controlled drug because its wrong use is dangerous. It is illegal to use meth without medical supervision. Speed, ice, crystal meth, and crank are street names for meth. Ice, or crank, is a pure form of meth that stays in the body a long time. It produces a long-lasting stimulation. Unlike cocaine, meth remains unchanged by the body. It accumulates in the body with repeated use and builds up to dangerous levels.

Meth misuse and abuse harms health. These drugs are stimulants. They produce extreme alertness. They cause deadly increases in heart rate, blood pressure, body temperature, and respiration. Meth can cause chest pain, irregular heartbeat, stroke, and bleeding into the brain. Users can slip into a coma. They can die from meth use.

A person who injects meth just one time might die from stroke, heart failure, or bleeding into the brain. Users who share a needle to inject meth are at risk for infection with HIV and viral hepatitis.

Users experience personality changes. They become impulsive, nervous, irritable, restless, and paranoid. They cannot sleep. The periods of stimulation last longer than those from cocaine. These are followed by long-lasting periods of severe depression. Meth is highly addictive because users want to stay high. Meth causes permanent brain damage. Meth also damages blood vessels.

Meth misuse and abuse is unsafe. Users are at risk for suicide during periods of depression. Meth use causes long periods of poor judgment. Users are at increased risk for motor vehicle accidents, suicides, burns, and falls. Personality changes cause users to become aggressive and violent. They are at increased risk for harming others.

speed

crank

ice

chalk

crystal meth

Why Is It Risky to Use LSD?

LSD is an illegal hallucinogen that can produce a trip and flashbacks. A trip is a period of mind-altering effects. A flashback is an effect of a drug that recurs long after the drug was taken. LSD is sold in many forms. A paper with liquid LSD on it is called blotter acid. It is cut into small squares and licked, swallowed, or chewed. Be cautious if someone offers you blotter paper. Microdots are tablets of LSD that are swallowed. Windowpanes are tiny gelatin chips that contain LSD. About ten of them are the size of an aspirin.

acid

windowpane

LSD use harms health. LSD produces hallucinations. During a trip, users experience color, space, and time abnormally. They are more sensitive to sounds and lights. They might speak of "seeing" sounds and "hearing" lights. Users also experience euphoria. They experience short-term memory loss and mood swings. Time seems to pass very slowly. Users can experience a "bad trip." They can become very anxious and fearful. They can become very depressed and paranoid. Users also can have flashbacks. For example, a user might experience a hallucination years after taking LSD.

LSD use is unsafe. Users cannot rely on their senses to warn them of danger. For example, LSD users cannot judge distances correctly. They often misjudge the source of sound. As a result, they are at increased risk for being injured or killed in accidents. They are more at risk for believing they are invincible. To be invincible is to be incapable of being harmed. Users might even think they have magical powers. You might have heard stories about users who believed they could fly from a building. This really happens and people die. Users who experience a "bad trip" are at risk for suicide.

Raves: What You Don't Know CAN Hurt You

blotter

A **rave** is an all-night underground party. The location of a rave is kept secret from teens who are not invited. Teens at raves use and sell controlled drugs and illegal drugs. They might slip drugs into other teens' food and beverages. Teens who eat and drink these foods and beverages do not know they are taking these drugs. The slipped drugs cause serious problems, including death.

microdots

Why Is It Risky to Use Ecstasy?

Ecstasy, also known as Adam or **MDMA,** is a stimulant and hallucinogen produced from methamphetamine. MDMA is considered a designer drug. A **designer drug** is a drug that is a changed form of a controlled drug. People who "design" these drugs do not want to follow the laws for controlled drugs. However, they are breaking the law by producing designer drugs. They do not show concern for teens who buy designer drugs and harm themselves. These drugs are taken in capsules or tablets. They sometimes are mixed with gelatin or juice and taken as a beverage.

Adam

XTC

love drug

MDMA misuse and abuse harms health.
The hallucinogenic effects of ecstasy and Adam are similar to those of LSD. These drugs also act as stimulants. They increase heart rate, blood pressure, and respiration. Users are at risk for having seizures and heart attacks. They experience insomnia, nausea, and anxiety. They sometimes have uncontrollable body movements. They sweat and have high fever and chills. Users might have hallucinations. They have euphoria that can last for several hours followed by severe depression. Ecstasy and Adam are addictive. Users develop physical and psychological dependence.

MDMA misuse and abuse is unsafe.
Ecstasy and Adam can cause personality changes. Users can believe they are invincible and might take foolish chances. As a result, they risk injury and death from accidents. They put others at risk for injury and accidents. Users of ecstasy and Adam have bouts of depression. They are at risk for making suicide attempts.

Herbal Ecstasy: What You Don't Know CAN Hurt You

Herbal ecstasy is an OTC stimulant made of herbs, ephedrine, and other ingredients. Ephedrine (i·FE·druhn) is a drug found in medicine to relieve asthma symptoms. Users get a quick reaction from herbal ecstasy. They are alert, very awake, and restless. Some teen users have become seriously ill. Some teen users have died. The FDA has issued a warning saying the use of herbal ecstasy is dangerous. Many states have banned the sale of herbal ecstasy.

cloud 9

essence

ultimate euphoria

Why Is It Risky to Use Roofies?

Roofie is a street name for the illegal drug flunitrazepam. **Flunitrazepam** (FLOO·nuh·TRA·zuh·pam) is an odorless, colorless sedative drug. **Drug slipping** is placing a drug into someone's food or beverage without that person's knowledge. Drug slipping is a crime. A person who does this can be prosecuted. A roofie might be slipped into a teen's food or beverage without the teen's knowledge. Roofies do not have a taste or odor. The teen could pass out and be raped while (s)he is unconscious. This is the reason roofies are known as one of the "date rape drugs."

rope
R2

Roofies misuse and abuse harms health. Roofies cause heart rate and respiration to decrease. Users become sleepy and relaxed. Their speech is slurred. They have bloodshot eyes.

Teens can overdose on roofies and slip into a coma or die.

Roofies misuse and abuse is unsafe. Roofies cause poor coordination. Users are at increased risk of accidents. Roofies can produce feelings of aggressiveness and fear-lessness. Users might take unnecessary risks. They might become violent and cause harm to themselves and to others.

GHB: What You Don't Know CAN Hurt You

GHB is an illegal depressant drug. GHB is one of the "date rape drugs." It causes sleepiness and loss of physical control. GHB is mixed into beverages that are marketed as "performance drinks" or "health formulas." Teens might drink these beverages, thinking the beverages will improve their performance. Instead, GHB causes headaches, vomiting, and diarrhea. It can cause seizures and short-term memory loss. GHB can cause coma and death.

Special K: What You Don't Know CAN Hurt You!

Special K is the street name of ketamine (KE·tuh·meen). Ketamine is a sedative used in human and veterinary medicine. Special K is taken in capsules or in powdered or liquid form. Users snort or inject it. Special K acts as a sedative and hallucinogen. It depresses the respiratory system. It causes vomiting, convulsions, sweating, chills, hallucinations, paranoia, and overdose. Its effects are similar to PCP. Special K can cause death.

roach
forget pill
rib
date rape drug

Why Is It Risky to Use Heroin? PCP?

Heroin is an illegal narcotic made from morphine. It looks like white or brown powder. It is injected, snorted, or smoked.

Heroin use harms health. Heroin reaches the brain very rapidly. It slows breathing and heart rate. It lowers body temperature. It causes chills, nausea, sweating, and a runny nose. It can cause coma.

Heroin can cause immediate death.

Users experience euphoria that lasts for about 30 minutes. They become depressed when the euphoria ends. Heroin is highly addictive because users want to stay high. Users who share a needle can become infected with HIV and viral hepatitis. Heroin use by pregnant females can harm the developing baby.

Heroin use is unsafe. Users who are high are in a dream-like state. They are forgetful and fall in and out of sleep. They are at increased risk of accidents. Users are at high risk of overdosing. They might accidentally buy heroin that is stronger than what they are used to and inject the same amount. They are at high risk of dying from overdoses.

PCP is an illegal hallucinogen that can speed up some body functions and slow down others. Angel dust is a street name for PCP. PCP can be snorted, smoked, taken by mouth, and injected. How long the effects of PCP last depends on the dose and how it is taken.

PCP use harms health. PCP can cause users to appear drunk. Users stagger, lose their coordination, and have slurred speech. PCP can depress the central nervous system. Users experience numbness in their arms and legs. They might not feel pain. PCP causes changes in personality. Users can become anxious and aggressive. PCP increases heart rate, blood pressure, and sometimes body temperature. Users are at risk for convulsions, lung failure, and heart failure. They are at risk for developing severe depression and mental health problems.

PCP can cause coma and death.

PCP use is unsafe. Users who cannot feel pain might be cut or burned without knowing it. They might not realize if they have broken a bone or strained a muscle. Because of personality changes, users are at risk for being very violent. They are at increased risk for suicide, assault, and murder.

smack **killer**

horse

garbage H

brown sugar

tea China white

angel dust wack

love boat peace

kibbart hog

Why Is It Risky to Get High on Inhalants?

An **inhalant** is a drug that is breathed in and produces immediate effects. Some inhalants are prescribed drugs. You might know a teen who has asthma and uses an inhaler under medical supervision. This is an example of a responsible use of inhalants. Inhalant abuse is inhaling solvents and gases to get a high. Such products usually are not intended to be used as drugs. Children sometimes abuse inhalants because they are easy to obtain.

Users breathe in inhalants by huffing, sniffing, and bagging. Huffing is breathing in inhalants through the mouth. Sometimes a user soaks a cloth with the inhalant and stuffs it in his or her mouth. Sniffing is breathing in inhalants through the nose from a bottle or a cloth soaked with the inhalant. Bagging is breathing inhalants from a paper bag.

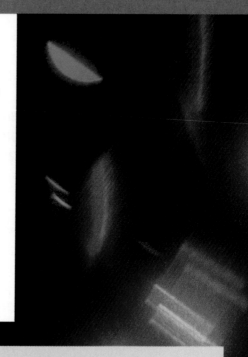

Getting high on inhalants harms health.
Inhalants can harm the heart, kidneys, blood, and bone marrow. They can cause leukemia (loo·KEE·mee·uh) and lead poisoning. They can cause nerve and brain damage. Inhalant abuse produces a brief euphoria. Inhalants depress the central nervous system. Users have headaches and hallucinations. They get shaky and have double vision. They get dizzy and vomit. They risk suffocating and choking on their own vomit.

Inhalant abuse can cause death.

Getting high on inhalants is unsafe.
Inhalant abuse can cause poor coordination. Users are at increased risk of falling and of having other accidents. Users who have ignited inhalant fumes have died from severe burns.

Examples of Inhalants

- Glue
- Paint thinner
- Dry cleaning fluid
- Shoe polish
- Correction fluid
- Felt-tip marker
- Whipped cream canister
- Hairspray
- Butane lighter fluid
- Propane tank
- Deodorant spray
- Nitrites, such as amyl nitrite (poppers)

Why Is It Risky to Use Anabolic Steroids?

Anabolic steroids are drugs that are used to increase muscle size and strength. Testosterone is a hormone that produces male secondary sex characteristics. Anabolic steroids fool the body into thinking it is producing more testosterone. Teens might take anabolic steroids to try to improve strength and athletic performance. Teens might take them to try to build muscles or to improve their appearance. Anabolic steroids are a controlled drug. It is illegal to take them without a prescription.

Anabolic steroid misuse and abuse harms health. Anabolic steroids can cause stroke and heart disease. They can cause acne, rashes, red spots, and bad breath. Teens who use anabolic steroids often stop growing. Users who inject anabolic steroids and share needles risk becoming infected with HIV and viral hepatitis. Male teens can have reduced sperm counts and shrinking testicles. Male teens can develop baldness and increases in breast size. This extra breast tissue can be permanent. Female teens can miss menstrual periods and grow hair on their face. Their voices can deepen and their breasts can shrink. Deepening of the voice can be permanent.

Anabolic steroid misuse and abuse is unsafe. Anabolic steroids cause changes in behavior. Users have wild mood swings. They become angry and aggressive. They might become violent and hurt someone. A **roid rage** is an outburst of anger caused by using anabolic steroids.

Anabolic steroids are banned throughout amateur and professional sports. Teens who use anabolic steroids can be kicked off athletic teams. They can be disqualified in competitions.

Corticosteroids

Corticosteroids (KOR·ti·koh·STER·OYDS) are drugs that are similar to a hormone produced by the adrenal glands. A physician might prescribe them to reduce inflammation after an injury. They are used to treat allergies, arthritis, and other diseases. Side effects include weight gain, headaches, and mood swings. Corticosteroids can cause ulcers, acne, and osteoporosis. Corticosteroids should be taken only when prescribed by a physician.

Activity

The Deadly Duo

Life Skill: I will not be involved in illegal drug use.

Materials: two glasses, bowl or pan, water, one-half cup of white vinegar, two tablespoons of baking soda for each group

Directions: Read the information in the box. Then follow the steps to demonstrate what happens when you mix drugs.

Drug Mixing

Suppose a teen takes a stimulant. The stimulant makes the teen feel anxious and stressed. The teen wants to relax. (S)he takes a sedative hypnotic. (S)he believes the sedative will cancel the effects of the stimulant. (S)he is wrong! **Drug mixing** is taking more than one kind of drug at one time. Drug mixing causes an effect called synergy. Synergy (SI·ner·jee) means that certain drugs taken together have a stronger effect than if taken individually. Drugs that are combined can create new substances. For example, cocaine mixed with alcohol forms cocaethylene. Cocaethylene increases the risk of sudden death.

1. **Get into a group of four people as instructed by your teacher.** Each group will perform the following experiment.

2. **Place a bowl or pan under an empty, upright glass.**

3. **Pour one-half cup of white vinegar into the glass.** The white vinegar represents alcohol that a teen is drinking.

4. **Pour one-half cup of water into another glass.**

5. **Add two tablespoons of baking soda to the water.** The baking soda represents a roofie that another teen has added to the glass of water.

6. **Pour the glass containing "roofies" into the glass containing "alcohol."** Observe what happens. This process represents a teen who drinks a beverage that contains a roofie after (s)he has alcohol in his or her body. The effect of mixing drugs is stronger than the effect of each drug.

What Are Ten Reasons I Will Avoid Being Involved in Illegal Drug Use?

1. **I want to protect my health.** Illegal drug use harms health. These drugs can harm the heart and blood vessels. They can cause brain damage and changes in personality. Long-term use can cause cancer, infertility, and mental illness.

2. **I want to follow the guidelines of my parents or guardian.** Responsible adults obey laws. They expect teens to obey laws. They expect teens to choose healthful and safe behaviors.

3. **I want to be in control of my thinking and decision-making.** Illegal drugs can cause hallucinations, confusion, and poor judgment. Teens who use drugs do not make responsible decisions.

4. **I want to have good character.** Teens who misuse and abuse drugs engage in illegal actions. They do not uphold responsible values.

5. **I want to maintain the respect of others.** Responsible people do not respect teens who misuse or abuse drugs. They avoid teens who misuse or abuse drugs because they want to stay safe. They want to stay out of trouble and keep a good reputation.

6. **I want to obey laws.** Teens who use, possess, make, or sell illegal drugs are breaking the law. Teens who use controlled drugs without medical supervision are breaking the law.

7. **I want to protect society from crime and violence.** Users might steal to get money for drugs. Users might become violent and hurt or even kill others.

8. **I want to be a responsible citizen without a criminal record.** Teens who use, possess, make, or sell illegal drugs can get stiff penalties and a criminal record.

9. **I want to protect myself from HIV infection.** Teens who share needles to inject drugs are at risk for HIV infection. Teens who use drugs have poor judgment. They might become sexually active. Their risk of getting HIV increases.

10. **I want to protect myself from infection with other STDs.** Teens who use drugs do not make responsible decisions. They often are sexually active, which increases the risk of getting an STD.

How Can I Resist Pressure to Be Involved in Illegal Drug Use?

1. **Say NO with confidence to illegal drug use.** Look directly at the person to whom you are speaking. Say NO in a firm voice. Be confident because you are being responsible.

2. **Give reasons for saying NO to illegal drug use.** Refer to the Ten Reasons Why I Will Avoid Being Involved in Illegal Drug Use on page 301.

3. **Be certain your behavior matches your words.** Do not do anything that suggests you might approve of illegal drug use.

   • Do not pretend to use illegal drugs. Even having those drugs in your possession is illegal.

   • Do not hang out with teens who use or sell drugs.

   • Do not listen to music that presents illegal drug use as acceptable behavior.

   • Do not wear clothing with drug-related pictures or words.

   • Do not join a gang.

4. **Avoid being in situations where teens will be involved in illegal drug use.** Do not attend parties where teens are using or selling illegal drugs. Do not hang out with gangs. Do not attend raves.

5. **Avoid being with teens who will pressure you to be involved in illegal drug use.** Choose friends who do not use or sell illegal drugs. They will not pressure you to be involved in illegal drug use.

6. **Resist pressure to be involved in actions that are illegal.** Do not have illegal drugs in your possession. Do not buy or sell illegal drugs. Do not hang out where illegal drugs are bought or sold.

7. **Influence peers to follow laws and resist illegal drug use.**

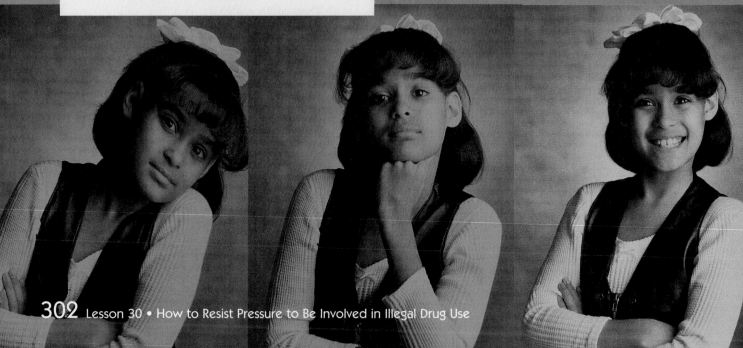

Review

Vocabulary Words

Write a separate sentence using each vocabulary word listed on page 290.

Health Content

1. Why is it risky to use marijuana? **page 291**

2. Why is it risky to use cocaine and crack? **page 292**

3. Why is it risky to use methamphetamine? **page 293**

4. Why is it risky to use LSD? **page 294**

5. Why is it risky to use MDMA? **page 295**

6. Why is it risky to use roofies? **page 296**

7. Why is it risky to use heroin? PCP? **page 297**

8. Why is it risky to get high on inhalants? **page 298**

9. Why is it risky to use anabolic steroids? **page 299**

10. What are ten reasons you will not be involved in illegal drug use? **page 301**

11. How can you resist pressure to be involved in illegal drug use? **page 302**

The Responsible Decision-Making Model™

Your friend offers you marijuana to smoke. He says that it is only an herb and is an all-natural high. Should you smoke the marijuana? Answer the following questions on a separate sheet of paper. Write "Does not apply" if the question does not apply to this situation.

1. Is it healthful to smoke marijuana? Why or why not?

2. Is it safe to smoke marijuana? Why or why not?

3. Is it legal to smoke marijuana? Why or why not?

4. Will you show respect for yourself if you smoke marijuana? Why or why not?

5. Will your parents or guardian approve if you smoke marijuana? Why or why not?

6. Will you demonstrate good character if you smoke marijuana? Why or why not?

What is the responsible decision to make in this situation?

Health Literacy

Self-Directed Learning

Look through newspapers and magazines or search the Internet. Find an article about a famous person who died from illegal drug use. Write a summary about the article. Share the summary with your classmates.

Unit 6 Review

Health Content

Prepare for the Unit Test. Review your answers for each Lesson Review in this unit. Then write answers to each of the following questions:

1. What are six consequences you might experience if you misuse or abuse drugs? **Lesson 26 page 253**

2. What happens during a formal intervention? **Lesson 26 page 254**

3. Why is it risky to be around someone who is involved in drug trafficking? **Lesson 27 page 257**

4. What should you do if you think you have been slipped a drug? **Lesson 27 page 258**

5. Why is it risky to use tobacco even one time? **Lesson 28 page 267**

6. Why is it risky to smoke a cigar? **Lesson 28 page 268**

7. How does drinking alcohol increase the risk of premature death? **Lesson 29 page 279**

8. How can drinking alcohol affect your decision to practice abstinence? **Lesson 29 page 281**

9. What are ten reasons to avoid illegal drug use? **Lesson 30 page 301**

10. Why is it risky to use cocaine? **Lesson 30 page 292**

Health Behavior Contract

Make a health behavior contract for one of the life skills in this unit. Review your health behavior contract with your parents or guardian.

Vocabulary Words

Number a sheet of paper from 1–10. Select the correct vocabulary word and write it next to the corresponding number. DO NOT WRITE IN THIS BOOK.

overdose	codependence
intoxication	rave
herbal ecstasy	cyberbar
sidestream smoke	tolerance
drug slipping	nicotine patch

1. _____ is an OTC stimulant made of herbs, ephedrine, and other ingredients. **Lesson 30**

2. _____ is the condition of being drunk. **Lesson 29**

3. _____ is an all-night underground party. **Lesson 30**

4. _____ is smoke that is given off by a burning cigarette, pipe, or cigar. **Lesson 28**

5. _____ is a mental disorder in which a person denies feelings and copes in harmful ways. **Lesson 27**

6. _____ is a Web site in which people pretend they are at a bar. **Lesson 29**

7. A _____ is a skin patch that releases nicotine into the bloodstream. **Lesson 28**

8. _____ is a condition in which the body becomes used to a substance. **Lesson 26**

9. _____ is placing a drug into someone's food or beverage without that person's knowledge. **Lesson 27**

10. To _____ is to take an excess amount. **Lesson 26**

The Responsible Decision-Making Model™

You have gone to a movie with a teen who is old enough to drive. After the movie, she says, "Let's go through the drive-through and get some beer. I know this place where they don't check IDs." Answer the following questions on a separate sheet of paper. Write "Does not apply" if a question does not apply to this situation.

1. Is it healthful to buy beer at the drive-through? Why or why not?

2. Is it safe to buy beer at the drive-through? Why or why not?

3. Is it legal to buy beer at the drive-through? Why or why not?

4. Will you show respect for yourself if you buy beer at the drive-through? Why or why not?

5. Will your parents or guardian approve if you buy beer at the drive-through? Why or why not?

6. Will you demonstrate good character if you buy beer at the drive-through? Why or why not?

What is the responsible decision to make in this situation?

What should you do if the older teen decides to buy beer anyway?

Health Literacy

Effective Communication

Several slogans have been used with programs to encourage teens to avoid illegal drug use. One example of a slogan is "Just Say NO." Create your own slogan.

Self-Directed Learning

Write a two-page report on alcoholism. Include at least ten facts about this disease. Include a bibliography that contains at least three different sources of reliable information.

Critical Thinking

Write an article for your school newspaper about teen drinking and alcoholism. Include reasons why you believe the rate of alcoholism is high in people who drank as teens.

Responsible Citizenship

Imagine that tonight is New Year's Eve. Plan a drug-free party. Select a theme. Plan a menu with foods your friends enjoy. Create a list of ten non-alcoholic beverages to serve. Design an invitation for your party.

Multicultural Health

Select a country that you would like to visit. Research drug laws for that country. What are the laws regarding possession and use of marijuana? Cocaine? Heroin?

Family Involvement

Write a ten line drug-free pledge on paper. Include a place for you to sign your name and date. Include a place for one of your parents or your guardian to sign his or her name and date. Sign and date it. Have your parents or guardian sign and date it as a witness.

UNIT 7
Communicable and Chronic Diseases

PRACTICE
HEALTH STANDARD 7
Be a Health Advocate

Practice this standard at the end of this unit.

1. **Choose an action for which you will advocate.** List three reasons why you should be an advocate for the prevention of cancer.

2. **Tell others about your commitment to advocate.** Share with your teacher that you want to help promote the prevention of cancer and why you want to do this.

3. **Match your words with your actions.** Call your local chapter of the American Cancer Society and get some pamphlets about cancer. Get enough pamphlets so that you can distribute them to each member of your class to read and take home to their parents or guardians.

4. **Encourage others to take healthful actions.** Select one kind of cancer that has the most significance to people your age. Give a report to the class about ways to reduce the risk of getting this kind of cancer.

How to Reduce Your Risk of Communicable Diseases

Life Skills

- ◆ I will choose behaviors to prevent the spread of pathogens.
- ◆ I will choose behaviors to reduce my risk of infection with communicable diseases.
- ◆ I will keep a personal health record.

Vocabulary

communicable disease

pathogen

cold

influenza

pneumonia

strep throat

mononucleosis

personal health record

A **communicable disease** is an illness caused by pathogens that can be spread from one living thing to another. A **pathogen** is a germ that causes disease. Some bacteria, viruses, and fungi (FUHN·jy) are pathogens. You can choose behaviors to reduce your risk of becoming infected with pathogens. You can choose behaviors to reduce the risk of spreading pathogens.

The Lesson Objectives

- • Identify ways pathogens are spread.
- • Discuss ways to reduce the risk of spreading pathogens.
- • Outline information on the common cold, influenza, pneumonia, strep throat, and mononucleosis including causes, how the disease is spread, symptoms, diagnosis, treatment, and prevention.
- • Explain why you need to keep a personal health record.
- • List the information you should keep in your personal health record.

What Are Ways to Prevent the Spread of Pathogens?

The left side of the table below lists many of the ways pathogens are spread. The right side of the table lists actions you can take to reduce the risk of spreading pathogens.

Ways Pathogens Are Spread	Ways to Reduce the Risk of Spreading Pathogens
Contact with eye, nose, throat secretions	• Cover your mouth and nose with a tissue when you cough or sneeze. • Wash your hands with soap and water often. • Keep your fingers out of your eyes, nose, and mouth. • Do not share personal items such as toothbrushes. • Avoid people who have infections that are spread by coughing and sneezing.
Contact with body wastes	• Wash your hands with soap and water after using the bathroom and before eating. • Keep your fingers out of your eyes, nose, and mouth.
Contact with open sores	• Cover open sores with an adhesive bandage. • Wash your hands with soap and water if you touch your sores. • Do not touch sores on another person's body.
Contact with blood	• Wear latex gloves to keep from touching blood. • Do not use injecting drugs. • Do not share needles to make tattoos or to pierce ears or other body parts.
Intimate sexual contact	• Practice abstinence.
Contaminated food	• Follow tips to prevent foodborne illnesses (see Lesson 18). • Keep animals and insects away from food.
Insect bites	• Use mosquito repellent as needed. • Promptly remove ticks from pets. • Wash your hands with soap and water after you remove a tick.
Animal bites	• Check with your physician if you are bitten by an animal.

How Can I Reduce My Risk of Getting a Cold?

A **cold** is a viral infection that affects the lining of the upper respiratory tract.

What causes colds?

Colds are caused by over 200 different viruses.

How is a cold diagnosed?

- Symptoms
- Laboratory tests

How are colds spread?

- Putting your fingers or contaminated objects in your eyes, nose, or mouth
- Breathing droplets from an infected person who coughs or sneezes

What is treatment for a cold?

There is no cure for the cold. Antibiotics do not work against viruses.

- Over-the-counter products can make you more comfortable. Ask your physician which ones you should use.
- Get plenty of rest and drink lots of fluids.

What are the symptoms of a cold?

- Runny, stuffy nose
- Watery eyes
- Sore or scratchy throat
- Mild cough
- Tiredness

How can I prevent a cold?

- Wash your hands with soap and water often.
- Keep your fingers and objects out of your eyes, nose, and mouth.
- Avoid close contact with people who have colds.

Is It a Cold or Is It the Flu?

You might think you have the flu when you really have a cold. A cold usually causes no or slight fever, minor aches, minor tiredness, and stuffy nose. The flu usually causes high fever, severe aches, extreme tiredness, and sometimes a stuffy nose.

How Can I Reduce My Risk of Getting the Flu?

The flu or **influenza** (IN·floo·EN·zuh) is a viral infection of the respiratory tract.

What causes the flu?

Flu (short for influenza) is caused by the influenza virus.

How is the flu diagnosed?

- Symptoms
- Laboratory tests

How is the flu spread?

- Putting your fingers or contaminated objects in your eyes, nose, or mouth
- Breathing droplets from an infected person who coughs or sneezes

What is treatment for the flu?

There is no cure for the flu. Antibiotics do not work against viruses.

- Over-the-counter products can make you more comfortable. Taking aspirin has been associated with a rare but serious condition called Reye's syndrome. Ask your physician which products you should use.
- Get plenty of rest and drink plenty of fluids.

What are the symptoms of the flu?

- Fever (up to 104°F)
- Chills
- Headache
- Severe body aches
- Extreme tiredness
- Chest discomfort
- Cough

How can I prevent the flu?

- Wash your hands with soap and water often.
- Keep your fingers and objects out of your eyes, nose, and mouth.
- Avoid close contact with people who have the flu.
- Get the flu vaccine every year. A new vaccine must be given each year because the virus changes each year. Check with your physician first.

What Is Stomach Flu?

Have you ever had an upset stomach and called it stomach flu? There is really no such thing. What you probably had was gastroenteritis. Gastro-enteritis (GAS·troh·EN·tuh·RY·tuhs) is an illness with nausea, diarrhea, and/or vomiting. Gastroenteritis has many causes, for instance, food poisoning. You can have stomach upset when you are ill with influenza, but this is rare.

How Can I Reduce
My Risk of Getting Pneumonia?

Pneumonia (noo·MOH·nyuh) is an infection in the lungs caused by bacteria, viruses, or other pathogens.

What causes pneumonia?

Pneumonia is caused by bacteria, viruses, or other pathogens.

How is pneumonia diagnosed?

- Symptoms
- Laboratory tests
- Chest X-rays of the lungs
- Change in breathing sounds when heard through a stethoscope

Pneumonia is not always contagious. You can get pneumonia from germs that already live in your nose and throat. Normally these germs do not cause disease because your immune system defends you against them. But if you become ill or run down, your immune system might weaken. You might develop an infection, such as pneumonia, from germs that normally do not harm you.

How is pneumonia spread?

- Putting your fingers or contaminated objects in your eyes, nose, or mouth
- Breathing droplets from an infected person who coughs or sneezes

What is treatment for pneumonia?

Treatment varies with the pathogen involved.

- Antibiotics are prescribed for bacterial pneumonia.
- Acyclovir is an antiviral drug that is sometimes given for certain viral infections. Acyclovir might be given for severe cases of viral pneumonia.

What are the symptoms of pneumonia?

- Cough
- Chest pain
- Chills
- Fever
- Coughing up blood or thick mucus

How can I prevent pneumonia?

- Wash your hands with soap and water often.
- Keep your fingers and objects out of your eyes, nose, and mouth.
- Get plenty of rest and drink plenty of fluids if you have the cold or the flu. Pneumonia sometimes follows a cold or the flu.
- Check with your physician to see if (s)he advises the vaccine for pneumonia.

How Can I Reduce My Risk of Getting Strep Throat?

Strep throat is a bacterial infection of the throat.

What causes strep throat?

Strep throat is caused by bacteria.

How is strep throat diagnosed?

- Symptoms
- Laboratory tests

Why You Should Take All of Your Antibiotics

You are taking antibiotics for a bacterial infection. Your physician tells you to take all of your medication. Suppose you take only some of it. You stop taking it as soon as you feel better. Why take the rest? Taking only some of the antibiotics might kill only some of the bacteria. The bacteria that were not killed can become resistant to the antibiotic you took. If you get another infection with those bacteria, the antibiotic you took before might not work.

How is strep throat spread?

- Close contact, such as kissing, with a person who is infected
- Breathing droplets from an infected person who coughs or sneezes

Strep throat is not as contagious as a cold or the flu.

What is treatment for strep throat?

- Antibiotics are prescribed.

Heart or kidney damage can occur if strep throat is not treated.

What are the symptoms of strep throat?

- Sore, bright red throat
- Pus in the throat
- Pain when swallowing
- Fever
- Chills
- Headache

How can I prevent strep throat?

- Avoid close contact with people who have strep throat.

People who have strep throat usually are not contagious after one to two days of taking antibiotics.

How Can I Reduce My Risk of Getting Mononucleosis?

Mononucleosis (MAH·nuh·NOO·klee·OH·suhs) is a viral infection that causes extreme tiredness.

What causes mononucleosis?

Mononucleosis is caused by the Epstein-Barr virus or EBV.

How is mononucleosis diagnosed?

- Symptoms
- Blood test

How is mononucleosis spread?

- Close contact, such as kissing, with a person who is infected
- Sharing cups or utensils with a person who is infected

Mononucleosis is not as contagious as a cold or the flu.

What are the symptoms of mononucleosis?

- Extreme tiredness
- Fever
- Sore throat
- Swelling of the lymph nodes

A person can have the virus for months even after the person feels well.

The Importance of Handwashing

Handwashing is an action you can take to reduce the spread of pathogens. Use this technique for washing your hands:

- Wet hands with running water.
- Apply soap and vigorously rub hands together for 10 to 15 seconds.
- Rinse thoroughly.
- Use a paper towel, if available, to turn off the faucet in public restrooms.

You can recontaminate your hands by touching the faucet.

What is treatment for mononucleosis?

There is no cure for mononucleosis. Antibiotics do not work against viruses.

- Get plenty of rest.
- Avoid heavy lifting and contact sports because of the risk of rupturing the spleen.

How can I prevent mononucleosis?

- Avoid close contact with people who are infected.
- Do not share cups or utensils with other people.

What Information Should I Keep in My Personal Health Record?

A **personal health record** is a record of a person's health, health care, and health care providers. Information about your health is in one place when you keep a personal health record. You can get to this information quickly. You can take your personal health record with you when you have examinations. Your physician can review the information. The information will help your physician provide the best care for you. Always know the location of your personal health record. Suppose you need emergency care. You or someone in your family can locate your personal health record quickly to take with you.

Your personal health record should include the following information.

1. **A copy of your birth certificate**

2. **A detailed family health history** A family health history is information about the health of a person's blood relatives. Close blood relatives might include your biological parents, brothers, sisters, aunts, uncles, and grandparents. Write down diseases they have had. Include the age at which they had these diseases. Record the age at time of death.

3. **A record of the immunizations you have had** Record the dates you were immunized or had a booster for the following.

   • OPV (oral polio vaccine)
   • DTP (diphtheria, tetanus, pertussis)
   • MMR (measles, mumps, rubella)
   • Hib (*Haemophilus influenza* type B)
   • Hepatitis B
   • Varicella (chickenpox)

4. **Details about your health and habits** Write down your height, weight, and blood pressure. Keep results of vision and hearing tests. Keep details on your sleep, eating, and exercise habits. (Note whether you have experimented with alcohol, tobacco, or other drugs.) Write down any medications you take. Write down medications to which you have an allergic reaction.

5. **A record of your visits to health care providers** Write down the dates of the visits and the reasons for going. Keep the name, address, and phone number of each health care provider. You might need to contact them to get files.

6. **A copy of your family's health insurance policy and other policies** It is handy to have policies with you when you visit a health care provider or go to a hospital. You also might have a school policy for playing sports.

Anthrax: Frequently Asked Questions

Name: _____ **Date:** _____

Life Skill: I will choose behaviors to prevent the spread of pathogens.

Materials: paper and pencil
Directions: Below are some commonly asked questions and answers about anthrax. Pretend you are a reporter. List five more questions about anthrax. Do research to find an answer for each question. You can find information in the library or on the Internet.

Question: What is anthrax?
Answer: Anthrax is a disease caused by a bacterium that reproduces itself by producing spores. The spores can survive in the ground or on animals. Some countries have developed anthrax in labs. Anthrax spores can get into the body by inhalation or through the skin.

Question: What are the symptoms of anthrax?
Answer: The symptoms depend on how a person gets anthrax. Early symptoms of inhalation anthrax may resemble the common cold. Skin infection begins with an itchy bump that looks like a spider bite. A liquid sac forms after a day or two. The sac then becomes a painless sore.

Question: How is anthrax treated?
Answer: Certain medicines called antibiotics can treat anthrax. The sooner the treatment, the better the chances of recovery. Antibiotic treatment continues for 60 days. The treatment is so long because anthrax spores can stay in the lungs for a long time.

Review

Vocabulary Words

Write a separate sentence using each vocabulary word listed on page 308.

Health Content

1. What are ways pathogens are spread? **page 309**

2. What are ways to reduce the risk of spreading pathogens? **page 309**

3. Outline information on the common cold, influenza, pneumonia, strep throat, and mononucleosis. Include causes, how the disease is spread, symptoms, diagnosis, treatment, and how the disease is prevented. **pages 310–314**

4. Why do you need to keep a personal health record? **page 315**

5. What information should you keep in your personal health record? **page 315**

Health Literacy

Effective Communication

Create a booklet that explains ways to prevent the spread of communicable diseases. Ask your school media specialist if you can display your booklet in the school library.

The Responsible Decision-Making Model™

You wake up coughing and sneezing with a bad cold. You feel lousy. However, a celebrity is coming to the school today. You do not want to miss the show that is planned. Answer the following questions on a separate sheet of paper. Write "Does not apply" if a question does not apply to this situation.

1. Is it healthful for you to go to school when you have a bad cold? Why or why not?

2. Is it safe for you to go to school when you have a bad cold? Why or why not?

3. Is it legal for you to go to school when you have a bad cold? Why or why not?

4. Will you show respect for yourself, your classmates, and your teachers if you go to school with a bad cold? Why or why not?

5. Will your parents or guardian approve if you go to school with a bad cold? Why or why not?

6. Will you demonstrate good character if you go to school with a bad cold? Why or why not?

What is the responsible decision to make in this situation?

How to Prevent Sexually Transmitted Diseases

Life Skill

♦ **I will choose behaviors to reduce my risk of infection with sexually transmitted diseases.**

A **sexually transmitted disease** or STD is a disease caused by pathogens that are transmitted from an infected person to an uninfected person during intimate sexual contact. Some STDs also can be spread in other ways. When you practice abstinence, you reduce your risk of being infected with STDs. **Abstinence** is choosing not to be sexually active.

The Lesson Objectives

- Outline information on *Chlamydia,* NGU, gonorrhea, candidiasis, syphilis, genital herpes, viral hepatitis, genital warts, trichomoniasis, and pubic lice.

- List two STDs for which there is no cure.

- List two STDs that are linked to cancers.

- List ten reasons why you do not want to become infected with an STD.

Vocabulary

sexually transmitted disease (STD)

abstinence

Chlamydia

pelvic inflammatory disease (PID)

nongonococcal urethritis (NGU)

gonorrhea

candidiasis

syphilis

chancre

genital herpes

viral hepatitis

jaundice

genital warts

trichomoniasis

pubic lice

lice

What Should I Know About Chlamydia? About NGU?

Facts About Chlamydia

Chlamydia (kluh·MID·ee·uh) is an STD that causes inflammation of the reproductive organs. It is caused by a bacterium. *Chlamydia* is spread by having sexual contact with an infected partner. An infected and pregnant female can spread *Chlamydia* to her baby during vaginal delivery. The bacteria enter the baby's eyes and lungs. Babies born with *Chlamydia* must be treated. They can become blind and develop pneumonia if they are not treated.

Symptoms in males include painful urination, a discharge from the penis, and swelling in the scrotum. These symptoms usually disappear in one to three weeks. Some males do not have any symptoms, but still can infect a partner. Half of infected females have no symptoms. Those who have symptoms usually experience a discharge from the vagina and burning during urination.

To diagnose *Chlamydia,* a cotton swab is used to collect a sample of the discharge. The discharge is allowed to "grow" in a lab to detect the bacteria. Antibiotics are used for treatment of *Chlamydia.* A follow-up checkup should be done. Complications of *Chlamydia* include infertility and PID. **Pelvic inflammatory** (in·FLA·muh·TOR·ee) **disease (PID)** is a serious infection of the internal female reproductive organs. PID can cause scarring of organs.

Facts About NGU

Nongonococcal urethritis (NAHN·GAH·nuh·KAH·kuhl YUR·i·THRY·tuhs) or NGU is an STD that causes inflammation of the urethra. *Chlamydia* causes about one third of cases. Some cases of NGU are caused by other pathogens such as *Trichomonas.*

NGU is spread by sexual contact with an infected partner. The symptoms are the same as they are for *Chlamydia.* A physician will make a diagnosis based on a patient's symptoms and laboratory testing. Treatment varies depending on the pathogen that is identified in the lab test.

Females with NGU might develop inflammation of the cervix, PID, and infertility. Males with NGU might develop narrowing of the urethra, inflammation of the epididymis, and infertility.

I Will Practice Abstinence

I Will Practice Abstinence

What Should I Know About Gonorrhea? About Candidiasis?

Facts About Gonorrhea

Gonorrhea (GAH·nuh·REE·uh) is an STD that infects the linings of the genital and urinary tracts. It is caused by a bacterium. Gonorrhea is spread by having sexual contact with an infected partner. An infected pregnant female can spread gonorrhea to her baby during vaginal delivery. The bacteria enter the baby's eyes and can lead to blindness.

Symptoms in males include a milky discharge from the penis and painful urination. Some males have no symptoms, but they still can infect a partner. Many infected females do not have symptoms. Those who have symptoms experience burning during urination and a discharge from the vagina. Without treatment, females can develop abdominal pain and bleeding between periods.

To diagnose this STD in males, the discharge is examined under a microscope. In females, bacteria from the discharge are grown and identified in the lab.

Antibiotics are used for treatment. However, there is concern that some strains of the bacteria are not responding to the antibiotics. Most states require that medication be put in the eyes of newborn babies to prevent blindness.

Complications of gonorrhea include PID in females and sterility in males and females. Without treatment, the bacteria can spread and infect the heart valves, joints, and brain.

Facts About Candidiasis

Candidiasis (KAN·duh·DY·uh·suhs) is a fungal infection that causes itching and burning. The fungi that cause this infection are normally present in the vagina. They multiply if a female takes antibiotics or uses vaginal sprays and douches.

Candidiasis can be spread by sexual contact. Symptoms in females include itching, burning, and a discharge with an odor. In males, there can be itching and burning during urination. To diagnose this STD, a physician checks the symptoms. Special creams and tablets are used for treatment.

I Will Practice Abstinence   I Will Practice Abstinence   I Will Practice Abstinence

What Should I Know About Syphilis?

Facts About Syphilis

Syphilis (SI·fuh·luhs) is an STD that produces chancres in the genital area and damage to organs if untreated. A **chancre** (SHANG·ker) is a hard, round, painless sore. Syphilis is caused by a spiral-shaped bacterium. This STD is spread by having sexual contact with an infected partner. An infected pregnant female can spread syphilis to her developing baby. The bacteria enter the baby's bloodstream.

Syphilis goes through different stages. Symptoms of the first stage appear in ten days to three months after sexual contact with an infected person. Chancres appear where the bacteria entered the body. In males, chancres appear on the penis. In females, they can appear outside the vagina or inside where they cannot be seen. Chancres can appear in the mouth, too. Chancres will go away in a few weeks if there is no treatment. But the disease does not go away if it is not treated. The second stage begins three to six weeks after the chancres go away. A skin rash develops in both males and females. It can cover the whole body or part of the body. There might be fever, tiredness, headache, sore throat, and swollen glands. These symptoms also go away if there is no treatment.

A blood test is used to diagnose syphilis. Syphilis is treated with antibiotics. Follow-up blood tests are given to make sure a person is cured.

Complications can be serious. Untreated syphilis progresses to a third stage. During this stage, body organs are damaged. The heart, eyes, brain, nervous system, bones, and joints can be damaged. The third stage of syphilis can cause mental illness, blindness, paralysis, heart disease, liver damage, and death.

If a pregnant female has syphilis, the fetus is at risk. The pregnancy might result in a miscarriage, stillbirth, or fetal death. If the baby lives, (s)he is at risk for:

- **Mental retardation**
- **Deafness**
- **Liver failure**
- **Excessive bleeding**
- **Anemia**
- **Skin sores and rashes**

I Will Practice Abstinence

I Will Practice Abstinence

What Should I Know About Genital Herpes? About Viral Hepatitis?

Facts About Genital Herpes

Genital herpes is an STD caused by a virus that produces cold sores and blisters on the sex organs or in the mouth. Genital herpes is spread by having sexual contact with an infected partner. An infected pregnant female can spread genital herpes to her baby during vaginal delivery.

Symptoms appear about a week after sexual contact. Clusters of small, painful blisters appear on the genital organs. The blisters break open after a few days and become red, painful open sores. There can be burning during urination. Other symptoms are tiredness, fever, headache, and swollen glands. Symptoms last about two to four weeks.

To diagnose genital herpes, fluid from the blisters is examined under a microscope. There is no cure for genital herpes. Antiviral drugs are used to reduce the severity of the outbreak.

The consequences of being infected with genital herpes are severe. There is no cure for genital herpes. The symptoms can recur when a person is stressed or ill. This STD can be spread even when there are no symptoms. When the blisters break, it is easy for other pathogens, such as HIV, to enter the open sores.

Facts About Viral Hepatitis

Viral hepatitis (HE·puh·TY·tuhs) is a viral infection of the liver. Different viruses cause viral infection. Some of these viruses are spread by sexual contact. Often there are no symptoms. When symptoms are present, they include mild fever, muscle aches, and tiredness. There also can be loss of appetite, vomiting, and diarrhea. The urine can be dark and the feces pale. There can be abdominal pain and jaundice. **Jaundice** (JAWN·duhs) is yellowing of the skin and whites of the eyes.

Blood tests confirm viral hepatitis. Treatment includes bed rest, a healthful diet, and no alcohol. Drugs are given to help the liver function. Vaccines are available for two kinds of hepatitis—A and B. Viral hepatitis increases the risk of developing liver cancer.

I Will Practice Abstinence

I Will Practice Abstinence

What Should I Know About Genital Warts? About Trichomoniasis?

Facts About Genital Warts

Genital warts is an STD that produces wart-like growths on the sex organs. Genital warts are caused by a virus and are spread during sexual contact. An infected pregnant female can infect her baby during vaginal delivery.

Symptoms appear three to eight months after infection. The warts are soft, red or pink, and look like cauliflower. In males, the warts appear on the penis and scrotum. In females, the warts appear on the external genitals and inside the vagina. A physician inspects the warts to make a diagnosis. Medication can be put on genital warts. They can be removed with liquid nitrogen and laser surgery.

The consequences of infection are serious. The virus remains in the body and genital warts can recur. A person who has had genital warts is at increased risk of cancers of the cervix or penis.

Facts About Trichomoniasis

Trichomoniasis (TRI·kuh·muh·NY·uh·suhs) is an STD that infects the urethra in males and the vagina in females. This STD is caused by protozoa (PROH·tuh·ZOH·uh). Trichomoniasis is spread by sexual contact and by sharing damp towels with the protozoa on them.

Symptoms in males include a thin, white discharge from the penis and painful urination. However, most males have no symptoms. About half of females have no symptoms. Females who have symptoms experience a green or gray vaginal discharge with an odor. They have painful urination and itching.

An infected pregnant female can have a low birth weight baby. To diagnose this STD, a smear of the discharge is examined under a microscope. A prescription drug is used for treatment.

Will Practice Abstinence **I Will Practice Abstinence** **I Will Practice Abstinence**

What Should I Know About Pubic Lice?

I Will Practice Abstinence

I Will Practice Abstinence

Pubic lice is the infestation of the pubic hair by lice. **Lice** are insects that attach to the skin and cause itching and swelling. Lice can be spread by having sexual contact with an infected partner. Lice can survive outside the body for as long as a day. They can be spread by sleeping in infested sheets, wearing infested clothing, or sharing an infested towel.

Symptoms include itching and swelling in the pubic area. The lice might be visible as little black dots. A physician examines the body to find the lice. A prescription drug is used as a shampoo to kill the lice. OTC shampoos also can be used.

Activity

This Might Not Happen If...

Life Skill: I will choose behaviors to reduce my risk of infection with sexually transmitted diseases.

Materials: paper, pen or pencil

Directions: Complete the following activity to reinforce why you should practice abstinence to avoid getting STDs.

1. **On a separate sheet of paper, copy the Ten Reasons Why You Do Not Want to Become Infected with an STD that appear on page 325.** After each reason, write "This might not happen if..." Leave 3–4 lines blank between each reason.

2. **Refer to the information on each STD in this lesson.** Complete the sentence "This might not happen if..." by referring to the information on each STD. Use the examples on the right as a guide. Make each sentence different.

Examples

- I want to live a long, productive, and healthful life. This might not happen if...*I get genital warts because I might develop cancer.*

- I want to keep my body healthy. This might not happen if...*I get syphilis because my body organs might be damaged.*

Review

Vocabulary Words

Write a separate sentence using each vocabulary word listed on page 318.

Health Content

1. Outline information on *Chlamydia*, NGU, gonorrhea, candidiasis, syphilis, genital herpes, viral hepatitis, genital warts, trichomoniasis, and pubic lice. Include causes, how the STD is spread, symptoms, diagnosis, treatments, and complications. **pages 319–324**

2. What are two STDs that have been linked to cancer? **pages 322–323**

3. What are two STDs for which there is no cure? **pages 322–323**

4. What are ten reasons why you do not want to become infected with an STD? **page 325**

5. How can you resist pressure to be sexually active? Refer to page 86. List the reasons for practicing abstinence that appear on that page.

The Responsible Decision-Making Model™

Suppose someone pressured you to have sex. Write a reply to the pressure. Include the resistance skills from page 86. Include at least three reasons why you do not want to become infected with an STD.

Ten Reasons Why You Do Not Want to Become Infected with an STD

1. I want to live a long, productive, and healthful life.
2. I want to keep my body healthy.
3. I want my reproductive organs to function as they should.
4. I want to keep my body free of recurring symptoms of STDs.
5. I want to maintain self-respect.
6. I want to avoid unnecessary medical expenses.
7. I want to be able to tell a future marriage partner that I have never been infected with an STD.
8. I want to have a healthful marriage without recurring symptoms of an STD.
9. I want to remain fertile so that I have the option of being a parent.
10. I do not want to infect my offspring with an STD.

How to Reduce the Risk of HIV Infection

Life Skill

◆ **I will choose behaviors to reduce my risk of HIV infection.**

Vocabulary

human immunodeficiency virus (HIV)

Acquired Immune Deficiency Syndrome (AIDS)

abstinence

injecting drug user

universal precautions

HIV status

HIV negative

HIV positive

ELISA

Western blot

opportunistic infections

pneumocystis carinii pneumonia (PCP)

Kaposi's sarcoma (KS)

AIDS dementia

ddi

AZT

protease inhibitors

resistance skills

Human immunodeficiency (I·myuh·noh·di·FI·shuhnt·see) **virus** or HIV is a pathogen that destroys infection-fighting T cells in the body. HIV infection causes AIDS. **Acquired Immune Deficiency Syndrome** or AIDS is a condition that results when infection with HIV causes a breakdown of the body's ability to fight other infections.

The Lesson Objectives

- List ways HIV is and is not spread.
- Explain why practicing abstinence protects you from HIV infection.
- Explain why saying NO to injecting drug use, alcohol and other drugs, sharing a needle to make tattoos or to pierce ears or other body parts protects you from HIV infection.
- Explain why you need to follow universal precautions to protect yourself from HIV infection.
- Discuss tests used to determine HIV status.
- Explain how HIV infection progresses to AIDS.
- Discuss the latest treatments for HIV and AIDS.
- Identify ways in which HIV and AIDS threaten society.
- Outline resistance skills you can use if you are pressured to choose risk behaviors for HIV infection.

What Are Ways HIV Is Spread and Not Spread?

People who are infected with HIV have HIV in most of their body fluids. HIV is spread from infected persons to others by contact with these body fluids. These body fluids are:

- **Blood**
- **Vaginal secretions**
- **Semen**
- **Breast milk (in a few cases)**

Ways HIV Is Spread

- Having sexual contact with a person infected with HIV

- Sharing a needle, syringe, or other injection equipment with a person infected with HIV

- Sharing a needle to make tattoos or to pierce ears or other body parts with a person infected with HIV

- Having contact with the blood or other body fluids, mucous membranes, or broken skin of a person infected with HIV

- Being born to a mother who is infected with HIV

Ways HIV Is Not Spread

To date, there have been no documented cases of HIV spread through saliva or tears. According to the Centers for Disease Control and Prevention (CDC), HIV is not spread through the following ways:

- Closed mouth kissing
- Hugging
- Touching, holding, or shaking hands
- Coughing or sneezing
- Sharing food or eating utensils
- Sharing towels or combs
- Having casual contact with friends
- Sharing bathroom facilities or water fountains
- Sharing a pen or pencil
- Being bitten by insects
- Donating blood
- Eating food prepared or served by someone else
- Attending school
- Using a telephone or computer used by someone else
- Swimming in a pool
- Using sports and gym equipment

Why Does Practicing Abstinence Protect Me from HIV Infection?

REASON: Because I could become infected with HIV if I have sex with a person who is infected with HIV.

A male who is infected with HIV has HIV in his semen. A female who is infected with HIV has HIV in her vaginal secretions. You can become infected with HIV if you have sex with someone who has HIV. Remember that you cannot tell by looking at someone if (s)he is infected with HIV. And you might not get an honest answer even if you ask.

Don't ignore these facts:

- A person who is infected with HIV can appear healthy.
- A person who is infected with HIV might not know (s)he is infected.
- A person who is infected with HIV might know (s)he is infected and tell you (s)he is not.

Increased risks involved in sexual contact include:

- **Having multiple sex partners** The more sex partners a person has, the greater the risk of HIV infection.
- **Having other sexually transmitted diseases** STDs that produce sores or lead to bleeding or discharge provide openings through which HIV can spread more easily.

Abstinence is choosing not to be sexually active.

Someday You Might Marry

Marriage partners protect their health and their marriage when they keep their promise to have sex only with each other.

The Centers for Disease Control and Prevention warns against open-mouth kissing with a person infected with HIV because of the possibility of contact with HIV-infected blood.

Why Does Saying NO to Drug Use Protect Me from HIV Infection?

REASON #1: Because I could become infected with HIV if I share a needle, syringe, or injection equipment that has been used by a person who is infected with HIV.

An **injecting drug user** is a person who injects illegal drugs into the body with syringes, needles, or other injection equipment. These drugs include anabolic steroids. Anabolic steroids are drugs that are used to increase muscle size and strength. Suppose a person is infected with HIV. HIV-infected blood can remain on a needle, syringe, or injection equipment this person uses. If a second person uses the same needle, syringe, or injection equipment, the HIV-infected blood will get into the second person's body. This person will then be infected with HIV.

REASON #2: Because I could become infected with HIV if I drink alcohol or use other drugs. I could make a wrong decision and, as a result, have sex with someone who is infected with HIV.

You know that practicing abstinence is the best way to protect your health. You know that practicing abstinence will prevent sexual transmission of HIV. But suppose you make a wrong decision and drink alcohol or use other drugs. Even drugs you do not inject, such as alcohol and marijuana, are risky. They affect the part of your brain used for clear thinking and reasoning. They dull your decision-making skills. In that condition, you might not consider the risks of being sexually active—HIV infection, STDs, and unwanted pregnancy. Teens who have made a mistake and have been sexually active often were drinking at the time. Stay in control of your decisions. Do not drink alcohol or use other drugs.

Why Does Saying NO to Sharing a Needle to Make Tattoos and to Pierce Body Parts Protect Me from HIV Infection?

REASON: Because I could become infected with HIV if I shared a needle that has been used on or by a person who is infected with HIV.

Suppose you decide to get a tattoo. You might make the tattoo yourself or you might have someone else do it. People might share needles to make tattoos. The person making your tattoo might use a needle that was used to make a tattoo on someone you do not know. The person making your tattoo might not tell you that (s)he used the needle on someone else's body. The needle might have been used on a person who is infected with HIV. That needle might have droplets of HIV-infected blood on it that would be too small to see. If that needle is used to make a tattoo on you, these droplets of blood could get into your body and you could be infected with HIV.

Think ahead about the consequences of getting a tattoo. Do you want to risk being infected with HIV? NO. Will you want to have the tattoo for the rest of your life? NO. Do your parents or guardian want you to get a tattoo? NEVER get a tattoo without asking permission.

Suppose you decide to pierce your ears or another body part. You might do it yourself or you might have someone else do it. Sometimes people share needles to do ear or body piercing. The needle might have been used on a person who is infected with HIV. That needle could have droplets of HIV-infected blood on it that might be too small to see. If that needle is used to pierce your ears or another body part, the droplets of blood could get into your body. Then you would be infected with HIV.

Always get permission from your parents or guardian if you consider getting a tattoo or piercing your ears or other body parts.

There are people who are licensed to make tattoos and pierce ears. They are required to use sterile equipment.

Why Do I Need to Follow Universal Precautions to Protect Myself from HIV Infection?

REASON: Because you can become infected with HIV if you have contact with the blood or other body fluids, mucous membranes, or broken skin of a person who is infected with HIV.

You usually have no way of knowing whether or not a person is infected with HIV. Let's look at some examples. Suppose you are playing softball and a teammate is injured and begins to bleed. You do not know whether or not this person is infected with HIV. Suppose you are in study hall and the person next to you has a nosebleed. You do not know whether or not this person is infected with HIV. Suppose you are giving first aid to someone who has open wounds. You do not know whether or not this person is infected with HIV.

But there is something you do know. You know that you can become infected with HIV if you have contact with the blood or other body fluids of a person who is infected with HIV. You also know that you can become infected with HIV if you have contact with the mucous membranes or broken skin of a person who is infected with HIV.

However, you might want to help a person. What should you do? Would you appear foolish if you did something to protect yourself? NO WAY. But you would be foolish if you did not think ahead.

Universal precautions are steps taken to keep from having contact with pathogens in body fluids. These steps help protect you from HIV. Practice the universal precautions on the right in any situation in which you might have contact with blood and other body fluids.

Practice the following universal precautions in any situation in which you might have contact with blood and other body fluids.

1. Wear disposable latex or polyurethane gloves.
2. Do not wear disposable gloves more than once.
3. Wash your hands well with soap and water after you remove the gloves.
4. Wear a face mask or shield if you give first aid for breathing.
5. Do not use a face mask or shield more than once without disinfecting it.
6. Cover any cuts, scrapes, and rashes on your body with plastic wrap or a sterile dressing.
7. Do not eat or drink anything while giving first aid.
8. Do not touch your mouth, eyes, or nose while caring for a victim.

What Tests Are Used to Determine a Person's HIV Status?

You cannot tell if people are infected with HIV by the way they look. They might appear healthy because there are no symptoms at first. However, a person who is infected with HIV and has no symptoms can spread HIV to someone else. Any person who has chosen risky behaviors should be tested for HIV. Risky behaviors are being sexually active, using injecting drugs, or sharing a needle. Other persons who have certain signs or symptoms also should be tested.

Suppose a person is infected with HIV. The immune system will begin to make HIV antibodies. Tests are necessary to determine that person's HIV status. A person's **HIV status** is the result of testing for HIV antibodies in the blood. **HIV negative** is a term used to describe a person who does not have HIV antibodies in the blood. **HIV positive** is a term used to describe a person who has HIV antibodies in the blood. **ELISA** (ee·LY·suh) is a test used on blood or mouth fluids to check for HIV antibodies. **Western blot** is a test used to confirm ELISA.

Other Tests

- The oral test for HIV uses a cotton swab to get a tissue sample from between the cheek and gums.

- Another test measures the amount of HIV in the blood. The more HIV that is present, the faster a person will develop AIDS. This test helps physicians decide how a patient is doing and when to change medicines. This test is not used to diagnose HIV infection.

HIV Test Results

There is something important to know about HIV test results. After infection occurs, it takes from two weeks to several months for the immune system to make enough HIV antibodies to get an accurate test. Most people develop detectable antibodies within three months. In some cases, it could take six months. This means a person who is infected with HIV might not test positive at first. Any person who has been involved in risky behaviors needs to be tested as soon as (s)he thinks (s)he has been exposed to HIV. (S)he should be retested several times up to six months after the last exposure. This person CAN spread HIV to someone else before (s)he tests HIV positive.

How Does HIV Infection Progress to AIDS?

The signs of HIV infection might appear right away or they might take twelve or more years to appear. Early signs are similar to those of the flu. They include tiredness, fever, swollen glands, rash, and headaches.

Opportunistic (AH·puhr·too·NIS·tik) **infections** are infections that develop when a person has a weak immune system. **Pneumocystis carinii** (NOO·muh·SIS·tis kuh·REE·nee) **pneumonia (PCP)** is a type of pneumonia found in people who have AIDS. PCP makes it very difficult to breathe. **Kaposi's** (KA·puh·seez) **sarcoma (KS)** is a type of cancer in people who have AIDS. KS causes purple spots to develop on the skin. **AIDS dementia** (di·MENT·shuh) is a loss of brain function caused by HIV infection. It causes changes in thinking, memory, and coordination.

According to the Centers for Disease Control and Prevention, a person infected with HIV has AIDS when (s)he has 200 or fewer helper T cells per microliter of blood or an opportunistic infection.

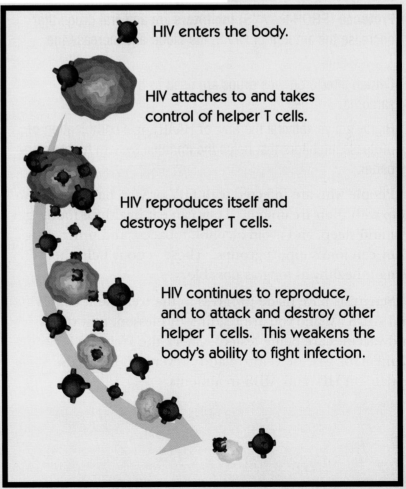

HIV enters the body.

HIV attaches to and takes control of helper T cells.

HIV reproduces itself and destroys helper T cells.

HIV continues to reproduce, and to attack and destroy other helper T cells. This weakens the body's ability to fight infection.

What Are the Latest Treatments for HIV and AIDS?

To date, there is no cure for HIV infection or AIDS. Early treatment is important. Treatments can slow the rate at which the virus multiplies. These treatments extend the life of a person who is infected with HIV. The amount of quality time for the person increases.

You might read about the following drugs for HIV and AIDS in the newspaper or hear about them in a news report.

- **ddi** is a drug that slows down the rate at which HIV multiplies.
- **AZT** is a drug that slows down the rate at which HIV multiplies.
- **Protease** (PROH·tee·AYS) **inhibitors** are antiviral drugs that decrease the amount of HIV in the blood and increase the T cell count.
- Certain interferon type drugs are used to treat Kaposi's sarcoma.
- Highly active antiviral therapy, or HAART, is a combination of protease inhibitors that helps the immune system function better.

People who are infected with HIV or who have AIDS can help with their treatment. They can eat healthful foods, get rest and sleep, and avoid alcohol, tobacco, and other drugs. They can join support groups. These actions help them remain healthy as long as possible.

Scientists have made progress in the treatment of HIV and AIDS. While you are reading this lesson, new drugs and vaccines are being tested. Check the Web site for the Centers for Disease Control and Prevention to get the latest update on HIV and AIDS treatments.

Activity

HIV and AIDS Tears Society Apart

Life Skill: I will choose behaviors to reduce my risk of HIV infection.

Materials: paper, pen or pencil, scissors

Directions: Complete the following activity to review ways in which HIV and AIDS threaten society.

1. **Cut a large round pie shape from a sheet of notebook paper.**

2. **Write "society" in the center of the pie.**

3. **With a pen or pencil, divide your pie into seven pieces.**

4. **Label each of six of the pieces with one of the ways in which HIV and AIDS threaten society.** (See the box.)

5. **Label the seventh piece of the pie with an additional way you think HIV and AIDS threaten society.** Tell your teacher your idea so (s)he can add it to the list of ways that are listed in the box.

6. **Listen as your teacher reads aloud your list of ways in which HIV and AIDS threaten society.**

   • Your teacher will pause after (s)he reads each way HIV and AIDS threaten society.

   • Tear the corresponding piece from your pie.

   • Each time you tear a piece, you are tearing away a part of society.

7. **Discuss the following question with classmates.**

   • How will society benefit if teens practice abstinence to protect themselves from HIV infection?

Ways in Which HIV and AIDS Threaten Society

• Increase health care costs

• Cause people to die at a young age

• Cause families to grieve the loss of a loved one

• Cause friends to grieve the loss of a loved one

• Cause people who are infected to suffer from illness

• Cause babies to be born infected with HIV or with AIDS

How Can I Resist Pressure to Choose Risk Behaviors for HIV Infection?

Use resistance skills if you are pressured to choose risk behaviors for HIV infection. **Resistance skills** are skills that are used to say NO to an action or to leave a situation.

1. **Be confident and say, "NO, I do not want to risk becoming infected with HIV."**

2. **Give reasons you will not choose risk behaviors for HIV infection.**

    • I will not be sexually active. I do not want to become infected with HIV.

    • I will not be involved in injecting drug use. I do not want to become infected with HIV.

    • I will not drink alcohol because drinking can affect my ability to make decisions about sex. I do not want to be sexually active and become infected with HIV.

    • I will not share a needle to get a tattoo. I do not want to become infected with HIV.

    • I will not share a needle to pierce my ears or other body parts. I do not want to become infected with HIV.

3. **Repeat your reasons for NOT choosing risk behaviors for HIV infection.**

4. **Do not send a mixed message.** Never lead someone to believe that you *might* change your mind.

5. **Avoid situations in which there might be pressure to choose risk behaviors for HIV infection.** Stay away from situations in which you think you might be pressured to have sex, to use injecting drugs, or to share a needle to make a tattoo or to pierce your ears or other body parts. Stay away from situations where teens drink or use other drugs that affect clear thinking.

6. **Break off a relationship when someone continues to pressure you to choose risk behaviors for HIV infection.**

7. **Influence others to AVOID risk behaviors for HIV infection.**

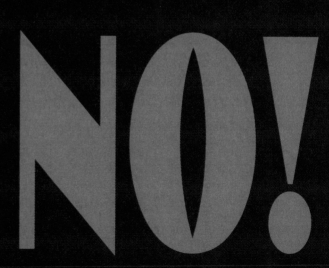

Review

Vocabulary Words

Write a separate sentence using each vocabulary word listed on page 326.

The Responsible Decision-Making Model™

An older teens tells you he can make a tattoo on your arm. He says he has made them for other teens and they are really "in." Answer the following questions on a separate sheet of paper. Write "Does not apply" if a question does not apply to this situation.

1. Is it healthful to have an older teen make a tattoo on your arm? Why or why not?

2. Is it safe to have an older teen make a tattoo on your arm? Why or why not?

3. Is it legal to have an older teen make a tattoo on your arm? Why or why not?

4. Will you show respect for yourself if you have an older teen make a tattoo on your arm? Why or why not?

5. Will your parents or guardian approve if you have an older teen make a tattoo on your arm? Why or why not?

6. Will you demonstrate good character if you have an older teen make a tattoo on your arm? Why or why not?

What is the responsible decision to make in this situation?

Health Content

1. What are ways HIV is spread? **page 327**

2. What are ways HIV is not spread? **page 327**

3. Why does practicing abstinence protect you from HIV infection? **page 328**

4. Why does saying NO to injecting drug use protect you from HIV infection? **page 329**

5. Why does saying NO to drinking alcohol or using other mood-altering drugs protect you from HIV infection? **page 329**

6. Why does saying NO to sharing a needle to make tattoos protect you from HIV infection? **page 330**

7. Why does saying NO to sharing a needle to pierce ears or other body parts protect you from HIV infection? **page 330**

8. Why do you need to follow universal precautions to protect yourself from HIV infection? **page 331**

9. What are eight universal precautions? **page 331**

10. What tests are used to determine HIV status? **page 332**

11. What are three opportunistic infections? **page 333**

12. How does HIV infection progress to AIDS? **page 333**

13. What are the latest treatments for HIV and AIDS? **page 334**

14. What are six ways in which HIV and AIDS threaten society? **page 335**

15. What are resistance skills you can use if you are pressured to choose risk behaviors for HIV infection? **page 336**

How to Reduce Your Risk of Cardiovascular Diseases and Cancer

 Life Skills

- ◆ I will choose behaviors to reduce my risk of cardiovascular diseases.
- ◆ I will choose behaviors to reduce my risk of cancer.

Cardiovascular diseases are diseases of the heart and blood vessels. **Cancer** is a group of diseases in which cells divide in an uncontrollable manner. Many kinds of cardiovascular diseases and cancer are considered lifestyle diseases. A **lifestyle disease** is a disease that is more likely to develop in a person who engages in specific risk behaviors. It is important to know what behaviors will reduce your risks of having a lifestyle disease.

The Lesson Objectives

- Discuss ways to reduce your risk of developing high blood pressure.
- Discuss ways to reduce your risk of having a stroke.
- Discuss ways to reduce your risk of developing atherosclerosis.
- Identify risk factors for cardiovascular diseases.
- Discuss ways to reduce your risk of developing cancers.

Vocabulary

cardiovascular diseases

cancer

lifestyle disease

high blood pressure

stroke

atherosclerosis

plaque

angina

heart attack

coronary artery

risk factor

tumor

malignant melanoma

ozone layer

How Can I Reduce My Risk of Developing High Blood Pressure? Having a Stroke?

Facts About High Blood Pressure

High blood pressure is a condition in which the pressure against the artery walls is above normal when the heart beats. Your normal blood pressure varies according to your height, age, and sex. Your physician can tell you whether or not you have high blood pressure. You are at higher risk for developing high blood pressure if family members have a history of high blood pressure.

High blood pressure can damage your heart, blood vessels, and kidneys. High blood pressure can cause stroke, blindness, heart attack, and kidney failure. You can reduce your risk of developing high blood pressure by taking the following actions.

- Lose weight if you are overweight.
- Participate in regular physical activity.
- Choose foods low in fat, cholesterol, and sodium.
- Do not use stimulants such as caffeine and nicotine.
- Do not drink alcohol.
- Do not use tobacco products.
- Avoid secondhand smoke.
- Learn to manage stress.
- Know your family health history.

Facts About Stroke

A **stroke** is a condition caused by a blocked or broken blood vessel in the brain. Brain cells near the blocked or broken blood vessel do not receive the oxygen they need. The brain cells die and the part of the body controlled by these cells cannot function. You are at higher risk for having a stroke if family members have a history of strokes. You can reduce your risk of having a stroke by taking the following actions.

- Maintain your normal blood pressure.
- Lose weight if you are overweight.
- Participate in regular physical activity.
- Choose foods low in fat, cholesterol, and sodium.
- Do not use tobacco products.
- Avoid secondhand smoke.
- Learn to manage stress.
- Know your family health history.

How Can I Reduce My Risk of Developing Atherosclerosis?

Atherosclerosis (A·thuh·ROH·skluh·ROH·suhs) is a disease in which fat deposits on artery walls. The fat can harden and form plaque. **Plaque** is hardened deposits that form on the inner walls of blood vessels.

Plaque narrows artery walls and reduces blood flow to the heart muscle. The heart muscle receives less oxygen. **Angina** (an·JY·nuh) is chest pain that results from decreased blood flow to the heart. A **heart attack** is the death of heart muscle caused by a lack of blood flow to the heart.

Plaque buildup also increases the likelihood that blood clots will form. A heart attack can result if blood clots form and lodge in the coronary arteries. A **coronary artery** is a blood vessel that carries blood to the heart muscles. Plaque also can break off and move through blood vessels, causing them to become blocked.

Plaque does not build up suddenly in later life. The buildup of plaque in artery walls may begin as early as two years of age. You can reduce your risk of developing atherosclerosis by taking the following actions.

- **Participate in regular physical activity.**
- **Choose foods low in fat, cholesterol, and sodium.**
- **Eat foods containing fiber to lower cholesterol.**
- **Do not use tobacco products.**
- **Maintain a normal blood sugar level if you have diabetes.**
- **Learn to manage stress.**
- **Learn to lessen angry feelings. Adrenaline is released when you are stressed or have angry feelings. Adrenaline causes your blood vessels to narrow and your heart to beat faster. This might cause your blood pressure to rise. Continued high blood pressure can damage artery walls. Plaque is more likely to deposit on damaged arteries. This increases your risk of having a stroke or a heart attack.**

Activity

The "Risk Facto" Game

Life Skill: I will choose behaviors to reduce my risk of cardiovascular diseases.

Materials: ten index cards per student, pen or pencil

Directions: Read the box that contains information on risk factors for cardiovascular diseases. Then play the game to help you remember these risk factors.

Risk Factors for Cardiovascular Diseases

A **risk factor** is something that increases the chance of a negative outcome. The American Heart Association has identified risk factors for cardiovascular disease. Some of these risk factors are listed below. Some of these risk factors can be controlled. Other risk factors cannot be controlled.

Some risk factors that can be controlled:

- Using tobacco products
- Having high blood pressure
- Having high blood cholesterol
- Eating fatty foods
- Not exercising regularly
- Being overweight

Some risk factors that cannot be controlled:

- Increasing age
- Being a male
- Having diabetes
- Having relatives who have heart disease

1. **Your teacher will organize the class into groups of four and give each student ten index cards.**

2. **Copy the risk factors from the lists on the left, one risk factor per card.** Your teacher will give each group one card on which is written "heart attack."

3. **Have one person in the group shuffle that group's cards (including the "heart attack" card).** That person deals the cards face down until all the cards are distributed. Do not let anyone else see your cards.

4. **Examine the cards in your hand for pairs.** Select any cards that you can pair and place them face down in front of you.

5. **Start to play Risk Facto with the dealer.** Continue around the group clockwise. The dealer selects a card (without seeing the cards) from the player on his or her left. If the card matches a card in the dealer's hand, the dealer removes both cards. The dealer places them face down in front of him or her.

6. **Play continues until one player gets rid of all cards in his or her hand.** The person who loses the game is the one holding the card that reads "heart attack."

How Can I Reduce My Risk of Developing Cancer?

All cells in a person's body usually divide in a controlled manner to produce more cells. Cancer is a group of diseases in which cells divide in an uncontrolled manner. These uncontrolled cells can form a tumor. A **tumor** is an abnormal growth of tissue. Cancer cells can break away from a tumor and spread to other parts of the body. You can reduce your risk of cancer by choosing the healthful behaviors on these two pages.

Eat five or more servings of fruits and vegetables a day. Why? Fruits and vegetables:

- provide fiber that helps you have a daily bowel movement. This reduces your risk of colon cancer;

- contain antioxidants. Antioxidants are substances that help prevent cancer;

- are lower in calories and help you maintain a desirable weight.

Limit the amount of beef, lamb, and pork you eat to three ounces or less per day. Why? Diets high in animal fat increase the risk of colon and rectal cancer.

Limit the amount of fatty foods you eat. Why? A high-fat diet increases the risk of cancers of the colon, rectum, lung, breast, and prostate.

Limit the amount of table salt you use. Why? Foods high in salt increase the risk of stomach cancer.

Limit the amount of food you eat that is grilled, smoked, or contains nitrites. Why? These foods can contain substances that increase the risk of cancers of the esophagus and stomach.

Do not eat food that appears to be moldy. Why? The food could contain aflatoxins. An aflatoxin (A·fluh·TAHK·suhn) is a substance produced by mold that increases the risk of liver cancer.

Avoid drinking alcohol. Why? Drinking alcohol increases the risk of cancers of the liver, breast, and digestive tract. Drinking alcohol also robs the body of vitamins.

Maintain a desirable weight. Why? Being obese increases the risk of cancers of the uterus, breast, gallbladder, prostate gland, and colon.

Participate in regular physical activity. Why? Regular physical activity helps prevent obesity and cancers associated with obesity.

Avoid tobacco products, such as cigarettes and smokeless tobacco, and secondhand smoke. Why? Tobacco is the number one cause of cancers of the lung, mouth, throat, and digestive tract.

Do not use anabolic steroids. Why? Anabolic steroids increase the risk of cancers of the liver and prostate gland.

Avoid infection with HIV and other sexually transmitted diseases. Why? People who are infected with HIV are at increased risk of developing several types of cancer. Females who have had genital warts or genital herpes are at increased risk for developing cervical cancer. Practice abstinence to keep from becoming infected with HIV and other STDs.

Protect yourself from ultraviolet or UV radiation. Why? Exposure to UV radiation is the main cause of skin cancer. Use a sunscreen with an SPF (sun protection factor) of at least 15 when outdoors. Wear sunglasses. Do not use sunlamps or tanning salons.

Avoid exposure to household chemicals. Why? Exposure to household chemicals increases your risk of certain cancers. Wear rubber gloves and a mask when using cleaning products. Use glues, paints, and thinners in well-ventilated areas.

Get regular physical examinations. Why? Your physician might be able to detect cancer early. Cancers are easier to treat if discovered early.

Check your home for radon. Why? Radon increases your risk of cancer of the lungs. Radon is an odorless, colorless radioactive gas that is released by rocks and soil. It can collect and become trapped in basements and crawl spaces.

Have water in your home checked if it looks or smells strange. Why? Drinking water that is polluted with certain chemicals increases your risk of cancer.

Avoid breathing exhaust from cars, buses, and trucks. Why? Exhaust from motor vehicles contains many substances that increase the risk of cancer.

Know your family's cancer history. Why? You might have an increased risk of developing certain cancers. Tell your physician if a family member has had cancer.

Contact a physician if you have one of the seven warning signs of cancer. Why? Cancers are easier to treat if discovered early. Having one of these signs does not necessarily mean you have cancer. Your physician can determine the reason for your symptoms. The first letters of the seven warning signs of cancer spell out the word CAUTION.

- **C**hange in bowel or bladder habits
- **A** sore that does not heal
- **U**nusual bleeding or discharge
- **T**hickening or lump in a breast or elsewhere
- **I**ndigestion or difficulty in swallowing
- **O**bvious change in a wart or mole
- **N**agging cough or hoarseness

How Can I Reduce My Risk of Developing Skin Cancer?

Skin cancer is one of the most common cancers. Ultra-violet (UV) radiation is the main cause of skin cancer. UV radiation comes from the sun, sunlamps, tanning beds, and tanning booths. **Malignant melanoma** (muh·LIG·nuhnt ME·luh·NOH·muh) is a serious form of skin cancer. It is the form of skin cancer that is most often fatal. It affects the cells that produce melanin. Melanin is a substance that protects skin and gives it color.

The number of cases of skin cancer in the United States has increased. One reason for this increase is the thinning of the ozone layer. The **ozone layer** is a layer of ozone in the upper atmosphere that filters UV radiation from the sun. Ozone is a form of oxygen produced when sunlight reacts with oxygen. More UV radiation is now reaching the earth. You can protect yourself from UV radiation. You can reduce your risk of developing skin cancer.

- Limit your time in the sun between 10 a.m. and 3 p.m.
- Wear sunscreen with SPF (sun protection factor) of at least 15.
- Cover up with a hat, long pants, and long sleeves when you are in the sun.
- Be aware that certain medications, such as antibiotics, increase the chance of sunburn.
- Do not use sunlamps or tanning salons. UV radiation from these sources causes the same skin damage as the sun.
- Wear sunglasses that protect against UV radiation. Melanoma can occur in the eye.
- Check your skin regularly for signs of skin cancer. Signs of skin cancer are a change on the skin or a sore that does not heal.

- Examine moles by using the following ABCD system from the American Cancer Society.

  A is for asymmetry (AY·SI·muh·tree). One half of the mole does not match the other half.

  B is for border. The edges of the mole appear ragged, uneven, or blurred.

  C is for color. The mole might appear to have different colors, usually different shades of brown and black. The colors red, white, and blue might be present.

  D is for diameter. The mole is wider than the tip of a pencil eraser.

Review

Vocabulary Words

Write a separate sentence using each vocabulary word listed on page 338.

Health Content

1. How can you reduce your risk of developing high blood pressure? **page 339**

2. How can you reduce your risk of having a stroke? **page 339**

3. How can you reduce your risk of developing atherosclerosis? **page 340**

4. What are ten risk factors for cardiovascular diseases? **page 341**

5. What are 20 ways to reduce your risk of developing cancers? **pages 342–343**

The Responsible Decision-Making Model™

Your friend visits a tanning salon. (S)he says it's healthier than tanning in the sun. You are thinking about visiting a tanning salon. Answer the following questions on a separate sheet of paper. Write "Does not apply" if a question does not apply to this situation.

1. Is it healthful to visit a tanning salon? Why or why not?

2. Is it safe to visit a tanning salon? Why or why not?

3. Is it legal to visit a tanning salon? Why or why not?

4. Will you show respect for yourself if you visit a tanning salon? Why or why not?

5. Will your parents or guardian approve if you visit a tanning salon? Why or why not?

6. Will you demonstrate good character if you visit a tanning salon? Why or why not?

What is the responsible decision to make in this situation?

What should you say to your friend?

Health Literacy

Critical Thinking

Visit a library or search the Internet. Find the five most common cancers for males and females. Make a graph and post it in your classroom.

Responsible Citizenship

List all the dietary recommendations in this lesson to reduce the risk of cancer. Post the list in your kitchen so your family can see it.

How to Manage Chronic Health Conditions

Life Skills

- ◆ I will recognize ways to manage chronic health conditions.
- ◆ I will recognize ways to manage asthma and allergies.
- ◆ I will choose behaviors to reduce my risk of diabetes.

Vocabulary

chronic health condition

asthma

asthma triggers

asthma attack

exercise-induced asthma (EIA)

headache

migraine headache

allergy

Type I diabetes

epilepsy

chronic fatigue syndrome (CFS)

sickle cell anemia

systemic lupus

Many teens have chronic health conditions. A **chronic health condition** is a health condition that lasts a long time or keeps coming back. Teens who have chronic health conditions must learn to manage them. They might need regular examinations and medications. They might need to follow a special diet or exercise plan. Some teens who have chronic health conditions need assistance. You can learn about chronic health conditions. Then you can be helpful and supportive of others.

The Lesson Objectives

- Explain how a chronic health condition differs from other health conditions.

- Discuss asthma, including signs of an asthma attack, asthma triggers, and ways to avoid asthma triggers.

- Outline the definition of, signs and symptoms of, and ways to manage the following chronic health conditions: headache, allergy, Type I diabetes, epilepsy, chronic fatigue syndrome, sickle cell anemia, and systemic lupus.

How Can a Teen Manage Asthma?

Asthma is a chronic condition in which breathing becomes difficult. **Asthma triggers** are substances or conditions that can cause asthma attacks. An **asthma attack** is an episode of coughing, wheezing, and shortness of breath. Breathing might be so difficult that first aid is needed. The signs and symptoms of an asthma attack include:

- Coughing
- Shortness of breath
- Rapid breathing
- Wheezing (whistling sound)
- Tightness in the chest
- Itchy or sore throat

Teens who have asthma should avoid asthma triggers to prevent asthma attacks. Some asthma triggers are:

- Cockroach droppings
- Dust mite droppings
- Dander from cats and dogs
- Pollen
- Colognes
- Dust and mold
- Cigarette smoke
- Aspirin and other OTC drugs
- Household cleaning products
- Emotional stress
- Tiredness
- Cold weather

Exercise-induced asthma (EIA) is a condition in which vigorous physical activity causes a person to have asthma attacks. Breathing cold, dry air during exercise increases the risk of having an asthma attack.

Teens with asthma can take these steps to manage their asthma.

- Avoid asthma triggers.
- Take medications and follow all advice from your physician.
- Always keep medications with you.
- Know the warning signs and symptoms of an asthma attack.
- Know when and how to get medical help for severe asthma attacks.
- Check with your physician before taking over-the-counter medicine.
- Do not smoke or inhale secondhand smoke.
- Get regular physical activity if your physician recommends it. Try swimming and other indoor water sports if you have EIA. Your physician might recommend that you breathe in puffs of medication from your inhaler before you exercise.
- Practice stress management skills.

What Are Some Common Chronic Health Conditions in Teens?

Disease or Condition

Signs and Symptoms

Ways to Manage

A **headache** is head pain with many causes. Some causes are tiredness, stress, loud noises, and certain foods. A **migraine headache** is severe head pain caused by widening of blood vessels in the brain.

- A dull, constant ache and tender spots on the head and neck
- Severe throbbing, nausea, and vomiting in migraine headache

- Taking medication to reduce pain
- Resting in a quiet, dark room
- Practicing stress management skills
- Avoiding eating foods that trigger headaches

An **allergy** is a condition in which the body overreacts to a substance. Most allergies are caused by airborne substances such as pollen and dust mite droppings. Some allergies are caused by foods.

- Allergies to airborne substances: sneezing, runny nose, stuffy nose, and itchy eyes
- Food allergies: skin rashes, stuffy nose, and difficulties breathing

- Eliminating the substance causing the allergy
- Taking medication to relieve symptoms
- Avoiding eating foods that cause allergic reactions

Type I diabetes (DY·uh·BEE·teez) is a disease in which the body produces little or no insulin. It usually occurs before age 30. Insulin is a hormone that helps the body use sugar from foods for energy. As a result, sugar levels build up in the blood instead of going to body cells.

- Extreme thirst, frequent urination, extreme hunger, weight loss, and tiredness

- Taking daily injections of insulin
- Eating a special diet
- Exercising regularly
- Testing blood sugar regularly

Disease or Condition

Signs and Symptoms

Ways to Manage

Epilepsy is a condition in which nerve messages in the brain are disturbed for a brief time. Epilepsy can be caused by head injury, brain tumor, brain infection, or poisoning.

- Seizures: A seizure is a brief loss of control over the mind and body due to a disturbance of nerve messages in the brain. A seizure can involve shaking of the entire body.

- Taking medication to control seizures
- Getting adequate rest and sleep
- Being active
- Informing school personnel of the condition
- Having surgery

Chronic fatigue syndrome (CFS) is a condition in which recurring tiredness makes it difficult to function.

- Tiredness, sore throat, fever, weakness, tender lymph glands, muscle and joint aches, and inability to concentrate

- Eating a balanced diet
- Getting adequate rest and sleep
- Having limited physical activity
- Practicing stress management skills
- Taking medications

Sickle cell anemia is an inherited blood disease in which the red blood cells carry less oxygen. The red blood cells are sickle-shaped and do not easily pass through tiny blood vessels. Sickle cell anemia occurs primarily in African Americans.

- Tiredness, headache, and shortness of breath
- In children, pneumonia and other infections

- Having oxygen therapy
- Taking antibiotics to protect against bacterial infections
- Taking medications to reduce pain
- Drinking fluids to prevent dehydration during physical activity, sickness, and hot weather
- Having regular physical exams

Systemic lupus is a disease that affects fat tissue, bones, ligaments, cartilage, and blood. The body produces antibodies against its own cells. The cause is unknown. Systemic lupus occurs most often during the teen years and is more common in females than in males.

- Tiredness, fever, loss of appetite, nausea, joint pain, and weight loss
- Red, blotchy rash on the cheeks and nose
- Bleeding in the central nervous system
- Heart and kidney failure

- Taking medications to reduce inflammation and fever
- Taking medications to relieve skin rashes
- Having the support of family members and friends

Activity

Management Match Game

Life Skill: I will recognize ways to manage chronic health conditions.

Materials: paper and marker for each student

Directions: Play the Management Match Game to review how to manage chronic diseases.

1. **Your teacher will divide the class into teams of five.** Each team will choose a team name. Your teacher will write the names of the teams on the chalkboard.

2. **Each student will write on a sheet of paper a question about how to manage a chronic disease.** The question must have more than one possible answer. An example is, "What is one asthma trigger?" Your teacher will collect the questions.

3. **Your teacher will call out each question.** On another sheet of paper, write one answer. Team members may NOT look at what anyone else on their team or on another team is writing.

4. **When everyone is finished writing, your teacher will ask each team to hold up its answers.** Your teacher will count the number of correct matches per team. A match is two correct identical answers. Each team gets one point for each correct match. If two students on the same team write "pollen" and three students write "dander from dogs," the team would get two points.

5. **The team with the most points wins.**

Vocabulary Words

Write a separate sentence using each vocabulary word listed on page 346.

Health Content

1. How does a chronic health condition differ from other health conditions? **page 346**

2. What are signs that indicate a person is having an asthma attack? **page 347**

3. What are different kinds of asthma triggers? How can a person avoid them? **page 347**

4. What triggers exercise-induced asthma (EIA)? **page 347**

5. Divide a sheet of paper into three columns. List the following chronic health conditions in the first column: headache, allergy, Type I diabetes, epilepsy, chronic fatigue syndrome, sickle cell anemia, and systemic lupus. Write the signs and symptoms for each chronic health condition in the second column. Write ways to manage them in the third column. **pages 348–349**

Self-Directed Learning

Select a chronic disease in which you are interested. Visit a library or search on the Internet. Start a file on the disease. Include articles you have copied or printed out. Continue to add to your file as you find new information.

The Responsible Decision-Making Model™

Your friend has asthma. During lunch, your friend has difficulty breathing. You tell your friend to go to the office. Your friend does not want to miss the rest of lunch period, so (s)he can socialize with friends. Answer the following questions on a separate sheet of paper. Write "Does not apply" if a question does not apply to this situation.

1. Is it healthful for your friend to ignore signs of an asthma attack? Why or why not?

2. Is it safe for your friend to ignore signs of an asthma attack? Why or why not?

3. Is it legal for your friend to ignore signs of an asthma attack? Why or why not?

4. Will your friend show respect for himself or herself if (s)he ignores signs of an asthma attack? Why or why not?

5. Will your friend's parents or guardian approve if your friend ignores signs of an asthma attack? Why or why not?

6. Will your friend demonstrate good character if (s)he ignores signs of an asthma attack? Why or why not?

What is the responsible decision to make in this situation?

Unit 7 Review

Health Content

Prepare for the Unit Test. Review your answers for each Lesson Review in this unit. Then write answers to each of the following questions:

1. Why should you avoid taking aspirin if you get the flu? **Lesson 31 page 311**

2. What is the proper technique for handwashing? **Lesson 31 page 314**

3. What are the consequences of being infected with genital herpes? **Lesson 32 page 322**

4. What are the consequences of being infected with genital warts? **Lesson 32 page 323**

5. Why does practicing abstinence protect you from HIV infection? **Lesson 33 page 328**

6. Why should you follow universal precautions if you give first aid for bleeding? **Lesson 33 page 331**

7. What are six risk factors for heart disease that you can control? **Lesson 34 page 341**

8. What are the seven warning signs of cancer? **Lesson 34 page 343**

9. What are the signs and symptoms that a person is having an asthma attack? **Lesson 35 page 347**

10. What causes allergies? **Lesson 35 page 348**

Health Behavior Contract

Make a health behavior contract for one of the life skills in this unit. Review your health behavior contract with your parents or guardian.

Vocabulary Words

Number a sheet of paper from 1–10. Select the correct vocabulary word and write it next to the corresponding number. DO NOT WRITE IN THIS BOOK.

pneumonia	HIV status
genital herpes	angina
universal precautions	strep throat
lifestyle disease	pubic lice
migraine headache	exercise-induced asthma (EIA)

1. _____ is an infection in the lungs caused by bacteria, viruses, or other pathogens. **Lesson 31**

2. _____ is the result of testing for HIV antibodies in the blood. **Lesson 33**

3. _____ is an STD caused by a virus that produces cold sores and blisters on the sex organs or in the mouth. **Lesson 32**

4. _____ is a bacterial infection of the throat. **Lesson 31**

5. _____ are steps taken to keep from having contact with pathogens in body fluids. **Lesson 33**

6. A _____ is severe head pain caused by widening of blood vessels in the brain. **Lesson 35**

7. A _____ is a disease that is more likely to develop in a person who engages in specific risk behaviors. **Lesson 34**

8. _____ is the infestation of the pubic hair by lice. **Lesson 32**

9. _____ is chest pain that results from decreased blood flow to the heart. **Lesson 34**

10. _____ is a condition in which vigorous physical activity causes a person to have asthma attacks. **Lesson 35**

The Responsible Decision-Making Model™

Your neighbor falls in your home and is bleeding. Your family has a first aid kit that contains disposable latex gloves. You grab the kit and put the gloves on. Your neighbor says, "Take those gloves off. I don't have AIDS!" Answer the following questions on a separate sheet of paper. Write "Does not apply" if a question does not apply to this situation.

1. Is it healthful to give first aid for bleeding without wearing gloves? Why or why not?

2. Is it safe to give first aid for bleeding without wearing gloves? Why or why not?

3. Is it legal to give first aid for bleeding without wearing gloves? Why or why not?

4. Will you show respect for yourself if you give first aid for bleeding without wearing gloves? Why or why not?

5. Will your parents or guardian approve if you give first aid for bleeding without wearing gloves? Why or why not?

6. Will you demonstrate good character if you give first aid for bleeding without wearing gloves? Why or why not?

What is the responsible decision to make in this situation?

Health Literacy
Effective Communication

Select three agencies that deal with chronic diseases. Check to see if the agencies have a symbol or logo. Then create your own symbol or logo for each agency.

Self-Directed Learning

Select a disease you consider to be a lifestyle disease. Write a two-page paper containing at least five facts about this disease. Discuss ways to prevent this disease.

Critical Thinking

Imagine that you are a physician who hosts a call-in show. Write a response to a caller who asks, "Why is the number of cases of people who have skin cancer increasing?"

Responsible Citizenship

A person who has a disability might not do things in the same way as others. For example, a person with multiple sclerosis might not walk long distances. This person might need to park in a handicapped space. Make a list of five services your community provides for people who have a disability.

Multicultural Health

List two countries whose borders are closest to the country in which you live. List two countries that are far away. Find out the immunizations that are needed to enter these countries.

Family Involvement

Design a card that lists the universal precautions found in the margin on page 331. Place the card in an appropriate place in your family's living space.

UNIT 8
Consumer and Community Health

PRACTICE
HEALTH STANDARD 2

Access Valid Health Information, Products, and Services

Practice this standard at the end of this unit.

1. **Identify health information, products, and services you need.** Suppose you are interested in finding out information about a career in health.

2. **Locate health information, products, and services.** Name some organizations that can provide information about a specific health career.

3. **Evaluate health information, products, and services.** Do the organizations provide all the information you need? For example, what level of education is needed to pursue a career in the health profession you selected? Is there information on the need for people in this health profession?

4. **Take action when health information is misleading.** Take action when you are not satisfied with health products and services. Suppose an organization provides incomplete information. Write a letter to the organization requesting the information you need.

How to Evaluate Health Information and Develop Media Literacy

Life Skills

- ◆ I will evaluate sources of health information.
- ◆ I will develop media literacy.

Vocabulary

CD-ROM

Internet

modem

World Wide Web (WWW)

Web site

electronic mail (e-mail)

newsgroup

media

media literacy

target audience

accurate message

Some sources of health information are more reliable than others. You need to be able to identify reliable sources of health information. Think about where you gain information about health. Do you talk to health professionals? Do you read magazine articles? Do you use the Internet? Do you watch television programs? You need to know how to evaluate the media messages you see and hear.

The Lesson Objectives

- Identify reliable sources of health information.
- Explain ways to use technology to gain health information.
- Recognize and evaluate media messages.
- Produce accurate messages about health.

What Are Reliable Sources of Health Information?

Use the following questions to decide whether or not a source of health information is reliable.

1. **What is the source of the information?** Reliable sources include health care professionals such as physicians and dentists, government agencies, community agencies, and professional organizations.

2. **Is the information based on current research and scientific evidence?** The information should not be based on someone's opinion. You should be able to get copies of the research if you request them.

3. **Do reputable physicians, dentists, and other health care professionals endorse the information?** Ask your own physician or dentist if the information is reliable. Talk to other health care professionals and other scientists.

4. **Are you able to get more information if you request it?** People who are sources of reliable health information will be able to suggest additional sources to prove their information.

5. **What is the purpose of the information?** The purpose of reliable health information is to inform you. Reliable health information does not try to persuade you to buy a specific product or service.

6. **Does the information make realistic claims?** Reliable health information does not claim to cure problems for which medical science does not have cures.

Some Reliable Sources of Health Information

- Your physician, dentist, or other health care professional
- Centers for Disease Control and Prevention (CDC)
- National Health Information Center
- American Red Cross
- American Heart Association
- American Cancer Society
- American Medical Association
- American Association for Health Education
- Books, such as this textbook
- Medical journals
- Computer products and services such as CD-ROMs and the World Wide Web
- Your health teacher

How Can I Use Technology to Gain Health Information?

You can gain health information and have fun at the same time by using technology. You might use videos, TV programs, CD-ROMs, or the Internet to gain health information.

Gaining Health Information from Videos

You can find health-related videos at your local library or video store. You also can borrow health-related videos from local health agencies or professional organizations.

Gaining Health Information from CD-ROMs

A **CD-ROM** is a computer disc that stores computer programs that might include text, graphics, music, and animation. CD-ROM stands for Compact Disc Read-Only Memory. Many CD-ROMs contain information on health-related topics. You can watch video clips, listen to sounds, look at photos, and read text using a CD-ROM. You need a computer with a CD-ROM drive to use CD-ROMs.

Gaining Health Information from TV Programs

Many educational programs on TV focus on health-related topics. These programs often are reliable sources of health information. However, some programs try to sell you products that they claim will improve your health. Remember to evaluate all information you learn from TV programs.

Gaining Health Information from the Internet

The **Internet** is a worldwide system of computer networks. To use the Internet, you need a computer, a modem, a telephone line, communications software, and an Internet account. A **modem** is a device that allows a computer to exchange information with another computer over the telephone lines. Always get permission from your parents or guardian before using the Internet.

Parts of the Internet include the World Wide Web, e-mail, and newsgroups. The **World Wide Web (WWW),** or Web, is a computer system that allows a person to view information as text and/or graphics. A **Web site** is a collection of files or "pages" kept on a computer called a Web server. Suppose you use a program called a search engine to search for the words "Centers for Disease Control and Prevention (CDC)." You would find the agency's Web site. Then you could click your mouse on various words or pictures to look at health information, publications and software products, health information for travelers, or other parts of the CDC's Web site. Schools, businesses, agencies, organizations, and individuals can have Web sites.

Electronic mail or e-mail is a message delivered quickly from one computer to another. You can send e-mail to a friend, a relative, a teacher, or a health professional if you know his or her e-mail address. A **newsgroup** is an area on the Internet where people post messages on a specific subject for other people to read. There are newsgroups on thousands of subjects.

Sources of Health Information on the World Wide Web

- Centers for Disease Control and Prevention (CDC)
- American Red Cross
- American Cancer Society
- National Safety Council
- World Health Organization
- American Medical Association
- MedAccess
- American Heart Association
- Medline

Always use the questions on page 357 to evaluate the information you find by using technology.

How Can I Evaluate the Messages in Media?

Media are the various forms of mass communication. Examples of media include magazines, newspapers, television, radio, billboards, and the Internet. Health knowledge is available through various media. You must evaluate carefully any health information you learn about in media. Anyone can post information on the World Wide Web, regardless of whether the information is true. Companies pay to advertise their products in magazines and newspapers, and on television, radio, and billboards.

You need to have media literacy skills. **Media literacy** is the ability to recognize and evaluate the messages in media. Use the *Questions to Evaluate Media Messages*™.

Questions to Evaluate Media Messages™

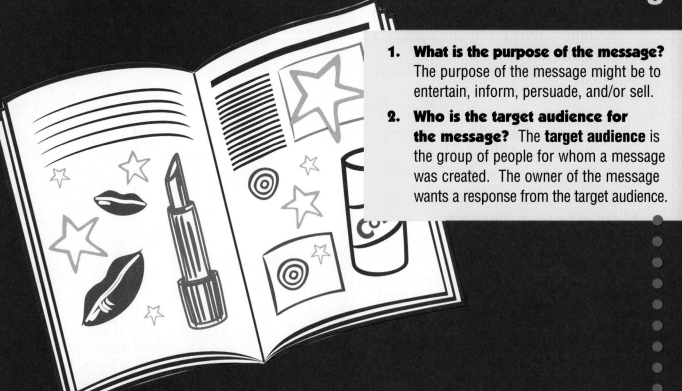

1. **What is the purpose of the message?** The purpose of the message might be to entertain, inform, persuade, and/or sell.

2. **Who is the target audience for the message?** The **target audience** is the group of people for whom a message was created. The owner of the message wants a response from the target audience.

3. **Who will profit if members of the target audience are influenced by the message?** Someone owns and pays for the messages in media. The owner might be a nonprofit organization, such as the American Cancer Society. Or the owner might be a company or businessperson that uses the media to advertise products, services, or entertainment. The owner intends to make a profit for the company or businessperson. The target audience might or might not profit from the message.

4. **Does the message encourage members of the target audience to choose responsible behavior? How?** Does the message encourage members of the target audience to behave in ways that are healthful? That are safe? That are legal? That are respectful of self and others? That follow the guidelines of parents or guardians? That demonstrate good character? A media message can influence your behavior.

5. **What techniques are used to make the message appealing to the target audience? Why?** Techniques that use sound, video images, lighting, camera angles, editing, wording, setting, characters, and props make messages appealing. The message must appeal to the target audience or the audience will not respond the way the message owner desires.

6. **What information is missing from the message? Why?** Messages have different purposes. Depending on those purposes, messages might not contain all the possible details about the issue being discussed. Think about what information might be missing from the message. Suppose you see an ad for a "miracle acne cure." The purpose of this ad would be to sell the acne cure. But the ad does not mention that scientific research has found no cure for acne. By thinking about what information is missing, you also can decide whether the message promotes responsible behavior. Would it be responsible to buy such a "miracle cure"?

7. **Is this message consistent with messages found in other media on the same subject? How?** Suppose you see a television program about an "amazing" new vitamin. Check other sources of health information to see if the same message appears there. You might read a magazine article or look up information about the vitamin on the World Wide Web. Suppose you find other reliable sources with the same information about the vitamin. Then you know the message is more likely to be accurate.

Activity
Produce Accurate Messages

Life Skill: I will evaluate sources of health information.

Materials: paper, pen or pencil, computer (optional)

Directions: Having media literacy skills includes being able to produce accurate messages. An **accurate message** is a message that is based on scientific research and is supported by several different sources. You will produce an accurate message about a health issue.

1. **Choose a disease or condition from the following list.**

cold	high blood pressure
influenza	atherosclerosis
mononucleosis	skin cancer
strep throat	diabetes
pneumonia	asthma
stroke	

2. **Research your topic.** You should use at least three reliable sources. You might choose sources from the lists on pages 357 and 359, or you might use other sources. Use the questions on page 357 to decide whether or not your sources are reliable.

3. **Write a two-page report on your topic.** Your report should describe the condition you chose. It also should include ways to reduce the risk of having the condition. Include a bibliography listing your sources.

4. **Present your report to your class.** Tell which sources you used. Explain how you know those sources are reliable.

Vocabulary Words

Write a separate sentence using each vocabulary word listed on page 356.

Health Content

1. How can you decide whether or not a source of health information is reliable? **page 357**

2. What are five examples of reliable sources of health information? **page 357**

3. What are four ways you can use technology to get health information? **pages 358–359**

4. What are five sources of health information on the World Wide Web? **page 359**

5. What are the seven *Questions to Evaluate Media Messages™?* **pages 360–361**

Health Literacy

Responsible Citizenship

Design a poster that motivates people to use technology to gain health information. Be creative.

Critical Thinking

Find an advertisement in a magazine or newspaper for a health-related product. Evaluate the advertisement using the questions on page 357. Write a one-page paper explaining whether or not the advertisement provides reliable health information.

The Responsible Decision-Making Model™

You are shopping with a friend. You spot a display featuring a new brand of toothpaste. Your friend says, "Let's get some of that toothpaste! I saw an ad that said it actually fills in cavities." Answer the following questions on a separate sheet of paper. Write "Does not apply" if a question does not apply to this situation.

1. Is it healthful to buy the toothpaste? Why or why not?

2. Is it safe to buy the toothpaste? Why or why not?

3. Is it legal to buy the toothpaste? Why or why not?

4. Will you show respect for yourself if you buy the toothpaste? Why or why not?

5. Will you follow the guidelines of your parents or guardian if you buy the toothpaste? Why or why not?

6. Will you demonstrate good character if you buy the toothpaste? Why or why not?

What is the responsible decision to make in this situation?

How to Spend Time and Money Wisely

Life Skills

- ◆ I will make a plan to manage time and money.
- ◆ I will choose healthful entertainment.

Vocabulary

time management

time management plan

empowered

budget

income

expenses

healthful entertainment

desensitization

Everyone spends time and everyone spends money. Managing your time and money wisely is an important health investment you should make. You promote your health when you have a budget and manage your money. You promote your health when you make time for important health habits. And you promote your health when you choose to spend your time and money on healthful entertainment.

The Lesson Objectives

- Explain why you need to follow a time management plan.

- Explain why you need to have a budget and manage money wisely.

- Design a time management plan in which you make time for healthful habits.

- Discuss reasons why you need to choose healthful entertainment.

- Identify *Guidelines for Choosing Entertainment That Promotes Responsible Behavior.*

Why Do I Need to Follow a Time Management Plan?

Have you ever wanted to do something and then found you just could not get around to it? **Time management** is organizing time to do the things that matter to a person. A **time management plan** is a plan that shows how a person will spend time. You benefit from making and following a time management plan.

You keep your priorities straight. Your priorities are those things that matter most to you. When you list your priorities, you make time for them. You keep your life balanced. You identify and eliminate activities that waste your time. You follow your plan and reflect on it. You go back and see if your plan is working.

You are less stressed. Most likely, you are a busy person. The number of homework assignments that you have has increased. Your parents or guardian expect you to do more to help out at home. There are social activities you want to enjoy. How can you do everything? Use your time management plan to do what matters to you. You do not waste your time worrying about getting important things done.

You make time for healthful habits. Sometimes you might be tempted to skip healthful habits to make time for other things. But taking care of your health will save time in the long run. You will have more energy to get things done and spend less time being ill. Plan time for regular exercise. Get adequate sleep. Get up early enough to pack a healthful lunch and to appear well groomed. Make time to spend with family and friends. Arrange some leisure time for yourself.

You sleep better. You get important things done when you follow a time management plan. You are able to relax when you go to bed. You are not worried that you are behind on important projects. You feel more positive because you have made time to take care of your social and mental health.

You accomplish more. You eliminate time wasters such as watching hours of television. You focus your time on your priorities. You feel competent because you complete your goals. Your self-confidence increases. You are in control of your time. You are taking care of your mental health.

Why Do I Need to Manage Money Wisely?

Here's a pop quiz. Managing money wisely can help you: a) buy a video game; b) have fun at an amusement park; c) achieve optimal health. Are you surprised that the correct answer is "all of the above"? You might have heard that money cannot buy health. But that is only partly true. Managing your money wisely can help you protect your health. Managing money wisely means you do not spend more money than you have. It means you are more likely to have money to buy what you need. It means you buy things you want only when you have the money. You need to manage your money wisely for the following reasons.

You experience less stress. You are better able to buy things you need. You do not spend more money than you have. You are less worried about paying bills. You can concentrate on more enjoyable areas of life. You are less likely to develop premature heart disease or cancer because of stress.

You become empowered. To be **empowered** is to be energized because a person has some control over his or her decisions and behavior. You increase your sense of control because you are making wise decisions about how to spend your money. You do not let spending control you. You control spending.

You are more likely to have the money you need for items that promote physical, social, and mental health. You can buy sports equipment, grooming products, or a ticket to an amusement park. Your family has money to get health care.

You achieve one of the developmental tasks for becoming a responsible adult. Managing money wisely is a skill you need to become independent from your parents or guardian in the future.

A **budget** is a written plan for saving and spending money. A budget helps you manage money wisely. A budget has two parts—income and expenses. **Income** is money received. You might get money from allowances, part-time jobs, and gifts. **Expenses** are amounts of money needed to purchase or do something. Follow these three steps to prepare and follow a budget.

- **Make a list of your sources of income.**

- **List the amount you spend and what you purchase each time you spend money.**

- **Compare your expenses to your income.** Suppose your expenses are greater than your income. Develop ways to cut back on your spending. Ask your parents or guardian to help you.

Activity

Health Behavior Contract

> **Copy the health behavior contract on a separate sheet of paper.**
> DO NOT WRITE IN THIS BOOK.

Name:_____ **Date:**_____

Life Skill: I will make a plan to manage time and money.

Effect on My Health: My life will be balanced because I will keep my priorities straight. I will be less stressed. I will make time for healthful habits. I will sleep better. I will accomplish more.

My Plan: On a separate sheet of paper, I will list activities I do to promote my health. I will assign each activity to a time slot on my calendar. I will do that activity during that time. I will list activities to promote my health that I do not practice. I will make time for those activities by assigning each one to a time slot. I will be certain to plan time for all activities I need to do to promote my health. My calendar is my time management plan. I will follow the plan for a week.

	M	T	W	Th	F	S	S
My Calendar							

How My Plan Worked: (Complete after one week)_____

_____

_____

Why Do I Need to Choose Healthful Entertainment?

Healthful entertainment is entertainment that promotes physical, mental, or social health. Choosing healthful entertainment helps keep you from being bored. Healthful entertainment makes you a more interesting person. It gives you interesting things to talk about. It provides opportunities for building social skills. You need to choose healthful entertainment for four reasons.

Healthful entertainment can influence your thinking in a positive way. Positive thinking causes biochemical changes that help build your immune system. They also cause you to have a feeling of well-being. You might feel charged up when you surround yourself with upbeat music. You might be motivated to play tennis after watching a tennis match.

Healthful entertainment can influence the way you make decisions. Healthful entertainment promotes responsible decision-making. It motivates you to choose behaviors that are healthful, safe, legal, show respect for yourself and others, follow the guidelines of your parents or guardian, and demonstrate good character.

Healthful entertainment can influence what you believe is right and wrong. It is important for you to know the standards society upholds. You see people using self-control to act on responsible values. This motivates you to use self-control to act on responsible values.

Healthful entertainment can influence how you think people should treat others. You reinforce responsible values when you choose entertainment that shows people respecting one another. You are motivated to choose nonviolent ways of solving problems.

Desensitization (DEE·sent·suh·tuh·ZAY·shuhn) is the effect of reacting less and less to the exposure to something. Children and teens who continually watch TV and movie violence might gradually stop feeling shocked. They might become numb to the horror of pain and death that results from violence. They might see violence as an acceptable way of life. Some children and teens might imitate the violence to which they have been exposed. They might commit violent acts or behave aggressively toward others.

Guidelines for Choosing Entertainment That Promotes Responsible Behavior

- Entertainment should be approved for your age group.
- Entertainment should be approved by your parents or guardian.
- Entertainment should not present harmful drug use as acceptable behavior.
- Entertainment should not present violence as acceptable behavior.
- Entertainment should not lead you to believe sex outside of marriage is acceptable behavior.

Vocabulary Words

Write a separate sentence using each vocabulary word listed on page 364.

Health Content

1. What are five benefits of making and following a time management plan? **page 365**

2. What are four reasons to manage money wisely? **page 366**

3. What should you include in a budget? **page 366**

4. What are four reasons you need to choose healthful entertainment? **page 368**

5. What are five *Guidelines for Choosing Entertainment That Promotes Responsible Behavior?* **page 368**

Health Literacy

Responsible Citizenship

Help a younger brother or sister make a time management plan to practice healthful habits.

Self-Directed Learning

Check the library or Internet for information about how to save money for a long-term goal such as a car or college education. Develop a plan to save regularly a portion of your income (even if it is small) toward this goal.

The Responsible Decision-Making Model™

You are listening to a new compact disc (CD) your friend just bought. One song describes how to beat up a girlfriend. Answer the following questions on a separate sheet of paper. Write "Does not apply" if a question does not apply to this situation.

1. Is it healthful to listen to music that presents violence as acceptable behavior? Why or why not?

2. Is it safe to listen to music that presents violence as acceptable behavior? Why or why not?

3. Is it legal to listen to music that presents violence as acceptable behavior? Why or why not?

4. Will you show respect for yourself if you listen to music that presents violence as acceptable behavior? Why or why not?

5. Will your parents or guardian approve if you listen to music that presents violence as acceptable behavior? Why or why not?

6. Will you demonstrate good character if you listen to music that presents violence as acceptable behavior? Why or why not?

What is the responsible decision to make in this situation?

How to Be an Assertive Consumer

Life Skills

◆ I will recognize my rights as a consumer.

◆ I will take action if my consumer rights are violated.

A **consumer** is a person who uses information, products, and services. As a consumer, you have rights. **Consumer rights** are the privileges that a consumer is guaranteed. These include the right to choose, the right to be heard, the right to be safe, and the right to be informed. You can protect your rights by being assertive. To be **assertive** is to make one's expectations clear using positive actions.

The Lesson Objectives

• Identify four rights you can expect as a consumer.

• List questions you should ask before you buy something.

• Discuss actions you can take if you are not satisfied with something you have bought.

• Identify and discuss agencies that protect your consumer rights.

• Discuss appeals and claims that might indicate quackery.

Vocabulary

consumer

consumer rights

assertive

Food and Drug Administration (FDA)

product recall

Federal Trade Commission (FTC)

Consumer Product Safety Commission (CPSC)

United States Postal Service (USPS)

Council of Better Business Bureaus

Consumer's Union (CU)

Center for Science in the Public Interest (CSPI)

quackery

What Questions Should I Ask Before I Buy Something?

Imagine that you are starting a new exercise program. You would like to buy some exercise equipment and videotapes. And you think you will buy a new protein drink advertised on TV to give you more energy. Sound simple? Maybe not. Millions of health products are available for purchase. Many provide the health benefits claimed by the manufacturer. Some do not. Some health products waste your money. Others are harmful, even dangerous. How can you protect yourself? Ask yourself the following questions before you buy something.

1. **Do I really need the product?** You should not buy something just because your friends have it.

2. **Do I understand what the product does and how to use it?** You should read the directions or description carefully. Do not buy the product if the manufacturer makes a claim you know is false.

3. **Is the product safe?** You do not want to become sick or injured.

4. **Is the product worth the price?** You should compare the product to other similar products. Be sure to include tax and shipping and handling charges if they apply.

5. **Is the product well made?** You do not want the product to fall apart with normal use.

6. **What is the return policy of the company?** You should be able to get a refund or exchange the product if it is not satisfactory to you.

7. **What do consumer agencies have to say about this product?** See page 373 for agencies that provide information for consumers.

The Flip Side of Getting Your Coin's Worth

Do not buy an item you intend to return after one use. This is dishonest. Suppose you plan to go to a professional sports game with friends. You want to impress your friends by wearing a jacket with the team logo. You purchase the jacket, which is very expensive. You wear it to the game. Then you take the jacket back to the store. You tell the sales clerk you have not worn the jacket. You get your money back. Were you being honest? Were you being fair? No. You must be fair if you expect manufacturers and store owners to be fair to you.

What Can I Do If I Am Not Satisfied with Something I Bought?

You have the right to complain when you are not satisfied with something you bought. Here is what you can do:

- Make sure you know the store's policy on returns. Some stores will not give a refund or an exchange after a certain time.

- Talk with your parents or guardian and agree on what you will do.

- Take the product and receipt back to the store.

- Tell the salesperson exactly what happened. Be assertive. Use a calm tone of voice. Do not yell or insult the salesperson. Stick to the facts. Do not exaggerate. You might say, "I bought this jump rope last week and used it twice. The handles broke off."

- Tell the salesperson you want a refund or exchange.

What can you do if the salesperson refuses to give you a refund or exchange? Ask to speak to the manager. Repeat your request. Again, be assertive.

What if the store manager still refuses to give you a refund or exchange? Or what if you want a refund or an exchange for a mail-order product? Write a letter to the company. Type the letter or print it neatly. Keep a copy for your records. Include the following in your letter:

- **The address of the company's consumer office or headquarters**

- **The date you are writing the letter**

- **The name of the product, the serial or model number, the date you purchased the product, and the store where you purchased the product**

- **An explanation of why you are dissatisfied** Be brief. State the facts. Do not use an angry or threatening tone.

- **A statement of what you have done so far to correct the problem** Write the names of salespeople or managers you have spoken with.

- **A description of what you want the company to do** Do you want the product fixed or replaced, or your money back?

- **Your name, address, and home telephone number**

- **A copy of your receipt (not the original!)**

What Agencies Protect My Consumer Rights?

Suppose you buy a product and it breaks after only one use. You take it back to the store. The manager refuses to give you a refund or exchange. You write a letter to the company. You do not receive a reply. What more can you do? You can contact an agency that protects consumer rights. These agencies can help consumers in several ways. Some provide information about products. Some require manufacturers to correct defective products. Some keep and make public lists of businesses about which consumers have complained. Some agencies have information about products that are harmful or defective. You can report unsafe products to these agencies.

You can contact the following federal agencies to help you with a complaint.

- The **Food and Drug Administration (FDA)** is a federal agency that checks and enforces the safety of food, drugs, medical devices, and cosmetics. The FDA has the authority to recall products. A **product recall** is an order to take a product off the market because of safety concerns. The FDA Consumer Affairs Information Line is 1-800-532-4440.

- The **Federal Trade Commission (FTC)** is a federal agency that checks advertising practices. The FTC can stop certain advertising or force an advertiser to change the wording in advertisements.

- The **Consumer Product Safety Commission (CPSC)** is a federal agency that establishes and enforces product safety standards. The CPSC has the authority to recall products.

- The **United States Postal Service (USPS)** is a federal agency that protects the public when products and services are sold through the mail. Contact your local post office or call the Postal Crime Hotline at 1-800-654-8896.

The following private organizations can provide information.

- The **Council of Better Business Bureaus** is a private organization that checks consumer complaints and advertising and selling practices. This organization will provide a list of businesses about which consumers have complained.

- **Consumer's Union (CU)** is a private organization that tests products and publishes a magazine, *Consumer Reports*. CU provides books and pamphlets on consumer topics.

- The **Center for Science in the Public Interest (CSPI)** is a private organization that works to improve government policies on food, nutrition, and other health concerns.

Activity

False Claims

Life Skill: I will recognize my rights as a consumer.

Materials: paper and pencil, props as needed

Directions: Read the information in the box about quackery. Then complete this activity to help you recognize quackery.

1. **Your teacher will divide the class into five groups.** (S)he will assign each group two appeals or claims that might indicate quackery. These are listed in the box below.

2. **Each group will create two one-minute TV commercials.** Each group will try to sell a worthless product using the two methods it was assigned.

3. **Each group will perform their two commercials for the rest of the class.**

How to Recognize Quackery

Quackery (KWA·kuh·ree) is a method of selling worthless products and services. Quackery makes false appeals and claims. Quackery often is targeted at teens. Don't risk being hurt or injured by using worthless products or services. You can recognize quackery if you look for these appeals and claims before you buy a health product. Quackery might be at work!

Remedy Rip-Off The maker claims the product cures conditions for which there is no cure.

Sonic Bomb The maker claims the product gives quick and/or painless results.

Unique Mystique The maker claims the product works by a secret formula or in a mysterious way.

Snake Sell The product is sold over the telephone, door-to-door, or by mail-order.

Quack Backs The product is promoted on the back pages of magazines.

Tombstone Sidestepper People in the advertisement claim they were cured by the product.

Pot Luck The product does not provide directions or cautions about use.

Heart Rob The product is promoted by appealing to emotion.

Hocus Bogus The maker claims the medical profession does not recognize the product.

You Pay It, I'll Say It A celebrity endorses the product.

Review

Vocabulary Words

Write a separate sentence using each vocabulary word listed on page 370.

Health Content

1. What are four rights you have as a consumer? **page 370**

2. What are seven questions you should ask before you buy something? **page 371**

3. What can you do if you are not satisfied with something you bought? **page 372**

4. What are seven agencies that protect your consumer rights? What does each of these agencies do? **page 373**

5. What are ten appeals or claims that might indicate quackery? **page 374**

The Responsible Decision-Making Model™

You buy and play a compact disc (CD) for a party. A friend tells you to take it back to the store and tell the salesperson you did not play it. Answer the following questions on a separate sheet of paper. Write "Does not apply" if a question does not apply to this situation.

1. Is it healthful for you to return the CD and get your money back? Why or why not?

2. Is it safe for you to return the CD and get your money back? Why or why not?

3. Is it legal for you to return the CD and get your money back? Why or why not?

4. Will you show respect for yourself if you return the CD and get your money back? Why or why not?

5. Will your parents or guardian approve if you return the CD and get your money back? Why or why not?

6. Will you demonstrate good character if you return the CD and get your money back? Why or why not?

What is the responsible decision to make in this situation?

Health Literacy

Effective Communication

Suppose you have a friend who has difficulty returning products that do not work. How might you help your friend learn to be assertive?

Responsible Citizenship

Make a list of the ways to recognize quackery. Share the list with family members.

How to Investigate Health Care

Life Skills

- ◆ **I will make responsible choices about health care providers and facilities.**
- ◆ **I will evaluate ways to pay for health care.**

Everyone needs regular health care. It is important to know where and how to get health care before you need it. Be informed about the health care system that is available to you. The **health care system** is a system that includes health care providers, health care facilities, and payment for health care. You will know where to go, who can help you, and how you can pay when you need health care.

The Lesson Objectives

- Identify health care facilities that provide health care.
- Explain how to get and use health insurance.
- Identify different medical specialists.

Vocabulary

health care system

health care facility

health care provider

private office

physician

specialist

health center

urgent care center

emergency room

hospital

inpatient

outpatient

health insurance policy

policy owner

health insurance benefits

premium

deductible

co-payment

managed care

health maintenance organization (HMO)

What Are the Health Care Facilities That Provide Health Care?

A **health care facility** is a place where people receive health care. You and your family should know where these facilities are located in your community. You also should know when they are open, the services they provide, and the fees they charge. Health care facilities are staffed by health care providers. A **health care provider** is a professional who provides health care. You should know about five different health care facilities.

- A **private office** is a health care facility that is privately owned by one or more health care providers. A **physician** is a health care provider who is licensed to practice medicine. A **specialist** is a physician who has additional training in a particular area. Physicians, dentists, optometrists, and other health providers might have private offices.

- A **health center** is a health care facility with several health care providers or that provides health care for a special population. A primary care health center might be owned by a hospital and have several physicians on staff. A women's health center provides health care only to women.

- An **urgent care center** is a facility that provides care for minor injuries and short-term illnesses. Urgent care centers are open 12 to 24 hours seven days a week. Urgent care centers are convenient when your physician's office is closed or (s)he cannot see you immediately.

- An **emergency room** is a facility that provides service for major and minor medical emergencies. These facilities are located within hospitals.

- A **hospital** is a facility that provides care for many medical conditions. Hospitals are staffed and equipped to provide a greater variety of services than do other health facilities. An **inpatient** is a person who stays at the hospital while receiving health care. An **outpatient** is a person who comes to the hospital for treatment but does not stay overnight.

What Should I Know About Health Insurance?

A **health insurance policy** is a plan that helps pay the cost of health care. A **policy owner** is the person who owns the health insurance policy. A health insurance policy can be purchased through your parents' or guardian's employer or a private company. Ask the following questions to evaluate a health insurance policy.

1. **What benefits are included in the health insurance policy?** A health insurance policy will provide you with benefits. **Health insurance benefits** are the costs the insurance company will pay for specific health services. A health insurance policy can cover some or all of the costs of:

   • office visits to a health care provider;

   • visits to a health center;

   • visits to an urgent care center;

   • visits to an emergency room;

   • treatment at a hospital as an inpatient or outpatient.

2. **What will you pay for a health insurance policy?** Determine the premium. A **premium** is a set amount of money that the owner of a health insurance policy pays regularly. The premium guarantees that the insurance company will pay for the benefits stated in the policy.

3. **What additional costs might you have to pay?** A health insurance policy:

   • covers all costs;

   or

   • requires you to pay a deductible;

   or

   • requires you to make co-payments.

   A **deductible** is an amount the policy owner must pay before the insurance company makes payments. For example, every year a policy owner might have a deductible of $500. The policy owner will pay for the first $500 worth of health care. The insurance company will pay health care costs after the policy owner has paid the first $500 each year. A **co-payment** is the portion or amount of the fee for health care the policy owner must pay.

How Policy Holders Can Avoid Problems with Insurance Companies:

- **Policy holders should tell an insurance company important information about their health and the health of their families.** They should be honest with an insurance company about their health history. They should not lie to ensure that they will be covered.

- **Policy holders should always pay premiums on time.** Sometimes insurance companies will refuse to pay a claim. Policy owners can resubmit their bills to try to get insurance companies to pay.

- **Policy holders can ask their insurance company whether the company will pay for certain surgeries and procedures.** Many insurance companies have toll-free or local telephone numbers. Policy owners can call and ask over the phone about their insurance coverage.

- **Policy holders can call their state department of insurance to complain if an insurance company refuses to pay a bill.**

4. **Which health care providers can you choose?** A health insurance policy:

- allows you to choose any health care provider;

    or

- requires you to choose from an approved list.

    Health insurance that limits your choices is called managed care. **Managed care** is a system of health care services designed to control costs.

5. **What is a health maintenance organization?** A **health maintenance organization** or HMO is a plan in which a group of health care providers are paid to give health care. An HMO is a type of managed care. When you belong to an HMO, you:

- usually pay less for your premiums;

- usually do not have to pay a deductible;

- must choose a health care provider from an approved list;

- might have to make a co-payment for each health visit.

Activity

Is There a Doctor in the House?

Life Skill: I will make responsible choices about health care providers and facilities.

Materials: paper or wipe-off boards and markers

Directions: Read the information in the box. Then complete this activity to help you learn what each medical specialist does.

Medical Specialists

Here is a list of specialists and their specialty areas.

Cardiologist (KAHR·dee·AH·luh·jist)—the circulatory system

Endocrinologist (EN·duh·kri·NAH·luh·jist)—the endocrine system

Gastroenterologist (GAS·troh·EN·tuh·RAH·luh·jist)—the digestive system

Gynecologist (GY·nuh·KAH·luh·jist)—female reproductive health

Neurologist (nu·RAH·luh·jist)—the nervous system

Obstetrician (AHB·stuh·TRI·shuhn)—pregnant women

Orthopedist (OR·thuh·PEE·dist)—the skeletal system

Pulmonologist (PUL·muh·NAHL·oh·jist)—the respiratory system

Urologist (yu·RAH·luh·jist)—the urinary system

1. Your teacher will divide the class into groups of three or four students.

2. Your teacher will call out vocabulary words, such as parts of the body or diseases, that you have studied.

3. Your group will refer to the list of specialists and quietly discuss which specialist would care for that body part or disease. For example, if your teacher called out "amniotic sac," you would choose "obstetrician."

4. One person in each group will write down the kind of specialist the group agrees on. Each group will hold up their paper or board when asked by your teacher. Each group gets one point for each correct answer. The group with the most points wins.

Review

Vocabulary Words

Write a separate sentence using each vocabulary word listed on page 376.

Health Content

1. What are five health care facilities that provide health care? **page 377**

2. What are five questions to ask to evaluate a health insurance policy? **pages 378–379**

3. What is a premium, a deductible, and a co-payment? **page 378**

4. What does it mean to belong to a health maintenance organization (HMO)? **page 379**

5. What are nine kinds of medical specialists? What does each do? **page 380**

Health Literacy

Self-Directed Learning

Use a dictionary to identify the meanings of the beginnings of words, or prefixes, that mean a medical specialty or specialist. For example, "cardio" means heart. Find other medical specialties not listed in this lesson and identify their meanings.

Critical Thinking

Most of the costs of health care are used to diagnose and treat illnesses and injuries. Many of these illnesses and injuries can be prevented. How can practicing healthful behaviors reduce the costs of health care?

The Responsible Decision-Making Model™

Your friend's older brother is applying for health insurance through his college. The premiums are very low unless the customer participates in a risky sport. Your friend's brother skydives. He is thinking about lying about his skydiving on the application. Answer the following questions on a separate sheet of paper. Write "Does not apply" if a question does not apply to this situation.

1. Is it healthful to lie on an application for health insurance? Why or why not?

2. Is it safe to lie on an application for health insurance? Why or why not?

3. Is it legal to lie on an application for health insurance? Why or why not?

4. Will your friend's brother show respect for himself if he lies on his application for health insurance? Why or why not?

5. Will your friend's parents or guardian approve if your friend's brother lies on his application for health insurance? Why or why not?

6. Will your friend's brother demonstrate good character if he lies on his application for health insurance? Why or why not?

What is the responsible decision for your friend's brother to make in this situation?

How to Investigate Health Careers

- ◆ I will be a health advocate by being a volunteer.
- ◆ I will investigate health careers.

Vocabulary

career

health career

health advocate

volunteer

service learning

shadowing

mentor

endurance

license

certificate

A **career** is the work that a person prepares for and does through life. People should choose a career for which they have passion and commitment. Passion is a very strong feeling. Commitment is a promise or willingness to do something. You might find that you have passion and commitment for a health career. A **health career** is a profession or occupation for which one trains in the health field.

You can also be a health advocate. A **health advocate** is a person who promotes health for self and others. A health advocate can help others in the community by volunteering. A health advocate can encourage others to volunteer for a special cause, such as raising money for an organization that works to prevent certain diseases like heart disease or cancer.

The Lesson Objectives

- Explain ways you can benefit from service learning.
- Discuss ways a career mentor can help you.
- Identify questions to ask when you investigate health careers.
- Describe various health careers.
- Identify ways you can be a volunteer in your community.

What Are Ways I Can Benefit from Service Learning?

Have you ever picked up litter by a highway? Helped serve food in a homeless shelter? Or read to someone who was sick? If so, you were practicing the responsible behavior of helping others. You were a volunteer. A **volunteer** is a person who provides a service without pay. Did you know that you can connect your volunteer activities with what you are learning in school? **Service learning** is an educational experience that combines learning with community service without pay. For example, suppose you help plant trees around your community. You participate in an educational experience in which you learn about the environment. At the same time, you provide service without pay. Service learning provides you with many health benefits.

- **Service learning promotes positive feelings.** Positive feelings produce bio-chemical changes in your body that boost your immunity. These changes also create a feeling of well-being.

- **Service learning promotes feelings of confidence.** Suppose you use your artistic talent to make greeting cards for patients in a hospital. You are rewarded as you experience positive self-esteem.

- **Service learning helps you cope with stress.** You realize many people are less fortunate than you. You stop thinking about your own problems and appreciate your life more.

- **Service learning promotes satisfying personal relationships.** You feel connected to others. You do not feel isolated or angry. You reduce your risk of developing cardiovascular diseases.

- **Service learning can give you an idea of what some careers might be like.**

  Shadowing is spending time with a mentor as (s)he performs work activities. A **mentor** is a responsible person who guides another person. A mentor can help you by:

  - **telling you about his or her job and showing you how the job is performed;**
  - **allowing you to try new things;**
  - **motivating and encouraging you;**
  - **helping you develop endurance.**

  Endurance is the ability to continue despite hardship or stress. You might have doubts about whether or not you can complete a task. A mentor can help you when you doubt your abilities. You decide to stay with the task, and you feel good when you complete it. You have more confidence to tackle difficult tasks in the future.

What Are Health Careers I Might Consider?

A health career can be very rewarding. It also can be very demanding. Most careers in health require you to be able to handle responsibilities well. You must be able to work independently as well as part of a team. You must have sensitivity and compassion if you work with patients.

Most health careers also require specialized training. Some require a license or certificate. A **license** is a document granted by a government agency to a person for the right to practice or to use a certain title. A **certificate** is a document granted by a non-governmental agency to a person for the right to practice or to use a certain title. A person must meet educational requirements, pass an examination, and/or complete practical training to get a license or certificate.

You should ask yourself five questions when considering a particular health career.

1. Do my interests and abilities match the responsibilities of this health career?

2. What education and training will I need to become qualified for this health career?

3. How much time and money will I need to spend to become qualified for this health career?

4. What are my chances of finding a job in this health career?

5. Do I feel passion and commitment for this health career?

Biomedical Engineer

Are you interested in technology? Do you think you would like to help people by designing equipment? You might consider being a biomedical engineer.

Responsibilities

- Inventing new equipment, such as an artificial heart

- Finding new uses for technology, such as using laser beams for eye surgery

- Maintaining complex equipment for hospitals and research facilities

Qualifications

- Bachelor's degree in engineering

- State license in many states

Cytotechnologist

Are you interested in looking through microscopes? Do you think you would like to help people by identifying diseased body cells? You might consider being a cytotechnologist.

Responsibilities

- Preparing body tissue for examination using special stains

- Looking at slides through a microscope for signs of damage or disease, especially cancer

Qualifications

- Usually a bachelor's degree in medical technology or a life science

- Certification by most employers

- State license in some states

Health Careers

Environmental Health Inspector or Sanitarian

Are you interested in health and the environment? Do you think you would like to help people by making sure the environment is clean and safe? You might consider being an environmental health inspector.

Responsibilities

- Inspecting recreational areas, water, sewage, and handling of food
- Determining if water and air meet government standards
- Enforcing government standards of cleanliness and safety

Qualifications

- Bachelor's degree in environmental health, physical or biological science
- Additional specialized training
- State license in many states

Food Technologist

Are you interested in science, research, and nutrition? Do you think you would like to help people by improving food safety and quality? You might consider being a food technologist.

Responsibilities

- Developing methods to make food safe for the consumer
- Searching for ways to improve the flavor and nutritional value of food
- Conducting tests to make sure food meets government standards

Qualifications

- Bachelor's degree in food technology or in science with on-the-job training

Geriatric Social Worker

Are you interested in helping people solve their problems? Do you think you would like to work with senior citizens? You might consider being a geriatric social worker.

Responsibilities

- Helping senior citizens get health services
- Providing therapy to senior citizens for depression or anxiety
- Planning health services for senior citizens

Qualifications

- Associate's, bachelor's or master's degree with a specialty in gerontology (JER·uhn·TAH·luh·jee)
- Certificate, registration, or license required by all states

Medical Illustrator

Are you interested in art and medicine? Do you think you would like to help people by using your artistic abilities? You might consider being a medical illustrator.

Responsibilities

- Making detailed drawings of human anatomy, medical and surgical procedures, and body conditions
- Building models for use in teaching
- Helping to create artificial parts such as ears

Qualifications

- Bachelor's or master's degree with courses in art, biology, and physical science

Medical Record Technician

Are you interested in medicine without patient contact? Do you think you would like to help people by organizing patient information? You might consider being a medical record technician.

Responsibilities

- Collecting information from physicians about a patient

- Coding patient information and making sure it is accurate

- Helping other health professionals find patient information

Qualifications

- Associate's or bachelor's degree in medical record technology or another field with certification

- National examination required by most employers

Health Careers

Optometrist

Are you interested in working with equipment? Do you think you would like to help people see better? You might consider being an optometrist.

Responsibilities

- Examining eyes using special instruments

- Identifying eye health problems and defects in vision

- Prescribing eyeglasses and contact lenses

Qualifications

- Doctor of Optometry (O.D.) degree

- License required by all states

Music Therapist

Are you interested in music? Do you think you would like to help people by using your musical abilities? You might consider being a music therapist.

Responsibilities

- Helping people manage depression and anger by expressing themselves through music

- Helping people relate to others by having them play or move to music with others

- Teaching people to sing or play an instrument as part of therapy

Qualifications

- Bachelor's or master's degree in music therapy

- Certification required by most employers

Physiatrist

Are you interested in physical exercise? Do you think you would like to help people by using exercise and machines? You might consider being a physiatrist (FIZ·ee·AT·rist).

Responsibilities

- Determining and prescribing treatment to rehabilitate patients (Rehabilitation is treatment to improve the function of patients with impairments due to illness or injury.)

- Using exercise, machines, heat, and cold to rehabilitate patients

- Instructing therapists who give treatments

Qualifications

- Doctor of Medicine (M.D.) degree

- License to practice medicine

- Additional training in physical medicine

Respiratory Therapist

Are you interested in working with equipment and machines? Do you think you would like to help people with breathing difficulties? You might consider being a respiratory therapist.

Responsibilities

- Testing lung capacity
- Operating machines that give oxygen and gases to relieve breathing difficulties
- Connecting people to ventilators and caring for their breathing needs

Qualifications

- Usually an associate's or bachelor's degree in respiratory therapy
- License required by most states

Toxicologist

Are you interested in math, science, and research? Do you think you would like to help people by studying health effects of toxic substances? You might consider being a toxicologist.

Responsibilities

- Conducting research on the poisonous effects of substances on health
- Testing new products for toxicity
- Working with the government to regulate toxic waste disposal

Qualifications

- Doctorate in pharmacology, chemistry, or related field
- Doctor of Medicine (M.D.) degree
- License or certificate in toxicology

Surgical Technologist or Operating Room Technician

Are you interested in working with surgical equipment? Do you think you would like to help people during surgery? You might consider being a surgical technologist.

Responsibilities

- Setting up and maintaining the operating room with equipment and supplies
- Washing and shaving patients before surgery
- Assisting the surgeon during surgery

Qualifications

- Certificate, diploma, or associate's degree from a vocational school or hospital

Water and Wastewater Treatment Technician

Are you interested in working outdoors? Do you think you would like to help people by improving water quality? You might consider being a water and wastewater treatment technician.

Responsibilities

- Making sure water pollution standards are met
- Reviewing construction plans for water facilities
- Setting up equipment and conducting surveys

Qualifications

- Associate's degree with specialized training

Health Behavior Contract

Copy the health behavior contract on a separate sheet of paper.

DO NOT WRITE IN THIS BOOK.

Name:_____ **Date:**_____

Life Skill: I will be a health advocate by being a volunteer.

Effect on My Health: I will get positive feelings from volunteering. I will increase my self-confidence. I will develop satisfying relationships.

My Plan: I will obtain permission from my parents or guardian to volunteer in my community. I will select one of the places in the box below or choose one of my own. I will contact the place where I will volunteer and obtain a description of exactly what I will do. I will decide how many hours of volunteer work I want to complete. I will make a schedule.

Places to Volunteer

- **Hospital or extended care facility:** draw pictures, read books, deliver flowers, or visit patients

- **Social service organizations (for example, American Lung Association, homeless shelters):** help with fund-raising activities, participate in walk-a-thons, collect items to donate, serve food

- **Community:** pick up litter, plant trees, organize healthful activities for peers or younger children, write letters to elected officials about health issues

My Calendar	M	T	W	Th	F	S	S

How My Plan Worked: On another sheet of paper, I will keep a journal. I will write exactly what I did when I volunteered. I will record the dates and time I spent as a volunteer. I will list the benefits to me and to others of my volunteer experience.

Review

Vocabulary Words

Write a separate sentence using each vocabulary word listed on page 382.

Health Content

1. What are five ways you can benefit from service learning? **page 383**

2. What are four ways a career mentor can help you? **page 383**

3. What are five questions to ask yourself when you are investigating health careers? **page 384**

4. What are some different health careers you might consider? Which career appeals to you most? Why? **pages 384–387**

5. What are three places for volunteering where you live? **page 388**

The Responsible Decision-Making Model™

You and several friends collect soap, shampoo, and other grooming products for needy persons. One friend decides to take a bottle of donated shampoo for herself. She says, "It's the least I can get for doing this for nothing!" Answer the following questions on a separate sheet of paper. Write "Does not apply" if a question does not apply to this situation.

1. Is it healthful for your friend to take the shampoo? Why or why not?

2. Is it safe for your friend to take the shampoo? Why or why not?

3. Is it legal for your friend to take the shampoo? Why or why not?

4. Will your friend show respect for herself and others if she takes the shampoo? Why or why not?

5. Will your friend's parents or guardian approve if your friend takes the shampoo? Why or why not?

6. Will your friend demonstrate good character if she takes the shampoo? Why or why not?

What is the responsible action for your friend to take? What should you say to your friend?

Health Literacy

Effective Communication

Make a poster that lists the benefits of service learning. Obtain permission to display the poster in your school to encourage other students to volunteer.

Self-Directed Learning

Visit a library or the Internet to get more information about health careers. Find out which health careers have the greatest opportunities for growth.

Unit 8 Review

Health Content

Prepare for the Unit Test. Review your answers for each Lesson Review in this unit. Then write answers to each of the following questions:

1. How can you use the Internet to gain health information? **Lesson 36 page 359**

2. How can you decide if something you read contains accurate messages about health? **Lesson 36 pages 360–361**

3. What are three steps you can take to prepare and follow a budget? **Lesson 37 page 366**

4. Why should you avoid watching television and movie violence? **Lesson 37 page 368**

5. What actions can you take if a salesperson refuses to give you a refund or an exchange? **Lesson 38 page 372**

6. Why does the FDA recall some products? **Lesson 38 page 373**

7. When might you use an urgent care center? **Lesson 39 page 377**

8. What does it mean if a health insurance policy has a $250 deductible each year? **Lesson 39 page 378**

9. How might you benefit from participating in service learning? **Lesson 40 page 383**

10. How can a mentor help you learn more about a health career of interest to you? **Lesson 40 page 383**

Health Behavior Contract

Make a health behavior contract for one of the life skills in this unit. Review your health behavior contract with your parents or guardian.

Vocabulary Words

Number a sheet of paper from 1–10. Select the correct vocabulary word and write it next to the corresponding number. DO NOT WRITE IN THIS BOOK.

service learning	managed care
healthful entertainment	desensitization
consumer	product recall
accurate message	shadowing
co-payment	newsgroup

1. _____ is the portion or amount of the fee for health care the policy owner must pay. **Lesson 39**

2. _____ is spending time with a mentor as (s)he performs work activities. **Lesson 40**

3. _____ is entertainment that promotes physical, mental, or social health. **Lesson 37**

4. _____ is an educational experience that combines learning with community service without pay. **Lesson 40**

5. A _____ is a person who uses information, products, and services. **Lesson 38**

6. _____ is a system of health care services designed to control costs. **Lesson 39**

7. _____ is the effect of reacting less and less to the exposure to something. **Lesson 37**

8. A _____ is an order to take a product off the market because of safety concerns. **Lesson 38**

9. A _____ is an area on the Internet where people post messages on a specific subject for other people to read. **Lesson 36**

10. An _____ is a message that is based on scientific research and is supported by several different sources. **Lesson 36**

The Responsible Decision-Making Model™

Your friend's older brother rented a videotape. Your friend puts the videotape in the VCR. The movie contains sex and violence. Answer the following questions on a separate sheet of paper. Write "Does not apply" if a question does not apply to this situation.

1. Is it healthful to watch a videotape containing sex and violence? Why or why not?

2. Is it safe to watch a videotape containing sex and violence? Why or why not?

3. Is it legal to watch a videotape containing sex and violence? Why or why not?

4. Will you keep your self-respect if you watch a videotape containing sex and violence? Why or why not?

5. Will your parents or guardian approve if you watch a videotape containing sex and violence? Why or why not?

6. Will you demonstrate good character if you watch a videotape containing sex and violence? Why or why not?

What is the responsible decision to make in this situation?

What might you say to your friend?

Multicultural Health

Imagine that you are traveling to a foreign country of your choice. Suppose you purchase a product on your trip. The product breaks and you attempt to return it. The company who sold it to you will not offer a refund or an exchange. What organizations protect consumers in the country you are visiting?

Health Literacy
Effective Communication

Imagine that you are a store manager. A teen returns a dress and says it did not fit. Earlier you overheard the teen say she wore it to a school dance. On a sheet of paper, write what you would say to the teen.

Self-Directed Learning

Write a letter to one of the agencies on page 373 requesting more information about the agency.

Critical Thinking

Read the want ads that appear in a newspaper. Write a short paper to answer the following questions. How many different health careers were advertised in the want ads? What percentage of the want ads were advertisements for health careers? Why are many people needed for careers in the health field?

Responsible Citizenship

Select a movie or TV program to watch with family members that does not contain sex, violence, drug use, or other inappropriate content. Explain to family members the reasons you made your selection.

Family Involvement

Discuss time management with your parents or guardian. Evaluate the time you spent together last week. Discuss ways to guarantee that you spend quality time together.

UNIT 9
Environmental Health

PRACTICE
HEALTH STANDARD 3
Make a Health Behavior Contract

Practice this standard at the end of this unit.

1. **Tell the life skill you want to practice.** Use the life skill: *I will help conserve energy and natural resources.*

2. **Write a few statements describing how the life skill will affect your health.** Describe how conserving water in your home is beneficial to you and to the environment.

3. **Design a specific plan to practice the life skill and a way to record your** progress in making the life skill a habit. Use the information on page 403 as a guide to the behaviors you can practice to conserve water. Keep track of your progress for one week.

4. **Describe the results you got when you tried the plan.** After a week, write a paragraph describing how you saved the unnecessary use of water in your home.

How to Prevent Pollution

Life Skills

- ◆ I will help keep the air clean.
- ◆ I will help keep the water safe.
- ◆ I will help keep noise at a safe level.

Vocabulary

environment

pollution

pollutant

polluted air

fossil fuels

smog

acid rain

ozone

sick building syndrome (SBS)

secondhand smoke

radon

carbon monoxide

water pollution

water runoff

sewage

groundwater

decibel (dB)

noise

noise pollution

The **environment** is everything around a person. The environment includes air, water, soil, and the noise level. **Pollution** is any change in the environment that harms health. A **pollutant** is something that has a harmful effect on the environment. People pollute the environment. You can be aware of pollutants. You can help prevent pollution.

The Lesson Objectives

- Discuss ways you can help keep the air clean.
- Explain ways indoor air pollution can harm your health.
- Discuss ways you can help keep the water safe.
- Discuss ways noise pollution affects your health.
- Discuss ways you can help keep noise at a safe level.

What Are Ways I Can Help Keep the Air Clean?

"Go outside and get some fresh air." Someone has probably said this to you. But did you know that the air might not be so fresh? **Polluted air** is air contaminated with harmful substances. Most polluted air is caused by exhaust fumes from cars and by smoke from burning fossil fuels. **Fossil fuels** are coal, oil, and natural gas burned to produce energy. As these fuels burn, they produce gases that mix with rain and gases in the atmosphere.

Smog

Smog is a combination of smoke and fog. It forms from a mixture of car exhaust, smoke from burning fossil fuels, and other chemicals that react with sunlight. Smog can irritate the eyes and cause breathing problems. It is a special risk to children, older adults, and people who have asthma.

Acid Rain

Acid rain is rain and other precipitation (snow, sleet, hail) that has a high acid content. It forms when car exhaust and smoke from burning fossil fuels mix with water vapor in the atmosphere. Acid rain kills fish and plants, and damages buildings.

Upper Atmosphere Pollution

Earth's upper atmosphere contains a chemical called ozone. **Ozone** is a form of oxygen produced when sunlight reacts with oxygen. Ozone in the upper atmosphere protects us from some of the sun's UV rays. Gases found in some fire extinguishers and air conditioners destroy ozone in the upper atmosphere. As a result, more UV rays reach the earth. This increases the risk that people will develop skin cancer and eye cataracts.

Ways to Keep Air Clean

- Walk or ride a bicycle instead of having a parent or guardian drive you short distances.
- Use public transportation if it is available and safe.
- Form a carpool.
- Do not burn trash or yard waste.
- Plant trees to produce oxygen and absorb carbon dioxide.

How Can Indoor Air Pollution Harm My Health?

Do you think air pollution only occurs outdoors? There are many indoor air pollutants that can harm health. **Sick building syndrome (SBS)** is an illness that results from indoor air pollution. Symptoms include headaches, nausea, and irritated eyes. Getting out of a building can help people with SBS. The following agents are indoor air pollutants.

Secondhand Smoke

Secondhand smoke is sidestream smoke and smoke that a person exhales while smoking. It can cause lung cancer. Secondhand smoke also can cause pneumonia, bronchitis, and ear infections. Secondhand smoke harms people who have asthma, and it might cause children to develop asthma.

Radon

Radon is an odorless, colorless, radioactive gas. Radon can enter buildings through dirt floors, drains, pumps, and cracks in foundations. If radon builds up in a house, the people who inhale it might develop lung cancer.

Carbon Monoxide

Carbon monoxide is an odorless, colorless, poisonous gas. Inhaling carbon monoxide can cause headaches, dizziness, weakness, nausea, confusion, fatigue, unconsciousness, and death. Carbon monoxide is present in secondhand smoke. It also can be found in smoke from space heaters, gas stoves, wood stoves, and fireplaces that are not ventilated correctly.

Household Chemicals

Cleansers, disinfectants, paints, varnishes, waxes, glues, and other products all contain chemicals. Some chemicals can cause irritated eyes and lungs, headaches, dizziness, and memory problems in people who inhale the fumes. Some chemicals used in household products cause cancer in animals, and might cause cancer in people.

Ways to Keep Indoor Air Clean

- Do not smoke. Encourage others not to smoke.
- Follow safety instructions when using space heaters.
- Use exhaust fans for gas stoves.
- Install a carbon monoxide detector in your home.
- Get a radon testing kit and test your home for radon.
- Follow the directions on the labels of household products.
- Use cleansers, glues, or other chemicals only in a well-ventilated area.
- Use non-toxic glues and paints.
- Store household chemicals in a well-ventilated area away from children.

What Are Ways I Can Help Keep the Water Safe?

If the water you drink is not safe, you might be drinking many harmful substances. **Water pollution** is the contamination of water with sewage, waste, gases, or chemicals that harm health. You can help keep the water safe.

Water runoff causes a lot of water pollution. **Water runoff** is water that runs off land into a body of water. As water runoff moves over land, it carries chemicals from the ground. Some chemicals that might be carried by water runoff are pesticides from crops and lawns, acid rain, and any chemicals dumped on the ground. Water runoff can pollute drinking water.

Sewage also can pollute water. **Sewage** is waste liquids or matter carried off in sewers. Some people dump harmful chemicals into bodies of water or on the ground. Chemicals dumped on the ground can seep into groundwater. **Groundwater** is water in natural underground reservoirs. Once groundwater is polluted, there is almost no way to clean it. Some drinking water comes from groundwater. Drinking polluted water can cause cancer, blood diseases, and liver and kidney damage.

Ways to Keep Water Safe

- Do not dump anything into water or on the ground. Chemicals, oils, or other products dumped on the ground can be carried by water runoff into bodies of water or can seep into groundwater.

- Do not pour harmful chemicals down the drain or down the toilet. They will pollute drinking water. Take harmful chemicals to a facility that safely disposes of hazardous waste.

- Do not use a lawn service that sprays harmful chemicals. The chemicals can run off into bodies of water or seep into groundwater.

- Call your local health department if your tap water is orange, red, brown, or smells strange.

What Are Ways I Can Help Keep Noise at a Safe Level?

A **decibel (dB)** is a unit used to measure the loudness of sound. **Noise** is sound that produces discomfort or annoyance. Sounds that are louder than 70 dBs cause noise pollution. **Noise pollution** is loud or constant noise that causes hearing loss and stress. Noise pollution also causes headaches, tension, and sleep disturbances. It can increase blood pressure and cholesterol level. If noise pollution reaches 120 dBs, it can cause immediate and permanent hearing loss.

Keep Noise at a Safe Level

- Keep the volume low enough to hear someone talking when using headphones.
- Sit away from the speakers or wear earplugs at a concert.
- Wear earplugs when using machinery like a lawnmower.
- Cover your ears if there is loud noise.

Activity
Noticing Noise

Life Skill: I will help keep noise at a safe level.

Materials: paper, pen or pencil

Directions: Complete this activity to estimate your exposure to noise pollution.

1. List all the loud or prolonged noises you hear for one day.
2. Write the approximate decibel level next to each noise you hear. Use the chart on the right to help you estimate the decibel level of each noise.
3. Write a paragraph to tell how you might reduce your exposure to noise pollution.

Noises That Contribute to Noise Pollution

Noise	dBs
Power lawnmower	85
Vacuum cleaner	85
City traffic	90
Chain saw	90
Car horn	110
Loud stereo in car	115
Jackhammer (3 ft. away)	120
Loud setting on earphones	125
Loud rock music	130
Air raid siren	140
Gunshot	140

Vocabulary Words

Write a separate sentence using each vocabulary word listed on page 394.

Health Content

1. What are five ways you can help keep the air clean? **page 395**

2. How can indoor air pollution harm your health? **page 396**

3. What are four ways you can help keep the water safe? **page 397**

4. How can noise pollution harm your health? **page 398**

5. What are four ways you can help keep noise at a safe level? **page 398**

The Responsible Decision-Making Model™

At a concert your friends want to stand right in front of the stage, next to the speakers. You do not have earplugs. Answer the following questions on a separate sheet of paper. Write "Does not apply" if a question does not apply to this situation.

1. Is it healthful to stand next to the speakers? Why or why not?

2. Is it safe to stand next to the speakers? Why or why not?

3. Is it legal to stand next to the speakers? Why or why not?

4. Will you show respect for yourself if you stand next to the speakers? Why or why not?

5. Will you follow the guidelines of your parents or guardian if you stand next to the speakers? Why or why not?

6. Will you demonstrate good character if you stand next to the speakers? Why or why not?

What is the responsible decision to make in this situation?

Health Literacy

Self-Directed Learning

Using the library or Internet, research a law designed to reduce pollution. For example, you might choose the Clean Air Act. Write a two-page paper describing what the law is intended to do. Who supports the law? Who opposes it?

Responsible Citizenship

Design a six-month calendar. For each month, draw or describe a way to reduce indoor air pollution. Use information from reputable sources, such as the Environmental Protection Agency. Post the calendar in your home.

How to Conserve Resources

Life Skills

- ◆ I will precycle, recycle, and dispose of waste properly.
- ◆ I will help conserve energy and natural resources.
- ◆ I will be a health advocate for the environment.

Resources are substances that cannot be replaced once they are used. Many resources are used to make products you use every day. For example, the production of paper uses trees, water, and energy. It is important to conserve and not to waste the resources we have. When you conserve the amount of paper you use, you are conserving trees, water, and energy. A **health advocate for the environment** is a person who takes action to protect the environment. When you conserve resources, you are protecting the environment.

The Lesson Objectives

- Discuss ways to precycle, reuse, and recycle.
- Discuss ways to dispose of waste.
- Discuss ways to conserve water.
- Discuss ways to conserve energy.
- Identify ways to be a health advocate for the environment.

Vocabulary

resources

health advocate for the environment

solid waste

precycling

reusing

recycling

landfill

biodegradable product

incinerator

medical waste

composting

humus

energy

accurate message

environmental issues

What Are Ways I Can Precycle, Reuse, and Recycle?

Many resources are used to make a single product. For example, paper is made from trees. But it also takes lots of water and energy to make paper. By conserving paper, you also conserve water, energy, and other resources.

Solid waste is discarded solid material such as paper, metal, and yard waste. You can reduce the amount of solid waste you throw away by precycling, reusing, and recycling products.

Precycling is a process of reducing solid waste by purchasing fewer products and by purchasing products that use fewer resources. Precycling reduces the amount of waste that needs to be thrown out or recycled.

Reusing is using items again instead of throwing them away and buying new ones.

Recycling is changing waste products so they can be used again. Recycling reduces the amount of energy and water used to make new products. It reduces pollution and the amount of space needed for landfills. Many communities offer curbside pickup of recyclable materials such as metal and glass. If yours does not, check to see if there is a facility where you can take recyclable materials.

Items That Can Be Recycled

- **Plastic bottles and jugs**
- **Glass bottles and jars**
- **Food and beverage cans**
- **Beverage cartons and boxes**
- **Newspapers, magazines, and other paper**
- **Yard waste**

Ways to Precycle and Reuse

1. Pack your lunch in reusable containers instead of in plastic wrap or bags. Use reusable dishes instead of paper or plastic dishes.

2. Buy recycled, recyclable, or reusable items.

3. Use cloth dishcloths, towels, and handkerchiefs instead of paper towels or tissues.

4. Buy items that have little or no packaging.

5. Use cloth bags instead of paper or plastic bags.

6. Buy food in large containers and divide it into single servings. Buying food such as pudding or applesauce in small containers wastes packaging.

7. Repair damaged items instead of buying new ones.

8. Reuse containers such as jars and margarine tubs instead of throwing them away or recycling them.

9. Use both sides of a sheet of paper.

What Are Ways I Can Dispose of Waste?

Some products cannot be recycled or reused. They must be thrown away. When you throw an item away, it usually goes to a landfill.

A **landfill** is a place where wastes are dumped or buried. The waste then is broken down by bacteria. Hazardous waste should not be thrown away in a landfill. Most areas have facilities where you can safely dispose of hazardous waste. A **biodegradable product** is a product that can be broken down by organisms to become part of Earth's natural resources. Materials that are not biodegradable should not be sent to a landfill, because bacteria and other organisms cannot break them down. However, much of the waste that currently is sent to landfills is not biodegradable. Much of it could be recycled or reused.

Some waste is sent to incinerators. An **incinerator** is a furnace in which solid waste is burned. Most medical waste is incinerated. **Medical waste** is infectious waste from medical facilities. Some incinerators use the energy from burning waste to make electricity. However, incinerators release pollutants into the air.

Organic products such as fruit peels, eggshells, and grass trimmings can be composted. **Composting** is a method of changing organic garbage into humus. **Humus** (HYOO·muhs) is the organic material in soil. It provides nutrients to the soil and loosens it. You can make a compost pile at home. Your community might even have a composting facility.

Stop That Waste!

When people hand out fliers and other information on the street, do not take them if you do not want them. Remember, a product is never free. Someone always pays for a product. By taking items you plan to throw away, you contribute to the problem of waste.

Precycle, reuse, recycle, and compost to reduce the amount of solid waste you send to a landfill.

What Are Ways I Can Conserve Water?

Did you know that on average each person uses between 80 and 100 gallons of water each day? You drink water. You wash yourself, your dishes, and your clothing with it. You flush water down the toilet. Your family uses about 74 percent of its daily water by bathing and flushing toilets. You might think that there is plenty of water on Earth. It is true that about two-thirds of Earth is covered with water. However, about 97 percent of that water is salt water and about 2 percent is frozen in polar ice caps. This water cannot be used. Everyone needs to help conserve water.

Nine Ways to Conserve Water

1. **Take short showers instead of baths.**

2. **Do not let the water run while you are brushing your teeth or washing dishes.** An average faucet releases about five gallons of water every two minutes.

3. **Run the dishwasher or washing machine only for full loads.** You can save 10 to 20 gallons of water by running the dishwasher only for a full load. Adjust the water level in your washing machine for the load size if the machine allows you to do so.

4. **Water your lawn only when absolutely necessary, and then at the coolest part of the day.**

5. **Do not run water from the faucet until it gets cold.** Keep a pitcher of water in the refrigerator instead.

6. **Make sure your faucets and pipes do not drip or leak.**

7. **Exchange your regular shower head for a low-flow shower head.** A low-flow shower head can save your family about 20,000 gallons of water each year. Ask your water company about other water-saving devices you might install.

8. **Plant trees in your yard to help store water.** Roots store water and then release it into the ground.

9. **Turn off the water while you are scrubbing if you wash the family car at home.** You can save up to 150 gallons of water this way.

What Are Ways I Can Conserve Energy?

Do you leave the TV on when you are not in the room? Do you keep lights on even when you are not using them? Actions such as these waste energy. **Energy** is the ability to do work. It takes energy to heat buildings, run cars, and produce electricity. Energy costs money. Producing energy requires lots of natural resources. Conserving energy saves money and conserves natural resources.

Twelve Ways to Conserve Energy

1. Turn off lights, stereos, TVs, and other electric devices when you leave a room or when you are not using them.

2. Use light bulbs with a low wattage except when you read.

3. Use lamps, not overhead lights, when you read.

4. Wear warm clothes in cold weather, instead of turning up the heat.

5. Use the thermostat to turn down the temperature when your family is not at home.

6. Seal cracks around windows and doors to keep warm air from leaking out in winter. Air leaking through cracks around windows can cause your house to lose as much heat as if a large window were open.

7. Suggest that your parents or guardian make sure your house has enough insulation.

8. Use fans instead of air conditioning in hot weather.

9. Use manual appliances, such as can openers, instead of electric appliances.

10. Ride your bicycle, walk, use public transportation, or form carpools whenever possible.

11. Use a clothesline instead of a dryer to dry your clothes in warm weather.

12. Use compact fluorescent light bulbs instead of standard incandescent bulbs.

Activity

Energy Leak

Life Skill: I will help conserve energy and natural resources.

Materials: paper, pen or pencil

Directions: Rate the amount of energy your family uses by completing the activity below.

1. **Copy the following questions on a separate sheet of paper.** Use them to check your home for energy loss. A lot of energy is wasted in a home. Write YES or NO after each question. DO NOT WRITE IN THIS BOOK.

> 1. Are there lights on when no one is using them?
>
> 2. Is the TV on when no one is watching it?
>
> 3. Is a stereo or radio on when no one is listening to it?
>
> 4. In cold weather, is it warm enough in your home to wear only a thin layer of clothing?
>
> 5. In warm weather, is it cool enough in your house that you need to put on a sweater or long pants?
>
> 6. In cold weather, can you feel cold air through cracks around windows and doors?
>
> 7. In warm weather, can you feel warm air through cracks around windows and doors?
>
> 8. Do you use electric appliances to do things that could easily be done by hand, such as sharpening a pencil or opening a can?
>
> 9. Do you dry your clothes in a dryer in warm weather?
>
> 10. Do you use air conditioning in warm weather?

2. **If you answered YES to any of the questions, you probably are wasting energy.** Use the tips on page 404 to conserve energy.

3. **Make up a rating scale for people who answer YES to a certain number of the above questions.** For example, a person who answers YES to all the questions might be called a "major energy waster." Decide where you fall on your rating scale.

How Can I Be a Health Advocate for the Environment?

A health advocate for the environment is a person who takes actions to protect the environment. Health advocates for the environment avoid actions that might harm the environment. There are several ways you can be a health advocate for the environment.

You can make sure your actions serve as an example to others. You can precycle, reuse, and recycle. You can encourage other people to precycle, reuse, and recycle. You can conserve energy and water, and encourage others to do the same. By the same token, you can avoid taking any actions that might harm the environment. For example, you can dispose of hazardous waste at a collection facility instead of dumping it down the drain. You can encourage others to dispose of hazardous waste properly.

You can work on environmental projects in your community. For example, you can pick up trash in a park or along a road or stream. You can plant trees. You can organize or improve a community recycling program. You can join an organization that works on environmental projects. Ask your teacher and your parents or guardian about environmental projects for which you might volunteer. Remember to get permission from your parents or guardian before working on environmental projects.

You can produce accurate messages about the environment. An **accurate message** is a message that is based on scientific research and is supported by several different sources. You can research environmental topics that interest you and share your findings with others. You can write letters to companies and elected officials about environmental issues. When you produce accurate messages, you can encourage other people to promote a healthful environment.

Environmental issues are environmental concerns that can affect the quality of life for people. You can learn about environmental issues by reading journals and newspapers and watching TV programs about the environment. You can join organizations that focus on environmental issues. You will learn more about environmental issues in Lesson 43.

Vocabulary Words

Write a separate sentence using each vocabulary word listed on page 400.

Health Content

1. What are ways you can precycle? Reuse? Recycle? **page 401**

2. What are two ways you can dispose of waste? **page 402**

3. What are nine ways you can conserve water? **page 403**

4. What are twelve ways you can conserve energy? **page 404**

5. How can you be a health advocate for the environment? **page 406**

The Responsible Decision-Making Model™

Your community has a recycling program, but your sister refuses to recycle. "It's too much work," she says. Answer the following questions on a separate sheet of paper. Write "Does not apply" if a question does not apply to this situation.

1. Is it healthful to recycle? Why or why not?

2. Is it safe to recycle? Why or why not?

3. Is it legal to recycle? Why or why not?

4. Does recycling show respect for yourself and others? Why or why not?

5. Does recycling follow the guidelines of your parents or guardian? Why or why not?

6. Does recycling demonstrate good character? Why or why not?

What is the responsible decision to make in this situation?

What might you say to your sister?

Health Literacy

Effective Communication

Find out where your garbage goes when you throw it out. Does it go to a landfill? An incinerator? Learn whether your community has a recycling program or other program for reducing solid waste. Design a flier explaining your community's method of solid waste disposal.

Critical Thinking

How does conserving energy help everyone in your community?

How to Improve the Quality of Life

Life Skills

- ◆ I will stay informed about environmental issues.
- ◆ I will protect the natural environment.

The **natural environment** is everything around a person that is not made by people. It includes trees, grass, wildlife, flowers, mountains, streams and lakes. When you protect the natural environment, you improve the quality of life for yourself and others. You also improve your quality of life when you stay informed about environmental issues. **Environmental issues** are environmental concerns that can affect the quality of life for people.

The Lesson Objectives

- Identify three steps you can take to stay informed and clarify your viewpoints about environmental issues.
- Discuss ways people are working together on the issue of global warming.
- Explain why poverty is an environmental issue.
- Explain why the use of forests is an environmental issue.
- Discuss ways you can protect the natural environment.

Vocabulary

natural environment

environmental issues

greenhouse effect

global warming

poverty

developing country

developed country

habitat

visual pollution

graffiti

How Can I Stay Informed About Environmental Issues?

Quality of life is a concern for everyone. This is the reason there are several pressing environmental issues. Environmental issues are environmental concerns that can affect the quality of life for people. People usually have different viewpoints about environmental issues.

- **They might disagree about the effects certain actions have on the environment.**

- **They might disagree about what actions to take to protect the environment.**

Three Steps to Help You Stay Informed and Clarify Your Viewpoints about Environmental Issues

1. **Obtain information about environmental issues.** Read newspaper and magazine articles. Watch television programs. Read journals, magazines, and bulletins published by government agencies and other organizations. Access the Web sites of government agencies and other organizations.

2. **Review the available information on both sides of an issue.** Get a clear understanding of the different viewpoints people hold.

3. **Process what you have learned with a responsible adult.** Discuss environmental issues at home with your parents or guardian. Share the information you have gathered. Ask your parents or guardian why they hold the viewpoint they do.

What Are Three Environmental Issues About Which I Need to Be Informed?

This part of the lesson includes information about three environmental issues. Study this information. Review additional information on both sides of these issues. Then share what you have learned with your parents or guardian.

Issue: The Effects of Global Warming

Have you ever been in a greenhouse? The glass roof traps the sun's rays inside the greenhouse. This warms the air in the greenhouse so that plants grow and thrive. There is a natural occurrence in our atmosphere called the greenhouse effect. The **greenhouse effect** is the trapping around the earth of the heat from the sun by gases, such as carbon dioxide. The greenhouse effect keeps Earth warm enough to support life. Earth would be very cold without this natural occurrence.

Over the last two centuries, Earth's temperature has increased slightly. **Global warming** is an ongoing slight increase in Earth's temperature. People disagree about the causes and effects of global warming. For example, some people believe that human activity is largely responsible for global warming. They point to the chemicals that are being released when fossil fuels are burned. They point to the increasing amount of exhaust from cars. Other people are not as concerned about the effects of human activity on Earth's temperature.

People also disagree about the current effects of global warming and what future effects might be. Some people believe that global warming has caused recent extreme weather conditions in parts of the world. They believe global warming will cause temperatures to rise and glaciers to melt. Other people do not expect these changes to occur.

People are working together on the issue of global warming. In 1997, several countries signed an agreement in Kyoto, Japan to reduce the amount of harmful gases that are released. The effects of the treaty remain to be seen. Other actions also have been taken. Some companies are finding new ways to make electricity and heat buildings. Some companies are looking at alternatives to using fossil fuels in vehicles. Other companies are developing appliances and automobiles that require less energy.

Issue: The Appropriate Actions to Take to Reduce Poverty

Poverty is a condition in which people do not have enough resources to live in a healthful way. Poverty is an important issue for a number of reasons. People living in poverty often have a poor health status. They might be without food, clothing, or shelter. They might be stressed or depressed about their living conditions. They might be malnourished. They might not get the vaccines they need to protect their health. As a result, they develop diseases. People who live in poverty also are less likely to have access to education. They might not know ways to protect their health or to improve their environment.

There are people who live in poverty in both developing countries and developed countries. A **developing country** is a country that is working to reach an acceptable standard of health conditions. A **developed country** is a country that has reached an acceptable standard of health conditions. More than two-thirds of the world's people live in developing countries. Populations are growing faster in developing countries.

Issue: The Appropriate Actions for Using Forests

Forests are an important part of the natural environment. This is the reason the use of forests has become an environmental issue. Consider the ways people want to use forests. Some people want to preserve forests as a natural habitat for trees, plants, and animals. A **habitat** is a place where an animal or plant normally lives. Some people want to preserve forests for their enjoyment. Many parks were built in locations where there were forests. Some people want to preserve forests to prevent further global warming. Trees absorb carbon dioxide and produce oxygen. Less carbon dioxide remains in the air. This might help slow global warming.

Other people want to clear forests and use the land for farmland or mining. Or they want to cut down some or all of the trees to use the wood for lumber and fuel. Some people are committed to planting more trees and finding other ways to reduce the greenhouse effect.

How many forests should be preserved? How many trees should be cut? How much forest land should be cleared for other uses? The debate continues over how to use forests.

What Are Ways I Can Protect the Natural Environment?

Perhaps you have walked along a trail next to a bubbling stream, or have seen an area carpeted with wildflowers. You might have listened to wind sighing in treetops high above your head, and heard birds singing. Your walk took place in a natural environment.

Spending time in a natural environment, such as a park, can improve your health status. You might watch birds, collect leaves and rocks, or take a nature walk. You might enjoy a natural environment with members of your family or friends. Together you might participate in physical activity or have a picnic.

Follow all rules when you spend time in a natural environment. The rules are intended to keep the area safe and pleasant for everyone. Rules might be posted on signs or stated in a brochure. For example, you might see a sign telling you to stay on the trail.

Be considerate of other people when you spend time in a natural environment. Allow them to enjoy their experience in peace and quiet. Do not feed any wild animals. Do not eat wild plants, or drink water out of lakes or streams. Build a fire only in a place where you are permitted to build one. Keep the fire small. Make sure you put the fire out before you leave.

Do not create visual pollution in the natural environment. Visual pollution is sights that are unattractive. Do not litter. Do not write graffiti on walls, trees, benches, or any other surfaces. **Graffiti** (gruh·FEE·tee) is writing or drawing on a public surface. Visual pollution and graffiti will be discussed in Lesson 44.

Activity

Design a Park

Life Skill: I will protect the natural environment.

Materials: large sheet of butcher paper, colored markers

Directions: Follow the steps below to design a park and show ways to protect the natural environment.

1. **Design a park in which people can enjoy the natural environment.** Draw your park on a sheet of butcher paper using your markers. Include a nature trail through woods, fields, or near water. Draw wildflowers, birds, plants, butterflies, and other living things that you might find in this park. Include a playground and picnic tables if you wish.

2. **Brainstorm rules that must be followed to protect the natural environment in your park.** For example, a rule might say, "Stay on the nature trail" or "Do not pick the wildflowers." Identify at least five rules you expect visitors to follow.

3. **Draw five signs with these rules in the appropriate place in your park.**

4. **Show your classmates the park you have drawn and explain the five signs posting the rules.** Tell your classmates why each rule must be followed to protect the natural environment.

Vocabulary Words

Write a separate sentence using each vocabulary word listed on page 408.

Health Content

1. What are three steps you can take to stay informed and clarify your viewpoints about environmental issues? **page 409**

2. How are people working together on the issue of global warming? **page 410**

3. Why is poverty an environmental issue? **page 411**

4. Why is the use of forests an environmental issue? **page 411**

5. What are at least four ways you can protect the natural environment? **page 412**

The Responsible Decision-Making Model™

You are walking through a park with a friend. A sign is posted asking you not to remove plants or flowers from the park. Your friend eats the leaves of a plant and suggests that you do, too. Your friend says, "They're tasty and there are so many leaves, they won't be missed." Answer the following questions on a separate sheet of paper. Write "Does not apply" if a question does not apply to this situation.

1. Is it healthful to eat the plant leaves? Why or why not?

2. Is it safe to eat the plant leaves? Why or why not?

3. Is it legal to eat the plant leaves? Why or why not?

4. Will you show respect for yourself and others if you eat the plant leaves? Why or why not?

5. Will you follow the guidelines of your parents or guardian if you eat the plant leaves? Why or why not?

6. Will you demonstrate good character if you eat the plant leaves? Why or why not?

What is the responsible decision to make in this situation?

Health Literacy

Responsible Citizenship

Design a one-page flyer in which you encourage people in your community to visit the nearest park. Also, include three actions people can take to protect the natural environment during their visit.

Critical Thinking

Research an environmental issue other than the three discussed in this lesson. List the arguments on both sides of the issue. Review what you have learned with your parents or guardian.

How to Improve the Visual Environment

Life Skill

◆ **I will take actions to improve my visual environment.**

Vocabulary

visual environment
graffiti
visual pollution
desensitization
empowered

The **visual environment** is everything a person sees regularly. A positive visual environment can improve your health by:

- sending messages that encourage responsible behavior;
- reducing stress;
- and generating feelings of well-being.

Be aware of your visual environment. Make every effort to keep it positive.

The Lesson Objectives

- Evaluate how messages in the visual environment can influence your behavior.
- Discuss ways to create a visual environment that reduces stress and promotes well-being.

How Can Visual Pollution Influence My Behavior?

What you see every day in your environment can influence how you feel. What do you see as you walk down your street? You are likely to feel calm and happy if you see a clean, tidy neighborhood. You might feel stressed and ill at ease if you see broken windows, abandoned buildings, litter, and graffiti. **Graffiti** (gruh·FEE·tee) is writing or drawing on a public surface. **Visual pollution** is sights that are unattractive. Visual pollution can have a negative effect on your health.

What you see also can influence what you do. There might be graffiti on buildings in your neighborhood. There might be litter on the ground. Seeing too much visual pollution can result in your desensitization. **Desensitization** (DEE·sent·suh·tuh·ZAY·shuhn) is the effect of reacting less and less to the exposure to something. Suppose you frequently are exposed to visual pollution. You might stop noticing it. You might accept it as normal. If that happens, you have become desensitized. People who are desensitized to visual pollution are more likely to contribute to it. They are more likely to write graffiti on buildings where there already is graffiti. They are more likely to throw litter in places where there already is litter.

Think about how messages in your visual environment might be intended to influence your behavior. For example, there might be a billboard advertising cigarettes near your home. The purpose of the billboard is to encourage people to smoke a certain brand of cigarettes. You might become desensitized to the billboard's message. You might accept it as normal. You might think smoking cigarettes is an acceptable behavior. But you would be wrong. Smoking cigarettes is not responsible behavior. Do not become desensitized to visual pollution.

Ways to Stop Visual Pollution

- **Clean up trash in your yard and neighborhood.**

- **Plant flowers or hang a bird feeder in your yard.**

- **Pick up clutter and trash in your home. Make sure your surroundings are neat and tidy.**

- **Organize a campaign to clean up your neighborhood.**

- **Write to elected officials and community organizations about visual pollution in your neighborhood. Suggest solutions. Offer to help in a clean-up effort.**

How Can I Create a Visual Environment That Reduces Stress and Promotes Well-Being?

Have you ever had a big project to do? Have you thought you couldn't even begin until your work area was clean? If you cleared off your desk, picked up trash on the floor, dusted shelves, and vacuumed the carpet, you would feel more in control. You would be less stressed. You would be able to tackle your project with ease.

When you create an orderly visual environment, you feel a sense of control over your environment. A sense of control reduces stress and makes you feel empowered. To be **empowered** is to be energized because a person has some control over his or her decisions and behavior. When you feel empowered, your well-being improves. You are able to make responsible decisions. You are able to focus on projects and complete them efficiently. You are able to do your best.

The way you treat the visual environment also affects other people. Suppose you leave your clutter all over your family's living room. Other members of your family might become stressed when they see the clutter. They cannot focus on their projects when they are surrounded by your clutter. They might slip or trip on your clutter. You show respect for other people when you keep your visual environment positive. Do not create visual pollution, even in your own home.

You might need to improve your visual environment. Making your visual environment neat and tidy is one way to improve it. Keep your visual environment positive after you have improved it. You will be less stressed if you keep your area neat and tidy. The diagram on page 417 shows ways you can make your bedroom or other space a pleasant visual environment.

Ways to Improve Your Visual Environment

Select colors you like. The colors that surround you can affect your mood. If you do not like the colors in your room, consider changing them. You might paint the room, or get a new bedspread or rug. Always get permission from your parents or guardian before painting or making major changes to your room.

Place pictures around you. Attractive or interesting pictures give you something positive to view. Use them to cover bare or ugly walls. Always get permission before hanging pictures on the walls.

Organize your living space and keep it clean. You might share a room or you might have your own room. Plan your visual environment with anyone who shares the space. Make your bed. Keep a trash can handy so you can throw away litter. You will feel empowered. You will not feel overwhelmed by clutter or projects you need to do.

Bring some nature inside. Put house plants or cut flowers in your living space. Plants and flowers add color and might improve the air quality. Or add an aquarium. Watching fish can be very relaxing.

Include positive reminders in your environment. You might place a photo on your desk of a family vacation or special ceremony. You might hang certificates or awards you have received. You might post positive quotations. These kinds of items can lift your spirits and encourage you.

Activity

What a View!

Life Skill: I will take actions to improve my visual environment.

Materials: butcher paper, colored markers

Directions: Follow the directions below to design a window shade that will improve your visual environment.

1. **Imagine a scene you would like to see from your bedroom window.** It might be a beach, a mountain range, or some other scene. Your scene does not have to be a real place. It should be a scene that calms you and helps you feel less stressed. It should not show or encourage behavior that is not responsible.

2. **Cut a piece of butcher paper to the approximate size of a window shade.**

3. **Draw the scene you imagined on the butcher paper using the colored markers.** Be creative.

4. **Share your drawing with your classmates.** Explain why you selected the scene you drew. Explain why the scene calms you.

5. **Attach your drawing to the inside of your bedroom window shade.** If you do not have a window shade, place the scene in another location where it can calm you. Remember to get permission from your parents or guardian before attaching the scene to a window shade or wall.

Vocabulary Words

Write a separate sentence using each vocabulary word listed on page 414.

Health Content

1. What are three ways a positive visual environment can improve your health? **page 414**

2. What are sources of visual pollution? **page 415**

3. How can exposure to visual pollution influence your behavior? **page 415**

4. What are ways to create a visual environment that reduces stress? **pages 416–417**

5. What are ways to create a visual environment that promotes feelings of well-being? **pages 416–417**

Health Literacy

Critical Thinking

Why might a pleasant visual environment be especially important for a person who is ill?

Self-Directed Learning

Research the meanings of different colors using the library or the Internet. For example, to many people red is considered the color of danger. This explains why stop signs are red. Write a two-page paper explaining some of the meanings you found.

The Responsible Decision-Making Model™

You are walking home from school with a friend. You pass a building that is covered with graffiti. Your friend takes out some markers and suggests you add to the graffiti on the building. "Lots of people have done it," (s)he says. "Why shouldn't we?" Answer the following questions on a separate sheet of paper. Write "Does not apply" if a question does not apply to this situation.

1. Is it healthful to write graffiti on the building? Why or why not?

2. Is it safe to write graffiti on the building? Why or why not?

3. Is it legal to write graffiti on the building? Why or why not?

4. Will you show respect for yourself and others if you write graffiti on the building? Why or why not?

5. Will you follow the guidelines of your parents or guardian if you write graffiti on the building? Why or why not?

6. Will you demonstrate good character if you write graffiti on the building? Why or why not?

What is the responsible decision to make in this situation?

What would you say to your friend?

How to Promote a Friendly Environment

 Life Skill

◆ **I will take actions to improve my social-emotional environment.**

Think about the contacts you have with others. When you enter a room, do you feel accepted? Are other people friendly to you? Are you friendly to others? The **social-emotional environment** is the quality of the contacts a person has with the people with whom (s)he interacts. When you have a positive social-emotional environment, your health and the health of others is promoted.

The Lesson Objectives

- Discuss ways your social-emotional environment can affect your health.

- Discuss what you can do if you are in a hostile environment.

- Discuss ways to get others to warm up to you.

- Discuss what to do if someone puts you down.

- Explain how to use humor to your advantage.

Vocabulary

social-emotional environment

hostile environment

I-message

beta-endorphins

appropriate joke

inappropriate humor

sarcasm

How Can My Social-Emotional Environment Affect My Health?

A positive social-emotional environment affects your health in several ways. Suppose you live in a positive social-emotional environment. Other people encourage you to do your best. They praise you for your good work. They notice your personal strengths. As a result, your self-respect is maintained and strengthened. Your responsible behavior is supported. You do not choose risk behaviors to cope or to get attention.

A positive social-emotional environment reduces your stress and prevents depression. When you feel valued by other people, you are less likely to feel lonely. You are more likely to feel positive and optimistic. You are resilient when problems arise.

In contrast, a negative social-emotional environment might cause you to feel discouraged or to choose wrong behavior. Suppose you live in a negative social-emotional environment. Other people put you down. They try to control your behavior. They gossip about you. They encourage you to behave in harmful ways. They might abuse you. They tell you that you cannot improve things around you. As a result, you might become stressed and depressed. You might get sick more often. You might feel worthless. You might choose risk behaviors to cope with your feelings or to get attention.

If you have a positive social-emotional environment, do everything you can do to maintain it. If you have a negative social-emotional environment, do everything you can do to improve it. You can improve your social-emotional environment by treating others with respect. Praise them when they do something well. Encourage them to do their best. Encourage others to choose responsible behavior. Identify people who might contribute to a positive social-emotional environment for you. Spend time with them. Limit the time you spend with people who have a negative outlook.

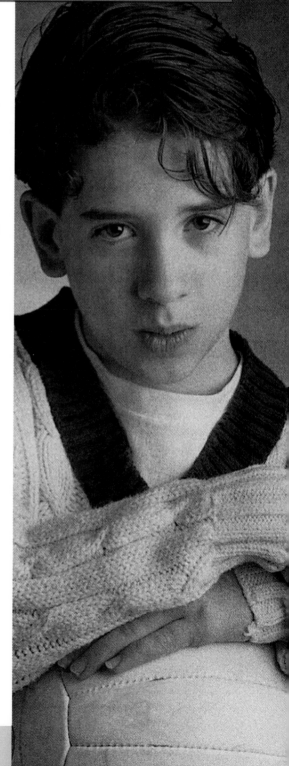

What Can I Do If I Am in a Hostile Environment?

Suppose you are in a hostile environment. A **hostile environment** is a threatening and unfriendly environment. Evaluate your own behavior. Are you contributing to the hostile environment? Are you encouraging others to act in harmful ways? If you are, you need to change your behavior. Set a good example. Stop the negative behavior. Encourage others to choose friendly behavior. Leave if a situation becomes dangerous.

Suppose some of your friends are negative. They always put you down. You need to change your social-emotional environment. Avoid contact with friends who are negative. Expand the group of people with whom you spend time. Make some new friends. Develop a hobby that puts you in contact with people who have similar interests. Join a club or organization where you can meet people who are positive and who do not put you down.

How can I get others to warm up to me?

Suppose you move to a new school. You might be afraid no one will talk to you. But if you are friendly, other teens will want to talk to you. They will want to spend time with you. They will want to be your friend.

There are several ways you can get others to be friendly to you. Smile at people you meet. Look them in the eye. Be a good listener. Ask questions that show you are listening to what they are saying. Have a neat appearance. Use social skills. Compliment others. Be pleasant to everyone, whether or not you agree with what they are saying. If you disagree, express your disagreement politely.

What can I do if someone puts me down?

There are several actions you can take if someone puts you down. Use I-messages to express your feelings. An **I-message** is a statement or message that contains a reference to a specific behavior or event, the effect of the behavior or event, and the feelings that result. Using an I-message allows you to tell the other person how you feel without accusing him or her.

Use self-statements to boost your self-respect. Pretend you are wearing a suit of armor that protects you from the person's words. Remind yourself that the person is simply trying to be unpleasant. Treat the person with respect. Do not respond by using put-downs. Talk to a trusted adult to determine if your behavior is appropriate. Avoid the person if (s)he continues to put you down.

How Can I Use Humor to My Advantage?

People who use humor are less likely to get stressed out. The use of humor improves relationships. It reduces anxiety and depression. It lowers stress levels. Research indicates that laughter triggers the release of beta-endorphins. **Beta-endorphins** (BAY·tuh·en·DOR·fuhnz) are substances produced in the brain that create a feeling of well-being.

There are several ways you might use humor to create a positive social-emotional environment. Read funny books. Tell appropriate jokes you hear or find in books or on the Web. An **appropriate joke** is a joke that does not make fun of anyone, does not put anyone down, and is not dirty. Read the comics in the newspaper and cut out funny comics to share with others. Laugh when other people tell appropriate jokes. This will make them more comfortable with you. You also should learn to laugh at yourself. You will be less stressed if you can laugh at yourself sometimes. Try to see the funny side of situations.

Avoid inappropriate humor. **Inappropriate humor** is humor that includes put-downs, dirty jokes, or jokes that make fun of certain groups of people. **Sarcasm** is a harmful form of inappropriate humor. Sarcasm is a taunting remark. Sarcasm can hurt the feelings of others. A person might mean to be funny when (s)he makes a sarcastic remark, but the results can be negative. For example, a teen might say, "Oh, yeah, she's a real winner." In this case, the teen's tone of voice indicates that (s)he does not think the other teen is a winner. The other teen's feelings might be hurt. Do not make fun of other people.

Activity

The Top Ten List of Ways to Make New Friends

Life Skill: I will take actions to improve my social-emotional environment.

Materials: paper, pen or pencil, poster board, colored markers

Directions: A person who has contact with many different people improves his or her social-emotional environment. Follow the directions below to make a list of ways you can expand the group of people with whom you spend time.

1. **Your teacher will divide the class into groups of three or four students.** (S)he will give each group a sheet of poster board and some markers.

2. **Each group will brainstorm ways a teen could meet new friends.** For example, a group might suggest that the teen go to camp, write to a pen pal, or join a club. Write all the group's suggestions on a piece of paper.

3. **Each group will select its ten best suggestions.**

4. **One person from each group will write the top ten suggestions on the piece of poster board using the markers.** Title the poster "The Top Ten List of Ways to Make New Friends."

5. **Each group will share its poster with the class.** Each group will explain how it selected its Top Ten List of Ways to Make New Friends.

Vocabulary Words

Write a separate sentence using each vocabulary word listed on page 420.

Health Content

1. What are ways your social-emotional environment can affect your health? **page 421**

2. What can you do if you are in a hostile environment? **page 422**

3. How can you get others to warm up to you? **page 422**

4. What can you do if someone puts you down? **page 422**

5. How can you use humor to your advantage? **page 423**

The Responsible Decision-Making Model™

Your classmate is making fun of another teen. You are tempted to join in. Answer the following questions on a separate sheet of paper. Write "Does not apply" if a question does not apply to this situation.

1. Is it healthful to make fun of another teen? Why or why not?

2. Is it safe to make fun of another teen? Why or why not?

3. Is it legal to make fun of another teen? Why or why not?

4. Will you show respect for yourself and the other teen if you make fun of him or her? Why or why not?

5. Will you follow the guidelines of your parents or guardian if you make fun of another teen? Why or why not?

6. Will you demonstrate good character if you make fun of another teen? Why or why not?

What is the responsible decision to make in this situation?

What would you say to your classmate?

Health Literacy

Responsible Citizenship

A warm fuzzy is a positive statement given to another person. It is the opposite of a put-down. Plan to give at least three warm fuzzies every day. For one week write in a journal each time you give someone a warm fuzzy.

Critical Thinking

Suppose you are the author of a book on manners. On one page of the book, explain why people who have manners do not use inappropriate humor.

Unit 9 Review

Health Content

Prepare for the Unit Test. Review your answers for each Lesson Review in this unit. Then write answers to each of the following questions:

1. What are the symptoms of sick building syndrome? **Lesson 41 page 396**
2. What symptoms might you have if you inhale carbon monoxide? **Lesson 41 page 396**
3. What is the difference between precycling and recycling? **Lesson 42 page 401**
4. What items can you recycle? **Lesson 42 page 401**
5. Why do people living in poverty often have a poor health status? **Lesson 43 page 411**
6. What are the different ways in which people want to use forests? **Lesson 43 page 411**
7. What could happen if you became desensitized to visual pollution? **Lesson 44 page 415**
8. What are some ways you can improve your visual environment? **Lesson 44 page 417**
9. How might being in a negative social-emotional environment affect your health? **Lesson 45 page 421**
10. What can you do if someone puts you down? **Lesson 45 page 422**

Health Behavior Contract

Make a health behavior contract for one of the life skills in this unit. Review your health behavior contract with your parents or guardian.

Vocabulary Words

Number a sheet of paper from 1–10. Select the correct vocabulary word and write it next to the corresponding number. DO NOT WRITE IN THIS BOOK.

hostile environment	radon
pollutant	biodegradable product
graffiti	poverty
environmental issues	visual pollution
inappropriate humor	medical waste

1. A _____ is a threatening and unfriendly environment. **Lesson 45**
2. _____ is sights that are unattractive. **Lesson 44**
3. _____ is humor that includes put-downs, dirty jokes, or jokes that make fun of certain groups of people. **Lesson 45**
4. A _____ is something that has a harmful effect on the environment. **Lesson 41**
5. _____ is writing or drawing on a public surface. **Lesson 44**
6. _____ are environmental concerns that can affect the quality of life for people. **Lesson 43**
7. _____ is infectious waste from medical facilities. **Lesson 42**
8. _____ is a condition in which people do not have enough resources to live in a healthful way. **Lesson 43**
9. A _____ is a product that can be broken down by organisms to become part of Earth's natural resources. **Lesson 42**
10. _____ is an odorless, colorless, radioactive gas. **Lesson 41**

The Responsible Decision-Making Model™

Another teen constantly puts you down. A friend suggests that you stand up for yourself and get even. Your friend suggests that you trash this teen's locker. Answer the following questions on a separate sheet of paper. Write "Does not apply" if a question does not apply to this situation.

1. Is it healthful to get even by trashing the teen's locker? Why or why not?

2. Is it safe to get even by trashing the teen's locker? Why or why not?

3. Is it legal to get even by trashing the teen's locker? Why or why not?

4. Will you show respect for yourself if you get even by trashing the teen's locker? Why or why not?

5. Will you follow the guidelines of your parents or guardian if you get even by trashing the teen's locker? Why or why not?

6. Will you demonstrate good character if you get even by trashing the teen's locker? Why or why not?

What is the responsible decision to make in this situation?

What is another way to deal with this teen's put-downs?

Health Literacy
Effective Communication

Write a proposal to improve the visual environment in your school. Include at least one suggestion.

Self-Directed Learning

Find the name of a historical landmark listed in the National Registry. Obtain information about this landmark. Why do people want to keep this historical landmark part of their environment? Share your findings with classmates.

Critical Thinking

Imagine that you live in an apartment with very thin walls. Your neighbor plays drums. You guess that the sound level is over 75 decibels. You get headaches and have difficulty concentrating on your homework. What might you say to your neighbor? Write your response on a sheet of paper.

Responsible Citizenship

Design a NO SMOKING sign for a place in your community. Contact an appropriate person and arrange to have your sign displayed.

Multicultural Health

Draw a map of another country. Develop symbols to depict different resources, such as oil, forests, bodies of water. Place the symbols on the appropriate place on the map. How do this country's resources promote the health of its people? Other people in the world?

Family Involvement

Obtain permission from your parents or guardian. Plan a time when family members will work together to improve the visual environment in your living space. Pick up clutter. Arrange things neatly.

UNIT 10
Injury Prevention and Safety

PRACTICE

HEALTH STANDARD 1

Comprehend Health Facts

Practice this standard at the end of this unit.

1. **Study and learn health facts.** Study the information on pages 450-451. List six ways you can prevent unintentional injuries in your home.

2. **Ask questions if you do not comprehend health facts.** Write a question about a safety hazard in your home. Share your question with your parents or guardian.

3. **Answer questions to show you comprehend health facts.** Write an answer to the question, Why should you be careful when removing covers from foods that have been microwaved?

4. **Use health facts to practice life skills.** Suppose you often use a microwave oven to heat food. You want to practice this life skill: *I will follow safety guidelines to reduce the risk of unintentional injuries.* Use health facts to write two safety habits you can follow.

How to Prevent Violence

Life Skills

◆ **I will practice protective factors to reduce the risk of violence.**

◆ **I will practice self-protection strategies.**

◆ **I will respect authority and obey laws.**

◆ **I will participate in victim recovery if I am harmed by violence.**

Violence is the use of physical force to injure, damage, or destroy oneself, others, or property. The number of teens harmed by violence has increased in the past several years. There are ways you can help reverse this trend. You can respect authority and obey laws. You can learn to settle disagreements without violence. You can learn self-protection strategies to help keep you safe.

The Lesson Objectives

- Describe the behavior of a law-abiding person.
- Discuss protective factors that reduce your risk of being involved in violence.
- Identify self-protection strategies you can practice.
- Discuss guidelines you can follow to reduce the risk of rape.
- Explain steps to recover if you are a survivor of violence.

Vocabulary

violence
law-abiding person
conscience
moral guilt
fighting
assault
bullying
homicide
murder
random violence
protective factor for violence
self-respect
anger management skills
conflict resolution skills
self-protection strategies
stalking
restraining order
street smart
sexual harassment
rape
acquaintance rape
date rape
mixed message
victim of violence
victim recovery
survivor of violence
empowered

How Does a Law-Abiding Person Behave?

A **law-abiding person** is a person who respects authority and obeys laws. The actions of a law-abiding person are based on his or her conscience. A **conscience** is an inner sense of right and wrong that causes a person to behave responsibly or to feel moral guilt. **Moral guilt** is a pang of conscience a person experiences after an irresponsible or wrong action. Moral guilt reminds people to correct their wrong actions.

Suppose you find a jacket in a booth at a fast food restaurant. Another teen suggests you keep the jacket. After all, you do not know the person who left it. Your conscience should tell you that it is wrong to take the jacket. If you take the jacket, you should experience moral guilt. Moral guilt helps you think about what you have done when you have done something wrong. Moral guilt prompts you to correct wrong actions. In this case, you would know that it would be wrong to take the jacket. You would return it.

Unfortunately, all people are not law-abiding people. There are some people who do not know the difference between right and wrong. And some people do not experience moral guilt after they do something wrong. Why? Some people were raised by adults who did not teach them the difference between right and wrong. They might not have been disciplined for their wrong actions. Or they might have been treated in wrong ways themselves. They might have been abused or disciplined with violence. As a result, they do not know how to show respect for others. They might believe violent actions are appropriate or "right" in some situations. They might believe violence is an acceptable way to solve problems or to get what they want. And worse yet, they might not experience moral guilt if they have harmed others.

Violent behavior is wrong. You should experience moral guilt if you choose violent behavior. The following actions are examples of violent behavior.

- **Fighting** is taking part in a physical struggle. Teens who fight can be injured. Fighting is not a good way to settle a disagreement.

- **Assault** is a physical attack or a threat of an attack. An assault can lead to a fight. A teen might assault someone in order to commit another crime, such as theft. Or a teen might assault someone in order to harm him or her.

- **Bullying** is an attempt by a person to hurt or frighten people whom the bully considers smaller or weaker. Many teens have been bullied.

- **Homicide** is the killing of one person by another person.

- **Murder** is a homicide that is purposeful. Homicides and murders can result from fights or assaults.

What Are Protective Factors That Will Reduce My Risk of Being Involved in Violence?

Violence is a frequent topic in the media. Evening newscasts usually include a report of at least one shooting, robbery, or other incident. **Random violence** is violence over which a person has no control. For example, an innocent bystander who is injured in a drive-by shooting is a victim of random violence. But a lot of violence is not random. You can reduce your risk of being involved in violence. A **protective factor for violence** is an action or circumstance that decreases the likelihood that a person will be involved in violence. The following pledge includes nine protective factors for violence.

The Violence-Free Pledge

I will recognize violent behavior. First of all, you must know what actions are violent behavior. For example, kicking someone is violent behavior. Slapping someone in the face is violent behavior. When you understand what violent behavior is, you can avoid people who choose violent behavior. You recognize when someone else chooses violent behavior. Refer to the list of violent actions on page 431.

I will have self-respect. Self-respect is a high regard for oneself because one behaves in responsible ways. If you have self-respect, you do not allow others to harm you. You tell them to stop. If someone tries to harm you, tell a responsible adult. When you have self-respect, you are more likely to treat others with respect.

I will practice anger management skills. Anger management skills are ways to express anger without harming oneself or others. For example, you might use an I-message to tell someone you are angry instead of calling the person a name.

The Violence-Free Pledge

I will use conflict resolution skills instead of fighting.
Conflict resolution skills are steps that can be taken to settle a disagreement in a responsible way. For example, you might discuss and agree upon a solution rather than settling an argument with a fight. Lesson 7 discusses conflict resolution skills in more detail.

I will make responsible decisions. You should use *The Responsible Decision-Making Model™* to evaluate the effects of actions before you take them. Then you will be less likely to provoke others with your wrong actions. You will be less likely to respond to the actions of others with violent behavior.

I will avoid gangs and weapons. Gang members use weapons to engage in violent behavior. You reduce your risk of being involved in violence by staying away from gangs and weapons. You will learn more about gangs and weapons in Lesson 47.

I will participate in recovery if I am a victim of violence.
Suppose you are a victim of violence. You likely feel hurt and angry. You might want to keep your anger inside and forget the experience. But the anger can build up and cause you to explode or harm yourself. When you participate in recovery, you learn to cope with your anger in a healthful way. You do not treat others the way you were treated. Talk about your feelings with a responsible adult. See page 440 for more information about victim recovery.

I will change my behavior if I am not now a law-abiding person. You must respect authority and obey laws. If you currently do not, change your behavior right now. Talk to a responsible adult. Get a mentor to work with you.

I will avoid alcohol and other drugs. Drinking alcohol and using other drugs affects reasoning and judgment. Drinking alcohol and using other drugs can make angry feelings even stronger. Stay in control of your actions and your emotions.

What Are Self-Protection Strategies I Can Practice?

Violence is a fact of life. But you do not have to become a statistic. Protect yourself. Use self-protection strategies. **Self-protection strategies** are strategies that can be practiced to protect oneself from violence.

Q: What can I do if I have a gut feeling that a person or situation might be dangerous?

A: Trust your instincts. The person might even be someone you know. Avoid the person or situation. Be cautious whenever you are near the person or situation. Tell your parents or guardian about your feelings. They can help protect you. If you are threatened, get away from him or her. If necessary, scream to get attention. Go to a safe place immediately.

Q: What can I do to protect myself if I am at home alone?

A: Keep your windows and doors locked. Use deadbolt locks on the doors. Do not rely on chain locks. Do not hide extra keys under the doormat or outside your house. Have your keys ready when going to the door. Keep an outside light on at night so you can see to unlock the door. Do not enter your home if it looks like someone has broken in. Call the police. Keep inside lights on at night. Do not let strangers enter your home. Suppose you answer the phone or the door. Make it sound as if someone is at home with you. Suppose someone asks to come in and make an emergency phone call. Do not open the door. Offer to make the call yourself if you think the emergency is real. Suppose you receive a prank phone call. Hang up immediately. Call the police if the person continues to call. Make sure you have a list of emergency phone numbers next to the telephone.

Q&A

Q: What is stalking? What can I do if I am stalked?

A: **Stalking** is obsessing about a person with the intent to threaten or harm that person. A stalker might try to upset the other person. A stalker might try to develop a relationship with the other person. Stalkers usually are male. They usually stalk females. A stalker might injure or kill the other person.

Tell your parents or guardian immediately if you think someone is stalking you. Report stalking to the police. Press charges against the stalker. Try to get a restraining order. A **restraining order** is an order by a court that forbids a person from doing a particular act. Keep track of any stalking incidents. Write down the time, date, what happened, what the stalker said, and what you said. Save anything the stalker has sent you, such as letters. Save any answering machine tapes on which the stalker has left messages. Tell your teacher and principal about the stalking. They can help protect you. Join a support group for people who have been stalked.

Q: What can I do to be street smart?

A: To be **street smart** is to be aware of possible danger and to know what to do. A person who is street smart is less likely to be involved in violence. Pay attention to what is happening around you if you are in an area where you do not feel safe. Know where other people are, how close they are to you, and what they are doing. Plan your route ahead of time. Violent people will be less likely to target you if you appear confident. Look as if you know where you are going. Stay in safe, well-lighted areas when waiting for public transportation. Stay with a group of people. Go to a store or other busy place if you feel threatened. Do not turn your back toward a street or a lobby when you are using a public telephone. Turn your back toward the telephone.

Avoid walking alone, especially at night. Carry a flashlight if you must walk at night. You can use the flashlight to light suspicious areas. You also can use it as a weapon if you are attacked. Walk far enough away from buildings so that people cannot grab you or surprise you. Walk far enough away from the street so that people cannot grab you from a car. Carry items in only one hand. You can use the other hand to defend yourself, if necessary. Carry your purse under one elbow and hold it tightly. Give a robber a personal belonging if (s)he demands it. You do not want to risk being harmed by violence.

Q: **What can I do to stay safe when I am childsitting?**

A: If you are childsitting for your own siblings, follow the guidelines for staying safe when you are home alone. Suppose you are caring for someone else's children. Ask the parents or guardian to show you where everything is in the home. Note the locations of doors. Ask the parents or guardian what to do in case of emergency. Keep all windows and outside doors locked. Leave lights on in several rooms so it looks like several people are home. Do not let strangers in the house. Do not tell anyone who calls on the phone or knocks on the door that you are alone with the children.

Suppose you hear a suspicious noise or see a suspicious person. Call the police immediately. Do not leave young children alone in a room or outside. Do not let the children's parents or guardian drive you home if they have been drinking alcohol. Call your parents or guardian to pick you up. Call your parents or guardian and tell them you will be late if the child's parents or guardian do not come home on time. Suppose the children's parents or guardian do something that makes you feel uncomfortable. Call your parents or guardian to pick you up. Tell them what happened.

Q: **What can I do to protect myself when I exercise outdoors?**

A: Suppose you like to walk, jog, bicycle, or in-line skate. You need to take steps to stay safe. Always tell your parents or guardian where you are going and when you will return. Do not exercise alone at night or in deserted areas. Pay attention to your gut feelings. Suppose you feel that an area or person is not safe. Avoid the area or person. Do not use the same route every time you exercise. Vary your route, so you will be harder for a stalker to track. Stay away from places where a person could grab you from bushes or trees. Suppose someone in a car bothers you. Move quickly away from the person. Go to a place where there are other people. Carry a whistle or personal alarm to attract attention if someone threatens you. Consider taking a large dog with you when you exercise. Do not use a personal stereo with headphones. You might not hear an attacker or someone following you. Stay away from strangers. Always carry identification and enough change to make a phone call.

Q: **What can I do to stay safe when I am riding in a car?**

A: Do not get into a car with a stranger. Check the front and back seats before you get in a car to make sure no one is hiding inside. Keep the doors locked. Keep all valuable items out of sight. Do not yell or make nasty gestures at people in other cars. Do not distract the driver of your car.

Q: **What is sexual harassment? What can I do if I am sexually harassed?**

A: **Sexual harassment** is unwanted sexual behavior that ranges from making sexual comments to forcing another person into unwanted sex acts. Sexual harassment might include making sexual jokes, touching someone inappropriately, staring at someone's body, or making inappropriate gestures. Both males and females can be sexually harassed.

Suppose you are being sexually harassed. Ask the person who is harassing you to stop. Explain exactly what behavior is bothering you. Keep a record of what happened. Write down the date, time, what happened, and how you handled the situation. Save any notes, letters, or pictures from the person. Tell your parents or guardian what happened. Tell a teacher or principal what happened. Your school might have guidelines to deal with sexual harassment.

What Should I Know About Rape?

Rape is the threatened or actual use of physical force to get someone to have sex without giving consent. Both males and females can be raped. Rape is the fault of the person who commits rape. It is not the fault of the victim. **Acquaintance rape** is rape in which the rapist is known to the person who is raped. **Date rape** is rape that occurs in a dating situation. You can practice self-protection strategies to reduce your risk of being raped.

When you plan to spend time with a person you do not know well... Do not spend time alone with a person you do not know or do not trust. Spend time with that person in a group of friends. Never use alcohol or other drugs. Using alcohol or other drugs harms your ability to think clearly and to defend yourself. Do not spend time with any teens who use alcohol or other drugs.

When you want to express affection... Set clear limits for expressing affection and stick to them. Respect the limits of other people. Do not assume that another person's limits are the same as yours. Do not pressure another person to go beyond his or her limits for expressing affection. Do not tease another person or send mixed messages. A **mixed message** is a message that expresses two different meanings. Suppose someone does not respect your limits. Use physical force if necessary to defend yourself.

When you recognize disrespectful or controlling behavior... A person who does not respect you is more likely to harm you than is a person who shows respect for you. A person who tries to control your behavior or is very jealous might be likely to harm you. A person who is rough, violent, or abusive is likely to harm you. Suppose someone you know has these characteristics. (S)he might harm you. Avoid this person. Tell your parents or guardian about this person.

Talk to your parents or guardian about how to set clear limits for expressing affection. Discuss ways to avoid situations in which you risk being raped. You might attend workshops to learn self-defense techniques.

If you are raped... Tell your parents, your guardian, or another responsible adult immediately. Go to the hospital to have a medical examination. Report the rape to the police. Participate in a victim recovery program.

Activity

You Be the Judge

Life Skill: I will respect authority and obey laws.

Materials: paper, pen or pencil

Directions: Follow the directions below to learn why it is important to respect authority and obey laws.

1. Your teacher will divide the class into four groups. Each group will be a "jury."

2. Your teacher will assign each group a scenario from the following box. Read the scenario your teacher assigns to your group.

- A group of teens steals some bowling shoes from a bowling alley. They say that it is OK to steal the shoes because the bowling alley has lots of shoes.

- A teen carves his or her initials in a desk at school. The teen says his or her parents paid for the desk with their tax money, so (s)he can do whatever (s)he wants.

- A group of teens toilet-papers the house of another teen.

- A teen copies some software from a friend's computer. The teen says there is no need to purchase the software because it is easy to copy.

3. Each jury will decide whether or not its scenario describes wrong behavior. The members will list three reasons why the behavior is right or wrong.

4. Each jury will recommend an appropriate penalty if it determines that the behavior is wrong. Each jury will present its case to the judge (your teacher).

5. Each student will answer the following questions on a separate sheet of paper.

- What kinds of wrong actions do teens take that they do not believe are illegal?

- Are those actions in fact illegal?

- If the actions are not illegal, in what way are they wrong? Might they contribute to violence? Might they harm another person or property?

- Would a law-abiding person experience moral guilt if (s)he took any of these actions?

What Are Steps to Take to Recover If I Am a Survivor of Violence?

A **victim of violence** is a person who has been harmed by violence. Suppose you are a victim of violence. You might feel depressed, angry, and afraid. You might cry a lot. You might have trouble sleeping or concentrating. You might have bad dreams and flashbacks. You might avoid spending time with other people. Your reaction might differ from the reactions of other victims, depending on the kind of violence and the way you usually react to different situations.

Victims might need help to recover from the effects of violence. **Victim recovery** is a person's return to physical and emotional health after being harmed by violence. Victim recovery helps victims heal the pain that resulted from the violence. Victims can proceed confidently with their lives.

There are several parts to victim recovery. First, victims must receive treatment for any physical injuries. They should be examined for infection with HIV or other STDs if they were raped.

Second, victims should receive treatment for emotional pain. Without help, they might have trouble trusting others. They might not believe they deserve respect. They might allow others to continue to harm them.

Third, victims will recover more completely if they have support from family and friends. Family and friends can help victims regain their self-respect. Victims can recover when they know people they can trust.

Fourth, victims should attempt to be repaid for money or property losses. Fifth, victims should educate themselves about self-protection strategies. Victims should avoid risk behaviors and develop their protective factors. Victims who do not recover completely are more likely to behave violently themselves. For example, teens who were earlier abused by their parents or guardian might abuse others if they do not participate in victim recovery.

Victim recovery helps victims become survivors of violence. A **survivor of violence** is a person who has been harmed by violence, participated in recovery, and feels empowered. To be **empowered** is to be energized because a person has some control over his or her decisions and behavior. Survivors of violence are able to put the violent incident behind them. They do not dwell on the violence. They are able to go on with their lives.

Review

Vocabulary Words

Write a separate sentence using each vocabulary word listed on page 430.

Health Content

1. How does a law-abiding person behave? **page 431**

2. What are some protective factors that will reduce your risk of being involved in violence? **pages 432–433**

3. What are some self-protection strategies you can practice? **pages 434–437**

4. What are guidelines you can follow to reduce the risk of rape? **page 438**

5. What are steps you can take to recover if you have been a survivor of violence? **page 440**

The Responsible Decision-Making Model™

A classmate calls you a nasty name. (S)he challenges you to a fight. (S)he says you will be a chicken if you do not fight. Answer the following questions on a separate sheet of paper. Write "Does not apply" if a question does not apply to this situation.

1. Is it healthful to fight your classmate? Why or why not?

2. Is it safe to fight your classmate? Why or why not?

3. Is it legal to fight your classmate? Why or why not?

4. Will you show respect for yourself and others if you fight your classmate? Why or why not?

5. Will you follow the guidelines of your parents or guardian if you fight your classmate? Why or why not?

6. Will you demonstrate good character if you fight your classmate? Why or why not?

What is the responsible decision to make in this situation?

Would a law-abiding person experience moral guilt if (s)he fought a classmate?

Health Literacy

Responsible Citizenship

Gather information from victim recovery programs in your area. Design a pamphlet describing the programs. Ask permission to place the pamphlet in your school nurse's office.

Critical Thinking

Why might a person who does not have a conscience be dangerous?

How to Protect Yourself from Gangs and Weapons

Life Skills

◆ I will stay away from gangs.
◆ I will not carry a weapon.

Vocabulary

gang
resistance skills
anti-gang gang
weapon

A **gang** is a group of people involved in violent and illegal activities. Being a member of a gang has serious outcomes. A gang member can be harmed or acquire a criminal record. If you wander into gang territory, there also can be serious outcomes. You can be harmed. Legal authorities might mistake you for a gang member. It might be difficult for you to prove you are not part of a gang. Protect yourself and your future. Stay away from gangs. Never carry a weapon.

The Lesson Objectives

- Discuss reasons why you will stay away from gangs.
- Explain how you can protect yourself from gang members.
- Outline resistance skills you can use if you are pressured to join a gang.
- Discuss reasons why you will not carry a weapon.
- Explain how to protect yourself if someone has a weapon.

How Can I Protect Myself from Gang Members?

Gang members are not law-abiding people. You must be able to identify gang members in order to protect yourself from them. There are several characteristics of gang members.

Gang members stick together and follow specific rules. They spend time only with members of their gang. They might use special signals and vocabulary to communicate with members of their gang. They follow rules set by the leaders of the gang. For example, the rules might require them to commit crimes. Gang members who break the rules face severe consequences from other gang members.

Gang members consider certain areas their territory. They defend their territory, or "turf," by harming or killing other people who enter it. They draw logos, special symbols, and other graffiti on buildings to mark their turf. They also use this graffiti to send messages to other members of the gang.

Gang members identify themselves with nicknames, tattoos, clothing, and colors. Gang members use their nicknames when they are involved in illegal activities. They get tattoos to show that they plan to be in the gang for life. The tattoos might include the gang's logo or other symbols.

Protect yourself from gang members by taking the following precautions. Be aware of and avoid gang territory. Stay away from gang members or people whom you suspect might be gang members. Know the colors of any gangs in your community, and avoid wearing those colors. Be home each night before it gets late. Do not listen to music that promotes gangs or gang activities. Do not draw graffiti. Do not use alcohol or other drugs. Obey laws and respect authority. Spend time with family members and responsible friends and adults. Make sure your parents or guardian know where you are at all times. Set goals and work toward them. Teens who have good relationships with their families and are working toward defined goals do not feel the need to join a gang for companionship.

How Can I Resist Pressure to Join a Gang?

You might be pressured to join a gang if you live in a community where there are gangs. Joining a gang is a wrong decision. Use resistance skills if you are pressured to join a gang. **Resistance skills** are skills that are used to say NO to an action or to leave a situation.

1. **Say NO in a firm voice to joining a gang.** Do not hesitate. You are making a responsible decision.

2. **Give reasons for saying NO to joining a gang.** You might say, "NO, I do not want a criminal record." Or you might say, "NO, I do not want to be harmed or to harm others."

3. **Be certain your behavior matches your words.** Do not show interest in or participate in gang activities. Do not commit crimes.

4. **Avoid situations in which there will be pressure to join a gang.** Participate in safe activities in your school or community. Stay away from gang territory. Avoid gang activities. Do not hang out with gang members.

5. **Avoid being with gang members.** Do not hang out with gang members. People will think you belong to a gang if you hang out with gang members. You might be blamed for their illegal activities. You might be harmed.

6. **Resist pressure to do something illegal.** Do not commit crimes. Do not use alcohol or other drugs. Remember, you can get a criminal record and be punished for illegal activities.

7. **Influence others to stay away from gangs.** Encourage your friends to stay away from gangs. Tell a responsible adult if you suspect a friend is thinking about joining a gang. Consider forming an anti-gang gang. An **anti-gang gang** is a group of teens who stay together to avoid pressure and to protect themselves from gang members. Members of an anti-gang gang stay together to be safe. They know that gang members are less likely to hassle them when they are together. They might plan safe activities to enjoy together.

Activity

Guilty by Association

Life Skill: I will stay away from gangs.

Materials: paper, pen or pencil, red water-based marker, blue water-based marker, water

Directions: Suppose you hang out with gang members. You might tell others you are not a gang member. But other people associate you with the gang. Follow the directions below to illustrate the concept of guilt by association.

1. **Color part of a sheet of paper with a red marker to represent gang territory.** What might you find in the gang territory? You might find graffiti or other signs of gangs.

2. **Color the area of the paper next to the red part with a blue marker to represent areas next to gang territory.** Do not let the colors overlap.

3. **Drip some water onto the part of the paper where the colors nearly touch.** Most likely, the colors will blur and run together. This represents a law-abiding teen wandering into gang territory. Even though the colors were not touching originally, they begin to mingle. It is difficult to tell where one stops and the other begins. When a teen spends time in gang territory or hangs out with gang members, it is difficult to tell whether or not that teen is a gang member. The teen's activities mingle with the activities of the gang. Other people associate the teen with the gang. They might associate the teen with crimes the gang commits, even if the teen was not involved with the crimes.

4. **On a separate sheet of paper, write three reasons why you should stay away from gang territory and gang members.**

What Are Reasons I Will Not Carry a Weapon?

A **weapon** is an instrument or device used for fighting. Kinds of weapons include guns, knives, clubs, bombs, and other items. Guns and knives are most commonly used by teens. Most states have made it illegal to sell guns to people younger than 18. It is illegal for anyone at any age to carry a weapon on school property.

Never purchase a weapon illegally. Do not carry a weapon. If you do, you increase your risk of being injured or killed. You increase your risk of injuring or killing someone else. You cannot undo an injury or death. For example, you might accidentally shoot someone because you did not know how to handle a gun. You might be showing off and shoot someone because you did not realize the gun was loaded. You might use a weapon to settle a fight. It is easy to think about using a weapon when you are angry and a weapon is available. Without the weapon, you would settle the fight differently. Also, someone might take the weapon and use it on you.

You might be tempted to use a weapon in a crime. If you do, you cannot undo any harm that results. Suppose you are depressed. You might think of committing suicide. Such thoughts usually pass. But if you have a weapon, you might use it. Suicide cannot be undone.

Do not pretend you have a weapon. For example, do not point your finger in your pocket as if you have a gun. Encourage others not to carry weapons.

How to Protect Yourself from Someone Who Has a Weapon

- **Stay away from people who carry or sell weapons.** You never know what they might do. People who sell weapons to teens are breaking the law. They are criminals. Avoid them.

- **Keep away from people who have weapons.** Do not argue with them or provoke them. Stay calm. Do not cause a person who has a weapon to become upset.

- **Avoid situations where people will have weapons.** If you know that other teens will have weapons at a place or event, stay away.

- **Avoid touching a weapon if you find one.** Do not move it. Tell a responsible adult about the weapon immediately.

Vocabulary Words

Write a separate sentence using each vocabulary word listed on page 442.

Health Content

1. What are reasons why you should stay away from gangs? **page 442**

2. How can you protect yourself from gang members? **page 443**

3. How can you resist pressure to join a gang? **page 444**

4. Why is it dangerous for you to carry a weapon? **page 446**

5. How can you protect yourself if someone has a weapon? **page 446**

Health Literacy

Responsible Citizenship

Find out if there are any anti-gang gangs in your community. If there are none, consider starting one. Design a poster that explains why it is risky to join a gang. Your poster should invite teens to join an anti-gang gang.

Self-Directed Learning

In several cities, local people have taken action against gang activities. Using the library or the Internet, find an article about one such effort. Read the article. Write a one-page paper explaining how the people handled the problem of gangs in their neighborhood.

The Responsible Decision-Making Model™

Your classmate shows you a gun he has in his locker. "Don't tell anyone," he says. "I just want to show it off." Answer the following questions on a separate sheet of paper. Write "Does not apply" if a question does not apply to this situation.

1. Is it healthful not to tell a responsible adult about the gun? Why or why not?

2. Is it safe not to tell a responsible adult about the gun? Why or why not?

3. Is it legal not to tell a responsible adult about the gun? Why or why not?

4. Will you show respect for yourself and others if you do not tell a responsible adult about the gun? Why or why not?

5. Will you follow the guidelines of your parents or guardian if you do not tell a responsible adult about the gun? Why or why not?

6. Will you demonstrate good character if you do not tell a responsible adult about the gun? Why or why not?

What is the responsible decision to make in this situation?

How to Prevent Unintentional Injuries

Life Skills

♦ I will follow safety guidelines to reduce the risk of unintentional injuries.

♦ I will follow guidelines for motor vehicle safety.

Vocabulary

unintentional injury

random event

speeding

burn

scald

poison

electrical injury

near drowning

An **unintentional injury** is an injury caused by an accident. Unintentional injuries are a leading cause of death and disability in teens. In most cases, unintentional injuries can be prevented. However, random events sometimes lead to unintentional injuries. A **random event** is an event over which a person does not have control. For example, a drunk driver might crash into the automobile in which a teen is riding.

The Lesson Objectives

• Discuss ways to prevent unintentional injuries when you are a passenger in a motor vehicle.

• Discuss ways to prevent unintentional injuries from falls, using a microwave oven, poisoning, and using electrical items.

• Discuss ways to prevent unintentional injuries when you are at an amusement park and when you are celebrating holidays and special occasions.

• Discuss ways to prevent near drowning and drowning.

• Make a fire escape plan for your home.

How Can I Prevent Unintentional Injuries When I Am a Passenger in a Motor Vehicle?

Motor vehicle crashes are the leading cause of death in teens. Death usually results from serious injury to the head, chest, and/or abdomen. Motor vehicle crashes also cause millions of nonfatal injuries each year. Some of these injuries can be severe, such as permanent brain damage or the loss of arms or legs. Three major factors that contribute to motor vehicle crashes are alcohol use, speeding, and not wearing a safety belt.

Alcohol is involved in 40 percent of fatal motor vehicle crashes. Drinking alcohol can slow reaction time and interfere with coordination. A driver who is drinking alcohol might not stop at red lights or stop signs. The driver might not keep the vehicle within the proper lane. The driver might speed or take other unnecessary risks.

Speeding is involved in 30 percent of fatal motor vehicle crashes. **Speeding** is exceeding the posted speed limit or driving too fast for conditions. For example, a driver who is going the posted speed limit might be speeding if the road is covered with ice. Speeding is dangerous. Drivers must have time to respond to traffic signs, animals in the road, curves and hills, and the actions of other drivers.

According to the Centers for Disease Control and Prevention, *teens are far less likely to use safety belts than any other age group.* Safety belts protect you by keeping you in place if a crash occurs. A safety belt includes the lap and shoulder straps. You are less likely to strike some part of the vehicle's interior when you wear a safety belt. You are less likely to be thrown out of the vehicle during a crash. Wear a safety belt at all times when you are riding in a motor vehicle. Most motor vehicle crashes occur within 25 miles of home and where the posted speed limit is 45 miles per hour or less.

You can prevent unintentional injuries when you are a passenger in a motor vehicle.

- Wear a safety belt at all times.
- Do not ride with a driver who has been drinking.
- Do not ride with a driver who speeds.
- Do not ride with a driver who races with other drivers.

Click!

How Can I Prevent Unintentional Injuries in My Home?

You have probably heard the expression "Home is where the heart is." Consider the following expression: "Home is where the hazards are!" Many unintentional injuries occur in a home. These include falls, burns from using microwave ovens, poisoning, and injuries from using electrical items.

Falls

Falls are the second leading cause of unintentional injuries. **You can prevent unintentional injuries from falls.**

Keep objects off stairways and floors where people walk. You walk through the rooms or go up and down stairs in your home. You assume the path is clear. You are familiar with the usual position of furniture and other items. You might not watch where you are walking. A misplaced object can cause you or someone else to trip and fall and be injured.

Place rubber mats or slip resistant stickers in the bathtub. Water makes surfaces slick. You risk serious head and bone injuries if you slip in a wet tub. Traction can be provided by special stickers or mats placed on the bottom of the tub.

Do not lean against window screens. A screen is not designed to withstand the weight of a person. It can give way, causing the person to fall out of the window.

Microwaves

A **burn** is an injury caused by heat, electricity, chemicals, or radiation. **You can prevent unintentional injuries from using a microwave oven.**

Stir foods often during microwaving. A **scald** is a burn caused by hot liquid or steam. Steam can build up when food is heated in a covered dish. The steam escapes when the cover is lifted. Remove covers carefully from foods that have been microwaved. Liquids heated in a microwave oven also can cause a scald. The container in which the liquid is heated might feel warm, not hot, and you could be scalded if you are not careful.

Handle items carefully that have been microwaved. Food heated in a microwave can warm unevenly. Parts of the food can develop hot areas, which can burn your mouth, throat, or esophagus.

Electrical Injuries

An **electrical injury** is an injury that occurs when electricity passes through the body. The heat from the electric current can severely burn and damage body tissues. **You can prevent unintentional injuries from electrical items.**

Do not use electrical items near water or when your body is wet. Because water is an excellent conductor of electricity, you might come in contact with the electrical current. This does not apply to appliances that are designed for wet conditions.

Do not use an electrical item if you think it has unsafe wiring. You might have an electrical cord that is frayed or worn. If so, the wires are not properly insulated. Such wires can conduct electricity to you if you touch them. Electrical items that repeatedly blow a fuse or trip a circuit breaker might have unsafe wiring. Outlets and switches that are very warm to the touch also might have unsafe wiring. Unsafe wiring should be repaired or replaced.

Poisoning

A **poison** is a substance that causes injury, illness, or death if it enters the body. Poisons can enter the body through breathing, eating, or drinking. They also can be absorbed through the skin. Poisons are the third leading cause of unintentional injuries. **You can prevent unintentional injuries from poison.**

Follow directions on the label when using a product. Some products, such as paint thinners, give off fumes that can be harmful. The labels on these products warn you to use the products in well-ventilated areas so that the circulating air will carry the fumes away from you. Products such as pesticides can harm you if they get on your skin. Labels on such products warn you to wear protective clothing such as gloves when you use the products.

Keep nonfood products in their original containers. You might mistake the product for a beverage if it has been transferred to a drinking glass or pop bottle.

Suspicious Mail

Be aware of harmful substances that can be sent through the mail. Suspicious mail may have:
- Too much postage.
- No name or only a title such as Resident.
- Words not spelled correctly.
- Stains, oil spots, or discoloration.
- No return address.
- Unevenly shaped envelope.
- Too much wrapping.
- A postmark different from the return address.

How Can I Prevent Unintentional Injuries When I Am Having Fun?

The last thing you want to think about when you are having fun is being injured. But preventing an injury should be the first thing you think about.

Holidays and Special Occasions

Holidays and special occasions can be enjoyable. But they also can present special hazards. You can prevent unintentional injuries when you are celebrating holidays and special occasions.

Follow safety guidelines when using decorations. Place burning candles away from trees, curtains, or other flammable items. Follow directions for spraying artificial snow. Artificial snow can irritate your lungs if you inhale it. Do not burn wrapping paper in a fireplace. Poisonous fumes can be released. Do not overload electrical circuits or extension cords. A fire might result. Do not place electrical cords under rugs. The cords can become worn and lead to a fire.

Take actions to prevent or deal with stress. You might feel more tired than usual. You might not be able to concentrate. You might hurry to finish preparations. When you are stressed, you are less cautious. You are more likely to be injured. Allow yourself time for preparations. Practice stress management skills. Be alert to careless actions by others who are stressed.

Amusement Parks

You can have lots of fun, food, and family togetherness at amusement parks. But you might get sick or injured if you do not follow health and safety guidelines. You can prevent unintentional injuries when you are at an amusement park.

Take actions to avoid dangers in your environment. You might trip and fall over litter or spilled beverages in your path. Wear shoes that provide good traction. Do not run. Wear head protection, sunglasses, and sunscreen during the day to prevent sunburn.

Follow guidelines while riding amusement park rides. Rides can cause severe injuries if you take unnecessary risks or do not follow instructions. Some rides are dangerous for young teens. Do not dangle arms and legs from rides. Do not stand up in rides when you should remain seated. Do not take risky dares. Do not go on rides for which you are too young or too small. Do not continue to ride rides if you become dizzy or nauseated. Do not go on rides with health warnings that apply to you.

Scooter Safety

If you ride a scooter, remember to follow scooter safety tips. Wear the correct equipment such as a helmet, knee pads, and elbow pads. Ride in safe places and only in daylight. Avoid gravel and dirt roads as it is easy to fall on these surfaces. If you must ride in the street, follow traffic rules.

How Can I Prevent Near Drowning and Drowning?

Do you think it is cool to dunk your friends in a swimming pool? How about swimming by yourself? Would you get a thrill diving into water without knowing how deep it is? NOT! Drowning is a major cause of unintentional deaths among teens. Near drowning can cause coma or permanent brain damage. **Near drowning** is being without sufficient oxygen for a long period of time under water but not dying. You can prevent near drowning and drowning.

Do not swim alone. You might become tired and unable to keep yourself above water. You might get caught in a strong current. No one would be available to help you.

Find out the depth of water before entering. What might you do if you find yourself in water over your head? You might be so startled that you forget to hold your breath. You might be frightened and inhale water. What might you do if you dive into water of unknown depth and hit your head on the shallow bottom? You might be knocked unconscious and drown. You might end up with brain damage or a spinal cord injury.

Do not dunk, push, or jump on others or allow others to do these things to you. You might inhale water if you are dunked. You might be injured and not be able to stay above water if you are pushed or jumped on.

Do not chew gum or eat while swimming, diving, or playing in the water. You might choke on the gum or food. You might breathe in water while you are fighting for air.

Swim in designated areas only. You might get caught by strong currents or hidden trash. You might be far from shore if a storm comes up suddenly.

Do not drink alcohol. Alcohol slows your reaction time and interferes with your coordination. You might not be able to keep yourself above water. Alcohol clouds your judgment. You might take unnecessary risks around water.

According to the Centers for Disease Control and Prevention, alcohol is considered a major contributing factor in 40 to 50 percent of drownings among male teens.

Activity

A Cool Plan for Escaping a Hot Fire

Life Skill: I will follow safety guidelines to reduce the risk of unintentional injuries.

Materials: paper, markers, poster board or white poster paper

Directions: A home fire occurs every 70 seconds. Someone dies in a home fire every two hours. Read the information in the box below. Then follow the steps to design a fire escape plan for your home.

My Fire Escape Plan

My fire escape plan should include:

1. the floor plan of my home;
2. two escape routes for each room;
3. the location of an outside family meeting place;
4. actions to take if my home catches fire.
   - Crawl to the nearest window or door if smoke is present.
   - Get out fast! Do not stop to get any belongings.
   - Go to the family meeting place.
   - Do not go back inside your home while it is burning.

1. **Draw the floor plan of your home on a sheet of paper.** Your teacher will provide you with an example. (You might need to do this step at home.)

2. **Use a colored marker to draw lines for the doors and windows.**

3. **Use a different colored marker to draw arrows showing two escape routes for each room.**

4. **Decide a place for your family to meet outside your home.** Create a symbol or picture to mark this place.

5. **Copy your plan onto a larger piece of poster paper.** Somewhere on your poster, write the actions to take if your home catches fire.

6. **Share your plan with your family.** Have your parents or guardian approve the plan. Make any changes they suggest. Practice the actions to take if your home catches fire every six months with your family.

Review

Vocabulary Words

Write a separate sentence using each vocabulary word listed on page 448.

Health Content

1. How can you prevent unintentional injuries when you are a passenger in a motor vehicle? **page 449**

2. How can you prevent unintentional injuries from falls? Using a microwave oven? Poisoning? Using electrical items? **pages 450–451**

3. How can you prevent unintentional injuries when you are at an amusement park? When you are celebrating holidays and special occasions? **page 452**

4. How can you prevent drowning and unintentional injuries from near drowning? **page 453**

5. What should you include in a fire escape plan for your home? **page 454**

The Responsible Decision-Making Model™

You and a friend are swimming in a lake. Your friend dares you to swim beyond the designated area. Answer the following questions on a separate sheet of paper. Write "Does not apply" if a question does not apply to this situation.

1. Is it healthful to swim beyond the designated area? Why or why not?

2. Is it safe to swim beyond the designated area? Why or why not?

3. Is it legal to swim beyond the designated area? Why or why not?

4. Will you show respect for yourself if you swim beyond the designated area? Why or why not?

5. Will your parents or guardian approve if you swim beyond the designated area? Why or why not?

6. Will you demonstrate good character if you swim beyond the designated area? Why or why not?

What is the responsible decision to make in this situation?

Health Literacy

Effective Communication

Call or write your state health department. Ask them for the number and types of unintentional injuries in your state over the past five years. Make a graph of this data. Display your graph in your classroom.

Critical Thinking

Poisoning is a leading cause of death in young children. Why do you think this is true? What are some things that can be done to prevent young children from being poisoned in the home?

How to Stay Safe in Severe Weather and Natural Disasters

Life Skill

♦ **I will follow safety guidelines for severe weather and natural disasters.**

What is the weather like today where you live? It might be sunny, cloudy, hot, or cold. **Weather** is the condition of the atmosphere at a particular time and place. The weather where you live is part of your environment. A **natural disaster** is an event caused by nature that results in injury, damage, or loss. You might live in an area where there has been a flood, landslide, or tornado. This lesson presents guidelines to help you stay safe in severe weather and natural disasters.

The Lesson Objectives

- Discuss ways to stay safe if you are in an electrical storm.
- Discuss ways to stay safe if you are in a tornado.
- Discuss ways to stay safe if you are in a hurricane.
- Discuss ways to stay safe if you are in a flood or a flash flood.
- Discuss ways to stay safe if you are in a landslide.
- Discuss ways to stay warm if the temperature is cold.
- Discuss ways to stay cool if the temperature is hot.

Vocabulary

weather

natural disaster

electrical storm

lightning

severe thunderstorm

severe thunderstorm watch

severe thunderstorm warning

tornado

tornado watch

tornado warning

hurricane

hurricane watch

hurricane warning

flood

flash flood

landslide

frostbite

hypothermia

winter storm

winter storm watch

winter storm warning

wind chill

heat exhaustion

heatstroke

How Can I Stay Safe in an Electrical Storm?

Thunder crashes. Lightning flashes. Rain pours down. An **electrical storm** is a storm that features lightning and thunder. **Lightning** is flashes of light caused by electricity in the air. An electrical storm can be beautiful, but it also can be dangerous.

Weather Warnings

The National Weather Service (NWS) monitors the weather and issues warnings in areas where conditions might produce electrical storms. A **severe thunderstorm** is an electrical storm with damaging winds of at least 58 miles per hour or hail at least three-fourths of an inch in diameter. A **severe thunderstorm watch** is a warning issued when weather conditions are such that a severe thunderstorm is likely to develop. A **severe thunderstorm warning** is a warning issued when a severe thunderstorm has been sighted or indicated by weather radar.

Make an Emergency Supply Kit

Include the following supplies in an emergency supply kit for your home. These supplies will be useful during any emergency discussed in this lesson.

- **First aid kit**
- **Flashlight**
- **Small battery-operated radio**
- **Extra batteries**
- **Nonperishable food and bottled water**
- **Necessary prescription medicines**
- **Manual can opener**
- **Money**
- **Sturdy shoes**
- **Blankets**

Staying Safe

Take the following precautions if a warning has been issued or if an electrical storm appears likely.

- **Stay indoors.** Go indoors if you are outdoors. If you cannot get indoors, go to an open space away from trees, power lines, and other tall structures. Crouch close to the ground.

- **Stay away from metal objects and appliances.** Avoid using the telephone, if possible. If lightning strikes power lines or telephone lines, the electricity can travel through the wires.

- **Do not swim, bathe, or stand in water.** Electricity travels through water.

- **Park away from trees and tall structures if you are in a car.** Stay in the car until the storm passes.

- **Listen to a battery-operated radio to keep up with the latest weather information.**

How Can I Stay Safe in a Tornado?

Powerful electrical storms sometimes cause tornadoes. A **tornado** is a violent, spinning windstorm produced by a severe thunderstorm. Most tornadoes have a visible, funnel-shaped cloud. Tornadoes can cause serious damage to property. They can cause injury and death. The NWS issues warnings when tornadoes are likely. A **tornado watch** is a warning issued when weather conditions are such that tornadoes are likely to develop. A **tornado warning** is a warning issued when a tornado has been sighted or indicated by weather radar. A tornado warning will be announced on the radio and on TV. Tornado sirens will be activated if a tornado warning is issued.

Pay attention to the weather if you are in a place where you cannot hear warning signals. Watch for large hail, a funnel-shaped cloud, or an approaching cloud of debris during a severe thunderstorm. These are signs of a possible tornado. A tornado also is possible if the storm suddenly dies down and the air becomes very still. A loud roaring noise that sounds like a freight train also can indicate a tornado. Suppose you hear a warning or see signs of a possible tornado. Use the following DOs and DON'Ts to stay safe.

DOs

- DO go to the basement or to a room on the ground floor of your home or a building. Stay in the center of the room, away from windows. Get under a piece of furniture, or cover your head and neck with your arms.
- DO get indoors immediately if you are outdoors. If you cannot get indoors, lie in a ditch or other low-lying spot, or crouch near a building.
- DO get out of a car and into a sturdy building. If you cannot get indoors, get out of the car and lie in a ditch or other low-lying spot, or crouch near a building.

DON'Ts

- DON'T stay in a mobile home. Go to a permanent building for shelter.
- DON'T try to outdrive a tornado. A tornado can toss a vehicle through the air.

How Can I Stay Safe in a Hurricane?

You might have heard about a hurricane that caused damage in a coastal area. A **hurricane** is a tropical storm with heavy rains and winds in excess of 74 miles per hour, or dangerously high water and rough seas. Most hurricanes in the United States occur in the southern Atlantic states. The hurricane season in that area is August, September, and October. But hurricanes can occur at other times. A **hurricane watch** is a warning that is issued when there is a threat of hurricane conditions within 24 to 36 hours. A **hurricane warning** is a warning that is issued when hurricane conditions are expected in 24 hours or less.

You might live in an area where hurricanes are possible. Make sure you have an emergency supply kit in your home. Be certain all members of your family know how to turn off electricity, gas, and water. Install permanent shutters to protect your windows in case of a hurricane. Make sure dead branches are trimmed from the trees near your house. Plan an evacuation route in case a hurricane forces your family to leave home.

Before a Hurricane

Suppose there is a hurricane watch in your area. Listen to a battery-operated radio to learn the latest weather conditions. Make sure you have plenty of emergency supplies. Remind your parents or guardian to make sure there is gas in your car. Bring any outdoor furniture, toys, tools, or other items indoors. Close shutters or board up your windows. Set your freezer and refrigerator to their coldest settings. Fill clean bathtubs, jugs, and bottles with water for drinking.

Staying Safe in a Hurricane

Stay indoors, away from windows and glass doors. Keep your emergency supply kit handy. Listen to a battery-operated radio to keep up with weather reports. Go to a permanent building if you live in a mobile home. Evacuate the area if safety officials suggest you do so. Before you leave, unplug all appliances and turn off the electricity and the main water valve. Tell someone away from the hurricane area where you are going. Bring your emergency supply kit, blankets, sleeping bags, and warm clothing when you leave.

How Can I Stay Safe in a Flood or a Flash Flood?

You might have heard about the "Great Flood of 1993" along the Mississippi River, or about the Red River flooding in 1997 in North Dakota and Minnesota. There could be a flood in your area after a period of heavy rain, or when a lot of snow melts. A **flood** is the overflowing of a body of water onto normally dry land. Flash floods might occur during and after a big electrical storm, tornado, or hurricane. A **flash flood** is a flood that occurs suddenly.

Before a Flood

Suppose you live in an area that has frequent floods. Make sure you know where to go in case of a flood. Learn any community flood evacuation plans that exist. Encourage your family to have supplies on hand for building barriers in case flood waters begin rising. Make sure there is plenty of gas in your car.

Staying Safe in a Flash Flood

Follow the guidelines for Staying Safe in a Flood. Be aware that a flash flood can happen during any big storm. Flash floods always occur suddenly. Do not walk or drive through water during a flash flood. Watch carefully for floodwaters if you travel during a storm.

Staying Safe in a Flood

Listen to a battery-operated radio to keep up with the latest weather information. Keep your emergency supply kit handy. Fill sinks, jugs, and clean bathtubs with water. Move all valuable items to the top floor of your home. Move outdoor items, such as furniture and toys, indoors.

Evacuate if authorities tell you to do so. Leave before floodwaters become too deep. Turn off power and gas lines before leaving. Go to a shelter on high ground. Do not walk or drive through any flood waters. If you are outdoors, go to high ground and stay there. Do not return to your home until authorities tell you it is safe to do so.

How Can I Stay Safe in a Landslide?

A **landslide** is a rapid movement of a mass of earth or rock down a slope. A landslide usually strikes with no warning. The results can be devastating.

Before a Landslide

You can help lessen the effects of a possible landslide by planting ground-cover on slopes. Ground-cover plants help keep soil from washing away. Build retaining walls to keep slopes from washing away. Keep your emergency supply kit handy. Watch for landslide warning signs. These include doors or windows that jam for the first time. New cracks might appear in the plaster, the bricks, or the foundation of your house. They might appear in the sidewalk or driveway. Outside stairs, walls, or walkways might pull away from the house. Underground utility lines might break. Bulging ground might appear at the base of a slope. Trees, poles, walls, and fences might tilt or move. Water might break through the ground in new places. A faint rumbling sound might grow louder as a landslide approaches, and the ground might begin to shift.

Staying Safe in a Landslide

If you are indoors, stay there. Get under a piece of sturdy furniture, such as a desk or table. If you are outdoors, get out of the path of the landslide. Run away from the path to the nearest high ground. Get to the nearest shelter, away from rocks and other debris. Curl into a tight ball and protect your head if you cannot get away from the landslide.

How Can I Stay Warm If the Temperature Is Cold?

Cold temperatures can be fun for skiing, ice skating, sledding, hockey, and other sports. Cold temperatures also can be dangerous. You need to know how to stay warm when the temperature is cold.

The two major dangers of cold temperatures are frostbite and hypothermia. **Frostbite** is the freezing of body parts, often the tissues of the extremities. **Hypothermia** (HEYE·puh·THER·mee·uh) is a reduction of the body temperature so that it is lower than normal. You can prevent frostbite and hypothermia. Stay inside when the temperature is extremely cold. Dress properly for the cold if you do go outside. Wear several layers of clothing so that if you get too hot, you can take off a layer. Your boots and gloves should be loose enough that blood can circulate properly. Wear a warm hat that covers your ears. You lose much of your body heat through your head. Wear warm mittens and socks. Wear earmuffs if your hat does not cover your ears. Frostbite is particularly likely in your hands, feet, and ears. You will learn first aid procedures for hypothermia and frostbite in Lesson 50.

Danger: Winter Storm Warning

A **winter storm** is a storm in winter that might include freezing rain or sleet, ice, winds, and heavy snowfall. Take extra precautions if a winter storm is predicted in your area. A **winter storm watch** is a warning that severe winter weather conditions might affect the area. A **winter storm warning** is a warning that severe winter weather conditions exist and will affect the area. If a winter storm is likely, make sure you have plenty of food and supplies on hand. Keep your emergency supply kit handy. If you must travel, be very cautious. Make sure the vehicle is in good condition. Make sure there is gas and antifreeze in the car. Be careful if you walk outside. The ground might be slippery.

Beware of the Wind Chill

You might have heard weather forecasters talking about the wind chill. **Wind chill** is the effect of wind that makes the air seem colder than the actual temperature. For example, suppose you hear that the actual temperature is 30°F with a wind-chill factor of 5°F. The air will feel as if the actual temperature were 5°F. Plan your activities and wear clothing accordingly.

How Can I Stay Cool If the Temperature Is Hot?

You probably look forward to warm temperatures. You might enjoy swimming and being outside all day. Your body cools itself by circulating blood close to the skin's surface. This allows the excess heat to escape into the air. Sweating also helps remove heat from the body. But on hot, humid days, your natural body processes might not keep your body cool enough. You need to keep your body cool on those days.

Use the following guidelines to stay cool if the temperature is hot. Drink plenty of water to replace fluids lost through sweating. Wear lightweight clothing. Avoid exercise or strenuous outdoor work during the hottest time of the day, usually between 10 a.m. and 3 p.m. Wait until evening to exercise, if possible. Wear a wide-brimmed hat and sunscreen with an SPF of at least 15 to protect yourself from sunburn. Sunburn slows your body's ability to cool itself. Stay in the shade or in the coolest part of your home or of another building. Use air conditioning or fans to cool the air in your home. Shade the windows to keep the sun from heating the house.

Recognize the signs and symptoms for heat exhaustion and heatstroke. **Heat exhaustion** is extreme tiredness due to the body's inability to regulate its temperature. A person with heat exhaustion has a body temperature that is lower than normal. His or her skin becomes pale or red, moist, and cool. (S)he might have nausea, dizziness, weakness, and a fast pulse.

Heatstroke is an overheating of the body that is life-threatening. A person with heatstroke has a body temperature that is higher than normal. (S)he has a fast pulse, fast breathing, and hot, wet skin. (S)he is dizzy and weak. Tell a responsible adult if you suspect a person has heat exhaustion or heatstroke. The person needs immediate medical attention. You will learn the first aid procedures for heat exhaustion and heatstroke in Lesson 50.

Activity

Weather Channel

Life Skill: I will follow safety guidelines for severe weather and natural disasters.

Materials: paper, pen or pencil, poster board (optional), colored markers (optional)

Directions: Use the following steps to teach younger students ways to stay safe in severe weather and natural disasters.

1. Your teacher will divide the class into groups of three students each.

2. Your teacher will assign each group a weather event or natural disaster from the following list.

tornado   forest fire

hurricane   earthquake

electrical storm   winter storm

flood   landslide

Your group will research the natural disaster you have been assigned. You should learn what causes the disaster, what happens when the disaster occurs, and what people should do to stay safe.

3. **Your group will present a television weather forecast about the natural disaster.** Your television weather forecast should be aimed at younger students. Your television weather forecast should include the cause of the natural disaster, what happens when it occurs, its effects, and how people can stay safe. Be creative. You might want to make a weather map or other illustration to use in your forecast.

4. **Your group will present your television weather forecast to a group of younger students.**

Vocabulary Words

Write a separate sentence using each vocabulary word listed on page 456.

Health Content

1. What are five ways you can stay safe in an electrical storm? **page 457**

2. How can you stay safe in a tornado? In a hurricane? **pages 458–459**

3. How can you stay safe in a flood or a flash flood? In a landslide? **pages 460–461**

4. How can you stay warm if the temperature is cold? **page 462**

5. How can you stay cool if the temperature is hot? **page 463**

Health Literacy

Self-Directed Learning

Your local American Red Cross chapter or other emergency management agency likely has plans for how to handle natural disasters that are common in your area. Request copies of these plans. Write a two-page paper about ways to stay safe during natural disasters in your area.

Effective Communication

Select a severe weather event or natural disaster that is common in your area. Write a public service announcement for the radio that tells people how to stay safe in the event or disaster you selected.

The Responsible Decision-Making Model™

There was a big snowstorm in your area last night. Your friend comes over to go sledding with you. As you are putting on your heavy wool hat, your friend says, "Don't wear that! Only dorks wear hats. Just wear earmuffs. You'll be fine." Answer the following questions on a separate sheet of paper. Write "Does not apply" if a question does not apply to this situation.

1. Is it healthful to go sledding without a hat? Why or why not?

2. Is it safe to go sledding without a hat? Why or why not?

3. Is it legal to go sledding without a hat? Why or why not?

4. Do you show respect for yourself if you go sledding without a hat? Why or why not?

5. Do you follow the guidelines of your parents or guardian if you go sledding without a hat? Why or why not?

6. Do you demonstrate good character if you go sledding without a hat? Why or why not?

What is the responsible decision to make in this situation?

How to Give First Aid

Life Skill ◆ **I will be skilled in first aid procedures.**

Vocabulary*

first aid

emergency

actual consent

implied consent

universal precautions

*A complete listing of vocabulary words appears on page 498.

First aid is the immediate and temporary care given to a person who has been injured or suddenly becomes ill. An **emergency** is a serious situation that occurs without warning and calls for quick action. *The First Aid Skills Checklist* includes first aid procedures for which you need skills. Being skilled in first aid procedures can help you:

- take safe actions to reduce your risk of illness or injury;
- prepare to respond in an emergency.

The Lesson Objectives

- Discuss what items should be kept in a first aid kit.
- Explain how to get consent to give first aid.
- Explain how to make an emergency telephone call.
- Explain how to follow universal precautions.
- Outline steps to take when you check a victim.
- Explain first aid procedures for: choking; rescue breathing; CPR; heart attack; stroke; bleeding; shock; poisoning; burns; fractures and dislocations; sprains and strains; vomiting; fainting; seizures; heat-related illnesses; frostbite; hypothermia.

The First Aid Skills Checklist

Training in First Aid Skills

A person who is skilled in first aid procedures needs training. Training can be obtained from your local chapter of the American Red Cross. People who successfully complete the standard first aid course receive a certificate from the American Red Cross. The following questions can be answered by a person who is skilled in first aid procedures.

What Should Be in a First Aid Kit?

It is important to keep first aid kits where they might be needed. Keep a first aid kit at home and in the family car. Carry a first aid kit when you participate in outdoor activities, such as camping and hiking. Ask where first aid kits are kept when you are away from home. You can purchase a first aid kit from a drugstore or the local chapter of the American Red Cross. You also can purchase items and put together a first aid kit yourself. Keep items needed to follow universal precautions in your first aid kit. Universal precautions are discussed later. Add special medicines you or family members need. Check the first aid kit often. Some of the items have expiration dates and will need to be replaced. Be certain flashlight batteries work.

activated charcoal

syrup of ipecac

plastic bags

Sting Relief Pads

triangular bandage

disposable gloves

gauze pads and roller

antiseptic ointment

adhesive tape

hand cleaner

adhesive bandages

small flashlight and extra batteries

cold pack

blanket

scissors and tweezers

How Do I Get Consent to Give First Aid?

You must have consent to give first aid. Consent means permission. There are two types of consent.

Actual Consent

Actual consent is oral or written permission from a mentally competent adult to give first aid. You must get actual consent before giving first aid.

- **If the victim is an adult who is conscious:** get consent from the adult. Tell the adult who you are, what you plan to do, and the first aid skills for which you have been trained. Do not give first aid if the adult says NO.

- **If the victim is a child:** get consent from the child's parent, guardian, or other adult with legal permission to care for the child. Do not give first aid if the parent, guardian, or other adult says NO.

- **If the victim is an adult who is not mentally competent:** get consent from the adult's parent, guardian, or other adult with legal permission to care for the adult. Do not give first aid if the parent, guardian, or other adult says NO.

Implied Consent

Implied consent is unspoken understanding that first aid may be given if no one who can give actual consent is conscious or present. You have implied consent to give first aid to:

- **a mentally competent adult who is unconscious;**

- **an adult victim who is not mentally competent, when no adult who can grant actual consent is present;**

- **an infant or child when no adult who can grant actual consent is present.**

How Do I Make an Emergency Telephone Call?

1. Remain calm and speak clearly.

2. Describe the exact location of the emergency.

3. Tell your name, what has happened, the number of people involved, the condition of the injured people, and the help that has been given.

4. Give the telephone number of the telephone you are using.

5. Listen carefully if you are told how to care for a victim. Write down directions if necessary.

6. Do not hang up the telephone until you are told to do so.

7. Return to the victim or victims. Provide care if appropriate. Stay with the victim or victims until help arrives.

How Do I Follow Universal Precautions?

Universal precautions are steps taken to keep from having contact with pathogens in body fluids. A victim's blood or other body fluids might contain pathogens. A victim might be infected with HIV or HBV. HBV is the pathogen that causes hepatitis B. HIV and HBV are in the semen, vaginal secretions, blood, and other body fluids of persons who are infected. You can help a victim and reduce your risk of becoming infected. You can follow universal precautions.

1. Wear disposable latex or polyurethane gloves.

2. Do not wear disposable gloves more than once.

3. Wash your hands well with soap and water after you remove the gloves.

4. Wear a face mask or shield if you give first aid for breathing.

5. Do not use a face mask or shield more than once without sterilizing it.

6. Cover cuts, scrapes, and rashes on your body with plastic wrap or a sterile dressing.

7. Do not eat or drink anything while giving first aid.

8. Do not touch your mouth, eyes, or nose while caring for a victim.

FOLLOW UNIVERSAL PRECAUTIONS
- **Wear Disposable Latex Gloves**
- **Always Use a Face Mask**

How Do I Check a Victim?

A **victim check** is a check of the injured or ill person to determine if:

- the victim has an open airway;
- the victim is breathing;
- the victim's heart is beating;
- the victim is severely bleeding;
- and the victim has other injuries.

FOLLOW UNIVERSAL PRECAUTIONS
- Wear Disposable Latex Gloves
- Always Use a Face Mask

1. **Call the local emergency number and obtain medical care immediately.**

Ask the victim what happened. A victim who is able to speak to you is breathing and has a pulse.

2. Tap the victim and shout loudly to see if the victim responds.

3. Check for breathing if the victim does not respond.

a) Place your finger under the nose or near the mouth to feel for air being exhaled.

b) Listen for signs of breathing.

4. **If there are no signs of breathing...**

Support the head and neck and position the victim on the back.

5.

Tilt the head back and lift the chin of the victim. The victim's mouth should be open.

6.

Make a five-second recheck for signs of breathing. (Repeat step 3.)

7.

If there are still no signs of breathing...

Wear a face mask or shield for protection. Follow instructions provided with the mask. Blow two slow breaths of air into the victim's mouth.

8.

Check to see if the victim has a pulse for five to ten seconds. Use your index and third finger and check the carotid artery in the victim's neck. The carotid artery is the large artery where the pulse can be felt.

9.

10.

Check the victim's body for severe bleeding. Be certain to follow universal precautions to avoid contact with the victim's blood.

Check for other injuries.

How Do I Give First Aid for Choking?

Choking is an emergency in which the airway is blocked. A piece of food or other small object can block the airway. A conscious victim will cough to try to dislodge it. If a victim can talk, the victim is getting enough air. Encourage the victim to continue trying to cough up the object. Call for help if the victim cannot cough up the object.

A victim might not get enough air to talk or cough. Or, the cough might be very weak. This tells you that the airway is completely blocked. The victim might indicate that (s)he is not breathing. The **universal distress signal** is a warning that a person has difficulty breathing and is shown by clutching at the throat with one or both hands.

The airway must be opened quickly when someone is choking. **Abdominal thrusts** are a series of thrusts to the abdomen that force air from the lungs to dislodge an object. The method of giving abdominal thrusts is different for adults, children, and infants.

If You Are Choking

Call the local emergency number and obtain medical care immediately.

1. Get the attention of someone around you. Use the universal distress signal.

2. Give yourself abdominal thrusts if no one can help you. Make a fist with one hand and grab the fist with your other hand. Give yourself five quick abdominal thrusts. Apply pressure inward and push up toward your diaphragm in one smooth movement. Repeat until the object is dislodged.

Call the local emergency number and obtain medical care immediately.

FOLLOW UNIVERSAL PRECAUTIONS
• **Wear Disposable Latex Gloves**
• **Always Use a Face Mask**

If an Adult or Older Child Is Conscious and Choking

1.

FOLLOW UNIVERSAL PRECAUTIONS
- **Wear Disposable Latex Gloves**
- **Always Use a Face Mask**

Call the local emergency number and obtain medical care immediately.

Ask the victim if (s)he is choking. Do not do anything if the victim can speak or cough easily. Encourage the victim to continue coughing to dislodge the object.

2.

If the victim cannot speak, breathe, or cough...

Stand behind the victim and wrap your hand around the victim's waist. Make a fist with one hand. Place the thumb side of the fist into the victim's abdomen above the navel and below the rib cage. Grab your fist with the other hand.

3.

Give five quick abdominal thrusts. Apply pressure inward and push up toward the victim's diaphragm in one smooth movement. Repeat the cycle of five abdominal thrusts until the object is dislodged.

The victim might need rescue breathing after the object is dislodged. Stay with the victim and watch for breathing difficulties.

First aid for choking in children and infants is done in a different way.

How Do I Give Rescue Breathing?

If a Victim Is an Adult or Older Child

A victim will become unconscious without oxygen after a period of time. The heart will stop beating and blood will stop circulating to body organs. The different body systems will fail and the victim will die. **Rescue breathing** is a way of breathing air into an unconscious victim who is not breathing, but has a pulse. Rescue breathing gives a victim the oxygen needed to stay alive.

FOLLOW UNIVERSAL PRECAUTIONS
- **Wear Disposable Latex Gloves**
- **Always Use a Face Mask**

1.

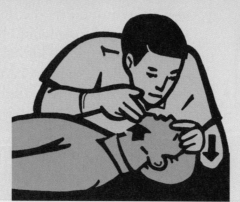

Call the local emergency number and obtain medical care immediately.

Roll the victim on his or her back. Tilt the victim's head back in the following way. Place one hand under the victim's chin and lift up while pressing down on the victim's forehead with your other hand. Pinch the victim's nostrils shut.

2.

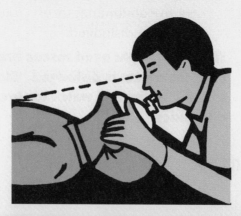

Wear a face mask or shield for protection. Follow instructions provided with the mask. Apply the mask. Open the airway. Give two slow breaths. Watch to see if the victim's chest slowly rises.

3. Check to see if the victim has a pulse. Use your index and third finger and find the carotid artery in the neck.

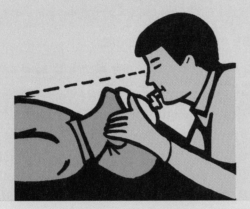

4. **If the pulse is present, but the victim is still not breathing...**

Give one slow breath about every five seconds. Remove your mouth after each breath so the victim can exhale.

5. Recheck pulse and breathing every minute. Continue rescue breathing as long as the victim is not breathing, but has a pulse.

If the victim does not have a pulse, the heart is not beating. CPR is needed. CPR is illustrated in the next section.

CPR should be used only if you are trained to use it.

Call the local emergency number and obtain medical care immediately.

How Do I Give CPR?

If a Victim Is an Adult or Older Child

When Am I Qualified to Give CPR?

Cardiopulmonary resuscitation (CPR) is a first aid technique that is used to restore heartbeat and breathing. CPR should be used only if you are trained to use it. Contact your local chapter of the American Red Cross to find out when CPR training classes are held.

FOLLOW UNIVERSAL PRECAUTIONS
- **Wear Disposable Latex Gloves**
- **Always Use a Face Mask**

1.

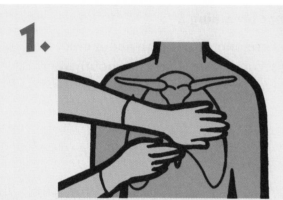

Make a victim assessment.

Call the local emergency number and obtain medical care immediately.

Roll the victim on his or her back. Find the lower part of the breastbone and measure up the width of two fingers from that point. Place the heel of your other hand on the sternum next to the fingers. Place the other hand on top of the first hand.

2.

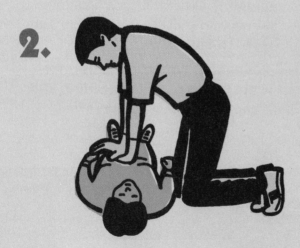

Position your shoulders over your hands to exert pressure straight down. Compress the chest 15 times (at a rate of 80 compressions per minute). Exert enough pressure to depress the breastbone one and one-half to two inches. Each compression forces blood from the heart to other parts of the body.

3.

Wear a face mask or shield for protection. Follow instructions provided with the mask. Apply the mask. Open the airway. Give two slow breaths. Watch to see if the victim's chest slowly rises. Remove the mouth to allow the victim to exhale.

4.

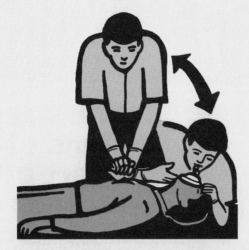

Do three more sets of 15 compressions and two slow breaths.

5.

Make a five-second check to see if the victim has a pulse and is breathing.

6.

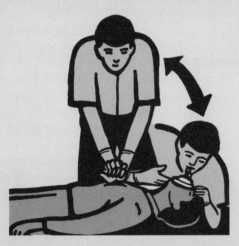

If the victim does not have a pulse...

Continue sets of 15 compressions and two slow breaths.

CPR for children and CPR for infants is done in a different way.

CPR should be used only if you are trained to use it.

Call the local emergency number and obtain medical care immediately.

How Do I Give First Aid for Heart Attack?

A **heart attack** is the death of heart muscle caused by a lack of blood flow to the heart. The blocked blood vessel prevents blood from getting to the heart tissue. Without blood, the heart tissue does not receive oxygen. This usually causes pain in the center of the chest, beneath the breastbone. **Cardiac arrest** is the death of the heart muscle. Prompt action must be taken for warning signs of heart attack to prevent cardiac arrest.

First aid for heart attack involves these steps:

Call the local emergency number and obtain medical care immediately.

1. Have the victim stop activity and rest in a comfortable position.

2. Ask the victim about his or her condition. Does the victim have a history of heart disease? Is the victim taking any medication?

3. Comfort the victim until help arrives.

4. Observe the victim for changes in condition.

If cardiac arrest occurs, the victim is not breathing and has no pulse...

A person who is trained in CPR should:

5. Perform CPR and rescue breathing.

The warnings signs of heart attack include:

- Persistent pain or pressure in the center of the chest that is not relieved by resting or changing position
- Pain that spreads from the center of the chest to the shoulder, arm, neck, jaw, or back
- Dizziness
- Sweating
- Fainting
- Difficulty breathing
- Shortness of breath
- Pale or bluish skin color
- Moist face
- Irregular pulse

FOLLOW UNIVERSAL PRECAUTIONS
- **Wear Disposable Latex Gloves**
- **Always Use a Face Mask**

CPR should be used only if you are trained to use it.

Call the local emergency number and obtain medical care immediately.

How Do I Give First Aid for Stroke?

A **stroke** is a condition caused by a blocked or broken blood vessel in the brain. A stroke can occur when a clot moves through the bloodstream and lodges in the brain. A clot can form inside one of the arteries in the brain, or a blood vessel in the brain can burst. A head injury or tumor can cause an artery to burst. Blood cannot get to all parts of the brain and some tissue dies.

The damage that occurs depends on the part of the brain that is affected. A victim might suffer a loss of vision or slurred speech. Body parts can become paralyzed. Sometimes blood cannot flow to parts of the brain that control heart rate or breathing and death results. Prompt action must be taken for signs of stroke to prevent disability and death.

First aid for stroke involves these steps:

Call the local emergency number and obtain medical care immediately.

1. Keep the victim lying down with the head and shoulders raised to relieve the force of blood on the brain.

2. Check the airway. Keep the victim's air passage open.

3. Position the victim on his or her side if there is fluid or vomit in the mouth.

4. Do not give the victim anything to drink.

5. Comfort the victim until help arrives.

The warning signs of stroke include:

- Slowed breathing rate
- Unequal size of pupils in the eyes
- Slurred speech
- Paralysis on one side of the body
- Blurred vision
- Severe headache

FOLLOW UNIVERSAL PRECAUTIONS
- **Wear Disposable Latex Gloves**
- **Always Use a Face Mask**

Call the local emergency number and obtain medical care immediately.

How Do I Give First Aid for Bleeding?

A **wound** is an injury to the body's soft tissues. The first priority in any wound is to stop severe bleeding and prevent germs from entering the wound. A person with a wound can bleed to death in a matter of minutes.

If a Victim Is Bleeding

1.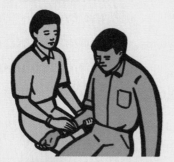

Call the local emergency number and obtain medical care immediately.

Cover the wound with a clean cloth or sterile dressing and apply direct pressure with your hand. Add more cloth if the blood soaks through, but do not remove the first piece of cloth. Do not remove any foreign objects that are lodged deep in the wound.

2.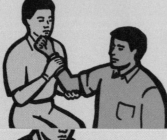

Raise the wounded body part above the level of the heart. This helps reduce blood flow to the area.

3.

Cover the cloth or sterile dressing with a roller bandage.

FOLLOW UNIVERSAL PRECAUTIONS
- **Wear Disposable Latex Gloves**
- **Always Use a Face Mask**

If a Victim Has a Nosebleed

A **nosebleed** is a loss of blood from the mucous membranes that line the nose. Many teens have nosebleeds. Most nosebleeds are caused by a blow to the nose or cracked mucous membranes in the nose. Nosebleeds are usually easy to control.

1. Have the victim sit with his or her head slightly forward and pinch the nostrils firmly together. Sitting slightly forward helps the blood flow toward the outside opening of the nose instead of backward down the throat.

2. The nostrils should be pinched firmly together for about five minutes before releasing. The victim should breathe through the mouth and spit out any blood in the mouth.

3. An ice pack may be applied to the bridge of the nose.

4. Repeat this procedure for another ten minutes if the bleeding does not stop.

5. Get prompt medical help if bleeding continues or if you suspect serious injury.

If a Tooth Is Knocked Out

A **knocked-out tooth** is a tooth that has been knocked out of its socket. There are various recommendations on how to respond to this emergency.

1. Place a sterile dressing in the space left by the missing tooth. Have the victim bite down to hold the dressing in place.

2. Place the tooth in a cup of cold milk, or in water if milk is not available. Do not touch the root of the tooth.

3. The victim should see a dentist immediately. The sooner the tooth is placed back inside the socket, the better the chance it can be saved.

FOLLOW UNIVERSAL PRECAUTIONS
- **Wear Disposable Latex Gloves**
- **Always Use a Face Mask**

How Do I Give First Aid for Shock?

Any serious injury or illness can lead to shock. **Shock** is a dangerous change in blood flow to the body. The body organs fail to function properly when they do not receive oxygen. Shock can lead to collapse, coma, and death if untreated. Signs of shock include:

- **Rapid, shallow breathing**
- **Cold, clammy skin**
- **Rapid, weak pulse**
- **Dizziness**
- **Weakness**
- **Fainting**

First aid for shock involves these steps:

Call the local emergency number and obtain medical care immediately.

1. Have the victim lie down. Elevate the legs about 8 to 12 inches above the level of the heart unless you suspect head, neck, or back injuries or broken bones in the hips or legs. Leave the victim lying flat if you are unsure of the victim's injuries.

2. Improve the victim's circulation.

   A Airway   Keep the victim's airway open.

   B Breathing   Perform rescue breathing if necessary. Remember to use a face mask or shield.

   C Circulation   If you have completed CPR training, perform CPR if the victim has no pulse.

3. Control for external bleeding. Wear disposable gloves.

4. Help the victim maintain normal body temperature. Cover the victim with a blanket if (s)he is cold.

5. Do not give the victim anything to eat or drink.

FOLLOW UNIVERSAL PRECAUTIONS
- **Wear Disposable Latex Gloves**
- **Always Use a Face Mask**

CPR should be used only if you are trained to use it.

Call the local emergency number and obtain medical care immediately.

How Do I Give First Aid for Poisoning?

A **poison** is a substance that causes injury, illness, or death if it enters the body. Poisoning can occur when a person:

- **swallows a poison;**
- **breathes a poison;**
- **has poison on the skin that is absorbed into the body.**

Most cases of poisoning occur when small children swallow medicines or products, such as cleaning solutions or pesticides. Some people are poisoned by certain foods, such as shellfish or mushrooms. Some substances cause poisoning in larger amounts. For example, a person can be poisoned by taking too many pills or by drinking too much alcohol in a short time. Combinations of drugs, such as alcohol and sleeping pills, can cause poisoning.

Poisoning also can occur from breathing the fumes of household products, such as glue, paints, and cleaners. Certain gases cause poisoning. For example, a well-known tennis athlete died from carbon monoxide poisoning. Chlorine that is added to swimming pools is dangerous to breathe. Fumes from certain drugs, such as crack cocaine, also can cause poisoning.

Some poisons get on the skin and are absorbed into the body. Products, such as pesticides and fertilizers, can cause poisoning if they get on the skin. People using these products should wear gloves and clothing to prevent poisoning. They also should wear a mask to keep from breathing in fumes from these products. Poisons from plants, such as poison ivy and poison oak, can get on the skin. They are absorbed into the body and cause a reaction. Bites or stings from insects, spiders, bees, snakes, and marine life can cause poisoning.

The signs of poisoning include difficulty breathing, nausea, vomiting, chest and abdominal pain, sweating, and seizures. Skin rashes and burns on the lips or tongue also can indicate poisoning.

CPR should be used only if you are trained to use it.

Call the local emergency number and obtain medical care immediately.

If a Victim Has Been Poisoned

First aid for poisoning involves these steps:

Call the local emergency number and obtain medical care immediately.

1. Be cautious. Protect your health and safety. Do not risk injury.

2. Move the victim to a safe location if necessary.

3. Treat the victim for life-threatening emergencies.

A Airway Keep the victim's airway open.

B Breathing Perform rescue breathing if necessary. Remember to use a face mask or shield.

C Circulation If you have completed CPR training, perform CPR if the victim has no pulse.

4. Gather information about the cause of poisoning. Determine the type of poison. Ask the victim what the type of poison might be. Be on the lookout for empty bottles and containers or needles. Try to determine how much poison has been taken and when. Recognize fumes and odors that might be the cause. Be alert to the environment. Are there bees, snakes, or poisonous plants in the area?

> CPR should be used only if you are trained to use it.

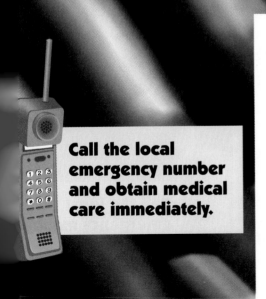

Call the local emergency number and obtain medical care immediately.

A poison center will tell you whether or not to induce vomiting in the victim. Victims who have swallowed acid substances, bleach, or gasoline products should not vomit. These substances can burn the esophagus, mouth, and throat if the victim vomits. A victim with seizures or who is unconscious or semiconscious might be advised not to vomit. You might be advised to dilute the poison by having the victim drink water or milk.

Syrup of ipecac is a liquid used to induce vomiting in victims who have swallowed certain poisons. It can be bought at local drugstores. **Use syrup of ipecac only if told to do so by a poison control center.** The poison center will tell you how much to give. The victim usually vomits within 20 minutes after taking the syrup.

If a Victim Has Touched a Poisonous Plant

Touching poisonous plants, such as poison ivy, poison sumac, or poison oak, can result in skin redness, swelling, and itching. If you touch a poisonous plant do the following.

1. Wash the affected body parts with soap and water immediately.

2. Remove any clothing that might have some of the poison on it.

3. Use over-the-counter drugs to relieve the reactions that result.

4. Call a physician if the reactions are severe.

CPR should be used only if you are trained to use it.

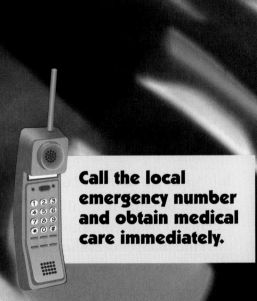

Call the local emergency number and obtain medical care immediately.

If a Victim Has a Snakebite

Poisoning can occur from being bitten by a poisonous snake, such as a coral snake or a pit viper. Examples of pit vipers are rattlesnakes, copperheads, and water moccasins. Symptoms of a bite from a poisonous snake include pain at the site of the wound, rapid pulse, dimmed vision, vomiting, and shortness of breath. The victim might experience shock and become unconscious.

Call the local emergency number and obtain medical care immediately.

1. Treat for shock.

2. Keep the victim still. This will reduce the speed with which the poison can travel through the body.

3. Keep the bitten area below the level of the heart.

4. Get prompt medical care for the victim of a snakebite.

If a Victim Has a Bee Sting

Stings from bees are one of the most common insect-related problems. The bee will leave its stinger in the skin when it stings. Bee stings can create a serious health problem for people who are allergic. These people should carry medication to prevent a serious allergic reaction. They also should wear a Medic Alert tag. Most people do not have an allergic response to bee stings.

Call the local emergency number and obtain medical care immediately.

1. Remove the stinger. Do not try to remove the stinger with a tweezer. The tweezer will force the bee's venom into the body. Flick the stinger away with a nail file, fingernail, credit card, or a similar object. Hornets, wasps, and yellow jackets do not leave stingers in the skin.

2. Place something cold over the area to relieve the pain.

Call the local emergency number and obtain medical care immediately.

FOLLOW UNIVERSAL PRECAUTIONS
- **Wear Disposable Latex Gloves**
- **Always Use a Face Mask**

CPR should be used only if you are trained to use it.

If a Victim Has a Spider Bite

Being bitten by a black widow spider can be deadly. A bite from this spider will produce a dull, numbing pain. Headache, muscular weakness, vomiting, and sweating can occur.

Call the local emergency number and obtain medical care immediately.

1. Wash the bitten area with soap and water.

2. Apply ice to relieve the pain.

3. Get prompt medical help. Antivenin might be given. Antivenin is a medicine that reduces the effects of the poison.

A bite from the brown recluse spider also is dangerous. A bite from this spider produces an open ulcer. Chills, nausea, and vomiting might follow.

1. Wash the affected part with soap and water.

2. Get prompt medical help.

If a Victim Has a Marine Animal Sting

Stings from marine animals, such as the sting ray, sea urchin, spiny fish, jellyfish, sea anemone, or man-of-war, can cause serious allergic reactions. Breathing difficulties, heart problems, and paralysis can result. A victim should be removed from the water as soon as possible.

Call the local emergency number and obtain medical care immediately.

First aid for stings from a sting ray, sea urchin, or spiny fish involve these steps:

1. Remove the sting ray, sea urchin, or spiny fish.

2. Flush the area of the sting with water.

3. Do not move the injured part.

4. Soak the injured area with hot water for 30 minutes to relieve pain.

5. Clean the wounded area and apply a bandage.

6. Seek medical attention. A tetanus shot might be required.

First aid for stings from a jellyfish, sea anemone, or man-of-war involve these steps:

1. Remove the victim from the water as soon as possible.

2. Soak the area with vinegar as soon as possible. Vinegar offsets the effects of the toxin from the sting. Rubbing alcohol or baking soda can be used if vinegar is not available.

3. Do not rub the wound. Rubbing spreads the toxin and increases pain.

Call the local emergency number and obtain medical care immediately.

CPR should be used only if you are trained to use it.

Prompt medical attention is needed for a victim who:

• does not know what stung him or her;

• has had a previous allergic reaction to a sting;

• has been stung on the face or neck;

• has difficulty breathing.

FOLLOW UNIVERSAL PRECAUTIONS
• **Wear Disposable Latex Gloves**
• **Always Use a Face Mask**

If a Victim Has a Tick Bite

A tick is an insect that attaches itself to any warm-blooded animal. It feeds on the blood of the animal. There is great concern about diseases spread by ticks. Two such diseases are Lyme disease and Rocky Mountain spotted fever. **Lyme disease** is a bacterial disease transmitted through a tick. Mice and deer can carry the ticks that cause Lyme disease. The ticks are very small. The bacteria that cause Lyme disease are transmitted through the bite of an infected tick. A rash starts and can grow to be about seven inches long. The center of the rash is light red and the outer ridges are darker red and raised. A victim might have fever, headaches, and weakness. Prompt medical attention is needed. Antibiotics are used for treatment.

Rocky Mountain spotted fever is a potentially life-threatening disease carried by a tick. Cases of this disease are not confined to the Rocky Mountain region. Symptoms include high fever, weakness, rash, leg pains, and coma. Prompt medical attention is needed. Antibiotics are used for treatment.

How to Remove a Tick

A tick should always be removed from the body.

1. Grasp the tick with tweezers as close to the skin as possible.
2. Use a glove or plastic wrap to protect your fingers if you do not have tweezers.
3. Pull the tick slowly away from the skin.
4. Wash the area with soap and water. Also, wash your hands with soap and water.
5. Apply an antibiotic ointment or antiseptic to the area to prevent infection.
6. Observe the area for signs of infection.
7. Obtain medical help if the tick cannot be removed or if part of it remains under the skin. Medical help also is needed if signs of Lyme disease or Rocky Mountain spotted fever develop.

How Do I Give First Aid for Burns?

A **burn** is an injury caused by heat, electricity, chemicals, or radiation. Burns are usually described as first-degree burns, second-degree burns, or third-degree burns. These descriptions help explain the seriousness of the burn.

If a Victim Has a First-Degree Burn

A **first-degree burn** is a burn which affects the top layer of skin. Most sunburns are first-degree burns. The skin becomes red and dry and the area might swell. The area is painful to touch. First-degree burns usually heal in six days without permanent scarring.

First aid for a first-degree burn involves these steps:

1. Stop the burning. Get the victim out of the sun. Put out flames that are burning clothes or skin.

2. Cool the burned area with water as soon as possible. Soak the area with tap water, a garden hose, or have the victim get into the bath or shower. Use sheets or towels soaked in cold water to cool a burn on the face or other areas that cannot be soaked. Keep adding cool water to the area.

3. Wear disposable gloves. Loosely bandage the area with a dry, sterile dressing.

4. Place cotton or gauze between burned fingers and toes.

FOLLOW UNIVERSAL PRECAUTIONS
• Wear Disposable Latex Gloves
• Always Use a Face Mask

Call the local emergency number and obtain medical care immediately.

If a Victim Has a Second-Degree Burn

A **second-degree burn** is a burn that involves the top layers of the skin. The skin becomes red. Blisters form and can open and discharge a clear fluid. The skin appears wet and mottled. Second-degree burns usually heal in two to four weeks. Slight scarring can occur.

First aid for a second-degree burn involves these steps:

Call the local emergency number and obtain medical care immediately.

1. Stop the burning. Remove the victim from the source of the burn.

2. Cool the burned area with cool water or cold cloths. Keep the cover loose. This helps prevent infection and reduces pain. Do not break blisters or remove tissue.

3. Raise the burned area above heart level.

4. Cover the victim with clean, dry sheets if burns cover large parts of the body. Treat for shock.

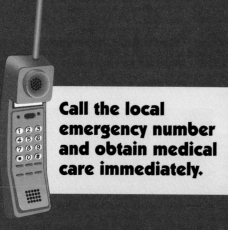

Call the local emergency number and obtain medical care immediately.

FOLLOW UNIVERSAL PRECAUTIONS
- **Wear Disposable Latex Gloves**
- **Always Use a Face Mask**

If a Victim Has a Third-Degree Burn

A **third-degree burn** is a burn that involves all layers of the skin and some underlying tissues. The skin becomes darker and appears charred. The underlying tissues can appear white. A third-degree burn is painless if nerve endings are destroyed. It also can be very painful. Third-degree burns can take months or years to treat. Permanent scarring often occurs requiring skin grafting and plastic surgery.

First aid for a third-degree burn involves these steps:

Call the local emergency number and obtain medical care immediately.

1. Treat the victim for shock.

2. Check immediately if the victim is breathing. Give rescue breathing if necessary. Do not open blisters or remove pieces of tissue. Do not apply cold cloths or cool water.

3. Cover the burned area with a dry, sterile dressing, clean cloth, or sheet.

How Do I Give First Aid for Fractures and Dislocations?

If a Victim Has a Fracture

A **fracture** is a break or crack in a bone. An **open fracture** is a fracture in which there is a break in the skin. A **closed fracture** is a fracture in which there is no break in the skin. A fracture can be very serious if a break in a bone damages an artery or interferes with breathing. The signs of a fracture include pain, swelling, loss of movement, and deformity. Signs of a fracture of the skull include bleeding from the head or ears, drowsiness, and headache.

First aid for fractures involves these steps:

Call the local emergency number and obtain medical care immediately.

1. Treat for bleeding and shock.

2. Keep the injured part from moving. Use a splint when appropriate. Keep a victim with a head injury still.

3. Apply ice to the break or crack to prevent swelling.

4. Follow universal precautions. Control bleeding.

5. Get prompt medical help.

If a Victim Has a Dislocation

A **dislocation** is the movement of a bone from its joint. Dislocations often are accompanied by stretched ligaments. The signs of a dislocation are pain, swelling upon movement, loss of movement, and deformity.

First aid for a dislocation involves these steps:

Call the local emergency number and obtain medical care immediately.

1. Splint above and below the dislocated joint.

2. Apply cold compresses.

How Do I Give First Aid for Sprains and Strains?

If a Victim Has a Sprain

A **sprain** is an injury to the ligaments, tendons, and soft tissue around a joint caused by undue stretching. The signs of a sprain include pain that increases with movement or weight bearing, tenderness, and swelling.

First aid for sprains involves these steps:

1. Follow the RICE Treatment.

2. Get prompt medical help if a fracture is suspected.

If a Victim Has a Strain

A **strain** is an overstretching of muscles and/or tendons. One of the most common strains involves the muscles of the back. Signs of strain include pain, swelling, stiffness, and firmness to the area.

First aid for strains involves these steps:

1. Follow the RICE Treatment.

2. Get prompt medical help for a severe strain.

How to Use the RICE Treatment

Rest: Rest the injured part for 24 to 72 hours. Longer rest is required for severe injuries. Do not exercise the injured area until there is complete healing.

Ice: Apply cold water, a cold compress, or ice pack for 20 minutes as soon as possible after the injury occurs. Apply several times a day for one to three days. Wrap ice in a cloth before placing on the skin. Applying cold water reduces pain, swelling, inflammation, and tissue damage.

Compression: Wrap the injury with an elastic bandage to limit swelling. The compression should not be too tight so as to restrict blood flow. Remove the wrap periodically and check.

Elevation: Raise the injured body part above the level of the heart to reduce swelling and to drain blood and fluid from the area.

Call the local emergency number and obtain medical care immediately.

How Do I Give First Aid for Vomiting? Fainting? Seizures?

Sudden illness is an illness that occurs without warning signals. It is difficult to determine if the situation is an emergency. Signs of sudden illness can include dizziness and confusion, weakness, changes in skin color, nausea, vomiting, and diarrhea. Seizures, paralysis, slurred speech, difficulty seeing, and severe pain can also indicate sudden illness.

First aid for sudden illness involves these steps:

Call the local emergency number and obtain medical care immediately.

1. Give first aid for life-threatening conditions.
2. Keep the victim calm.
3. Cover the victim with a blanket if (s)he is chilled.
4. Do not try to give an unconscious victim anything to eat or drink.
5. Get prompt medical attention.

Call the local emergency number and obtain medical care immediately.

FOLLOW UNIVERSAL PRECAUTIONS
- **Wear Disposable Latex Gloves**
- **Always Use a Face Mask**

If a Victim Is Vomiting

Turn the victim on his or her side.

If a Victim Has Fainted

Put the victim on his or her back. Raise the victim's legs 8 to 12 inches above the level of the heart. (Do not raise the legs if you suspect a head or back injury.) Loosen tight clothing. Do not splash water on the victim, slap the victim's face, or use smelling salts.

If a Victim Has Seizures

A **seizure** is a brief episode in which a person loses control over mind and body. A seizure can cause twitching of a body part or shaking of the entire body. If a victim has a seizure, move things around the victim out of the way. Place something soft under the victim's head. Turn the person on his or her side. Loosen the clothing around the victim's neck. Do not hold down the victim. Do not place anything in the victim's mouth or between the teeth. Send someone to find an adult.

How Do I Give First Aid for Heat-Related Illnesses?

If a Victim Has Heat Cramps

Heat cramps are painful muscle spasms in the legs and arms due to excessive fluid loss through sweating.

First aid for heat cramps involves these steps:

1. Have the victim rest in a cool, shaded area.
2. Give the victim cool water to drink.
3. Stretch the muscle gently.

If a Victim Has Heat Exhaustion

Heat exhaustion is extreme tiredness due to the body's inability to regulate its temperature. Heat exhaustion can be life-threatening. Signs of heat exhaustion include cool, moist, pale, or red skin; nausea; headache; dizziness; fast pulse; weakness; and a body temperature below normal.

First aid for heat exhaustion involves these steps:

Call the local emergency number and obtain medical care immediately.

1. Have the victim rest in a cool place.
2. Have the victim lie down and raise his or her feet.
3. Give the victim cool water to drink.
4. Observe the victim for signs of heatstroke.

If a Victim Has Heatstroke (Sunstroke)

Heatstroke is an overheating of the body that is life-threatening. Sweating stops and the body cannot regulate its temperature. Signs of heatstroke include hot, dry skin; headache; dizziness; weakness; rapid pulse; and a high body temperature.

First aid for heatstroke involves these steps:

Call the local emergency number and obtain medical care immediately.

1. Have the victim rest in a cool place.
2. Remove heavy clothing.
3. Wrap the victim in cool, wet towels or sheets.
4. Place ice packs near the neck, armpits, and groin.
5. Continue cooling the victim.
6. Treat life-threatening emergencies.

FOLLOW UNIVERSAL PRECAUTIONS
- **Wear Disposable Latex Gloves**
- **Always Use a Face Mask**

Call the local emergency number and obtain medical care immediately.

How Do I Give First Aid for Frostbite? Hypothermia?

If a Victim Has Frostbite

Frostbite is the freezing of body parts, often the tissues of the extremities. Frostbite can involve the fingers, toes, ears, and nose. People exposed to subfreezing temperatures or snow are at risk for developing frostbite. Signs of frostbite include numbness in the affected area, waxy appearance of skin, and skin discolored and cold to touch.

First aid for frostbite involves these steps:

Call the local emergency number and obtain medical care immediately.

1. Do not attempt rewarming if a medical facility is nearby. Take the following steps if medical help is not available.

2. Remove any clothing or jewelry that interferes with circulation.

3. Handle the affected area gently.

4. Soak the affected body part in warm water for 25 to 40 minutes.

5. Apply warm, moist cloths to warm the ears, nose, or face.

6. Do not rub the affected area.

7. Slightly raise the affected part.

8. Place dry, sterile gauze between the toes and fingers to absorb moisture and avoid having them stick together.

9. Do not allow a victim to walk on frostbitten toes or feet, even after rewarming.

If a Victim Has Hypothermia

Hypothermia (HEYE·puh·THER·mee·uh) is a reduction of the body temperature so that it is lower than normal. Hypothermia results from overexposure to cool temperatures, cold water, moisture, and wind. The victim shivers and feels cold. The pulse rate slows down and becomes irregular. Eventually, a victim can become unconscious and die if hypothermia is not treated.

First aid for hypothermia involves these steps:

Call the local emergency number and obtain medical care immediately.

1. Get the victim into a warm environment.

2. Handle the victim gently.

3. Remove any wet clothing and replace it with dry clothing.

4. Place something warm above and below the victim, such as blankets.

5. Cover the victim's head.

For mild hypothermia (body temperature above 90°F [32.2°C]):

1. Use an electric blanket or warm tub of water to warm the victim. Do not cover or submerge the victim's arms or legs.

2. Place hot packs on the victim's head, neck, chest, and groin.

For profound hypothermia (body temperature below 90°F [32.2°C]) transport the person to a medical facility within 12 hours.

Activity

First Aid Headline News

Life Skill: I will be skilled in first aid procedures.

Materials: paper, pen or pencil

Directions: This activity will help you review your knowledge about first aid and safe actions you can take to prevent illness or injury.

1. You will get into groups of four or five as instructed by your teacher.

2. Your teacher will give an index card to each group. The card will list five to seven vocabulary words from the list below.

3. Your group will write a script that is a lead story for a television news program. Two people in the group will act as reporters. The others will pretend to have experienced and received first aid for the illnesses or injuries listed on the card. Your group will write a script in which the reporters interview the victims. Include the following in your script about each illness or injury: events leading to the illness or injury, definition of the illness or injury, symptoms, the first aid that was given to the victim, and what (if anything) could have been done to prevent the illness or injury. Each person should have a complete script.

4. Perform your news story for the class.

Vocabulary Words

first aid	rescue breathing	poison	sprain
emergency	cardiopulmonary	Lyme disease	strain
actual consent	resuscitation (CPR)	burn	sudden illness
implied consent	heart attack	first-degree burn	seizure
universal precautions	cardiac arrest	second-degree burn	heat cramps
victim check	stroke	third-degree burn	heat exhaustion
choking	wound	fracture	heatstroke
universal distress	nosebleed	open fracture	frostbite
signal	knocked-out tooth	closed fracture	hypothermia
abdominal thrusts	shock	dislocation	

Vocabulary Words

Write a separate sentence using each vocabulary word listed on page 466.

Health Content

1. What are two reasons you need to be skilled in first aid procedures? **page 466**

2. What should be in a first aid kit? **page 468**

3. How do you get consent to give first aid? **page 469**

4. How do you make an emergency telephone call? **page 470**

5. How do you follow universal precautions? **page 471**

6. How do you check a victim? **pages 472–473**

7. What are first aid procedures for: choking; rescue breathing; CPR; heart attack; stroke; bleeding; shock; poisoning; burns; fractures and dislocations; sprains and strains; vomiting; fainting; seizures; heat-related illnesses; frostbite; and hypothermia? **pages 474–497**

Health Literacy

Effective Communication

Choose an illness or injury in this lesson. Interview an emergency medical technician (EMT). Ask the following questions about the illness or injury: What causes the illness or injury? How often is first aid given for it? What are the steps to give first aid for it? Write a summary and share it with your class.

The Responsible Decision-Making Model™

You and a friend are shopping when a customer grabs her chest and faints. The manager dials 911 and asks if anyone knows how to give CPR. Your friend has studied CPR in this lesson but has not had training. Your friend tells the manager (s)he knows how to give CPR. Answer the following questions on a separate sheet of paper. Write "Does not apply" if a question does not apply to this situation.

1. Is it healthful for your friend to give CPR? Why or why not?

2. Is it safe for your friend to give CPR? Why or why not?

3. Is it legal for your friend to give CPR? Why or why not?

4. Will your friend show respect for himself or herself and others if (s)he gives CPR? Why or why not?

5. Will your friend's parents or guardian approve if your friend gives CPR? Why or why not?

6. Will your friend demonstrate good character if (s)he gives CPR? Why or why not?

What is the responsible decision for your friend to make in this situation?

What would you say to your friend?

Unit 10 Review

Health Content

Prepare for the Unit Test. Review your answers for each Lesson Review in this unit. Then write answers to each of the following questions:

1. What is a person's conscience? **Lesson 46 page 431**

2. Why don't some people experience moral guilt? **Lesson 46 page 431**

3. What is the purpose of an anti-gang gang? **Lesson 47 page 444**

4. What can happen to your reputation if you hang out with gang members? **Lesson 47 page 445**

5. What is the leading cause of death in teens? **Lesson 48 page 449**

6. How can you stay safe if you ride the roller coaster at an amusement park? **Lesson 48 page 452**

7. What is the difference between a hurricane watch and a hurricane warning? **Lesson 49 page 459**

8. How will the air feel if the temperature is 15°F with a wind-chill factor of -10°F? **Lesson 49 page 462**

9. What supplies should be kept in a first aid kit? **Lesson 50 page 468**

10. Why do you need to follow universal precautions if a friend has a severe nosebleed? **Lesson 50 page 471**

Health Behavior Contract

Make a health behavior contract for one of the life skills in this unit. Review your health behavior contract with your parents or guardian.

Vocabulary Words

Number a sheet of paper from 1–10. Select the correct vocabulary word and write it next to the corresponding number. DO NOT WRITE IN THIS BOOK.

moral guilt	weapon
near drowning	law-abiding person
anti-gang gang	speeding
universal precautions	landslide
flash flood	implied consent

1. A _____ is an instrument or device used for fighting. **Lesson 47**

2. _____ is exceeding the posted speed limit or driving too fast for conditions. **Lesson 48**

3. A _____ is a person who respects authority and obeys laws. **Lesson 46**

4. _____ are steps taken to keep from having contact with pathogens in body fluids. **Lesson 50**

5. An _____ is a group of teens who stay together to avoid pressure and to protect themselves from gang members. **Lesson 47**

6. A _____ is a rapid movement of a mass of earth or rock down a slope. **Lesson 49**

7. _____ is a pang of conscience a person experiences after an irresponsible or wrong action. **Lesson 46**

8. _____ is unspoken understanding that first aid may be given if no one who can give actual consent is conscious or present. **Lesson 50**

9. _____ is being without sufficient oxygen for a long period of time under water but not dying. **Lesson 48**

10. A _____ is a flood that occurs suddenly. **Lesson 49**

The Responsible Decision-Making Model™

You are standing in line with a friend to ride a scary roller coaster. A posted sign reminds you to put the safety bar down and stay seated. A friend dares you not to use the safety bar. Your friend says, "Don't lock the safety bar in place. Then we can stand up together at the first incline." Answer the following questions on a separate sheet of paper. Write "Does not apply" if a question does not apply to this situation.

1. Is it healthful to ride the roller coaster standing and with the safety bar ajar? Why or why not?

2. Is it safe to ride the roller coaster standing and with the safety bar ajar? Why or why not?

3. Do you obey the posted sign if you ride the roller coaster standing and with the safety bar ajar? Why or why not?

4. Will you keep your self-respect if you accept the dare and ride the roller coaster standing and with the safety bar ajar? Why or why not?

5. Will your parents or guardian approve if you ride the roller coaster standing and with the safety bar ajar? Why or why not?

6. Will you demonstrate good character if you ignore the posted sign, stand, and leave the safety bar ajar? Why or why not?

What is the responsible decision to make in this situation?

Health Literacy

Effective Communication

There is a hurricane warning in your community. Tape record a radio broadcast in which you outline procedures for residents to follow to stay safe.

Self-Directed Learning

Clip five articles from your local newspaper that discuss violence. Write one summary statement for each article.

Critical Thinking

Give a short oral report in class. Focus on two questions. Why are motor vehicle accidents the leading cause of death in teens? How can teens reduce their risk of injury and death from motor vehicle accidents?

Responsible Citizenship

Make a poster to be displayed at a mall. Give a tip for staying safe while shopping at a mall. Ask a store owner to display your poster.

Multicultural Health

Get permission from your parents, guardian, and teacher. Access the Internet. Find the leading cause of teen death in another country.

Family Involvement

Design a notepad to be used to record information your family might need in an emergency. For example, you might write the telephone number of the local poison control center.

Glossary

Sound	As in	Symbol	Example
ă	cat, tap	a	salivary (SA·luh·vehr·ee)
ā	may, same	ay	trachea (TRAY·kee·uh)
a	wear, dare	ehr	beta carotene (BAY·tuh KEHR·uh·teen)
ä	father, top	ah	amniotic (am·nee·AH·tik)
ar	car, park	ar	artery (AR·tuh·ree)
ch	chip, touch	ch	childbirth (CHYLD·berth)
ĕ	bet, test	e	melanin (MEL·uh·nuhn)
ē	pea, need	ee	emphysema (em·fuh·SEE·muh)
er	perk, hurt	er	hypothermia (HEYE·puh·THER·mee·uh)
g	go, big	g	malignant (muh·LIG·nuhnt)
ĭ	tip, live	i	cilia (SI·lee·uh)
ī	side, by	y, eye	angina (an·JY·nuh)
j	job, edge	j	cartilage (KAR·tuhl·ij)
k	cook, ache	k	quackery (KWA·kuh·ree)
ō	bone, know	oh	alveoli (al·vee·OH·ly)
ô	more, pour	or	beta-endorphins (BAY·tuh·en·DOR·fuhnz)
ȯ	saw, all	aw	audiologist (AW·dee·AH·luh·jist)
oi	coin, toy	oy	roid (ROYD) rage
ou	out, now	ow	power (POW·er)
s	see, less	s	cerebrum (suh·REE·bruhm)
sh	she, mission	sh	shadowing (SHA·doh·ing)
ŭ	cup, dug	uh	medulla (muh·DUH·luh)
u	wood, pull	u	pulmonary (PUL·muh·nehr·ee)
ü	rule, union	oo	nutrient (NOO·tree·uhnt)
w	we, away	w	water (WAH·ter)
y	you, yard	yu	urethra (yu·REE·thruh)
z	zone, raise	z	physician (fuh·ZI·shun)
zh	vision, measure	zh	malocclusion (MA·luh·KLOO·zhuhn)
ə	around, mug	uh	epididymis (e·puh·DI·duh·muhs)

A

abandonment: removing oneself from those whose care is one's responsibility.

abdominal thrusts: a series of thrusts to the abdomen that force air from the lungs to dislodge an object.

abstinence: choosing not to be sexually active.

abuse: the harmful treatment of another person.

abusive relationship: a relationship in which one person harms another person with cruel words or actions and the other person endures this behavior.

accurate message: a message that is based on scientific research and is supported by several different sources.

acid rain: rain and other precipitation (snow, sleet, hail) that has a high acid content.

acne: a skin disorder in which pores in the skin are clogged with oil.

acquaintance rape: rape in which the rapist is known to the person who is raped.

Acquired Immune Deficiency Syndrome (AIDS): a condition that results when infection with HIV causes a breakdown of the body's ability to fight other infections.

actual consent: oral or written permission from a mentally competent adult to give first aid.

addiction: the compelling need to continue a behavior even if it is harmful.

adrenal (uh·DREE·nuhl) **glands:** glands that secrete a hormone that helps the body react to emergency situations.

adrenaline (uh·DRE·nuhl·uhn): a hormone that prepares the body for quick action.

advertisement: or ad, is a paid announcement about a product or service.

aerobic exercise: one in which large amounts of oxygen are used for an extended time.

affection: a fond or tender feeling for another person.

agility: the ability to move quickly and easily.

AIDS dementia (di·MENT·shuh): a loss of brain function caused by HIV infection.

alcohol: a depressant drug found in some beverages.

alcoholism (al·kuh·HAW·LI·zuhm): a disease in which there is dependence on alcohol.

allergy: a condition in which the body overreacts to a substance.

alveoli (al·vee·OH·ly): small air sacs in the lungs through which oxygen enters the blood and carbon dioxide leaves the blood.

amniotic (am·nee·AH·tik) **sac:** a pouch filled with fluid that surrounds a developing baby.

amotivational syndrome: a loss of ambition and motivation.

anabolic steroids: drugs that are used to increase muscle size and strength.

anger: a feeling of being irritated or annoyed.

anger cue: a body change that occurs when a person is angry.

anger management skills: ways to express anger without harming oneself or others.

angina (an·JY·nuh): chest pain that results from decreased blood flow to the heart.

anorexia nervosa (a·nuh·REK·see·uh nehr·VOH·suh): an eating disorder in which a person starves himself or herself and has a low body weight.

anthrax: a disease caused by a bacterium that reproduces itself by developing spores.

antibody: a special protein in blood that helps fight infection.

anti-depressant: a drug that corrects chemical imbalances in the brain that cause depression.

anti-gang gang: a group of teens who stay together to avoid pressure and to protect themselves from gang members.

antioxidants: substances that protect cells from being damaged by oxidation.

antiperspirant: a product used to reduce the amount of perspiration.

appropriate joke: a joke that does not make fun of anyone, does not put anyone down, and is not dirty.

artery (AR·tuh·ree): a blood vessel that carries blood away from the heart.

artificial nails: products used to make nails longer or more attractive.

assault: a physical attack or a threat of an attack.

assertive: to make one's expectations clear using positive actions.

asthma: a chronic condition in which breathing becomes difficult.

asthma attack: an episode of coughing, wheezing, and shortness of breath.

asthma triggers: substances or conditions that can cause asthma attacks.

astigmatism (uh·STIG·muh·TI·zuhm): a condition in which irregular shape of the cornea causes blurred vision.

atherosclerosis (A·thuh·ROH·skluh·ROH·suhs): a disease in which fat deposits on artery walls.

audiologist (AW·dee·AH·luh·jist): a professional who tests hearing ability and helps correct hearing loss.

authority figure: a person who has the power and right to apply rules and laws.

AZT: a drug that slows down the rate at which HIV multiplies.

balance: the ability to keep from falling.

B cell: a white blood cell that produces antibodies.

beta carotene (BAY·tuh KEHR·uh·teen): a substance found in food that is changed to vitamin A in the body.

beta-endorphins (BAY·tuh·en·DOR·fuhnz): substances produced in the brain that create a feeling of well-being.

binge eating disorder: an eating disorder in which a person frequently stuffs himself or herself with food.

biodegradable product: a product that can be broken down by organisms to become part of Earth's natural resources.

biological age: a measure of how well a person's body parts function.

birthmark: an area of discolored skin present from birth.

blackout: a period in which a person cannot remember what has happened.

body composition: the percentage of fat tissue and lean tissue in the body.

body image: the feeling a person has about his or her appearance.

bonding: a process in which two people develop feelings of closeness for each other.

bookie: a person who takes bets and gets a percentage of the money.

braces: devices that are cemented or bonded to the teeth and wired together to bring the teeth into correct alignment.

brain: the organ that is the control center for the body.

brain stem: the part of the brain that controls the functions of inner organs.

breast self-examination (BSE): a monthly check for lumps and changes in the breasts.

bronchial (BRAHN·kee·uhl) **tubes:** two short tubes through which air enters the lungs.

budget: a written plan for saving and spending money.

bulimia nervosa (boo·LEE·mee·uh nehr·VOH·suh): an eating disorder in which a person stuffs himself or herself and then rids the body of food.

bullying: an attempt by a person to hurt or frighten people whom the bully considers smaller or weaker.

burn: an injury caused by heat, electricity, chemicals, or radiation.

button pusher: a person who pushes the "hot button" of another person to cause trouble.

C

calculated risk: a chance that is worth taking after careful consideration of the possible outcomes.

calorie: a unit of energy produced by food and used by the body.

Calories from Fat: the listing of the number of calories from fat in one serving of the food.

Calories Listing: the listing of the number of calories in one serving of the food.

Campylobacteriosis (KAM·pi·loh·bak·ter·ee·OH·sis): a foodborne illness caused by consuming food contaminated by *Campylobacter* (kam·pi·loh·BAK·ter) bacteria.

cancer: a group of diseases in which cells divide in an uncontrollable manner.

candidiasis (KAN·duh·DY·uh·suhs): a fungal infection that causes itching and burning.

capillary (KA·puh·lehr·ee): a tiny blood vessel that connects arteries and veins.

carbohydrates (KAHR·boh·HY·drayts): nutrients that are the main source of energy for the body.

carbon monoxide: an odorless, colorless, poisonous gas.

carcinogen (kar·SI·nuh·juhn): a substance that causes cancer.

cardiac arrest: the death of the heart muscle.

cardiopulmonary resuscitation (CPR): a first aid technique that is used to restore heartbeat and breathing.

cardiorespiratory endurance: the ability to do activities that require oxygen for extended periods of time.

cardiovascular diseases: diseases of the heart and blood vessels.

career: the work that a person prepares for and does through life.

caregiver: a person who provides care to someone who needs assistance.

cartilage (KAHR·tuhl·ij): soft material at the ends of bones that keeps them from rubbing together.

cataract: a clouding of the lens of the eye that affects vision.

CD-ROM: a computer disc that stores computer programs that might include text, graphics, music, and animation.

Center for Science in the Public Interest (CSPI): a private organization that works to improve government policies on food, nutrition, and other health concerns.

cerebellum (ser·uh·BEL·uhm): the part of the brain that controls how muscles work together.

cerebrum (suh·REE·bruhm): the part of the brain that controls the ability to reason and to make judgments.

certificate: a document granted by a non-governmental agency to a person for the right to practice or to use a certain title.

cervix: the lower part of the uterus that connects to the vagina.

chancre (SHANG·ker): a hard, round, painless sore.

character: a person's use of self-control to act on responsible values.

childbirth: the process by which the baby moves from the uterus out of the mother's body.

childsitter: a person who provides care for someone else's children.

Chlamydia (kluh·MID·ee·uh): an STD that causes inflammation of the reproductive organs.

choking: an emergency in which the airway is blocked.

cholesterol: a fatty substance that is made by the body and is found in dairy products and animal products.

chronic fatigue syndrome (CFS): a condition in which recurring tiredness makes it difficult to function.

chronic health condition: a health condition that lasts a long time or keeps coming back.

chronological age: the number of years a person has lived.

cilia (SI·lee·uh): tiny hairs that line the air passages.

circulatory system: the body system that transports oxygen, food, and waste products throughout the body.

circumcision: the surgical removal of the foreskin.

cirrhosis (suh·ROH·suhs): a disease of the liver in which cells are damaged.

closed fracture: a fracture in which there is no break in the skin.

cocaine: a stimulant made from leaves of the coca bush.

code of conduct: the expected standard of behavior.

codependence: a mental disorder in which a person denies feelings and copes in harmful ways.

codependent relationship: a relationship in which one person acts in wrong ways and the other person, the enabler, denies or supports the wrong actions.

cold: a viral infection that affects the lining of the upper respiratory tract.

commitment: a pledge or promise to do something.

communicable disease: an illness caused by pathogens that can be spread from one living thing to another.

communication: the sharing of feelings, thoughts, and information with another person.

composting: a method of changing organic garbage into humus.

conception: the union of a sperm and an ovum.

conflict: a disagreement.

conflict resolution skills: steps that can be taken to settle a disagreement in a responsible way.

conflict style: the particular way a person responds to conflict.

conscience: an inner sense of right and wrong that causes a person to behave responsibly or to feel moral guilt.

consumer: a person who uses information, products, and services.

Consumer Product Safety Commission (CPSC): a federal agency that establishes and enforces product safety standards.

consumer rights: the privileges that a consumer is guaranteed.

Consumer's Union (CU): a private organization that tests products and publishes a magazine, *Consumer Reports.*

controlled drug: a drug for which possession, manufacture, and sale is regulated by law.

controlling relationship: a relationship in which one person has the power and the other person gives up all power.

cool-down: five to ten minutes of reduced physical activity after a workout.

coordination: the ability to use body parts and senses together for movement.

co-payment: the portion or amount of the fee for health care the policy owner must pay.

coronary artery: a blood vessel that carries blood to the heart muscles.

Council of Better Business Bureaus: a private organization that checks consumer complaints and advertising and selling practices.

Cowper's glands: two small glands that secrete a clear fluid into the urethra.

crack: an illegal drug that is a smokable form of cocaine.

crisis intervention program: a program in which a trained team of adults offers assistance to help people who experience severe difficulty.

cross contamination: the transfer of pathogens from a contaminated food or surface to another food.

cruciferous (kroo·SI·fuh·ruhs) **vegetables:** vegetables that belong to the cabbage family.

cuticle: the non-living skin that surrounds and protects the nails.

cyberbar: a Web site in which people pretend they are at a bar.

D

dandruff: a condition in which dead skin is shed from the scalp and becomes visible.

dare: a request to do something as a test of courage.

date rape: rape that occurs in a dating situation.

dating: having social plans with another person.

ddi: a drug that slows down the rate at which HIV multiplies.

death: the end of life when vital organs no longer function.

decibel (dB): a unit used to measure the loudness of sounds.

deductible: an amount the policy owner must pay before the insurance company makes payments.

denial: refusing to admit there is a problem.

dental plaque: an invisible, sticky film of bacteria on teeth, especially near the gum line.

deodorant: a product that reduces body odor and perspiration.

depression: the feeling of being sad, unhappy, or discouraged.

dermatologist: a physician who specializes in the care of the skin.

desensitization (DEE·sent·suh·tuh·ZAY·shuhn)**:** the effect of reacting less and less to the exposure to something.

designer drug: a drug that is a changed form of a controlled drug.

desirable weight: the weight that is most healthful for a person.

developed country: a country that has reached an acceptable standard of health conditions.

developing country: a country that is working to reach an acceptable standard of health conditions.

developmental task: a task that a person must master at a given age.

diabetes (DY·uh·BEE·teez)**:** a disease in which the body produces little or no insulin or cannot use insulin.

Dietary Guidelines: recommendations for diet choices for healthy Americans who are age two or older.

digestive system: the body system that breaks down food so that it can be used by the body.

dislocation: the movement of a bone from its joint.

diuretic (DY·yuh·RE·tik)**:** a drug that increases the amount of urine the body excretes.

doggie bag: a container of leftovers from a meal.

domestic violence: violence that occurs within a family.

drug: a substance other than food that changes the way the body or mind functions.

drug abuse: the intentional use of a drug when no medical or health reasons exist.

drug dependence: the compelling need to take a drug even though it harms the body, mind, and relationships.

drug-free lifestyle: a lifestyle in which a person does not misuse or abuse drugs.

drug-free role model: a person who does not misuse or abuse drugs and encourages others to be drug-free.

drug misuse: the incorrect use of a prescription or OTC drug.

drug mixing: taking more than one kind of drug at one time.

drug slipping: placing a drug into someone's food or beverage without that person's knowledge.

drug trafficking: the illegal production, distribution, sales, and purchase of drugs.

dysfunctional relationship: a relationship that *does not* promote mutual respect and responsible behavior.

E

eating disorder: an emotional disorder in which a person chooses harmful eating patterns.

eating habits: a person's usual ways of eating.

eating trigger: something that causes a person to feel the urge to eat.

E. coli O157:H7: a strain of *E. coli* that can cause hemorrhagic colitis.

ecstasy: an illegal drug that can act as a stimulant or hallucinogen.

ejaculation: the passage of semen from the penis.

electrical injury: an injury that occurs when electricity passes through the body.

electrical storm: a storm that features lightning and thunder.

electronic mail (e-mail): a message delivered quickly from one computer to another.

ELISA (ee·LY·suh): a test used on blood or mouth fluids to check for HIV antibodies.

emergency: a serious situation that occurs without warning and calls for quick action.

emergency room: a facility that provides service for major and minor medical emergencies.

emotional abuse: "putting down" another person and making the person feel worthless.

emphysema (EMP·fuh·ZEE·muh): a condition in which the air sacs in the lungs become damaged.

empowered: to be energized because a person has some control over his or her decisions and behavior.

enabler: a person who supports the harmful behavior of another person.

endocrine system: the body system made up of glands that produce hormones.

endurance: the ability to continue despite hardship or stress.

energy: the ability to do work.

environment: everything around a person.

environmental issues: environmental concerns that can affect the quality of life for people.

epididymis (e·puh·DI·duh·muhs): a structure on the top of the testes where sperm mature.

epilepsy: a condition in which nerve messages in the brain are disturbed for a brief time.

esophagus (i·SAH·fuh·guhs)**:** a tube through which food passes from the mouth to the stomach.

estrogen: a hormone that produces female secondary sex characteristics and affects menstruation.

euphoria (yoo·FOHR·ee·uh)**:** a feeling of intense happiness and well-being.

exercise-induced asthma (EIA): a condition in which vigorous physical activity causes a person to have asthma attacks.

expenses: amounts of money needed to purchase or do something.

fad diet: a quick weight-loss diet that is popular.

Fallopian (fuh·LOH·pee·uhn) **tube:** a four-inch-(ten-centimeter-) long tube through which ova move from an ovary to the uterus.

family guidelines: rules a family makes to help members live in a responsible way.

fan: a person who watches and supports sports.

fast food: food that can be served quickly.

fats: nutrients that provide energy and help the body store vitamins.

Federal Trade Commission (FTC): a federal agency that checks advertising practices.

feeling: an emotion.

female reproductive system: the organs in the female body that are involved in producing offspring.

fetal alcohol syndrome (FAS): the presence of birth defects in a baby born to a mother who drank alcohol during pregnancy.

fetal smoking syndrome: the presence of birth defects in a baby born to a mother who smokes cigarettes during her pregnancy.

fiber: the part of grains and plant foods that cannot be digested.

fighting: taking part in a physical struggle.

first aid: the immediate and temporary care given to a person who has been injured or suddenly becomes ill.

first-degree burn: a burn which affects the top layer of skin.

fitness skills: skills that can be used in sports and physical activities.

flash flood: a flood that occurs suddenly.

flexibility: the ability to bend and move the joints through a full range of motion.

flood: the overflowing of a body of water onto normally dry land.

flossing: the removal of dental plaque and bits of food from between the teeth using a string-like material called floss.

flunitrazepam (FLOO·nuh·TRA·zuh·pam)**:** an odorless, colorless sedative drug.

Food and Drug Administration (FDA): a federal agency that checks and enforces the safety of food, drugs, medical devices, and cosmetics.

foodborne illness: an illness caused by consuming foods or beverages that have been contaminated with pathogens or toxins produced by pathogens.

food group: foods that contain similar nutrients.

Food Guide Pyramid: a guide that shows how many servings are needed from each food group each day.

food label: a panel of nutrition information found on foods.

food poisoning: a foodborne illness caused by toxins produced by pathogens.

formal intervention: an action by people who want a person to get treatment for a problem.

fossil fuels: coal, oil, and natural gas burned to produce energy.

fracture: a break or crack in a bone.

frostbite: freezing of body parts, often the tissues of the extremities.

gang: a group of people involved in violent and illegal activities.

garbage eater: a person who mostly eats foods that are high in sugar, fat, and salt.

general adaptation syndrome (GAS): a series of changes that occur in the body when stress occurs.

genital herpes: an STD caused by a virus that produces cold sores and blisters on the sex organs or in the mouth.

genital warts: an STD that produces wart-like growths on the sex organs.

GHB: an illegal depressant drug also known as one of the date rape drugs.

glamorize: to associate something with desirable qualities.

global warming: an ongoing slight increase in Earth's temperature.

gonorrhea (GAH·nuh·REE·uh)**:** an STD that infects the linings of the genital and urinary tracts.

gorger: a person who eats large portions of food at a time.

graffiti (gruh·FEE·tee)**:** writing or drawing on a public surface.

gratitude: feeling thankful for a favor or for something that is pleasing.

grazer: a person who eats small portions of food several times a day.

greenhouse effect: the trapping around the earth of the heat from the sun by gases, such as carbon dioxide.

grief: an emotional reaction to a loss or misfortune.

grieve: to express feelings of grief.

grooming: taking care of the body and having a neat appearance.

grooming product: an item that helps a person have a neat appearance and that keeps the body clean.

groundwater: water in natural underground reservoirs.

guideliner: a person who follows the Dietary Guidelines.

habitat: a place where an animal or plant normally lives.

hangnail: a piece of skin torn near the fingernail.

hangover: the aftereffect of using alcohol.

headache: head pain with many causes.

health: the condition of a person's body, mind, emotions, and relationships.

health advocate: a person who promotes health for self and others.

health advocate for the environment: a person who takes actions to protect the environment.

health behavior contract: a written plan to develop the habit of practicing a specific life skill.

Health Behavior Inventory: a personal assessment tool that shows which life skills a person practices.

health career: a profession or occupation for which one trains in the health field.

health care facility: a place where people receive health care.

health care provider: a professional who provides health care.

health care system: a system that includes health care providers, health care facilities, and payment for health care.

health center: a health care facility with several health care providers or that provides health care for a special population.

healthful behavior: an action that promotes health; prevents illness, injury, and premature death; and improves the quality of the environment.

healthful body composition: having a high ratio of lean tissue to fat tissue in the body.

healthful entertainment: entertainment that promotes physical, mental, or social health.

healthful relationship: a relationship that promotes mutual respect and responsible behavior.

health history: recorded information about a person's past and present health status.

health insurance benefits: the costs the insurance company will pay for specific health services.

health insurance policy: a plan that helps pay the cost of health care.

health knowledge: facts about health.

health literate person: a person who has skills in effective communication, self-directed learning, critical thinking, and responsible citizenship.

health maintenance organization (HMO): a plan in which a group of health care providers are paid to give health care.

health-related fitness: the ability of the heart, lungs, muscles, and joints to perform well.

health status: the condition of a person's health.

hearing loss: the inability to detect some or all sounds at normal levels of loudness or frequency.

heart: a muscular organ that pumps blood to the body.

heart attack: the death of heart muscle caused by a lack of blood flow to the heart.

heat cramps: painful muscle spasms in the legs and arms due to excessive fluid loss through sweating.

heat exhaustion: extreme tiredness due to the body's inability to regulate its temperature.

heatstroke: an overheating of the body that is life-threatening.

helper T cell: a white blood cell that signals B cells to produce antibodies.

hemorrhagic colitis (HE·muh·RA·jik koh·LY·tuhs): inflammation of the large intestine with pain and bloody diarrhea.

herbal ecstasy: an OTC stimulant made of herbs, ephedrine, and other ingredients.

heredity: the passing of characteristics from biological parents to their children.

heroin: an illegal narcotic made from morphine.

high blood pressure: a condition in which the pressure against the artery walls is above normal when the heart beats.

high density lipoproteins (ly·poh·PROH·teens) **(HDLs):** substances in blood that carry cholesterol to the liver for breakdown and excretion.

HIV negative: a term used to describe a person who does not have HIV antibodies in the blood.

HIV positive: a term used to describe a person who has HIV antibodies in the blood.

HIV status: the result of testing for HIV antibodies in the blood.

holistic (hoh·LIS·tik) **effect:** a term used to describe the effects one health behavior can have on total health.

homicide: the killing of one person by another person.

honest talk: the open sharing of feelings.

hormone: a chemical messenger that is released into the bloodstream and regulates body activities.

hospital: a facility that provides care for many medical conditions.

hostile environment: a threatening and unfriendly environment.

human immunodeficiency (I·myuh·noh·di·FI·shuhnt·see) **virus (HIV):** a pathogen that destroys infection-fighting T cells in the body.

humus (HYOO·muhs): the organic material in soil.

hurricane: a tropical storm with heavy rains and winds in excess of 74 miles per hour, or dangerously high water and rough seas.

hurricane warning: a warning that is issued when hurricane conditions are expected in 24 hours or less.

hurricane watch: a warning that is issued when there is a threat of hurricane conditions within 24 to 36 hours.

hyperopia (hy·puh·ROH·pee·uh): a vision problem in which close objects appear blurred and distant objects are seen clearly.

hypothermia (HEYE·puh·THER·mee·uh): a reduction of the body temperature so that it is lower than normal.

I

illegal drug: a drug for which possession, manufacture, and sale is against the law.

illegal drug use: the wrong use, possession, manufacture, or sale of controlled drugs, and the use, possession, manufacture, or sale of illegal drugs.

I-message: a statement or message that contains a reference to a specific behavior or event, the effect of the behavior or event, and the feelings that result.

immune system: the body system that removes harmful organisms from the blood and fights pathogens.

implied consent: unspoken understanding that first aid may be given if no one who can give actual consent is conscious or present.

inappropriate humor: humor that includes put-downs, dirty jokes, or jokes that make fun of certain groups of people.

incinerator: a furnace in which solid waste is burned.

income: money received.

indication for use: a symptom or condition for which an OTC drug should be used.

infertile: incapable of producing offspring.

influenza (IN·floo·EN·zuh): a viral infection of the respiratory tract.

inhalant: a drug that is breathed in and produces immediate effects.

injecting drug user: a person who injects illegal drugs into the body with syringes, needles, or other injection equipment.

injection drug use: drug use that involves injecting drugs into the body.

inpatient: a person who stays at the hospital while receiving health care.

inpatient care: treatment that requires overnight stay at a facility.

insecure: to feel uncertain or to lack confidence.

insomnia: a condition in which a person has difficulty falling asleep or staying asleep.

instant gratification: choosing an immediate reward regardless of the possible harmful effects.

integumentary (in·teh·gyuh·MEN·tuh·ree) **system:** the body system that covers and protects the body.

Internet: a worldwide system of computer networks.

intoxication: the condition of being drunk.

invincible (in·VIN·suh·buhl): incapable of being harmed.

jaundice (JAWN·duhs): yellowing of the skin and whites of the eyes.

joint: a point at which two bones meet.

Kaposi's (KA·puh·seez) **sarcoma (KS):** a type of cancer in people who have AIDS.

kidneys: organs through which blood circulates as wastes are filtered.

knocked-out tooth: a tooth that has been knocked out of its socket.

labor: a series of stages that result in the birth of a baby.

landfill: a place where wastes are dumped or buried.

landslide: a rapid movement of a mass of earth or rock down a slope.

large intestine: the organ in which undigested food is stored until it leaves the body.

law-abiding person: a person who respects authority and obeys laws.

laxative: a drug that helps a person have a bowel movement.

learning style: a person's way of gaining knowledge and skills.

lice: insects that attach to the skin and cause itching and swelling.

license: a document granted by a government agency to a person for the right to practice or to use a certain title.

life expectancy: the number of years a person can expect to live.

lifelong learning: being involved in gaining knowledge and skills throughout life.

life skill: a healthful action that is learned and practiced for a lifetime.

lifestyle disease: a disease that is more likely to develop in a person who engages in specific risk behaviors.

ligaments: tough bands of tissue that attach bones together at joints.

lightning: flashes of light caused by electricity in the air.

liver: a gland that produces bile to break down fats.

low birth weight: a weight at birth that is less than 5.5 pounds (2.5 kilograms).

LSD: an illegal hallucinogen that can produce a trip and flashbacks.

lungs: two organs that supply the blood with oxygen and rid the blood of carbon dioxide.

Lyme disease: a bacterial disease transmitted through a tick.

lymph: a clear liquid that surrounds body cells and circulates in lymph vessels.

lymph node: a structure that filters and destroys pathogens.

macrophage (MAK·roh·fahj)**:** a white blood cell that surrounds and destroys pathogens.

male reproductive system: the organs in the male body that are involved in producing offspring.

malignant melanoma (muh·LIG·nuhnt ME·luh·NOH·muh)**:** a serious form of skin cancer.

malocclusion (MA·luh·KLOO·zhuhn)**:** an abnormal fitting together of teeth when the jaws are closed.

managed care: a system of health care services designed to control costs.

marriage: a legal commitment a man and woman make to love and care for one another.

maximum heart rate: 220 beats per minute minus a person's age.

MDMA: a stimulant and hallucinogen produced from methamphetamine.

media: the various forms of mass communication.

media literacy: the ability to recognize and evaluate the messages in media.

mediator: a responsible adult who helps people resolve conflicts.

medical waste: infectious waste from medical facilities.

medulla (muh·DUH·luh): the part of the brain that controls involuntary actions, such as heart rate and breathing.

melanin (ME·luh·nuhn): a substance that protects skin and gives it color.

menstrual cycle: a monthly series of changes that involves ovulation, changes in the uterine lining, and menstruation.

menstruation (men·stroo·WAY·shuhn): the period during which the menstrual flow leaves the body.

mental alertness: the sharpness of the mind.

mental health: the condition of a person's mind and emotions.

mentor: a responsible person who guides another person.

metabolism: the rate at which food is converted to energy in the cells.

methamphetamine (ME·tham·FE·tuh·MEEN): a stimulant that can produce short-lived euphoria, followed by depression.

migraine headache: severe head pain caused by widening of blood vessels in the brain.

minerals: nutrients that are involved in many of the body's activities.

miscarriage: a natural early ending of a pregnancy.

mixed message: a message that expresses two different meanings.

modem: a device that allows a computer to exchange information with another computer over the telephone lines.

mole: a small dark skin growth that develops from melanin.

monogamous (muh·NAW·guh·muhs) **traditional marriage:** a marriage in which a husband and wife have sex *only with each other.*

mononucleosis (MAH·nuh·NOO·klee·OH·suhs): a viral infection that causes extreme tiredness.

mood swings: emotional ups and downs caused by changing hormone levels.

moral guilt: a pang of conscience a person experiences after an irresponsible or wrong action.

murder: a homicide that is purposeful.

muscle cramp: a sudden tightening of a muscle.

muscular endurance: the ability to use muscles for an extended period of time.

muscular strength: the ability to lift, pull, push, kick, and throw with force.

muscular system: the body system composed of skeletal muscles that provide motion and maintain posture.

myopia (my·OH·pee·uh): a vision problem in which distant objects appear blurred and close objects are seen clearly.

N

natural disaster: an event caused by nature that results in injury, damage, or loss.

natural environment: everything around a person that is not made by people.

near drowning: being without sufficient oxygen for a long period of time under water but not dying.

neglect: failure to provide proper care and guidance.

nervous system: the body system for communication and control.

newsgroup: an area on the Internet where people post messages on a specific subject for other people to read.

nicotine: an addictive stimulant drug found in tobacco.

nicotine patch: a skin patch that releases nicotine into the bloodstream.

noise: sound that produces discomfort or annoyance.

noise pollution: loud or constant noise that causes hearing loss and stress.

nongonococcal urethritis (NAHN·GAH·nuh·KAH·kuhl YUR·i·THRY·tuhs) **(NGU):** an STD that causes inflammation of the urethra.

nonverbal communication: the use of actions to express oneself.

nosebleed: a loss of blood from the mucous membranes that line the nose.

nursing home: a live-in facility that provides medical care, food, and social activities.

nutrient: a substance in foods that builds, repairs, and maintains body tissues; helps with body processes; and provides energy.

nutrition: the study of what people eat and the effects of food on health.

Nutrition Facts: the title of the information panel that is required on most foods.

obesity: a weight more than 20 percent over desirable body weight.

one-sided relationship: a relationship in which one person does most of the taking and the other person does most of the giving.

open fracture: a fracture in which there is a break in the skin.

ophthalmologist (AHF·thuhl·MAH·luh·jist): a physician who specializes in care and treatment of the eye.

opportunistic (AH·puhr·too·NIS·tik) **infections:** infections that develop when a person has a weak immune system.

optimal health: the highest level of health a person can achieve.

optimistic: tending to expect positive outcomes.

optometrist (ahp·TAH·muh·trist): a professional who tests vision and prescribes corrective lenses.

orthodontist (AWR·thu·DAHN·tist): a dentist who specializes in detecting and treating malocclusion.

osteoporosis (AHS·tee·oh·puh·ROH·suhs): a disease in which the bones become thin and brittle.

out-of-order death: the death of a person that occurs at an unexpected time in his or her life cycle.

outpatient: a person who comes to the hospital for treatment but does not stay overnight.

outpatient care: treatment that does not require overnight stay at a facility.

ovaries: two glands that produce estrogen and ova.

overdose: to take an excess amount.

overload: including exercise beyond what a person usually does to obtain added benefits.

over-the-counter (OTC) drug: a drug that can be purchased from a legal source without a prescription.

overweight: a weight above a person's desirable weight.

ovulation (ahv·yuh·LAY·shuhn)**:** the release of a mature ovum from an ovary.

ozone: a form of oxygen produced when sunlight reacts with oxygen.

ozone layer: a layer of ozone in the upper atmosphere that filters UV radiation from the sun.

pancreas (PAN·kree·uhs)**:** a gland that secretes juices that break down some foods and secretes insulin, which regulates blood sugar.

Pap smear: a screening test for cancer of the cervix.

parathyroid glands: two glands that secrete a hormone that controls the amount of calcium and phosphorous in the body.

pathogen: a germ that causes disease.

PCP: an illegal hallucinogen that can speed up some body functions and slow down others.

peer pressure: influence that peers place on others to convince them to behave in certain ways.

peers: people of similar age or status.

pelvic inflammatory (in·FLA·muh·TOR·ee) **disease (PID):** a serious infection of the internal female reproductive organs.

penis: the male sex organ used for reproduction and urination.

Percent Daily Value: the portion of the daily amount of a nutrient provided by one serving of the food.

perfectionism: the compelling need to be accurate.

personal health record: a record of a person's health, health care, and health care providers.

personality: a person's unique blend of traits.

personal reflection: serious or careful thought about oneself.

perspiration: a mixture of water, salt, and waste products.

pharmacist: a health professional who is licensed to prepare and sell prescription drugs.

phobia: an excessive fear of an object, situation, or person.

physical abuse: harmful treatment that results in physical injury to the victim.

physical activity: body movement produced by muscles and bones that requires energy.

physical dependence: repeated drug use that causes tolerance.

physical examination: a series of tests that measure health status.

physical fitness: the condition of the body that results from regular physical activity.

physical health: the condition of a person's body.

physician: a health care provider who is licensed to practice medicine.

pigging out: stuffing oneself with a large amount of food.

pitcher's shoulder: a tearing and swelling of the muscles and tendons that hold the upper arm in the shoulder joint.

pituitary (puh·TOO·uh·TER·ee) **gland:** a gland that secretes growth hormone and hormones that control other glands.

placenta: a structure that attaches the ovum to the inner wall of the uterus.

plaque: hardened deposits that form on the inner walls of blood vessels.

pneumocystis carinii (NOO·muh·SIS·tis kuh·REE·nee) **pneumonia (PCP):** a type of pneumonia found in people who have AIDS.

pneumonia (noo·MOH·nyuh): an infection in the lungs caused by bacteria, viruses, or other pathogens.

poison: a substance that causes injury, illness, or death if it enters the body.

policy owner: the person who owns the health insurance policy.

pollutant: something that has a harmful effect on the environment.

polluted air: air contaminated with harmful substances.

pollution: any change in the environment that harms health.

popular, to be: to be liked by others.

poverty: a condition in which people do not have enough resources to live in a healthful way.

power: the ability to combine strength and speed.

precycling: a process of reducing solid waste by purchasing fewer products and by purchasing products that use fewer resources.

pregnancy: the time period between conception and birth.

premature birth: the birth of a baby before it is fully developed.

premature death: death that occurs before a person reaches his or her life expectancy.

premium: a set amount of money that the owner of a health insurance policy pays regularly.

prenatal care: care that is given to a mother-to-be and her developing baby before birth.

prescription: a written order from a licensed health professional.

prescription drug: a medicine that can be legally obtained only with a prescription.

private office: a health care facility that is privately owned by one or more health care providers.

processed food: a food that has been specially treated or changed.

product recall: an order to take a product off the market because of safety concerns.

prostate gland: a gland that produces fluid that helps keep sperm alive.

protease (PROH·tee·AYS) **inhibitors:** antiviral drugs that decrease the amount of HIV in the blood and increase the T cell count.

protective factor: something that increases the chance of a positive outcome.

protective factor for violence: an action or circumstance that decreases the likelihood that a person will be involved in violence.

proteins: nutrients that are needed for growth and repair of body cells.

psychological dependence: a desire for a drug for emotional reasons.

puberty: the period of growth when secondary sex characteristics appear.

pubic lice: the infestation of the pubic hair by lice.

Q

quackery (KWA·kuh·ree): a method of selling worthless products and services.

quality of life: the degree to which a person lives life to the fullest capacity.

R

radon: an odorless, colorless, radioactive gas.

random event: an event over which a person does not have control.

random violence: violence over which a person has no control.

rape: the threatened or actual use of physical force to get someone to have sex without giving consent.

rave: an all-night underground party.

reaction time: the time it takes to move after a person hears, sees, feels, or touches a stimulus.

recovery program: a group that supports members as they change their behavior to become responsible.

recycling: changing waste products so they can be used again.

referee: an official who enforces rules in a sports event.

regular physical activity: physical activity that is performed on most days of the week.

relapse: a return to harmful behavior.

relationship: a connection a person has with another person.

repetitions: the number of times an exercise is performed.

reputation: what most people think of the person.

rescue breathing: a way of breathing air into an unconscious victim who is not breathing, but has a pulse.

resilient (ri·ZIL·yuhnt): to bounce back and learn from misfortune or change.

resistance exercise: an exercise in which a force acts against muscles.

resistance skills: skills that are used to say NO to an action or to leave a situation.

resources: substances that cannot be replaced once they are used.

respected, to be: to be held in high regard by others because one behaves in responsible ways.

respiratory system: the body system that provides the body with oxygen and removes waste carbon dioxide from the body.

responsible: accountable and dependable.

responsible decision: a choice that leads to actions that are healthful, are safe, are legal, show respect for self and others, follow the guidelines of parents and other responsible adults, and demonstrate good character.

Responsible Decision-Making Model™, *The:* a series of steps to follow to assure that decisions lead to actions that promote health, protect safety, follow laws, show respect for self and others, follow guidelines set by responsible adults, such as a person's parents or guardian, and demonstrate good character.

responsible drug use: the correct use of legal drugs to promote health and well-being.

responsible value: a standard or belief that guides a person to behave in responsible ways.

restitution: making good for any loss or damage.

restraining order: an order by a court that forbids a person from doing a particular act.

retainer: a plastic device with wires that keeps the teeth from moving back to their original places.

retirement community: a group of homes in which older people live.

reusing: using items again instead of throwing them away and buying new ones.

RICE Treatment: a technique for treating injuries that involves rest, ice, compression, and elevation.

risk: a chance that a person takes that has an unknown outcome.

risk behavior: an action that threatens health; increases the likelihood of illness and premature death; and harms the quality of the environment.

risk factor: something that increases the chance of a negative outcome.

roid rage: an outburst of anger caused by using anabolic steroids.

runner's knee: a condition in which the kneecap rubs against the thighbone.

S

salivary (SA·luh·vehr·ee) **glands:** glands that produce saliva to soften foods.

Salmonellosis (SAL·muh·ne·LOH·suhs): a foodborne illness caused by consuming food contaminated by *Salmonella* (sal·muh·NE·luh) bacteria.

sarcasm: a harmful form of inappropriate humor.

saturated fat: a type of fat from dairy products, solid vegetable fat, and meat and poultry.

scald: a burn caused by hot liquid or steam.

scoliosis (skoh·lee·OH·sis): an S-shaped curvature of the spine.

scrotum: a sac-like pouch that holds the testes and helps regulate their temperature.

sebum (SEE·buhm): a fatty substance secreted by the skin.

secondary sex characteristics: physical and emotional changes that occur in puberty.

second-degree burn: a burn that involves the top layers of the skin.

secondhand smoke: sidestream smoke and smoke that a person exhales while smoking.

seizure: a brief episode in which a person loses control over mind and body.

self-control: the degree to which a person regulates his or her own behavior.

self-esteem: a person's feelings about his or her worth.

self-protection strategies: strategies that can be practiced to protect oneself from violence.

self-respect: a high regard for oneself because one behaves in responsible ways.

self-sufficient: to have the skills and financial resources to take care of oneself.

semen: a mixture of sperm and fluids from the seminal vesicles, prostate gland, and Cowper's glands.

seminal vesicles (SE·muh·nuhl VE·si·kuhls): two small glands that secrete a fluid rich in sugar that nourishes and helps sperm move.

sense of humor: an ability to see the funny side of a situation.

service learning: an educational experience that combines learning with community service without pay.

Serving Size: the listing of the amount of food that is considered a serving.

Servings Per Container: the listing of the number of servings in the container or package.

severe thunderstorm: an electrical storm with damaging winds of at least 58 miles per hour or hail at least three-fourths of an inch in diameter.

severe thunderstorm warning: a warning issued when a severe thunderstorm has been sighted or indicated by weather radar.

severe thunderstorm watch: a warning issued when weather conditions are such that a severe thunderstorm is likely to develop.

sewage: waste liquids or matter carried off in sewers.

sex role: the way a person acts and his or her feelings and attitudes about being male or female.

sexual abuse: sexual contact that is forced on a person.

sexual feelings: feelings that result from an attraction to another person.

sexual harassment: unwanted sexual behavior that ranges from making sexual comments to forcing another person into unwanted sex acts.

sexually transmitted disease (STD): a disease caused by pathogens that are transmitted from an infected person to an uninfected person during intimate sexual contact.

shadowing: spending time with a mentor as (s)he performs work activities.

shin splint: a condition in which the muscles along the lower leg or shin are damaged.

shock: a dangerous change in blood flow to the body.

sick building syndrome (SBS): an illness that results from indoor air pollution.

sickle cell anemia: an inherited blood disease in which the red blood cells carry less oxygen.

side effect: an unwanted body change.

sidestream smoke: smoke that is given off by a burning cigarette, pipe, or cigar.

silent treatment: ignoring or indirectly fighting with a person with whom one has a disagreement.

skeletal system: the body system that consists of bones that provide a support framework.

skill-related fitness: the ability to perform well in sports and physical activities.

small intestine: the organ in which most digestion takes place, and in which digested food is absorbed into the blood.

smegma (SMEG·muh): dead skin and secretions that collect under the foreskin.

smog: a combination of smoke and fog.

smokeless tobacco: tobacco that is chewed.

snuff: a tobacco product that is placed between the cheek and gums.

social-emotional environment: the quality of the contacts a person has with the people with whom (s)he interacts.

social health: the condition of a person's relationships.

sodium: a mineral that is found in table salt and prepared foods.

solid waste: discarded solid material such as paper, metal, and yard waste.

specialist: a physician who has additional training in a particular area.

speed: the ability to move quickly.

speeding: exceeding the posted speed limit or driving too fast for conditions.

spinal cord: a thick band of nerve cells through which messages enter and leave the brain.

spinal nerves: nerves that branch from the spinal cord and convey messages to and from the spinal cord.

spleen: an organ that filters foreign matter from the blood and lymph.

sports participant: a person who plays sports.

sports physical: a physical examination to determine a person's health status before participation.

sports spectator: a person who watches and supports sports.

sprain: an injury to the ligaments, tendons, and soft tissue around a joint caused by undue stretching.

stalking: obsessing about a person with the intent to threaten or harm that person.

starch: a substance that is made in plants.

static stretching: stretching the muscle to a point where it pulls, and then holding the stretch for 15–30 seconds.

stomach: the organ that releases digestive juices to break down food.

strain: an overstretching of muscles and/or tendons.

street smart: to be aware of possible danger and to know what to do.

strep throat: a bacterial infection of the throat.

stress: the body's reaction to the demands of daily living.

stressor: a cause of stress.

stroke: a condition caused by a blocked or broken blood vessel in the brain.

stroke volume: the amount of blood the heart pumps with each beat.

sudden illness: an illness that occurs without warning signals.

sudden infant death syndrome (SIDS): the sudden, unexpected death of a seemingly healthy infant.

suicide: the intentional taking of one's own life.

suicide prevention strategies: ways to help prevent a person from attempting or committing suicide.

sulker: a person who uses the silent treatment.

sunscreen: a product that protects the skin from the sun's rays.

survivor of violence: a person who has been harmed by violence, participated in recovery, and feels empowered.

sweat glands: glands in skin that help maintain a healthful body temperature.

syphilis (SI·fuh·luhs)**:** an STD that produces chancres in the genital area and damage to organs if untreated.

systemic lupus: a disease that affects fat tissue, bones, ligaments, cartilage, and blood.

T

tamper-resistant package: a package that is sealed for safety.

tar: a sticky fluid that is formed when tobacco is burned.

target audience: the group of people for whom a message was created.

target heart rate: a heart rate of 75 percent of a person's maximum heart rate.

tendons (TEN·duhnz): tough tissue fibers that connect muscles to bones.

tennis elbow: damage to the tendons that move the wrist, and causes pain to the elbow and forearms.

terminal illness: an illness that will result in death.

testes: two glands that produce testosterone and sperm cells.

testicular self-examination (TSE): a check for lumps or tenderness in the testes.

testosterone: a hormone that produces male secondary sex characteristics.

THC: a compound that produces changes in a person's mind and body.

third-degree burn: a burn that involves all layers of the skin and some underlying tissues.

thymus gland: a gland that secretes a hormone that helps the parts of the body that fight disease.

thyroid gland: a gland that secretes a hormone that controls metabolism.

time bomb: a person who has a quick temper and is ready to explode without warning.

time management: organizing time to do the things that matter to a person.

time management plan: a plan that shows how a person will spend time.

tobacco: a plant that contains nicotine.

tobacco cessation program: a program to help a person quit smoking or using tobacco products.

tolerance: a condition in which the body becomes used to a substance.

tornado: a violent, spinning windstorm produced by a severe thunderstorm.

tornado warning: a warning issued when a tornado has been sighted or indicated by weather radar.

tornado watch: a warning issued when weather conditions are such that tornadoes are likely to develop.

toxemia of pregnancy: a disorder of pregnancy that causes high blood pressure, tissue swelling, and protein in the urine.

toxic shock syndrome (TSS): a severe illness resulting from toxins secreted by *Staphylococcus* (sta·fuhloh·KAH·kuhs) bacteria.

trachea (TRAY·kee·uh): the windpipe through which air travels to the lungs.

training ceiling: the maximum amount of overload required to obtain fitness benefits without risking injury or illness.

training threshold: the minimum amount of overload required to obtain fitness benefits.

training zone: the range of activity required to obtain fitness benefits.

tribute: something done to pay respect to someone.

trichomoniasis (TRI·kuh·muh·NY·uh·suhs): an STD that infects the urethra in males and the vagina in females.

tumor: an abnormal growth of tissue.

Type I diabetes (DY·uh·BEE·teez): a disease in which the body produces little or no insulin.

U

umbilical (uhm·BI·li·kuhl) **cord:** a rope-like structure that connects the placenta to the developing baby.

unintentional injury: an injury caused by an accident.

United States Postal Service (USPS): a federal agency that protects the public when products and services are sold through the mail.

universal distress signal: a warning that a person has difficulty breathing and is shown by clutching at the throat with one or both hands.

universal precautions: steps taken to keep from having contact with pathogens in body fluids.

unnecessary risk: a chance that is not worth taking after careful consideration of the possible outcomes.

unsaturated fat: a type of fat obtained from plant products and fish.

urethra (yu·REE·thruh): a narrow tube through which urine and semen pass out of the body.

urgent care center: a facility that provides care for minor injuries and short-term illnesses.

urinary bladder: a muscular organ that stores urine.

urinary system: the body system that removes liquid wastes from the body.

urine: liquid waste that collects in the urinary bladder.

uterus (YOO·tuh·ruhs): a muscular organ that receives and supports a fertilized ovum during pregnancy.

V

vaccine: a substance containing dead or weakened pathogens that is introduced into the body to prevent a disease.

vagina: a muscular tube that connects the uterus with the outside of the body.

vas deferens (VAS DE·fuh·ruhnz): one of two long, thin tubes that act as passageways for sperm and that store sperm.

vein (VAYN): a blood vessel that returns blood to the heart.

vertebral column: a column of bones that encloses, supports, and protects the spinal cord.

victim check: a check of the injured or ill person to determine if the victim has an open airway; the victim is breathing; the victim's heart is beating; the victim is severely bleeding; and the victim has other injuries.

victim of violence: a person who has been harmed by violence.

victim recovery: a person's return to physical and emotional health after being harmed by violence.

violence: the use of physical force to injure, damage, or destroy oneself, others, or property.

viral hepatitis (HE·puh·TY·tuhs): a viral infection of the liver.

visual acuity (uh·KYOO·uh·tee): sharpness of vision.

visual environment: everything a person sees regularly.

visual pollution: sights that are unattractive.

vitamins: nutrients that help the body use carbohydrates, proteins, and fats.

voluntary muscles: muscles that can be controlled.

volunteer: a person who provides a service without pay.

W-X-Y-Z

warm-up: three to five minutes of easy physical activity to prepare the muscles for more work.

water: a nutrient that makes up blood, helps digest food, helps with waste removal, regulates body temperature, and cushions bones and joints.

water pollution: the contamination of water with sewage, waste, gases, or chemicals that harm health.

water runoff: water that runs off land into a body of water.

weapon: an instrument or device used for fighting.

weather: the condition of the atmosphere at a particular time and place.

Web site: a collection of files or "pages" kept on a computer called a Web server.

weight management: a plan used to have a healthful weight.

Wellness Scale, The: a scale that shows the range of possible health conditions from premature death to optimal health.

Western blot: a test used to confirm ELISA.

wind chill: the effect of wind that makes the air seem colder than the actual temperature.

winter storm: a storm in winter that might include freezing rain or sleet, ice, winds, and heavy snowfall.

winter storm warning: a warning that severe winter weather conditions exist and will affect the area.

winter storm watch: a warning that severe winter weather conditions might affect the area.

withdrawal symptoms: unpleasant reactions experienced when drug use is stopped.

workaholism: the compelling need to work.

World Wide Web (WWW): a computer system that allows a person to view information as text and/or graphics.

wound: an injury to the body's soft tissues.

wrong decision: a choice that leads to actions that harm health, are unsafe, are illegal, show disrespect for self and others, disregard the guidelines of parents and other responsible adults, and do not demonstrate good character.

you-message: a statement or message that blames or shames another person.

Index

F